TA RA
FERGIE

FULL TIME FROM
THE MAN WHO
HELD UP THE
BANNER

TENBURY-TE

TA RA FERGIE

FULL TIME FROM THE MAN WHO HELD UP THE BANNER

FOREWORD BY JIM WHITE

PETE MOLYNEUX

The
History
Press

*I would like to dedicate this book to
Bill Molyneux, Robert Gregan and Andy Towler.*

Cover illustration of Alex Ferguson © Getty Images

First published 2013

The History Press
The Mill, Brimscombe Port
Stroud, Gloucestershire, GL5 2QG
www.thehistorypress.co.uk

British Library Cataloguing in Publication Data.
A catalogue record for this book is available from the British Library.

ISBN 978 0 7524 5759 8

Typesetting and origination by The History Press
Printed in Great Britain

CONTENTS

FOREWORD
BY JIM WHITE

We all make mistakes. Though few of us have made one as visible as Pete Molyneux did.

It was 9 December 1989 and Pete had had enough. A Manchester United fan to his bootstraps, Pete had been a home and away follower of the Reds for nigh on twenty years, doing his time on the terraces since the days of Matt Busby. And he was suffering. Alex Ferguson had been manager for three years, and Pete simply couldn't see any progress. Despite spending heavily in the transfer market, Ferguson had apparently marooned United in mediocrity; they were an outfit recently caned by their crosstown rivals and seemingly heading nowhere. The very idea of challenging Liverpool for the title was laughable. At the rate United were going they'd be lucky to achieve mid-table security. And there seemed to be one principal explanation: the manager wasn't up to the job. Sure Pete had no idea what was going on behind the scenes. But from what he could see, things were getting desperate. He was so fed up he decided to communicate his feelings in the most visible way he could. There was no setting up a Facebook protest group in 1989, no whinging on Twitter, no calling 6-0-6 to have a moan. What Pete did to articulate his feelings was purloin a bedsheet from home and some paint from the garden shed and give vent to his anger by making a banner.

After taking it along in a carrier bag to a couple of previous matches, his banner of protest was unfurled at the home game against Crystal Palace. 'Three years of excuses and it's still crap. Ta Ra Fergie' it read. The thing is, much as he may have been mocked subsequently for his total lack of prescience, at the time there were many among the 33,000 disgruntled Reds gathered in the stadium who felt the same. Few criticised the sentiment, many slapped him on the back for saying what they were thinking; the applause when the banner was spotted was the most prolonged of the afternoon. The football was crap, no one could deny that. Things had to change.

As history records, change they almost immediately did and in the most glorious, unexpected, life-enhancing fashion. A month after Pete had waved his banner, United embarked on the FA Cup run that was to deliver the first of thirty-eight trophies of the Ferguson era. As this book recounts, Pete, his faith restored, was there to savour almost every moment of success.

The bedsheet protest may look ridiculous in hindsight, but at the time no one could foresee the consistent joys Ferguson would deliver to United fans. Over the next two decades, the manager fundamentally altered the mindset of the United fan: Pete, like everyone of red affiliation, came to believe that in football anything is possible. He relished glorious victories, improbable comebacks and a mountain of unimagined glory. And, as he has long ago recognised, that is all thanks to the greatest manager the English game has ever known. How many times in those subsequent years has Pete sent up a silent prayer that no one in the Old Trafford board room at the time paid any heed to his grumbly complaint.

Indeed, when Ferguson finally retired long, long after the bedsheet protest, Pete paid homage in the only appropriate way: he made another banner. This time it read: '23 years of silverware and we're still top: Ta Ra Fergie'.

As this book explains, there really was nothing else to say.

Jim White, May 2013

ACKNOWLEDGEMENTS

In 2002, when Sir Alex decided not to retire, I wondered if there was time to put together a collection of stories about my fifty years following United. The book would be called *Ta Ra Fergie*, it would start with the 1989 'banner' story and its release, tied in with the great man's resignation in May 2013.

You are now holding a book much heavier than originally intended, written at a more leisurely pace and packed with wonderful tales of my time following Manchester United.

I would like to express my sincere appreciation to the many people who have helped me tell this story. In particular, my wife Louise and my children Bethany and Jessica, for listening to my football tales at almost every meal time during the last ten years. Their love, support, encouragement and suggestions (well, the ones that were physically possible) have been priceless. My sister Michelle for providing some of the missing details about our parents and early years, oh and for not telling me dad I locked her in the wardrobe when she was seven.

I would like to thank the following: Pete Seymour, Terry Lomax, Keith Byrom and Simon Rumsey for providing photos old and new; Iain McCartney and Richard Kurt for good advice when I needed good advice; Andrew Fowles of rem*creative* for his ideas and early illustrations; The History Press for having faith in me and being patient while Fergie kept on winning trophies; StretfordEnd.co.uk for being an invaluable source of stats when my brain turned into a colander; the spirit of Sir Matt and his Babes who set the bar; all the Manchester United heroes who lit up my life as a child, teenager and adult; Sir Alex Ferguson for being Alex Ferguson and finally ... all the United supporters whose company I have shared and enjoyed over six decades.

We had joy, we had fun ...

ABOUT THE AUTHOR

Pete Molyneux was raised in Salford and educated at Stand Grammar School, Whitefield. His father took him to watch George Best in United's youth team in 1963 and nine-year-old Pete was immediately hooked on football and Manchester United in particular. The love grew into obsession – Pete has seen United play over 2,000 games and once went nine years without missing a single competitive match that United played in the UK.

A season ticket holder for over thirty years, Pete has followed United across Europe since 1974, including trips to Romania, Poland, Turkey, Ukraine and Moscow. He has attended all six of United's European Finals. When it comes to supporting the Reds, Pete can honestly say, 'I was there!'.

Pete's career in the Energy Industry lasted thirty-six years before a change of direction led him to fulfil his ambition to write a book about his travels and his love for the 'greatest football team in the world'. He has always felt blessed being a Manchester United supporter and has had the time of his life following the team. The adventure has been packed with funny stories, great moments, amazing characters, times of sadness and even tragedy. This book is his chance to put the story out there for others to enjoy.

Pete lives in Worsley in Salford with his wife and two teenage daughters.

1

ANGER IS AN ENERGY!

It was an ordinary goal in an ordinary game in an ordinary season, but Mark Bright's fifty-fifth-minute strike for Crystal Palace against Manchester United would spark the most famous protest in Old Trafford's 103-year history. The date was 9 December 1989 and United, my glorious beloved United, had just gone 2-1 down to a Palace team hovering at the foot of the table.

'This is it lads, let's go!' I shouted to five mates who sat alongside me in United's notorious J Stand. Within seconds we were standing on our seats holding aloft a huge banner proclaiming '3 Years of Excuses And It's Still Crap Ta Ra Fergie'.

The adrenaline was really pumping. Though outwardly defiant, I was shaking inside with a mix of emotions. I was angry. Angry that the team I love had been reduced to a dour, shambolic outfit by a manager who had spent a fortune trying to assemble a side that would restore our former glories. I felt embarrassed. I am a loyal Red, yet here I was at Old Trafford publicly slagging off manager Alex Ferguson. Fear played a part too. I didn't know how the protest would be received; I had never done anything like it before and couldn't recall a similar incident at Old Trafford in twenty-five years watching United. By far, though, my over-riding emotion was anger. I'd had enough, there was no turning back – the protest was on!

Our seats were high up towards the back of J Stand, just under the old electronic scoreboard, diagonally opposite the players' tunnel. The area is now imaginatively labelled the 'North-East Quadrant'. In those days there were no second tiers around the ground, we were as high up as it got, which meant the entire crowd could see the banner. The die-hards on the United Road terraces noticed it first; their spontaneous reaction was cheering and loud applause. Then the supporters in the stands around us also voiced their approval. Within seconds, cheers rippled round Old Trafford like one of those long lines of falling dominoes. The ovation grew in volume as it travelled, reaching a deafening crescendo at the Stretford End. I found the reaction reassuring. I had no doubts I was doing the right thing and knew many Reds who were equally dissatisfied but until you put your head above the parapet you can't be sure what people really think. My fear melted away. There were 33,514 in the ground that day and at least 95 per cent showed they were in favour of the protest against Fergie's tenure.

Later in the chapter I'll return to the build-up to the protest and its aftermath, but for now let's just press the pause button. Surely there are some questions that need answering? If I was such a loyal Red, how had I got to this state of football anarchy? How could any true United supporter ever consider getting rid of Fergie? Why such a public show of dissent for the manager right in our own back yard? Firstly, let me nail one theory, the action wasn't the sudden impulse of a crazed nutter or a fickle day-tripper. Anyone who knows me would tell you I'm United through and through, I never slag off the team even after bad performances. I always see the glass half full. Loyalty to United is in my DNA. When I decided to call for Fergie's head I knew exactly what I was doing. I fully understood that the scale and intensity of the protest could leave the manager severely embarrassed, possibly humiliated. I didn't take the decision lightly, it was the culmination of several months' frustrations.

Alex Ferguson had become United's manager on 6 November 1986. He had one remit – to make United champions of England again. This was becoming mission impossible. United had last won the league title in 1967 under the incomparable Matt Busby who had put United at the forefront of world football by playing the game with tremendous flair and skill. Five times in twenty-four years United won the league under his leadership and in 1968 his United team became the first from England to win the European Cup. Between Sir Matt departing in 1969 and Fergie arriving in 1986 five managers had tried to put United at the top again. All had failed. The supporters were aching for United to win the title; Fergie had just accepted the best and hardest job in football.

Alex Ferguson had been a decent player in the 1960s and early 1970s plying his trade as a striker with six Scottish clubs, including Glasgow Rangers, scoring 167 goals in 327 games. He went into football management and came to prominence with Aberdeen in the early 1980s when he famously broke the Glasgow duopoly of Celtic and Rangers by winning the Scottish League three times in six years. Aberdeen had won the league only once previously in their seventy-six-year history, in 1955. Under his management they also won four Scottish Cups and one Scottish League Cup. The cherry on the cake was a sensational night in Gothenburg where his young Aberdeen side defeated the majestic Real Madrid to win the 1983 European Cup Winners' Cup.

So the man's credentials were good but just to put the new challenge into further perspective, when United were last champions in 1967 they equalled the record held by Liverpool and Arsenal. All three clubs had seven championships to their names. By 1986 Liverpool had won sixteen titles, Everton nine and Arsenal eight. United were still stuck on seven. Furthermore, the European Cup had been won by three English clubs in that period – Liverpool four times, Nottingham Forest twice and Aston Villa once.

Fergie set about his task at United by giving the existing players a chance to prove themselves. In doing so, the team finished 1986/87 eleventh in the league, having been nineteenth when he took over. Supporters expected him to build on this in his first full season and sure enough, 1987/88 saw United finish runners-up to Liverpool. The squad had been strengthened by the arrival of defenders Viv Anderson and Steve Bruce, and striker Brian McClair, who became the first United player to score twenty league goals in a season since Georgie Best in the halcyon days of 1968. That was the good news; the bad news was we finished nine points behind a Liverpool team that didn't lose until Easter. By mid-January we were seventeen points adrift of the leaders but a great run of twelve wins and three draws in the last sixteen games shot us to second place. Realistically, we were never close to being champions. The progress, however, had been good and during the summer of 1988 Fergie signed Jim

Leighton, his trusted goalkeeper at Aberdeen, and ensured the return of prodigal son and local hero, Mark Hughes. The supporters believed United were ready for a concerted attack on that elusive number one spot.

Alas, that assault turned into a retreat as we struggled to a mediocre eleventh in the league in 1988/89. The disappointment left supporters with a familiar empty feeling. Despite our justified optimism, the team had gone backwards. There had been a glimmer of hope mid-season when we walloped reigning champions Liverpool 3-1 in a pulsating New Year's Day match at Old Trafford. Fergie had bloodied a couple of youngsters, notably a feisty Russell Beardsmore. Injuries forced his hand to play some more in the first few rounds of the FA Cup. Fergie's Fledglings – Tony Gill, Mark Robins, Lee Martin, Deiniol Graham, David Wilson, Lee Sharpe and Jules Maiorana – put in some valiant performances. The innocence of youth carried them along and the crowd loved it. A good run of results got United as high as third place in the league and we had our first decent cup run for three years until Nottingham Forest put us out of the FA Cup at the quarter-final stage. Ironically, as the regular first-teamers returned the good run faltered and league results faded badly.

So it was eleventh place for the second time in three seasons for Fergie but the supporters' disappointment went deeper than just the league placing. There were some worrying home-truths for United fans to confront. Firstly, in each of the five seasons before Fergie was appointed, United had been in the running for the league title. He had now strengthened that squad with the purchases of Anderson, Bruce, McClair, Hughes, Leighton and Donaghy. Six costly signings within fifteen months, yet we seemed further away than ever from being champions. A second concern was the shortage of goals; we scored a wretched forty-five times in thirty-eight league games in 1988/89. Since 1922, United had scored less than fifty goals in a league season on only two occasions, forty-four in 1972/73 and thirty-eight the following season when we suffered a rare relegation from the top flight.

A third source of anxiety was the attendances at Old Trafford. Since the Second World War, United had enjoyed a huge and passionate following. This had been nurtured by Busby with a brand of exciting and entertaining football that brought in the crowds and gave United a bedrock of loyal support. Since 1964, United had enjoyed the best average home attendance in England in all but six seasons. In Fergie's first two full seasons Liverpool had overtaken United as the best supported club. Our average league gate for 1988/89 was 36,487. This was 10,000 per game down on Ron Atkinson's last season, 15,000 down on the Doc's Red Army years but most significantly it was United's lowest average since 1962. The attendances were a telling barometer of the team's performances on the pitch. Fergie implored us to have faith and as much as we wanted to believe in him, the 1988/89 season raised questions about the manager's suitability for the United job. His tactics often baffled supporters. He appeared to be overly cautious in his approach to matches. Fergie persevered with too many ordinary, workmanlike players in the same team, then confounded and infuriated supporters by playing these guys out of position just to accommodate them in the side. The result was a compromise of Manchester United's legendary attacking flair.

The football landscape for United supporters in the summer of 1989 was desperately bleak. Not even a sniff of a trophy for four years, poor performances becoming the norm on the pitch, declining crowds, no league title for twenty-two years and still banned from European adventure following the dreadful events at Heysel in 1985. Contrast this to a decade of relentless success by our rivals just thirty-five miles down the road. The title went west in more ways than one as Liverpool and Everton dominated English football. A tell-tale measure of your team's lean years is what you celebrate during that period. In the second half of the 1980s there are two defining moments of unbridled joy for United supporters. One is Wimbledon beating Liverpool in the 1988 FA Cup Final; the second is Arsenal beating Liverpool at Anfield in May 1989 to snatch the league title from under their noses in the last few minutes. The scenes of elation the Michael Thomas goal sparked around Manchester that night probably exceeded those in N5. Sadly, this summed up where we were at. All we had to celebrate were the setbacks of our biggest rivals. Those parties were good while they lasted but when the hangover wore off the following day the reality was still depressing for United fans. If this paints a black picture, it was about to get darker still.

Fergie's no fool; he could see the writing on the wall. The poor form of 1988/89 convinced him that despite the extensive array of talent he had brought in, further changes were necessary.

The existing squad was not going to deliver United the league title and in the first half of 1989 he instigated a clear-out. Peter Davenport, Jesper Olsen and Gordon Strachan were sold then Fergie decided to deal with an issue that had been simmering for some time. Right from his first spell in management at East Stirling he had gained a reputation as a disciplinarian. It was an innate value and a cornerstone on which he leads his life as well as builds his teams. His view was simple, without discipline you have nothing, and in his early Old Trafford years he encountered two issues that challenged those beliefs. One was a concern about the general levels of fitness at Old Trafford; the other was the existence of a drinking club – a clique of senior players who enjoyed regular booze-ups. The fitness issue was remedied fairly simply with new training regimes but the drinking problem was a more complex issue. In the late 1980s a good drink was still an essential lifestyle choice for many top footballers in Britain. United were no different. But Fergie wanted to harness their talents not waste them. Evolution rather than revolution had been his initial approach; educate existing players in the virtues of a healthier lifestyle while bringing in players with the right attitude. Sounds good in theory but it wasn't working and Fergie became increasingly intolerant of the drinking culture he had inherited. The manager decided that maybe revolution would be more effective. Norman Whiteside and Paul McGrath were transferred to Everton and Aston Villa respectively in August 1989.

All this has been well documented over the intervening years and now Reds look back from the 'comfort' of new-found glories but at the time most supporters didn't know what was going on behind the scenes. We were simply trying to make sense of it as events unfolded. Fergie's revolution gathered pace in August and September 1989 when he went on a spending spree that took the footballing world by storm. United had always traded at the top end of the British transfer market and regularly broke the record. But this was something else. In came £7 million of talent that looked like a who's who of English football – Neil Webb, Paul Ince, Danny Wallace, Gary Pallister and Mike Phelan. That amount of money might just about buy an average reserve team player nowadays but in 1989 it was astronomical. A couple of weeks earlier, entrepreneur Michael Knighton had bid £10 million for the entire club! The influx of new players raised expectations to fever pitch. We had seen a few false dawns in the previous twenty years but this felt like the real thing. At last we would have a team that could mount a serious challenge for the championship.

United started the season with a glorious 4-1 romp in the sunshine against reigning champions Arsenal, followed by a point at Crystal Palace. But as the new players made their debuts we lost our way with a run of three defeats on the bounce which left United sixteenth in the league. In his programme notes Fergie referred to it as a 'grim record' given where we had hoped to be. But he asked us to persevere a little longer as the blip was just teething troubles. When we crushed Millwall 5-1 in mid-September we were convinced United would now march to the top. How wrong could we be? Saturday, 23 September 1989 was our 'wake up and smell the coffee' moment. Those doubts, fears and suspicions about Fergie that we had tried to suppress in the previous twelve months came back to haunt us. On a bright, sunny afternoon at Maine Road, United were taken apart by local rivals City in a 5-1 defeat. Neither set of fans could believe it. City supporters were cock-a-hoop, though little did they realise they would have to dine out on that result for the next thirteen years. For Reds it was a football catastrophe. That day, I stood in the Platt Lane End and watched the debacle with horror. I was sick to the stomach. It wasn't just the score; it wasn't just the opponents, the humiliation or even the bloody annihilation. It was a deeper, nauseating realisation that United's rightful place among England and Europe's finest was still light years away despite a succession of managers and millions of pounds invested in top players.

That afternoon, as a devoted United follower of twenty-five years, the frustration of so many failed attempts to recapture past glories welled-up inside of me. I just couldn't believe how bad we were. As the fifth City goal went in, I went tearing down the Platt Lane terraces right from the back to the front in an attempt to get on the pitch and get at Fergie. I deplore violence of any sort but I desperately wanted to get hold of the man and tell him what I thought of this utter shambles. I wanted him to feel my upset, my anger, my hurt. I wanted to express my disgust at what he'd done to my beloved team. I felt like I wanted to kill him! I wasn't the only one. Several hundred Reds decided they'd had enough and charged to the front. The police spotted the potential pitch invasion and quickly moved reinforcements in behind the goal. The chants and verbal bile towards Fergie were ugly and unpleasant but the police action prevented a full-scale riot, not to mention a lengthy jail term for this author. Tempers calmed as the match finished, we took the obligatory ribbing from the Blues and trudged home dejected.

United's original fixture list had us down to play at Liverpool the week after the derby but the game was re-arranged for December as part of the package for showing matches live on TV. While it gave Fergie more time than he wanted to reflect on the City result it was a blessing in disguise. A further calamity at Anfield could have brought the wrath of hell on the United manager. As it turned out the next two games were at home to Portsmouth and Sheffield Wednesday. Both ended 0-0, hardly the perfect antidote for the wounded Red Army and boos rang out at full time in both games. I couldn't bring myself to join in with those jeers but I fully supported the strength of feeling. We were well on target for another league season with less than fifty goals to cheer. Then came a 4-1 win at Coventry, football had become a teasing mistress for United fans. Four days later we were comprehensively beaten 3-0 at home by Spurs in a League Cup tie, the third consecutive home game in which we failed to score. Of the three competitions United entered that season we were already out of two and the leaves weren't off the trees yet. It was woeful.

The Spurs defeat was my epiphany moment. Since the City game I had stewed in a pot of simmering frustration. Now I had to do something. As football supporters we can always vote with our feet. A neutral might argue that no one is forcing you to go to the match, if it's that bad just stop going. But for the real supporter that just isn't an option. The commitment to your team, the love of your club, is unconditional. I had followed United throughout Britain and across Europe for twenty-five years. I had queued for countless hours in the cold and wet to get tickets for matches. I had bunked off school and taken time off work to watch United. I had been threatened, chased, bricked, and bottled by opposing fans, I had split with girlfriends, missed family weddings, been hospitalised and almost lost my life because of my devotion to the Reds. Yet no one asked me to do it. I did it simply because I love United. Manchester United, my team. No matter how bad things are, you don't walk away. You fight for what you cherish. Now my team was in a dreadful state. Results were erratic, performances often dire, the flair sacrificed for caution. Star quality was becoming a memory and the crowds at Old Trafford had dwindled to around 35,000. The once vociferous atmosphere on the Stretford End, United Road and Scoreboard End had been stifled and replaced with grumbling acceptance. The magic of Manchester United was disappearing fast.

The blame, in my opinion, lay fairly and squarely with manager Alex Ferguson but this was no knee-jerk reaction. Fergie had continually promised the fans he was getting things right. We had persevered but he hadn't delivered. Fergie had enjoyed the luxury of time and money; two vital resources for a manager. He had also had the support of the fans and, though blindly loyal, we were not stupid. I followed the manager's comments closely on TV, in match programmes and in the *Manchester Evening News*. Invariably, after each poor performance he made out that the situation wasn't so bad, that matters were improving and that there had been several pluses to take from the game. This frustrated and annoyed United supporters more than anything else. We know when we've seen a good game, or a bad one. We know instinctively if the players in those famous red shirts are good enough and committed enough. The supporters know if progress is being made or not, they couldn't be fooled by excuses.

My view was clear and simple – if you accept second-best in life, then you'll get second-best. Manchester United had become second-best and I couldn't sit back and do nothing. I believed Fergie had to go and decided to make my feelings known. There was a lot of speculation in the press about United's plight; many supporters voiced their dissatisfaction through the media or the emerging 'fanzines' such as *Red Issue* and *United We Stand*. I didn't get involved with that; writing a letter wasn't going to change anything. I wanted the protest to be direct and carry real impact. However, it had to be peaceful. Football was still reeling from the Hillsborough disaster and sensitivities were running high about any hint of hooliganism. I didn't want to lose the point of the protest with anything that could be construed as the action of a yob. Not on this occasion anyway!

The third anniversary of Fergie's appointment was approaching so I decided I would hold up a banner calling for his head at the home game nearest to that date. The game was Nottingham Forest on Sunday, 12 November 1989. One evening I dug out a blue king-size bed sheet, some black paint and sat there with a blank canvas pondering what to write. When I was a young lad in the mid-1960s, hooked on the magic of the Stretford End, there was a character called Nutty Norman. He was a legend among United fans and a sort of spiritual leader. Renowned for many daft antics, he once took his wife on a car trip to Liverpool for a United clash. She didn't follow football but Norman thought the company would be better than travelling alone. Several miles down the East Lancs Road he saw four United fans trying to hitch a lift to the game. Never one to see fellow Reds struggling, he stopped the car right away. Realising he couldn't fit all the lads in, he quickly convinced his wife it was his duty to get these sup- porters to Liverpool and asked did she mind hitching a lift back home in the other direction? I understand she agreed without argument. What a woman! What a guy!

Anyway, one of Nutty Norman's celebrated skills was the knack of coming straight to the point about any topic related to the beautiful game. Where others would wax lyrical about a subject or dance with flowery words he would summarise the main point brilliantly using a minimum of words, and the odd expletive. His concise insights often left the masses amazed and in awe.

My thoughts turned to Norman as I pondered over the blank bed sheet. I needed something brief that hit the right note. Well, Fergie been there three years, the football was dire and all we were being fed was excuses. That's it! '3 Years Of Excuses – And It's Still Crap' seemed to capture it per- fectly! I was considering finishing off with 'Fergie Out!' or 'Fergie Must Go!' but being a Salford lad I wanted the banner to convey some local culture. ITV's *Coronation Street* came to mind and the superb Bet Lynch who was at her peak as land- lady of the world famous Rovers Return. Her parting shot to all and sundry as they headed for the door of the Rovers was always an endearing 'Ta Ra cock, goodnight!' Perfect, it had to be 'Ta Ra Fergie!'

So the banner was ready. In the week running up to the game I contacted the mates who sat alongside me in the stands and tipped them off that I was planning a protest at the start of the next match. Tezzer Lomax, Brian Foy, Col Green, Pete Seymour and Steve Heywood, I had known these guys since the early 1970s. We had stood on the Stretford End together, followed United far and wide and shared the good times and the bad. They were loyal Reds who were also disenchanted at the state of our club, but I wanted their buy-in. A couple of the lads had doubts as to the timing of the protest, was it too soon or not? But overall they backed the idea and agreed to go along with it.

The plan was to start the protest as the referee and captains were tossing the coin and then keep the banner aloft for the first few minutes of the game. That would give the protest around five minutes of exposure and we would play the rest by ear. I concealed the banner in a big plastic bag as I entered the ground, took it to my seat and checked that the lads were ready for the big moment. Pete Seymour and I sat at either end of our little party. We would hold the top two corners of the banner with the other four in the middle. All was set and pulses were racing as the two teams came out onto the pitch. This was it!

Well, not quite it. The twenty-two players and officials walked to the centre circle and a solemn voice on the loudspeaker announced, 'There will now be two minutes' silence to remember all those who have given their lives for the peace and freedom we enjoy today.' It was bloody Remembrance Sunday! We were gutted. People around us must have been dismayed at our reaction. Why would six grown men at a football match be so bothered that a silence was being held to commemorate those fallen in battle? Anyway, there we stood for the next two minutes respectfully bemused. I mouthed to the other lads that the protest was off for now; it just wouldn't have had the same impact. The flag stayed in the bag. The next home game was on 25 November when the visitors were Chelsea but the great Jimmy Murphy had passed away that week and there was another minute's silence before the game. So the banner stayed at home.

Saturday, 9 December 1989 was a chilly, grey day in Manchester. The hours of daylight were receding fast with the advent of Christmas. In most seasons the prospect of a match at Old Trafford would lift the spirits and shine through the gloom. But hearts were heavy and the football mediocre. United were playing Crystal Palace and we stood twelfth in the league out of twenty teams. After such high expectation this was turning out to be a very poor season. But if our plight was bad, Palace's was grim. A sorry eighteenth and one point off the bottom, they hadn't won away from home that season and in September had lost 9-0 at Liverpool. I took the banner that day but with no real plan of attack.

The crowd was the lowest of the season so far. Fergie decided to drop Mark Hughes because the scoring combination with Brian McClair wasn't working. Nine minutes in, United took the lead through young Russell Beardsmore. We should have been on the way to equalling Liverpool's tally against Palace but squandered a hatful of chances. Five minutes before half-time the Londoners equalised through Mark Bright. On fifty-five minutes the same striker squeezed the ball between Jim Leighton and the post to give the visitors a 2-1 lead. For a second Old Trafford was stunned into absolute silence, unable to take in this latest setback. Instinctively I knew this was the moment. I got the banner out, threw one corner to the boy Seymour and there the six of us stood, loud and proud, proposing the demise of Alex Ferguson, manager of Manchester United.

Because the crowd's reaction was so loud and positive we kept the banner aloft for five or six minutes by which time it had become the focus of attention all around the ground. Then, out of the corner of my eye, I saw two policemen edging their way along the row to our seats. This was before stewards became the custodians of good behaviour across our football stadia. I had expected the police to get involved and had planned my response. I would remain calm, respectful but firm. I would explain we were making a peaceful protest as is our right as supporters and individuals. I knew that provided the protest remained peaceful we were not doing anything unlawful. I was ready.

'Take your flag down son!' shouted the first PC.

I ignored him at first, making out I couldn't hear him over the noise of the crowd.

'Oi, take your flag down!' He was up close and personal now.

'Sorry officer I can't do that, it's a protest, we're not causing any trouble,' I replied politely.

He repeated the request and I said, 'Look I'm not being funny or cocky but why?'

'Because it's causing offence,' said the officer

'Only to the person it's aimed at,' I said

The second PC then joined the debate and uttered sternly, 'Put your banner down, lad.'

'Sorry officer but why?' I questioned again.

'Because people behind can't see,' retorted the first PC, thinking on his feet.

By this stage the dynamics were changing. The coppers were young and inexperienced; they had taken a confrontational approach that they couldn't support with logic and were getting frustrated. Their attitude convinced me to stand my ground. More significantly though, the crowd who had supported the protest didn't take kindly to the police trying to censor it. Hearing the officer's comments about the banner blocking people's view, a group of lads in the rows behind us shouted, 'We don't mind, here mate, we'll hold up yer banner.' A couple of these lads grabbed hold of the flag, the police grabbed it too and a mini tug of war took place high up in the Old Trafford stands with me caught in the middle. Tempers were getting frayed and the next thing I saw was a copper's helmet spinning through the air over the heads of people sat in the rows below us. It all seemed to be happening in slow motion and I can remember thinking, 'Oh shit, that's the end of the peaceful protest then!'

Now, during the late 1980s and early 1990s there were some handy lads in J Stand. Like us they were thirty-somethings who had followed United passionately through the previous two decades and had moved from the Stretford End or United Road terraces to the seats. J Stand became the heartbeat of Old Trafford and a meaningful barometer of United supporters' views. The stand was laced with fanatical Reds and they all had attitude. Many also had police records, but it didn't make them bad people. Anyway, quite a tussle had broken out; the lad who had sent the police helmet into orbit was being arrested but clearly chose not to go quietly. The crowd in our stand were further incensed as they thought the police had arrested the guy with the banner, and to put it mildly the natives were very restless.

It took the two coppers what seemed like an eternity to get their man along the row to the steps that lead below the terracing. The three of them were just about to disappear from sight for the afternoon when I realised the coppers had taken my banner. I chased after the arresting party and shouted at the officers to give me the flag back. In the cold light of day, given what they had just gone through, it may not have been the wisest move. But it was my property; I had done nothing wrong and wanted it back. Understandably they were a little reluctant and said it would be used as evidence and stored at Stretford police station for collection sometime in the future. I carried on arguing the case but was getting nowhere and the coppers had moved down the steps to the concourse under the stand. I decided it was wise to stay at the top of the stairwell. Suddenly, one of the coppers had a change of heart, and shouted back up to me, 'Okay, you can have your flag!'

'Good, chuck it up then,' I said, rather surprised at this outbreak of compassion.

'You come down here and get it,' he bawled.

'Er, no thanks, just chuck it up,' I bartered.

'Come down here!' he bawled even louder. 'Come down here now!'

Just behind him I noticed a large platoon of Greater Manchester Police's finest entering the ground as back-up for their two stranded colleagues.

'Yer awright, mate,' I shouted. 'You can keep it!'

With that I turned and was away on my toes back to my seat. Seconds later dozens of police flooded our stand led by a very stern-looking sergeant. It is the one and only time at Old Trafford I've seen a police officer carrying a large baton to control the crowd. Several outraged supporters remonstrated with the sergeant and his men about the handling of the incident. It took them a further fifteen minutes before they got people back into their seats and restored civil order. All this time the game had been continuing, though how many people in the crowd were watching the match is debatable. Most were focused on the impromptu cabaret taking place in the stands. It was probably a welcome relief.

There was no further score and United lost 2-1. As the game ended, a United ground official came over to talk to me as I waited in my seat for the crowd to clear. I thought I was in for a bollocking but he told me he had seen what happened and thought we were perfectly in order to do what we did. He went on to say that the police didn't quite see it the same way and they were waiting by the exit to pick me off. He suggested I quickly jump over the wall into the adjacent stand and leave via a different exit. I took his advice and snuck off into the Manchester night.

In those days I had very long hair and a full curly perm – yeah I know it was ten years out of date but it's the still best hairstyle I've ever had so say what you will! Anyway, the point is, Charles II lookalikes were pretty rare on Trafford Road so it made me fairly easy to recognise. As I walked the couple of miles back to the car, several passing Reds shouted messages of support from their vehicles, others on foot thanked me for standing-up and letting the club know how the fans felt. The banner episode happened before Sky TV had wall-to-wall cameras at every ground in the country so there was no footage of the protest. Nowadays the whole thing would have been on YouTube before I got home for my tea. Nevertheless, the incident gained quite a few column inches in national and local newspapers and particularly the United fanzines over the next few months.

Of course, I never expected United's board to sack Fergie just on my say so. I simply wanted to get my frustration off my chest and put the strength of our dissatisfaction firmly on the agenda. In that respect the protest had the desired effect. It also served the purpose of polarising the views of anyone with a mild interest in Manchester United. It ended the covert rumblings among supporters and put the debate into the public domain. For the first time in living memory there had been a mass upsurge against the manager of Manchester United and you either agreed with it, or not. The protest provided a platform for supporters to voice their opinion. Remember, there were no blogs in those days!

Initially, Fergie thought the crowd's reaction was due to him dropping Mark Hughes. He referred to it in his programme notes the following Saturday as 'the worst experience of that nature of my career'. The truth is the team selection that day had nothing to do with it. The supporters' frustrations had welled-up for weeks. Displaying the banner was like lancing a boil. Four years later in his book, *Just Champion*, Fergie titled chapter three 'Black December' and ranks that month's events as 'the darkest period I have ever suffered in the game'. He recalls the Palace game and how he felt like a fugitive in a very hostile world when for the first time in his tenure the crowd turned against him. Well, dark as it may have been for Fergie, it wasn't half as black as the despair that gripped United supporters that winter.

Of course, what none of us knew in December 1989 is that the darkest hour was just before dawn. Just like the Mamas and Papas had told us on their 1967 classic 'Dedicated To The One I Love'. Soon Fergie would lead United into the Promised Land and a haul of trophies beyond our wildest dreams. My mates would revel in reminding me, and anyone else who cared to listen, that I was the prick who wanted to get rid of Alex Ferguson.

Understandably, the abuse increased with each piece of silver-ware the great man picked up. Anyway, thank God Fergie stayed. It doesn't bear thinking about where United would be today if he had heeded my words.

To be fair to Alex Ferguson, in those final days of the 1980s he bore the brunt of a decade of frustration from United's loyal following. Two FA Cups could never compensate for the failure to establish ourselves as the top team in England let alone Europe. Liverpool's collection of domestic and European trophies in that period magnified that failure. For many United supporters, including myself, the frustration went even further back than the 1980s. We had spent two decades yearning for a return to the days when United truly were the greatest.

2

THANK YOU FOR THE DAYS, THOSE ENDLESS DAYS, THOSE SACRED DAYS YOU GAVE ME

I doubt if alcoholics can identify the precise drink that sent them down the rocky road to addiction, or compulsive gamblers remember the initial wager that led to years of obsessive betting. For football junkies it's different. You can always recall an incident or occasion, usually in childhood, which triggered the link to your football team. From that moment on that is your team for life. You are not addicted at that stage but you have been hooked. My first recollection of Manchester United was an innocuous game of footie outside my house with the lad next door, David Hibbert. We often had a kick-about but one day we wanted to be proper teams. That day was 25 May 1963. I was 8 years old. My dad was watching a match on TV so we traipsed in and asked who was playing.

'Manchester United versus Leicester City, son, in the FA Cup Final at Wembley,' he replied.

'Wow, right, thanks,' I said and off we went to play our own version of the final. Neither of us could decide who we wanted to be so it was back to my old fella for more info.

'Dad, what colour do Manchester United play in?'

'Red shirts and white shorts, son,' came the life-changing response.

That was it, for some reason I had to be that team in red and white! I don't know why – maybe there were powers at work that we're just not meant to understand. Anyway, luckily for me and this story, young Mr Hibbert was happy to be Leicester City for the day. We played football for the next couple of hours, 'my' United beat 'his' Leicester then we went inside to find out that the real Reds had triumphed 3-1 to collect the FA Cup for the third time in their history. From that day United were my team. I didn't know it then but I had just embarked on a wonderful journey, one that will continue until I take my last breath. A flame had been lit that could never be extinguished.

I was never really any good at football. I thought I was, but I wasn't. However, my enthusiasm for the game was second to none. As well as playing whenever I could, I had a typical school-boy's thirst for knowledge about football and anything connected with it. This was satisfied mainly by reading magazines such as the classic *Charles Buchan's Football Monthly*, various soccer annuals and watching what I could on TV. It was the early 1960s and Sky Sports coverage was light-years away. *Match of the Day* was still twelve months from being launched and *FourFourTwo* was a maths ratio. Needless to say, Football Manager, PlayStations and Wii games didn't exist because personal computers hadn't been invented. But it wasn't all bad news and ignorance, we knew the earth wasn't flat and there was electric light in our homes. We also had *Grandstand* on a Saturday afternoon and *Sportsnight* on a Wednesday providing football fans with their weekly fix of action. Toy games such as Subbuteo and Waddington's Table Soccer brought our heroes to life in our bedrooms.

I realised at this early age I would probably never play for Manchester United, so my dream was to see them play live. My dad, Bill, was a keen United fan. I have early recollections of him going off to football matches on a Saturday afternoon with my uncles and his mates. After May 1963 I would ask if I could go with him but United were getting crowds of 60,000-plus and most of the ground was large areas of open terracing. My parents felt I was still too small. As a concession my dad took me to Saturday reserve games at Old Trafford during the 1963/64 season but the highlight was going to the evening matches in the FA Youth Cup. United had already established a great tradition in this competition having won it in each of its first five years from 1953–57. The atmosphere at night matches always seemed special. Football under floodlights has a magic of its own and United's red shirts were so bright it seemed like they had just been painted on a huge green canvas. The sense of smell brings back the most potent memories. We used to sit in the stands near the players' tunnel, as we approached the turnstiles the smell of footballers' liniment coming from the dressing room windows filled the air. Once inside my dad would buy us a cup of Bovril, a thick, salty, beef drink. Liniment and Bovril – a heady cocktail for a young lad! Anyway, we're in serious danger of nostalgia overload here so let's move on.

The main attraction was the football and United's youth team. I was dead lucky; in the autumn of 1963 the line-up contained George Best, who had just broken into the first team, David Sadler, Johnny Aston, John Fitzpatrick, Bobby Noble, Willie Anderson and Jimmy Rimmer. They all went on to play a part in United's success over the next decade. Best, Sadler, Aston and Rimmer playing a part in the team that won the European Cup in 1968. United took the 1964 youth competition by storm, walloping Manchester City 8-4 in the semi-final then overcoming Swindon 5-2 in the final before crowds in excess of 25,000. History shows that clubs winning the Youth Cup may have a couple of players progressing through to regular first team football. To get seven was exceptional and stirred memories of Busby's first bunch of Babes ten years earlier. After 1964 it would be another twenty-eight years before United lifted the Youth Cup again, this time with the fabled class of 1992.

So, my introduction to football at Old Trafford was good but it wasn't quite the real thing. I would avidly follow the results of the first team and dream of seeing them play at a packed Old Trafford. I kept pestering my dad to take me with him but he was having none of it. In May 1964, I got close to a first team fixture. Bert Trautmann, City's legendary German keeper, was given a testimonial and invited United as the opponents. My dad and uncles were split fifty/fifty between United and City and were all going to the match. There was a spare ticket and for a few days there was talk of me going but in the end one of my dad's friends had it and I was left at home. So near yet so far, it was torture.

Over the years we all get promised match tickets that don't materialise, it's a real sickener, but when you're trying to get to see your first game it's crushing. There's this tremendous anticipation of what going to a big match must be like and it grows and grows until you feel you'll burst if you don't get to one soon. Then you get to the point where you convince yourself it's never going to happen for you. In many ways it's a forerunner to trying to lose your virginity – it drives you stir crazy, then one day it happens when you least expect it.

My football 'first time' arrived on Saturday, 26 September 1964. I lived close to Sedgley Park Rugby Club in Whitefield. I wasn't interested in rugby but I used to set out the flags around the pitch before the game which earned me half a crown (12.5p) each weekend. For a 10-year-old it was a good little earner. Before I left the house to do that job, if United were playing at home, I would always ask if I could go to the match with my dad. I had got so used to the apologetic rejections that often I didn't wait for the reply before heading towards the door. But on this Saturday, late in September, I heard my dad say, 'What do you think, mum?' I couldn't believe it was even up for debate. Moreover I couldn't take in her reply when she said 'go on then', smiling and winking at my dad, 'but don't let him out of your sight whatever you do!' I shot round to the rugby club to tell them I couldn't put the flags out today … I was going to Old Trafford to see Manchester United play Tottenham Hotspur!

The heavens opened over Manchester that September day but I was the happiest kid in the world. We parked up somewhere on Trafford Road and set off walking to the ground. Every fourth or fifth step I would have to run to keep up with my dad. I was so full of anticipation and excitement that I started to wonder if I'd built it up too much in my mind. Could the experience end up as one of life's great disappointments? I needn't have worried. As we made our way up the steps and onto the uncovered 'popular side' on United Road the teams had just come out of the tunnel. My dad lifted me onto his shoulders and there before my eyes were my heroes – Harry Gregg, Shay Brennan, Tony Dunne, Paddy Crerand, Billy Foulkes, Nobby Stiles, Georgie Best, John Connelly, David Herd, Denis Law and Bobby Charlton. Not in black and white on a small TV set or a photo in a magazine. There they were live in glorious red and white. There were 53,000 at the match and the atmosphere was like nothing I had experienced or could have imagined.

My dad wormed his way through the packed terraces and got us close to one of the crash barriers. He sat me on the iron bar and stood behind making sure I didn't fall. The crowd roared every United move and it seemed to lift the red-shirted heroes to another level. There must have been some Spurs fans there but I don't remember seeing or hearing any in this partisan mass. When the goals went in the noise nearly blew me away. Everyone around just went ballistic. I found it an intoxicating potion of excitement and fear. I clung to my dad, cheering like mad, but holding on really tight so we didn't get separated. We survived each of the four United goals like that and when Spurs got a consolation I learned a few words I had not heard in the playground. What a start, a 4-1 mauling of London's top team, with two goals from King Denis and a rare double from Pat Crerand. At last I had seen United play! I couldn't contain my excitement, when I got home I followed my mum all round the house trying to tell her about it but all she was really interested in was that I had come back in one piece. After that I went with my dad to virtually all of United's home games, missing only five over the next three seasons.

Both my parents were from Salford, my dad from Irlams o' th' Height and my mum Elsie from Weaste, close to Salford docks. The Second World War probably delayed their marriage but in 1946 they tied the knot. My mother was very ambitious. Early in 1954 she convinced my father to embark on a new life in Australia. Brits were offered cheap fares and the promise of a great future by the Australian Government who needed to increase their labour market as post-war prosperity kicked in. I guess the UK at that time looked a bleak place by comparison. The war had been won but now families were experiencing the 'hard peace'. Lives and property were being rebuilt, food rationing was still in force and it would take another decade for Britain to recover economically from the devastation of the early 1940s. Anyway, off they sailed in April 1954 with a £10 one-way ticket. My mum kept one secret from the authorities – she was five months pregnant. Her doctor would have considered a six-week passage to Australia too risky and the new life they craved would have been put on hold for a year or so.

They set-up home in Adelaide, and on 11 August at the Victoria Hospital their first child Peter William Molyneux entered the world. The future looked bright for the Molyneux family. The great John Lennon once remarked that 'life is what happens while you're making plans'. My mother suffered increasingly from symptoms that would eventually be diagnosed as rheumatoid arthritis, a progressive disease affecting the joints and in advanced stages the loss of mobility. Even today, doctors don't know what causes it and there is no known cure. My parents tried to make a go of it but my father had become homesick and, combined with my mum's illness, they decided to return to the UK in 1956.

They bought a guest house on the A6 in Salford, a huge four-storey building, and for a time ran a good business frequented mainly by travelling salesmen. In 1957, my sister, Michelle, was born. My mum got significant relief from her symptoms during the pregnancy and it was hoped there would be some residual benefit after the birth. Sadly this wasn't the case. She was ailing slowly and cruelly; her mobility becoming more restricted. My parents sold the business in 1961 and we moved to a bungalow in Whitefield so my mum didn't have to climb stairs. I have no doubt the doctors did their best to treat the illness but much of it was experimental. Over time, the trials with drugs affected her kidneys. On 20 December 1965 my mum passed away in Hope Hospital Salford, the cause of death was renal failure. She was just 40 years of age. My father, at the age of 53, was faced with bringing up his two children alone. Michelle was 8 and I was 11, but kids are very resilient and though we were all devastated, with help from our wider family we battled on.

Football had become my absorbing passion. Over the next few years my interest in the game, and my devotion to Manchester United, increased obsessively. Nothing odd about that, teenagers have fallen madly in love with football teams since the professional game started in the late nineteenth century. However, the intensity of my passion and the addiction to watching United at all costs seemed to outstrip anything my friends felt. It would affect my life and many of the decisions I made. I'll never know, but I've often wondered, whether the loss of my mum at the start of my formative years triggered this compulsive devotion in United? I guess that's one for the psychiatrist's couch.

In 1964/65, my first season watching the first team, United won the league championship on goal average from Leeds United. The great Matt Busby was the manager; he had battled valiantly to put United back on top of the English game following the Munich air crash seven years earlier. The title race was fought out between three sides, Busby's attack-minded United,

Chelsea's exciting young team managed by the charismatic Tommy Docherty, and Leeds. The Yorkshire club were at the start of a decade that saw them win many of the game's top honours but their success was matched by the loathing and rage they evoked in other supporters. In short, Leeds became despised across the land. Formed in 1919, they were a mediocre provincial football team until Don Revie was appointed manager in 1961. After saving them from relegation to England's third tier he set about moulding a team by making average players believe in, and play above, themselves. He turned Leeds round, got them out of the Second Division as champions in May 1964 and by Christmas that year they sat at the top of the First Division.

But Leeds had 'something of the night' about them. This centred on their dirty play and gamesmanship. They were a very physical team and in time Billy Bremner, Norman Hunter, Paul Reaney and Jack Charlton would be renowned for their 'stop them at all costs' approach. Often the rough play was overt and there's plenty of TV footage from that period to bear witness to it. But they also knew how to be sneaky and resort to foul play when the referee wasn't looking or when the ball was at the other end of the pitch. Add to this a blatantly cynical approach to fair play; Leeds players would appeal for throw-ins, free kicks, offsides, anything, whether it was justified or not. I am not talking here about the odd game, this was a tactic callously and rigorously employed by Revie's teams for over a decade.

I first experienced a United versus Leeds match on 5 December 1964. The visitors came to Old Trafford lying third in the table, United were top after a run of eight straight league wins scoring twenty-three goals and conceding only five. It was a cold day and there was an eerie mist enveloping the ground. United bombarded the Leeds defence all afternoon but many attacks were broken up by continuous niggles and fouls. After fifty-five minutes Leeds scored against the run of play. As they hung on to that lead their tactics became more 'disruptive' and the large crowd resorted to collective booing and thunderous chants of 'dirty Leeds, dirty Leeds'. Although tame lyrics compared to later terrace songs, this was quite radical behaviour for Old Trafford. It wasn't just the vociferous Stretford End but the more sedate season ticket holders who were hurling down this abuse.

The fog thickened with the loss of daylight and ten minutes from time, referee Jim Finney called a halt to proceedings because visibility was so poor. As the players left the pitch the whole Leeds team and their entourage surrounded the referee berating him from all sides. I don't know what happened down in the tunnel but Leeds got their way when after eight minutes the players came back on the field to complete the match in farcical conditions. You couldn't see from one side of the pitch to the other. Leeds held on to win the game 1-0 but only after waves of derision from the United crowd.

Later that season the two sides met in the semi-final of the FA Cup. On a Hillsborough mud heap Leeds turned the showpiece into another fierce battle that boiled over when Law and Jack Charlton traded punches. Law played on with his shirt in tatters, ripped in the brutal tussle. This was my first away match and the game ended in a goalless stalemate. Four days later Leeds won the replay with a late goal from Bremner. The ugly side of football had won the day again so imagine our delight when United went to Elland Road five games from the end of that 1964/65 season and beat Leeds 1-0. The victory was part of a storming run which brought the Reds a sixth league title and robbed Leeds of top spot. The beautiful game eventually prevailed in 1965 but those matches set the tone for encounters between Manchester United and Leeds until Revie left in 1974. For a decade it would be English football's *Beauty and the Beast*, a clash of cultures and integrity, good versus evil.

During that first season I was introduced to another phenomenon that would have a lasting impact on me, but this was carved out of pure magic. United playing European opposition. I had listened with fascination when my dad and uncles had told me how United had led the way for English clubs by entering the newly formed European Cup in 1956. They had reached the semi-final stage at the first attempt and again the following year when the plane returning from the quarter-final had crashed on take-off at Munich on 6 February 1958. Eight players lost their lives. It knocked the heart out of the club for a while but by the mid-1960s the recovery was in its final stages.

In 1964/65, United entered the Inter-Cities Fairs Cup – a predecessor of the UEFA Cup – designed to promote trade between European cities. They romped through the competition, beating

Djurgardens 7-2, Borussia Dortmund 10-1, Racing Club Strasbourg 5-0 and, curiously, Everton 2-1 to reach the semi-final. Two games against the famous Ferencvaros club of Hungary resulted in a 3-3 stalemate. The away goals rule hadn't come in then and on Wednesday, 16 June United lost the play-off match 2-1 in Hungary. I was spellbound, these games had a charisma all of their own. Again under floodlight, just like those Youth Cup matches a year earlier, but this time against teams with exotic-sounding names and kits with different colours and styles to those we were used to in Britain.

The following season saw United back in Europe's prime competition, the European Cup, for the first time since 1958. United swept aside HJK Helsinki and ASK Vorwaerts and were drawn against the magnificent Benfica in the quarter-finals. The Lisbon side had appeared in four of the last five European Cup Finals, winning two. They provided over half the Portuguese national side and in Eusebio had the best player in Europe. But United were coming to the boil as a team capable of holding its own against any team at home or in Europe.

The first leg on 2 February drew 64,000 to Old Trafford with United edging it 3-2 but a one-goal lead was considered insufficient by many pundits. Enter George Best on to the world stage, dateline 9 March 1966, in the Stadium of Light, Lisbon. United shattered Benfica's 100 per cent European home record with a remarkable 5-1 triumph. Bestie destroyed their defence, scoring twice in the opening twelve minutes. History tells us a star was born in Portugal that night but in Manchester we had known about George's talents for three years. He had illuminated so many games already with his unique skills. In Lisbon, the world witnessed his immense talent and fell in love with our idol, our Georgie.

Reds expected a United procession to the Brussels final especially when we avoided giants Real Madrid and Juventus in the semi-final draw. We were paired against unfancied Partizan Belgrade but a poor performance in the first leg left us chasing a 2-0 deficit. We threw everything at them at Old Trafford but their defence was strong. The Yugoslav team beat United 2-1 on aggregate to become the first finalists from Eastern Europe. The dream was shattered; hard to take because this United team seemed ripe for the European prize. I honestly believed after that mauling of Benfica we were invincible. Perhaps the team did too; convinced they had done the hard part?

In truth we were dreadfully over-stretched as the season reached its climax. United were battling for the league, the FA Cup and the European Cup. Only one team had won the domestic double in the twentieth century and no English team had reached the final of the European Cup. It was a mammoth task and meant United had to play nine games in twenty-five days between 6 and 30 April 1966, including an FA Cup semi-final and the two legs against Partizan. The challenge became even harder when Bestie was injured in the first leg in Belgrade. His cartilage had gone, his season was finished. We badly missed his magic.

The 1965/66 finale ended in disappointment all round. United finished fourth in the league, ten points behind champions Liverpool and for the fourth time in five years our love affair with the FA Cup ended in heartbreak just one step from Wembley. However, the sad ending didn't lessen my affection for United, it left me craving more. United's style of football was often breathtaking and with Best, Law, Charlton, Herd, Stiles and Crerand in the team you knew you were going to be entertained. Add to that the passion of the Old Trafford crowd and the lure of European football nights – who wouldn't want more?

The 1966/67 season started with a hangover. Four of the first seven games were lost with the team shipping fourteen goals. Matt Busby moved quickly, bringing in goalkeeper Alex Stepney from Chelsea and promoting youth team captain Bobby Noble at left-back. The defence improved with every game. Early exits from the domestic cups and no European involvement left United with an uncluttered fixture list and we romped to another league title thanks to an undefeated twenty-game run in the second half of the season. We won all but one home match and drew all but one away from Old Trafford. Busby's formula of three points every two games proved spot-on and a 6-1 win at West Ham gave United a record-equalling seventh English league title.

My football world was taking on a new dimension. In three seasons to date my dad had taken me to four away matches – league games at City and Blackburn, a 4-2 cup win at Wolves and the 1965 semi-final against Leeds. These trips were different again to home games. The appeal was the travel and the different types of grounds but most of all it was the atmosphere. United were the team everyone wanted to beat and that galvanised the home supporters who wanted to see this glamorous side put to the sword by their own favourites.

United's visit often resulted in a full house and a record crowd. This was the era when travelling away to watch your team really took off. Previously, supporters had gone to away matches in large numbers mainly for big FA Cup games or local derbies but not for most league matches. The growing motorway network in Britain and affordable coach or rail fares made away matches part of the scene for the football supporter, particularly the teenage fans and those under thirty.

United always took a big following. On average 5,000 to 6,000 supporters but for some games it was 8,000 to 10,000. Entry was by payment at the turnstile on the day and the segregation of fans was non-existent. It was first come first serve and invariably the Manchester boys got there first in huge numbers before the home fans. This mix of home and away fans created a gladiatorial feel whenever United went on the road. When the Stretford Enders were in town it was exciting and a little dangerous but it didn't half give me a buzz. The away fixture at Burnley in February 1967 was a watershed. My dad didn't fancy going and I managed to convince him to let me go with my mate from school, Dave Kirk. Our parents chaperoned us to the coach for departure and collected us as it returned, but the freedom in between was the dawning of a new age for me and Kirky. Burnley was only twenty-four miles away from home but we couldn't have been more excited if we had flown to the Moon. We went behind the goal with the Stretford Enders, right in the middle with the singing, swaying, irreverent masses and loved every minute. Nothing I had experienced in my first twelve years had come anywhere close to matching the thrill of that day.

I had passed my exams at primary school and went to Stand Grammar, an all-boys school in Whitefield. Academically I had made an okay start; I was quite attentive and obedient at this stage. I found I had a natural gift for cross-country running which would later prove invaluable at some away grounds. I loved the sport but it tied me to Saturday morning school competitions and that made it tricky to get to away matches in the afternoon. I persevered for three years but finally fell out of love with cross-country when I had to represent Stand at a Saturday afternoon meeting in Lyme Park, Stockport. The date was 18 March 1967. It was an important race and I had done well to qualify but it clashed with a United home game against Leicester. I felt empty all afternoon. I just didn't want to be there. As soon as we finished the race I got United's result from a coach driver in the car park. We had won 5-2 to keep on track for the league title which was great, but I wasn't there to see it and that was painful. It felt wrong. My heart was with United and this was the first time I can remember wanting to do something I felt strongly about rather than what other people told me was right. It wouldn't be the last.

After missing that home match in March 1967 I attended every United first team home game until 19 October 1985, a run of eighteen and a half years. Not just league games, every home game including friendlies. The addiction was kicking in.

My third year at Stand in 1967 was a rite of passage between boy and teenager. Stand Grammar wasn't a rough school but it had some tough characters. Football-wise it was a mix of United, City and Bolton supporters. I didn't hang around with the older lads who followed United, but I heard lots of tales about their football trips. There were stories of 'jibbing' the train (not paying the fare), hitch-hiking to London, sleeping in motorway services and close encounters with other fans on the Underground. All this in the pursuit of seeing United play sounded like a fantastic adventure to an impressionable young lad. I desperately wanted to be part of it. I desperately wanted to be a Stretford Ender.

Being a Stretford Ender involved three criteria. Firstly, you had to watch United's home games from the Stretford End. The 'End' was a swaying mass of humanity that housed United's most loyal, patriotic, vociferous, foul-mouthed and sometimes violent supporters. In the days before all-seater stadia, it was the main standing area of the ground, accommodating 20,000 fans under one roof. It was the heartbeat of United's following. The problem was my dad didn't approve and I had to watch the Reds from the more tranquil and 'soft' Scoreboard End. Not cool at all.

Secondly, you had to be a hard lad. That meant fighting for the cause at home games if other fans dared approach the 'End' and running with the pack at away matches when we tried to take over the home terraces. Well, I wasn't hard, or even close to being hard. So I wasn't doing too well at this stage.

The third criteria could pass as an alternative to being hard. You had to look hard. Most of the great unwashed on the Stretford End wore second-hand combat jackets. These were dark green/grey camouflage, ex-US Army gear bought from a store in

Tib Street, Manchester. The jacket would be adorned with an assortment of United badges, stickers, metal pins spelling players' names, chains and various slogans written in thick felt tip. Some lads wore miner's helmets – without the lamp – painted red. This was good protection from the coins, bottles and paint cans that sometimes got exchanged between fans at certain grounds. If you were really hard you would wear other teams' scarves, all tied together, through the epaulets on the combat jacket. These had been nicked from rival supporters and were 'badges of courage'.

Many years later, on his acclaimed *Bat Out Of Hell* album, Meatloaf advocated 'Two out of Three Ain't Bad!' and in 1967 that was my strategy. My aim was to regularly stand on the Stretford End and to look the part. This would involve 'battling' with my dad for over a year to get what I wanted.

While I was still soppy 'Scoreboard End Pete' I got an unexpected taste of the tales I had heard at school. The opening game of 1967/68 was away at Everton. Dave Kirk and I got the thumbs-up to go to this highly charged fixture without parental supervision because Dave's older cousin Jenny was going on the coach and she would be able to keep an eye on us. I know it sounds a bit 'toy town' given our aspirations but we were only 13! Anyway, off we went with Fieldsend's Coach Travel to see the champions start their defence of the title. United got hammered that day with Alan Ball running the show and we were fortunate to come away with only a 3-1 defeat.

Dave and I had got separated from Jen before we even got in the ground but we knew our coach was parked near a cemetery with green railings round it. This was our first trip to Liverpool and little did we know that most of Stanley Park had walls with green railings. In fact there were miles of green railings and hundreds of coaches but no bloody cemetery. We searched and searched for our transport but to no avail. After an hour we realised we weren't going home by coach as the final bus drove off towards the East Lancs Road.

Now, many things have changed in the world since 1967 but that doesn't include the hospitality Mancs receive in Liverpool. We are as welcome as a dead fly in a salad, so we needed to keep a low profile. Neither of us had enough cash to buy a train ticket, we didn't want to phone home like the two stranded wallies we were, so we decided to hitch a lift home. Because we had hung around for so long most of the home fans had dispersed but it still felt like hostile territory and hitch-hiking on the East Lancs Road to Manchester was a bit of a give-away. This was mid-August, the sun was still shining brightly and the local scallies were out scavenging. We had little cover as we walked through the Liverpool suburbs and the newly built, high-rise slums. A couple of times we thought we had been 'spotted' and took sanctuary in local shops until the coast was clear. By the grace of God we escaped any serious antagonists, but it took an eternity to get a lift. The relief and sheer delight I felt as we sped away from Liverpool was indescribable. Funnily enough, more than forty-six years later, I still get the same feeling every time we play there!

In the end it took half a dozen lifts to complete the thirty-five-mile journey, arriving home around 9 p.m. to much relieved sets of parents. They had kept in touch by phone after Jen had sheep-ishly knocked on Mr Kirk's door a few hours earlier to report she had lost Dave and Pete. Apparently she had managed to get our coach driver to stay as long as he could but the natives on the bus got very restless and they had to leave us. It had been a pretty scary experience for Dave and me but there wasn't a trace of fear as we recounted the tale to our schoolmates when the new term started. The story reached the ears of Reds in the fourth and fifth years who seemed to be impressed by our venture behind enemy lines. They started to give us knowing nods of 'awright' as we passed around school. We had arrived!

Despite the Everton setback, United started 1967/68 in great form, by the end of February we were top by three points and through to the quarter-finals of the European Cup. The FA Cup wouldn't be a distraction thanks to a defeat to Spurs at the first hurdle. United's squad from the previous season had been bolstered by promising youngsters Brian Kidd, Francis Burns, Alan Gowling and Jimmy Ryan. With a bit of luck we could retain the league and land that elusive European Cup. March saw us overcome a very tough Gornik Zabrze 2-1 on aggregate in the quarter-final, the away leg attracting a crowd of 100,000 in the Polish mining city. But in the league we started to wobble. United lost at home to Chelsea, the first league defeat at Old Trafford for almost two years. In the remaining seven home league matches we lost three more times. Our lead at the top of the league was whittled away, on the season's final day United were pipped to the title by Manchester City.

Busby's United had their eyes on a greater prize. On 24 April we had managed a 1-0 first leg win over Real Madrid in the semi-final of the European Cup. The return leg in Madrid didn't take place until three weeks later, the Wednesday after we had lost the title to City. Like two years earlier in Lisbon we were taking a very slender lead into a cauldron against one of Europe's giants. The sceptics seemed to have called it right as United went in 3-1 down at half-time. With no live TV coverage, radio was still having its finest hour. I listened intently on the family radiogram. When either side attacked, the crowd got excited and the commentator was drowned out. Through the fuzzy noise, midway through the second half I heard Sadler had scored a second goal for United and we were level on aggregate. The tension was unbearable. With twelve minutes left the commentary went very faint. It mentioned United going forward with Best then faded and said Foulkes was involved. Bill Foulkes was a veteran centre-half and rarely ventured forward so I thought United's attack had broken down. 'Goal!' screamed the commentator. I was anticipating a 4-2 scoreline when it came through loud and clear that United had equalised and now led on aggregate. I couldn't believe we were so close to reaching the European Cup Final. Those remaining minutes were like hours but United held on and all hell broke loose across Manchester and a small corner of the Bernabeu.

My dad was at his sister's that evening so I phoned him after the game. He was really up for the final. My uncle Albert, a knowledgeable old Red, joined the conversation and was already speculating about how Best would have a field day on the wide-open spaces of Wembley in the final. We talked about going. My dad said we should be able to get tickets because we had collected enough tokens from the matches that season. I hardly slept a wink that night with excitement. Across the front page of the *Daily Express* the following day there was a great picture of Charlton and Kidd lying on the ground at the end of the match, exhausted, emotional but victorious. Approaching them was a United fan, arms aloft, white butchers' coat trailing, ready to share in the ecstasy with his heroes. It captured the moment perfectly. The impression stayed with me and for years, I wanted to be that guy. How fantastic to go to Madrid in the European Cup semi-final, see United pull back a 3-1 deficit, silence a crowd of that magnitude and get on to the pitch to share in the celebrations. I could only dream of such delights.

So United, the first English team to compete in the European Cup the previous decade, became the first English team to reach the final. There were only a couple of weeks between the semi and final and there were two important hurdles to overcome. The first was getting a ticket. Early on Sunday 19 May we queued with thousands of other supporters hoping there would be enough tickets. There was no electronic distribution of tickets in those days, that wouldn't come until the mid-1990s. There were no executive members taking priority, no loyalty pot, just 8,000 season ticket holders who had first choice then it was open to those who had enough tokens on a first come first serve basis. We got there well before the ticket office was due to open but the queue still went down Warwick Road (now Sir Matt Busby Way) to the junction with Trafford Wharf Road and along the railway tracks towards Trafford Park for about a quarter of a mile. My heart sunk when we joined the back of the queue but four nervous hours later a nice man at the office handed my dad two tickets. I was off to the European Cup Final at Wembley! – or so I thought.

The second hurdle to overcome was getting time off school. A big stink had been created in the media about whether school-children who had tickets should be given the day off to travel to the final. It started with a story in the *Manchester Evening News* about some schools who would be turning a blind eye to absentees on the day compared with those schools that were taking a hard-line stance and threatening to treat the matter as truancy. Suddenly, because it was a United story the whole nation had a view. Ex-army majors were writing to *The Times* about the issue and how it was an example of the country going downhill. Questions were asked in Parliament. I couldn't believe it. I know I'm biased but, my God, this was the bloody European Cup Final and Manchester United were playing in it! How in anybody's mind that couldn't take priority over one day's education was lost on me. The grammar schools took the moral high ground initially. My dad got cold feet and said he couldn't risk my future education at Stand for one football match. He decided I couldn't go.

The Suez Canal and Cuban Missiles crises put together didn't match the tension going on in the Molyneux household. I kept working on my dad explaining how much this meant to me and that we may never get another chance to live this dream but he was a stickler for doing 'the right thing'. I couldn't eat. With days to spare common sense prevailed, a few schools broke rank and decided that if parents wrote to the head confirming they had match tickets and requesting absence then it would be granted with no further action taken. The 'resistance' tumbled like a house of cards and the great and the good of Stand Grammar's governors followed suit. Now I was on my way, praise the Lord!

I was 13 when I watched United beat Benfica 4-1 in the 1968 European Cup Final. I wish I could remember every minute of 29 May but at that age you don't savour special occasions because you don't appreciate the historical significance or their impact on your life. What I do remember is it being a glorious day with brilliant sunshine. My dad and I went by Preston's coach from Whitefield. I remember thousands of shirt-sleeved Reds everywhere we stopped on the way down. Outside Wembley there were hundreds of home-made flags proclaiming United's rightful place among the elite or supporters' affection for Busby or the players. There was a huge following from Malta, singing and dancing with an enormous banner on the forecourt just under the twin towers. Inside Wembley it was a concoction of heat, excitement and noise. I got separated from my dad but that was okay.

United's all-blue kit for the night looked awesome in the fading sun and then under the Wembley floodlights and against the deep, rich green turf. The support was superb with at least 95 per cent of the stadium given over to United's cause. The first half was niggly and tense, the great Benfica uncharacteristically resorting to Leeds-like antics to stop Best. A goal by Charlton early in the second half seemed to have won it until Jaime Graca equalised with ten minutes left. A few moments later Alex Stepney made a superb save from Eusebio that has gone down in football folklore. In those last ten minutes United look tired and edgy but that was shrugged off as Busby's boys exploded into action with three goals in the first nine minutes of extra time. Best, Kidd and Charlton scored to give United an unassailable lead. On the terraces there was an outpouring of relief and joy that the European Cup was finally destined for Old Trafford.

It was also one of those rare occasions when your dream game doesn't end as a tense affair holding on to a slender lead or scrapping to get a winner. We were 4-1 up with over twenty minutes left to sing United home; and sing them home we did. Several older fans around me were crying with joy. I didn't fully understand the significance then, but I guess they had watched United through the early European games, the days of the Busby Babes and the crash at Munich. How poignant was that night for those supporters? As United went up Wembley's famous old thirty-nine steps it was difficult to pick out the players in their dark-blue, sweat-stained shirts. Suddenly, a huge spotlight lit up the players among the crowd as they climbed to the pinnacle of club football to receive the European Cup. When Charlton lifted the trophy it gleamed like a beacon and looked massive. I found my dad and we celebrated together. We stayed to watch the lap of honour and join the partying that seemed to go on forever. Yet forever wasn't long enough. Manchester United were champions of Europe and we sang loud and long to let the world know.

3

YESTERDAY HAS JUST DEPARTED, AND TOMORROW HASN'T STARTED, ALL THAT REALLY MATTERS IS RIGHT NOW

The euphoria of winning the European Cup left Reds on a high throughout the summer of 1968. That August, dad decided we needed to be nearer our relatives. He was struggling to hold down his job and look after two children so we moved back to Salford where relatives could help out with childcare. The move took me to the place I would call home for the next thirty years, 19 Minden Street at Irlams o' th' Height Salford 6. The Height was a fairly unspectacular district, famous for only one thing of note. Earlier that century it housed two factories that made turnstiles. The more famous, W.T. Ellison and Co. Ltd, were the sole manufacturers of Deluce's Patent Rush Preventive Turnstile. Not a great chat-up line I agree, but virtually every football ground in the country and many other stadia had turnstiles installed which had been manufactured at the Height. I bored many a turnstile operator over the years by pointing out the inscription on the equipment as I was passing through and telling them that's where I live. Some old relics still exist, check them out. That's the turnstiles of course not the operators!

Anyway, I now lived round the corner from my best mate Dave Kirk who I had known from primary school. We soon teamed up with some other Reds in the neighbourhood, Geoff Milloy, Ian McEwan and Dave Stockton, and travelled to home and away matches together. Just before the season started I finally persuaded my dad to let me buy a combat jacket. He didn't so much agree to it, he just reluctantly let me get on with it. My mates and I all went off to the Army and Navy stores and got kitted out. This was the 'uniform' of the Stretford Ender and it was the first 'fashion' item I longed for. Most guys my age were into smart hipster trousers, floral shirts and corduroy jackets. That was for the street not the terraces.

I loved my combat jacket and set about decorating it appropriately. I had two silver metal chains draped across the back held in place by silver studs. I put a large 'United – Champions of Europe' sticker above the chains and in thick felt-tip pen carefully printed 'Georgie', 'Fitz' and 'Kiddo' in large black letters. My dad said I looked ridiculous, I thought I looked great. We both knew how it made me look and each of us loved it or loathed it for that reason. My next move was to convince my dad to let me stand on the Stretford End with the other lads. Ironically, their parents hardly went to Old Trafford so didn't have a clue what the 'End' was all about. My old fella did go and didn't want me to be part of that sub-culture. He was mellowing on the matter when I scored a stupid 'own goal'.

On August Bank Holiday 1968 Salford Rugby Club were playing at home to Wigan. I wasn't into rugby but the other lads were, so off we went to the game bedecked in our new combat jackets looking like Salford's Reservoir Dogs. During the match talk turned to 'nicking' a scarf. The practice of stealing scarves from other fans was what some of the harder lads did at football matches. I wasn't up for the idea. I wish I could say it was because I knew it was wrong but the truth is Salford's scarves were red and white like United. We already had a United scarf so another one in the same colour wouldn't look like a trophy. I suppose we all egged each other on and maybe being the new kid in the neighbourhood I wanted to impress. At the final whistle youngsters our age used to invade the pitch to get close to their heroes. Kirky went for it and like a fool I followed. Out of the corner of my eye I saw Dave grab a scarf from a lad's neck and disappear into the crowd. I grabbed out at another lad, pulled his scarf from behind and tried to leg it when I was stopped dead in my tracks. The bloody scarf was tied in a knot at the front and I was unwittingly strangling this poor kid. An embarrassing scuffle took place, I got the scarf free but it had delayed my getaway. As I tried to escape I was apprehended by four adults who not only handed me over to a policeman, but kept banging on about not wanting football hooligans spoiling the good name of rugby. They had obviously read the stuff on the back of my new jacket.

I had never been in any real trouble before. I nearly wet myself. I was driven off in a police car to the Crescent Police Station, Salford. I gave my details and was told I would be charged with larceny. I didn't know what larceny was but it sounded serious. The police rang my dad to come and collect me. God, what a mess! I always respected my dad even when I was giving him a hard time as a teenager. Deep down I knew he was doing the best for Michelle and I in difficult circumstances and he was a decent man. Now he had a son just turned 14 who was turning into his worst nightmare. I will always remember the look on his face as he walked into the police station and saw me. It wasn't anger, upset or disgust, it was just abject disappointment. That hit me hard. His first words were, 'That bloody jacket's going in the bin as soon as we get home!' My coveted coat had become a symbol of all evil. I guess I had played into his hands on that matter. I chose not to argue.

Dad was pretty good about the whole incident – he could have torn into me but he knew that I realised I had done wrong. The charge of larceny would have meant a criminal record. I was told to report to the Crescent the following Saturday for the police's decision. When we arrived a very stern-looking sergeant took my dad and I into a side room. Dad started to explain how sorry I was but the sergeant politely cut him short, before turning to me and delivering a lecture I'll never forget. He made it clear that I was in danger of ruining the good opportunities I had been given in life by following the 'wrong' examples. He explained in very strong terms that I had let myself down, and my father too. He told me no charges would be brought but the misdemeanour would stay on police records and if there was a repeat I would be in serious trouble. I took the bollocking, apologised and we left. My passion for United didn't waver but I had to be on my best behaviour for a few months. I got the green light to still attend United matches but for the home games it was still the Scoreboard End. The combat jacket was banned but not binned. The Stretford End and the 'hard' look would have to wait.

On the pitch United started 1968/69 in mediocre form, hovering around mid-table. We thought it was just a blip and Reds were still wallowing in the after-glow of becoming European champions. The real distraction though was the prospect of being World Club Championship winners.

When Real Madrid won the 1960 European Cup 7-3 against Eintracht Frankfurt they were proclaimed the finest team in the world. The Spaniards had won the first five competitions. The South American football press thought different, 'prove it' they said, and the InterContinental Cup was born. The champions of Europe and South America would play an annual two-legged tie to determine the best club side in the world. In 1968, United were pitched against Argentina's Estudiantes de la Plata from Buenos Aires. The new competition was having its problems; games were becoming very heated affairs. The previous autumn Celtic's tie with Racing Club from Argentina had degenerated into a brawl with six players sent off amid chaotic scenes. There was still bad blood between England and Argentina from the 1966 World Cup game when Alf Ramsey famously branded the South Americans as 'animals'. Nevertheless this was a game to decide the champions of the world and that's how it felt to United supporters. We had long believed our team was the best on the planet and wanted to make it official.

Estudiantes were at the start of a great era in which they won the Copa Libertadores de América, the equivalent of the European Cup, three years in a row. The first leg took place in Buenos Aires on Wednesday, 25 September 1968. United travelled via Paris, Madrid and Rio de Janeiro and set-off immediately after the game against Newcastle on the previous Saturday. The match was broadcast live on BBC radio around 4 a.m. UK time. Thousands of Reds set their alarm clocks and tuned to the crackly commentary from 7,000 miles away.

As well as having some excellent players, Estudiantes also proved to be masters of cynical football. Their defenders were provocative in the extreme and most United attacks ended with callous fouls. Their crowd was really hostile and the atmosphere in Buenos Aires felt intimidating even sat in my dressing gown in Salford. Estudiantes won 1-0, with a header from Marcos Conigliaro in the twenty-seventh minute. Nobby Stiles, a member of the victorious England team two years before, had been demonised in the Argentine press in the weeks running up to the game. They nicknamed him the 'assassin' and throughout the game Estudiantes players tried to convince the referee the title was well deserved. Inevitably towards the end of the game, Stiles was sent off for throwing his arm up as a gesture of frustration after he was given offside. Some assassin, eh? Nevertheless, only a goal down we were confident United could turn it round in Manchester.

The Football League gave United a blank Saturday on 28 September to allow time to recover from the journey. This was unheard of as league fixtures were almost sacrosanct. The importance Matt Busby gave to the World Club Championship was underlined by the team selection for the league game at Anfield on the Saturday before the second leg. Six youngsters were brought in, three making their senior debut. The unfamiliar United line-up fought valiantly but lost 2-0 to Liverpool. Normally that would be a big setback but we had bigger fish to fry!

Busby appealed for calm ahead of the home leg against Estudiantes, pointing out his players had shown great restraint in Buenos Aires and asked the Old Trafford crowd to do the same. He added diplomatically, 'our opponents' attitude to soccer is totally different to our own'. The build-up to the game was immense and that was in less hyped-up times. Sky Sports would be hysterical about it nowadays. A fanatical 63,500 crammed into Old Trafford and the atmosphere was explosive as we roared United on.

We had been warned that their best player was a winger called Veron, nicknamed 'the wizard'. After seven minutes he scored a header to give Estudiantes a 2-0 lead. United had wave after wave of attacks but just as in Argentina their defenders were kicking lumps out of our forwards. In the last ten minutes it all erupted. Best had been 'assaulted' all evening. As the referee was booking one of their players for the umpteenth foul, George decided to exact his own justice, felled his opponent with a brilliant right hook and just walked off. The incident sparked a running brawl along the touchline as the Estudiantes players and backroom staff made a molehill into a mountain. All this disruption suited the opposition as the minutes ticked away. Willie Morgan equalised on 90 minutes and in a last valiant attempt Kidd scrambled the ball over the line only to find the ref had blown for full time.

Had that goal stood it would have taken us into a play-off in Amsterdam three days later. The dream of being world champions was over, but it was the manner of defeat that left such a bitter taste. We wanted another go at it next year to right the wrong. That made it even more important to retain the European Cup.

After my early season transgression at Salford Rugby Club, peace broke out between my dad and I that winter. I behaved myself and by Christmas I had 'migrated' to the Stretford End to join my mates and got my combat jacket back. I think he was giving me a bit more independence in the hope I would respond favourably. I constantly badgered him to let me follow United away and it was starting to bring results. The draw for the third round of the FA Cup would send us to Exeter on 4 January 1969. This tie really captured my imagination, a 250-mile trip to far-off Devon to see Exeter City, ninety-first in the English league, up against the European champions in the FA Cup. That excitement increased when the local coach company, Fieldsend's, advertised a trip leaving at midnight on the Friday night. I saved any money I got for Christmas and, surprisingly, my dad agreed to let me go. Dave Kirk's parents did the same. We couldn't believe our luck, we were 14 and free to spread our wings to the furthest away match in the country.

On the trip were a few fifth formers from school. One was 'Murph' who was 'cock' of the school. He was a big, tough, United fanatic whose warm welcome often involved grabbing your balls rather than the customary handshake. It was all done in a manly, jocular, Stretford End-type way and meant you were one of his mates. But it didn't half make your eyes water. Still, that was the price of having him on your side and you wouldn't want it any other way.

Travelling through the night made it a great adventure, few on the coach slept. The M6 only went as far south as Cannock then and just twenty-four miles of the M5 had been built, so several hours were spent travelling down the old A38. We stopped off at several greasy spoon cafés and entertained bleary-eyed regulars with our fine array of songs and ditties. Arriving in Exeter around 9 a.m. the first hour or so was whiled away with an impromptu game of football in the coach park. As each coach or minibus pulled in dozens more would join the kick-about. No one picked sides, few rules applied, it was a free-for-all reminiscent of medieval mob football from which our great game evolved. Later we toured the town, meeting up with other Reds as they arrived. The locals made us really welcome, a pleasant change from many first division venues we visited, and United's usually boisterous following responded in kind. Murph carried out his own per-sonalised charm offensive, greeting local males with a smile and a handshake then as they walked away he would chant, 'Exit, exit, Exeter! Exit Exeter!' Each one would look back and see his huge grin and a thumbs-up. For the girls he chose more seasonal greet-ings, rasping out a hearty 'all the breast, luv' or 'happy nude year'! Corny yeah, but it got a few laughs and we were still in the throes of puberty.

This was still the era when you fielded your best eleven for the FA Cup no matter who you were playing. Resting players was something that took place between Sunday and Friday. A crowd of 18,500 squeezed into Exeter's St James' Park to watch the champions of Europe in very unfamiliar settings. United's contingent occupied a big open end, and those who couldn't get in perched themselves in the several trees dotted around the stadium. After fourteen minutes Exeter's lively forward, Banks, headed his team into a 1-0 lead and United look ragged. The locals were in wonderland when Banks had the ball in the net again but the ref spotted a handball. Gradually, normal service resumed, Johnny Fitzpatrick pulled us level right on half-time and United's class and fitness won the day as we ran out 3-1 winners. The long journey back was much quieter as people caught up on lost sleep from the night before. We arrived home at 2 a.m. on Sunday, absolutely shattered but with memories to last a lifetime and a taste of freedom that whet our appetite for more United adventures.

Sometimes my dad would put his foot down; he stopped me going to the FA Cup fifth round tie at Birmingham that season. The match was postponed on the Saturday due to bad weather and played the following Tuesday. It would mean taking time off school to get there but my dad said no. I missed the game, my mates went and for a week I didn't speak to my father. I have still got the match ticket intact. But by and large I was getting to the games I wanted to. In March 1969, United played a re-arranged league game at Nottingham Forest on a Monday night. It was in the school holidays and I wanted to go. None of my mates were going, not even Kirky. No local coach companies were running a trip and there was no British Rail 'special' train which was rare for a United away game. Lingleys coaches, or to give them their full title Lingleys Sale-Away Touring Company, used to transport the team to away matches in those days. Based in Stretford, they also ran coaches for supporters and were running one to the game at Nottingham. I told my old fella I would have to go on my own and he agreed to it – another notable landmark.

On the coach that night were many of United's top lads. I don't mean fighters, although some were, I mean United's most loyal supporters who travelled anywhere no matter what. I was there among them and it felt great. I remember a big lad called 'Gibbo' who wore a sheepskin coat turned inside out with the sleeves cut off and several United slogans on the back. His mate was called 'Chink', a tall, thin lad with thick black hair and an olive complexion. They entertained the back half of the coach with their stories of previous trips, particularly the skirmishes they had encountered at West Ham two days earlier. As we reached the outskirts of Nottingham we passed several Forest fans who gestured their displeasure at our arrival in their fair city. Gibbo kept trying to get off the coach and discuss the matter. His mates managed to persuade him otherwise but I had seen enough to decide I was sticking with these guys once we got to the ground in case we got a hostile reception. In the end protection wasn't needed and United won 1-0 thanks to a George Best goal. It was one of only two away wins in twenty-one league games that season so I was extra pleased. On the coach home I had time to reflect. I was now doing what I wanted to do. I was following Manchester United home and away, singing and cheering my team on. I would travel with my mates where possible or on my own if it meant getting there. I wore the outfit I wanted and was running with the pack I wanted to run with. I was a Stretford Ender.

On Tuesday, 14 January 1969, Sir Matt Busby announced to the world that he would be retiring at the end of the season. At 59, he felt it was 'time to make way for a younger man … a tracksuited manager'. He said the pressures of managing a top-class team were becoming too great for a man of his age and he would now take on the role of general manager. 'United is no longer just a football club,' he said, 'It is an institution. I feel the demands are beyond one human being.' He had had enough and who could begrudge him a more leisurely lifestyle after what he had been through for Manchester United? His successor wasn't named immediately so the focus remained on Sir Matt winning a second successive European Cup. The final was scheduled for Madrid on his 6oth birthday. What a send-off that would be.

United had eased passed Waterford, Anderlecht and Rapid Vienna and were pitched against AC Milan in the semi-final. The Italians had played in two previous finals, winning in 1963 at Wembley. Italian teams had the edge over their English counterparts in the 1960s but many in Britain considered them to be negative, defensive and experts in cynical play. Some might even say cheats and in the following decade several stories emerged of referees taking bribes from wealthy Italian clubs. In a hard-fought first leg at the San Siro, Milan beat United 2-0. By the time the second leg came round on 15 May United's domestic season was complete bar one league game against Leicester. We were eleventh in the league and out of the FA Cup, so it was do or die and it certainly felt that way as the teams walked out into the Old Trafford sunlight. The Stretford End was at its very best that night – a thunderous, heaving mass of Red devotion. There is a YouTube clip from the game and it includes a few shots of the Stretford End, it is worth a view if you get the chance. Look at the crowd surge forward as Charlton's goal goes in, it's very special and sadly something that's gone forever.

United took the game to Milan but the Italians held out until midway through the second half when Best went on a mazy run towards the Stretford End. He threaded the ball to Charlton on the right who cannoned his shot high into the net. An over-used phrase in football is about 'the crowd going wild with delight'. Well that night the expression was pitifully inadequate. The din reached new heights even for Old Trafford, one more goal would level it. Milan were under siege and the supporters sensed blood. It was drama at its highest and most raw. Minutes later Denis Law, only a couple of yards out, side-footed a Crerand cross goalwards. A prostrate defender on the goal-line stretched a leg and scooped the ball out of the goal and into the keeper's arms. From where I was at the back of the Stretford End the ball looked to be a foot over the line. Six United players in the penalty area instinctively celebrated the equaliser. After a few seconds of confusion, the referee just waved play on.

Pandemonium broke out; 20,000 fans in the Stretford End felt they had seen United robbed of a legitimate equaliser and a possible place in the European Cup Final. Derision poured down on the referee and the Italian team. Coins, bolts and other objects also rained down but the chance had gone. Milan kept us to one goal to reach the final. Just like the World Club Championship, United had fought hard but come off second-best. Both games had ended in controversial fashion making the disappointment harder to swallow. We felt cheated. On both occasions United had played the better football but poor refereeing allowed Estudiantes' and Milan's tactics to win the day. Sir Matt wouldn't bow out in the Madrid sun with a second European title to his name after all.

The powerful romance with the European Cup had kept us spellbound for two seasons but it papered over cracks that had started to appear. United were still a team full of stars and on those European nights Charlton, Law, Morgan, Crerand, Kidd and the mercurial Best were majestic. The team was ageing but, more critically, it was losing its hunger for the run of the mill matches. In 1968/69 we lost fifteen league games out of forty-two and were second best to a number of very average teams.

The curtain came down on Sir Matt Busby's time as manager of Manchester United on 17 May 1969 win a 3-2 win over Leicester. In October 1945, at the age of 36 and with no management experience, he had taken charge of a club that had badly under-achieved since the early years of the twentieth century. Busby inherited a ground so badly damaged by the German Luftwaffe it couldn't be used for home matches until 1949 and a team full of veterans whose careers had been cut short by six years of war. He wisely retained those older players whereas several managers had a clear-out when peacetime resumed. With a couple of inspired signings he built a team that won the FA Cup in 1948. In Matt Busby's first six seasons, United were runners-up on four occasions and crowned champions in 1952. More importantly, Busby developed a brand of football that captured the public's imagination. His focus was on attack and a style that would win games and friends. The way the game should be played.

When his first great side grew old it was time to take the wraps off the young lads he had nurtured and the Busby Babes were born. In 1956 and 1957 United won back-to-back league titles. The average age of the 1956 team was just 22, unprecedented in the British game. The visionary Busby took United into Europe only for his beloved creation to be cruelly taken in the snows of Munich in February 1958. I was too young to see the Babes play but there is little doubt that team would have become England's finest ever side. Had it not been for the crash, Manchester United may have won the elusive treble forty years ahead of Fergie's finest hour. Critically injured at Munich, Busby was hospitalised for three months. Many men would have called it a day there and then but he fought back and by 1963 had fashioned his third great side. That team won the FA Cup, two league titles and the European Cup in a golden five-year spell that put the swing into Manchester's 1960s.

To thousands of Reds, Sir Matt Busby was Manchester United. His philosophy the catalyst that created the empire we see today. His great sides, the steady flow of trophies and the quality of football built United's tradition and brought the club worldwide admiration and interest. Furthermore, regular crowds of 50,000 to 60,000 brought in much needed cash after the ravages of war and then Munich. The money financed not only the playing staff but restored Old Trafford to the finest club ground in Britain. Matt Busby managed United for twenty-four and a half years, the statistics below show his overall record. It includes the second half of 1970/71 when he returned for a brief spell following the sacking of Wilf McGuinness but excludes the three months after the Munich crash when Jimmy Murphy took charge:

Played	W	D	L	F	A	W%	D%	L%
1141	576	266	299	2324	1566	51	23	26

I was born too late to catch the majority of the Busby years, but I count myself very fortunate to experience his last six years at Old Trafford. I never met Sir Matt to talk to but I wish I had. I got his autograph with a crowd of other schoolboys when I was 11 but was far too star struck to speak. Two particular incidents come to mind whenever I think of him. In January 1979, I was on the forecourt at Euston station waiting for the next train back to Manchester after a cup tie at Fulham had been postponed. There were hundreds of United fans milling around the station when a buzz went round that the team were coming through to board their train. Sure enough there was Dave Sexton followed

by the United stars of the day, Joe Jordan, Gordon McQueen,
Steve Coppell, Stuart Pearson, Martin Buchan and the Greenhoff
brothers, all struggling to reach the platform area.

Each player got a rousing cheer as the crowd surrounded their
heroes to pat them on the back or shake their hand. It was a bit
boisterous and undignified but all with good intent. The players
finally made it through and the supporters, who by now covered
the forecourt for as far as the eye could see, were belting out
United songs. Suddenly, a hush descended and the throng parted
like the Red Sea in biblical times. An elderly man came through
the middle, pulling his suitcase on a trolley. It was Sir Matt Busby.
There were no chants, no songs, no mobbing, just hundreds of
United fans of all ages standing in awe as the great man passed
by. Most remained silent and simply watched; those who did
speak whispered a respectful 'Sir Matt' and nodded their heads in
acknowledgement of his presence. He smiled to all, and every few
steps courteously said 'thank you, boys, thank you', appreciating the
path they had made for him. The hairs on my neck stood on end at
seeing him and witnessing the impact his presence had on people.

One evening in January 1994 I was driving through Stockport.
I was getting married later that year and had collected the invitations from the printers. It was a drab, forgettable winter's night
and a local radio station was my only company. A minute or so
into a record the DJ faded the music. The next few words seemed
unreal and I was completely unprepared for them, 'I regret to
announce, news is just coming in that Sir Matt Busby has passed
away at the age of 84.'

I carried on driving for a short distance before realising I wasn't
paying much attention to the road or anything else. I pulled over,
stopped the car, and sat there in a silent daze for several minutes.
Sir Matt hadn't been in the news much recently, he was club
president but kept a low profile and most people didn't know he
had been ill. Tears started to well-up in my eyes. I felt I had lost
someone very very close to me; someone I had respected since
I was a young boy. Now that era had come to an end. But what
an unprecedented era. What an extraordinary man. What a very
special life. Later that night I drove down to Old Trafford to pay
my respects.

4

LOOKS LIKE WE'RE IN FOR NASTY WEATHER, ONE EYE IS TAKEN FOR AN EYE

United took three months to announce Sir Matt's successor. On 9 April 1969, Wilf McGuinness was unveiled as the man to take over the reins from 1 June. A Manchester lad to the core, McGuinness had signed for United in 1953 on the same day as Bobby Charlton, making his debut at 17 and becoming an integral part of the Busby Babes. In 1957, he won a league championship medal and would represent England at all levels. A leg injury forced him out of the game for a long period in early 1958 and caused him to miss the fateful trip to Belgrade. Attempting a comeback the following year, he badly broke his leg in a reserve team match and he was forced to retire from playing at the age of 22. United made him youth team coach in 1961 and he also coached the England youth squad to a Junior World Cup win in 1964. This led to him being part of Sir Alf Ramsey's backroom staff for the successful 1966 World Cup tournament. At Old Trafford, he was promoted to reserve team manager.

The club realised that replacing Busby would be a daunting task and tried to mitigate that risk by appointing 31-year-old Wilf McGuinness as chief coach with Sir Matt moving up to a newly created post of general manager. At the time it appeared a logical approach. McGuinness had already served the club for sixteen years, groomed many of the current stars and worked closely with Matt Busby but he was still young with no experience as a manager.

McGuinness was given responsibility for team selection, coaching, training and tactics; Sir Matt was accountable for 'all other matters affecting the club' including spokesman.

In the summer of 1969, while most of the human race marvelled at man's Moon landing, United supporters pondered more earthly matters. Could Wilf take the giant leap into Sir Matt's shoes? Well, the initiation couldn't have been worse for the new regime. After a draw at Crystal Palace we lost the next two games at home, 2-0 to a good Everton side then 4-1 to lowly Southampton. Saints striker Ron Davies scored all four goals and gave veteran defender Bill Foulkes a torrid time. This turned out to be Foulkes' last game for United after eighteen seasons, a record of 688 first team appearances, four league titles and FA Cup and European Cup winners' medals. Bill Foulkes never attracted the big headlines but he had been a rock for United. He had survived the Munich crash and, with Harry Gregg, played on thirteen days later to help revive a club in crisis. He deserved a better finale, but that wasn't the manager's fault.

Wilf McGuinness' medium-term plan probably involved phasing out the ageing players he had inherited, but the abysmal start and injuries forced him to take drastic action immediately. For the return fixture away at Everton a week later he made five changes to the team but the news that reverberated around world football was the dropping of Denis Law and Bobby Charlton. Law, the 'King of The Stretford End', had never been dropped in his illustrious career and Charlton only once, nine years previously. As the team was announced at Goodison there was a buzz all around the ground. The Everton supporters' surprise quickly turned to delight, then mocking. For Reds it was a big shock and while many of us agreed the two superstars should be left out on form, we were amazed McGuinness had the balls to do it and so quickly. United were outclassed 3-0 by a strong Everton team that went on to win the title that season.

Law and Charlton were reinstated for the following game at Wolves but the new boss had sent a clear message – nobody was guaranteed a place in his side and he was prepared to make the tough decisions. The centre half spot had been troublesome for a couple of years, Bill Foulkes was 37 and several reserves had failed to establish themselves. Busby had tried to lure Welsh international Mike England from Blackburn a couple of seasons earlier but Spurs won race. Before the game at Molineux, United signed Ian Ure from Arsenal. A Scottish international, Ure was a rugged stopper who had some history against United after getting sent off with Denis Law at Old Trafford two years earlier. The two Scots gave supporters in the main stand a ringside seat at one of the best fights this side of Las Vegas. Ure's arrival steadied the defence, we stopped shipping goals and for a short time he became a terrace hero earning the nickname 'Iron Ore'.

By the start of December, United had clawed their way up to eighth in the table, only a couple of points off fourth spot. United supporters knew the title had already gone but qualification for Europe was a must for the fans. We had also put a good run together in the League Cup. The top clubs had treated this fledgling competition with contempt in the early 1960s, but since the final moved to Wembley in 1967 and the winners got automatic entry to Europe it had become a major trophy. United progressed to the semi-finals and were drawn against our old rivals, City.

As well as a managerial change, United fans were getting used to another new phenomenon. Growing up in the early 1960s in Manchester we had lauded it over City fans whose team had been in decline since the late 1950s and relegated to the Second Division in 1963. In January 1965 their future looked bleak with a record low home attendance of 8,015 against Swindon Town. That summer, City appointed a management team of Joe Mercer and Malcolm Allison. In their first season, City won the Second Division title and made shrewd signings in Tony Book, Mike Summerbee, Colin Bell and Francis Lee. They had a mediocre season back in the top flight, finishing fifteenth out of twenty-two. In recent years United had won two league titles, the FA Cup and had three ventures into Europe. Our team contained three European Footballers of the Year. We got gates of 60,000-plus, City averaged 35,000. Basically, United had the glamour, the style, the top players, the trophies, the crowds, the stadium, the lot. City had, well ... er ... a ground in Moss Side?

Nobody saw it coming but in 1967/68, Manchester City became champions of England for only the second time in their history. Even then United trumped it two weeks later by becoming the first English team to lift the European Cup. In 1968/69 both Manchester teams were in the European Cup. All summer long City fans were crowing about how great they were going to be. Some things never change, eh?

Coach Allison went even further and said they would 'terrify' Europe. Imagine our delight, and their crushing embarrassment, when they were knocked out in the first round by Fenerbahce of Turkey. In 1968, very few football fans had heard of Fenerbahce and Turkey was a third-rate footballing nation.

We had a huge repertoire of songs that ridiculed City, their ground and their insipid support. Derby matches were one long mickey-take. But a shift of power was taking place. City carried on winning trophies after 1968 whereas United stopped for almost a decade. It would be the first time in a generation that United weren't the dominant team in Manchester. Worse still, City had the upper hand on the pitch. In ten league games from 1969 to 1974 our record against the Blues was won one, drew three, lost six and some of those defeats were heavy ones. Through primary school and most of secondary school, City supporters really were invisible men in the playground. I couldn't buy an argument with them. Even Bolton fans used to wind them up! City's rise in the late 1960s plus our steady demise turned the tables dramatically. For Reds it was unbelievable, unbearable but undeniable. City had been the little kid brother you once looked down on who grew up overnight, stole your girlfriend and your best mate then gave you a bloody nose for good measure.

As much as we hated their resurgence, it didn't half increase the rivalry between the teams and supporters. City the cocky upstarts, United with their preened feathers slightly ruffled. The two derby fixtures each season brought plenty of passion and tension but in 1969/70 United and City would meet five times in all competitions. Pride was everything. We lost 4-0 away in the league meeting in November, a dreadful experience where City simply ran us ragged. The pairing in the League Cup semi-final in December was an early chance to exact revenge, knock the buggers out and get ourselves to a Wembley final. In the first leg at Maine Road a dodgy Franny Lee penalty two minutes from time gave City a 2-1 advantage but United had matched them and most Reds in the 63,000 Old Trafford crowd on 17 December 1969 believed Wembley still beckoned. United were 2-1 up with eight minutes left and the famous old ground was rocking. Another late goal, this time by Summerbee, put City through and denied us a final place.

Incredibly, five weeks later United played City again in the fourth round of the FA Cup at Old Trafford. The omens weren't good. They were the holders, cock-a-hoop after beating us twice already that season, George Best was suspended and Law was out injured. But United purred that day, trouncing City 3-0. Willie Morgan got a penalty but the man of the hour was Brian Kidd with two goals. Our pride was restored.

As the 1970s dawned, United's trinity of Best, Law and Charlton were still our heroes. However, a couple of young pretenders were challenging the status quo. Willie Morgan arrived in August 1968 for a huge fee of £118,000. He took a year to find his form but we saw some great displays from the right-winger. In 1970 and 1971 he was voted Supporters' Player of the Year. However, in January 1970 the player setting the terraces alight was 20-year-old local lad Brian Kidd and the two goals against City propelled him to stellar heights. Injury-hit Denis Law, the King of The Stretford End for seven years, managed only thirteen games in all competitions that season. scoring a very un-regal three goals.

United had a home fixture against Leeds two days after defeating City in the FA Cup. As the players were warming up in front of the Stretford End a lad ran on to the pitch and placed a makeshift crown on Brian Kidd's head. Some of the young turks on the 'End' started a new chant of 'King Brian' to Steam's number one hit 'Na Na Hey Hey Kiss Him Goodbye'. The press captured this coronation and went to town with stories of 'The King is Dead! Long Live The King!' the following day. In truth, Kiddo was in great form and growing in stature with the Old Trafford faithful but those guys who tried to shift Law's crown were premature and ill-advised. I found it embarrassing and annoying. You don't dismiss or disrespect a legend in that fashion and we certainly don't at United. The majority on the terraces and in the stands still revered Law and did so until the end of his days at United. Law returned to the Old Trafford throne after injury and reigned for another three seasons. A respectful nineteen years would pass before another true 'King' was deemed worthy of the title.

The FA Cup was United's only chance of silverware and the supporters were really up for it. We hadn't won the cup or even graced the final for seven years. Although I had been lucky enough to go to the 1968 European Cup Final with my dad, I desperately wanted to go to Wembley as a fully fledged Stretford Ender and with my mates. The fifth round hurdle was an away tie at Northampton.

George Best's suspension was over but during his five-match absence United clocked up three wins and two draws and were playing well. Some people were suggesting Best should be left out and the papers debated it all week. These were rebellious times, first Law now Best's contribution to the team being so openly questioned. Best was selected and one can only imagine the feeling of 'I'll show you' festering inside him as he ceremoniously cut Northampton to shreds on a muddy, windswept County Ground. United won 8-2 and Bestie rattled in six. The clips of those goals have been shown so many times they are part of the nation's psyche. I was fortunate enough to get in that day, at the Hotel End, and witness this piece of history and magic. Funnily enough, the pitch only had three enclosed sides because the football team shared its ground with Northamptonshire Cricket Club in those days. Given the score it seemed appropriate somehow.

Next up was a difficult trip to Middlesbrough but a Carlo Sartori equaliser got United a draw before we won a tight replay 2-1. Our first FA Cup semi-final for four years paired us with Leeds United who were on course for the treble. By the time United met Leeds at Hillsborough on 14 March 1970 we were sixteen games into an eighteen-game unbeaten run stretching back to early December. Players were back from injury and suspension and the defence had settled into a composed unit. The Leeds game ended 0-0 so it was off to Villa Park on Monday 23 March for the replay. Again it was goalless but United had a brilliant chance to score when Best lost his marker just inside the Leeds half and was bearing down on goal with only goalkeeper Sprake to stop him. About twenty-five yards out George simply tripped over the ball and the chance was gone. There was no extra time or penalties then so the two teams met again on the Thursday at Bolton's Burnden Park. Just as in the 1965 semi, Billy Bremner broke United hearts with a late goal. Leeds went on to lose to Chelsea in the final.

It was another case of so near yet so far. United's league form fell away and we finished eighth in the table. Some commentators coined it a 'respectable' eighth. Respectable? Maybe for other clubs, never for Manchester United. When eighth place becomes respectable we should abandon Old Trafford and let the council build houses on it! United's main problem was too many drawn games, seventeen out of forty-two, the most we had seen in a season since joining the Football League in 1892. Only once has it been surpassed, in 1981 when Dave Sexton's team managed eighteen draws.

At the end of Wilf McGuinness' first season in charge supporters were split. Many looked to the positives, a transitional season with a new manager taking over from a living legend. We had come very close to winning through to both domestic cup finals. United still had a good team with some great individual players. That summer, Sir Alf Ramsey named Charlton, Stiles, Kidd, Sadler, and Stepney in his World Cup squad for Mexico. Add to this Best, Morgan, Crerand, Ure, Dunne and Law plus several youngsters who had made a solid contribution to the cup runs. The squad was strong. Others took a more critical view, we were never in the race for the league, we failed to qualify for Europe and while the cup exits were unlucky, a trend was forming. In the last two seasons we had been 'unlucky' in all our key matches – Estudiantes, Milan, City and Leeds. Was it bad luck? It was starting to feel like an excuse for failure rather than a reason for optimism.

I felt McGuinness had done a decent job but United needed to be back among the winners soon. I was almost 15 and revelling in the great adventure of following United home and away. I was so besotted with everything United that blind faith had kicked in. Just getting to all the matches and talking about them took up most of my time. I didn't overly concern myself with which direction the team were heading, surely the mighty United would bounce back the following season?

I had my nose pressed firmly against the department store window and couldn't see that the walls and roof might be crumbling a little. The side was ageing; McGuinness released Foulkes, Brennan and Law at the end of the season (although Law didn't leave) but Crerand, Charlton and Ure were the wrong side of 30. I felt we could build on what we had already, but much would depend on the youngsters stepping up to the mark and earning the right to be called Manchester United players. The likes of Steve James, Carlo Sartori, Jimmy Rimmer, Don Givens, Alan Gowling and Paul Edwards weren't kids, they were in their early 20s and had been around the first team squad for a couple of years.

In August 1970, Wilf McGuinness was promoted to team manager and Busby remained general manager. Before the league season started we were treated to a little hors d'ouvre. The first in

a long line of 'Mickey Mouse' competitions was introduced by
the football authorities to boost revenue. The Watneys Invitation
Cup was the first commercially sponsored football tournament in
England. The Watney Mann brewers, famous for their Red Barrel
beer, stumped up £82,000 to get their name added to the new
competition. The pretence was to promote goalscoring, so the two
highest scoring teams from each of the four divisions would play
in a pre-season knockout competition. Teams who had qualified
for Europe or gained promotion were exempt. The games would
all be played within one week at the start of the season.

High-scoring United were invited and accepted. I feel a bit
embarrassed writing this now, but at the time I was really excited
about it. I have always loved going to different places following
United and this was a chance to visit grounds we wouldn't do
normally. In reality, it was embarrassing that two years after being
crowned champions of Europe, United even 'qualified' for the
invitation to a competition for teams who were top of the flops.

United were drawn away at Reading, so I ventured to Elm
Park on 1 August where we beat the Third Division side 3-2.
The following Wednesday it was off to Boothferry Park to play
Second Division Hull City in the semi-final. After 120 minutes
the tie stood at 1-1. The organisers had decided that any match
finishing level after extra time should go to a penalty shoot-out
and United out-gunned the Tigers 4-3 to go through. Over the
last forty years we've all watched penalty kicks decide cup-ties
at every level in football. Well, Hull versus Manchester United
in the Watney Cup in 1970 was the first competitive match anywhere in the world to be decided on penalties. Up to this point
drawn cup games were decided by replays, play-offs or by the toss
of a coin. The Football League had to get special permission from
UEFA and FIFA to use sudden-death penalties in the Watney
Cup. As a result of the experiment both organisations decided to
use penalties to decide drawn games in European and World Cup
competitions. It is fascinating how often United are involved in
footballing firsts, even in their less glamorous times.

United were in the Watney Cup Final away at Derby, the other
top flight team in the competition. United supporters knew it
was a tinpot cup but now it really seemed to matter. Thousands
travelled down to the Baseball Ground on a very hot August
day, only to see us trounced 4-1. Given our illustrious history it

seems a minor issue that United didn't win the Watney Cup. At the time, though, it was yet another step along the slippery road from the pinnacle of European football to also-rans. United fans don't just turn up and expect to win competitions, even in the golden years. We do, though, have high expectations and it hurt to be embarrassed even in a minor competition. Having been 'King of the Castle' for so long some Reds couldn't handle the pain of failure on the pitch. Throughout the second half at Derby, and after the match, United fans left a trail of destruction. They ransacked then demolished a refreshments hut inside the ground and ran riot around the streets outside. The scenes would become a feature of our decline.

Most football fans are in a state of perpetual denial. In our world hope springs eternal. There was a new season ahead and most of us believed United could hold their own despite the Watney Cup defeat. There were no new purchases despite lots of speculation, but Denis Law decided to stay and fight to regain his fitness and place. Sadly, after three league games United had only one point and hadn't even scored a goal. To misquote your average manager, 'It was déjà-vu all over again, Brian.' We picked up wins but it was very patchy through September, October and November. United didn't win two consecutive league games before Christmas and spent most of that time in the bottom half of the table.

Once again, salvation lay in the League Cup. After beating Aldershot and Portsmouth we met Chelsea at a rain-soaked and misty Old Trafford on 28 October 1970. This turned out to be a great game with an atmosphere to match. United played like the glory nights of the late 1960s with a forward line of Aston, Best, Charlton, Kidd and Law rolling back the years. This was the match where George Best scored the winner by waltzing through the Chelsea defence from the halfway line. On his way he withstood the crudest of scything tackles from Chopper Harris before rounding Bonetti, planting the ball in the net and sinking to his knees, arms aloft right in front of a captivated Stretford End. United won 2-1 and I remember going home to my bedroom and playing 'We Shall Not Be Moved' by The Seekers over and over again on my record player, adding 'we're on our way to Wembley' as I bellowed the chorus. Not exactly sex and drugs and rock 'n' roll but it got me through the night.

Crystal Palace were seen off 4-2 in the quarter-final and United drew Aston Villa in the semis. Villa were in the third tier having fallen from grace and were starting their 'fat Elvis' period. The twin towers were in sight and United were nailed-on favourites. In the run-up to the first leg United hit a dreadful patch in the league, winning only one of seven games which included a 4-1 thrashing at home to City. The League Cup was a chance for redemption but we could only manage a 1-1 draw in the first leg. In the return match at Villa Park, two days before Christmas, United had their best team out and when Kiddo gave us the lead we were ready to sing the lads home. But Villa hit back with headers from Andy Lochhead and Pat McMahon to go through to the Wembley final. Another humiliating defeat for United supporters everywhere and this time in a competition that did matter.

On Boxing Day, I went to Derby and witnessed a stunning 4-4 draw on a snow-covered Baseball Ground. The point left United eighteenth in the league. The cup exit had been the last straw for the board. On 27 December 1970, Wilf McGuinness was relieved of his duties as team manager and demoted back to reserve team trainer. Sir Matt reluctantly agreed to take over the reins until a new manager was found. United's succession plan was in tatters.

History has pigeon-holed Wilf McGuinness' tenure as that of a man who found it impossible to manage in the shadow of a legend. That's probably a fair summary but too simplistic. We know a lot more now than we did then. The team had deep-seated problems and it would take another two years of turmoil for the club to understand and accept the depths of the crisis. The idea of pairing Busby and McGuinness was sensible, the old head guiding the gifted and ambitious new manager. In such situations, however, there has to be a genuine and visible shifting of power from the old to the new. The board had a responsibility to ensure the shift took place but in that respect they failed. The role of the manager must be clear and unambiguous otherwise people will take advantage. With Busby still there as general manager, McGuinness' role was compromised.

There was an interesting, tell-tale sign right from the outset of Wilf's reign. The club's programme, *United Review*, still carried 'Sir Matt's Column' just inside the front page. Historically, this is where the manager gave his views on the current state of the side, the visitors and topical football titbits. Wilf McGuinness didn't have a column in the club programme and it stayed that way during his eighteen months at the helm. It might seem a small issue but in any organisation employees pick up on the message from the top – intended or unintended.

A more crucial issue was the lack of available funds. Wilf McGuinness identified that the team had lost its collective focus. We still had great players who could put on a show but not week in week out. From 1969 onwards key players lost some of the hunger having reached the pinnacle of their career with the European Cup win or carried injuries which limited their performance. The team needed new impetus. When McGuinness dropped the big names he brought in young lads who were still finding their way. He needed a couple of new leaders and winners brought into the club to support the change. In his book, *Manchester United Man and Babe*, McGuinness confirms that he identified three targets in the summer of 1970, defenders Colin Todd and Mick Mills and striker Malcolm McDonald. Because Sir Matt dealt with transfers Wilf could only make recommenda-tions and wait to see if they materialised. None of the players joined United. All three went on to have distinguished careers at the top of English football. A short time later there was talk of Ron Davies, a prolific scorer in that era, but a financial hitch scuppered the deal.

Ironically, United had been renowned for big money signings to back-up home-grown talent in the 1940s, 1950s and early 1960s. Yet during the period of transition post-1968 we spent just £80,000, on Ian Ure. United's only other significant signings since 1964 had been Willie Morgan and Alex Stepney. McGuinness was being asked to get United back to the top on a shoestring budget. Two months before his demotion, McGuinness sent out a team at Newcastle that cost just £5,000 in transfer fees. This must be a post-war record for Manchester United. Only Tony Dunne cost the club money. The full side that lost 1-0 at St James' Park on 31 October 1970 was: Rimmer, Edwards, Dunne, Fitzpatrick, James, Sadler, Burns, Best, Charlton, Kidd, Aston. Sub: Watson.

So why didn't the board provide McGuinness with the finan-cial backing? The club was still the best supported team in the country, if not Europe, with average crowds of 51,000. Perhaps the post-Munich spending had drained the club's resources?

Perhaps the board hoped the players coming through the ranks would replace the stars of the mid-1960s? Perhaps it reflected the board's lack of confidence in the manager? In contrast, Wilf McGuinness' successors were given huge funds to put United back at the top.

At the press conference to announce he was taking over the reins again, Sir Matt said how sad he was that it hadn't worked out for a man who he himself had recommended. Busby added, 'He might have been a wee bit raw.' The older players revered Busby and had won everything under him. Wilf just couldn't galvanise the players he had grown up with. Unfortunately, the younger players McGuinness had to put his faith in couldn't compete at the highest level and very few went on to play a significant part in United's history. As for the fans, well, most of us felt sympathy for Wilf McGuinness but our team had become mediocre. We had endured a dismal eighteen months, and the coup de grace was losing to Third Division Villa when one step from Wembley. We had grown accustomed to more, much much more.

United's playing record under Wilf McGuinness reads:

Played	W	D	L	F	A	W%	D%	L%
87	32	32	23	127	111	37	37	26

The facts put McGuinness thirteenth out of United's seventeen managers, based on win percentage. The draw percentage of thirty-seven is the highest of all seventeen managers, reflecting the mediocrity. His record in cup matches, however, tells a different tale. An incredible twenty-three games in only two seasons, thirteen wins, seven draws, and three defeats. But how telling those defeats were. Just one more goal in those semi-finals could have got United to a cup final and possible victory. A trophy and European football would have given Wilf McGuinness a foothold in management. It would have bought him time and possibly the money to deliver the transition. Remember it took Sir Alex four years to win any silverware in England. There is a very thin line between success and failure.

The demotion hit Wilf McGuinness badly. He felt he should have been given more time and backing from the board, a pain he carried for many years. He stayed at the club for a few months but his position was untenable and he took a job in Greece. Wilf McGuinness never managed at the top again, so the big question has to be, did he have the ability in the first place? If so, why didn't he resume his career after a break and find success with another big club? Or did the experience of those eighteen months crush his confidence so much that a total comeback was impossible? Maybe he just wasn't cut out for management? Football history is littered with good coaches who became failed managers. We can only speculate.

One thing that isn't in doubt is the passion Wilf McGuinness has for Manchester United. No United supporter should forget his commitment to the cause. The events around Christmas 1970 never affected his love of the club. He stayed loyal. Wilf is one of us. If anyone doubts that they should listen to his live radio commentary in the final minutes of the 1999 European Cup Final when those two late goals went in! He is a true Red.

5

SO I LEFT MY HOME,
I'M REALLY ON MY OWN AT LAST,
LEFT THE TRODDEN PATH AND
SEPARATED FROM THE PAST

New Year 1971 brought little cheer for United supporters. Sir Matt reluctantly took the manager's chair at Old Trafford for the second time and presided over a sorry state of affairs. Just picture his in-tray as he settled back into familiar surroundings. Busby's heir to the Old Trafford throne had been demoted as we languished fifth from bottom of the league. United had just lost a League Cup semi-final to a third tier side. The board, under pressure from the Football League, had closed part of the Stretford End directly behind the goal in response to a number of missile-throwing incidents. Before the New Year was a week old second tier Middlesbrough knocked us out of the FA Cup, effectively ending our season, and George Best walked out on United in the first of a series of vanishing acts.

Ray Charles, the great American soul singer, once said, 'If it wasn't for bad luck I'd have no luck at all!' and that's how it felt around Old Trafford as the festive season drew to a close. In the programme notes for his first game back Sir Matt acknowledged the challenges. His comments made heavy reading but nevertheless he finished his column with the traditional wishes for a happy New Year. If you were a Red, you had to see the funny side! Despite the gloom the players responded to Busby's stimulus and won eleven of the remaining nineteen league games to finish eighth. No new players were brought into the club; the manager

simply got the squad to gel again. The football was exciting in
those four months starting with a superb win at Stamford Bridge,
a 5-1 mauling of Southampton, a thrilling 5-3 comeback at
Palace and a much needed triumph over City at Maine Road in a
4-3 classic. The derby on 5 May 1971 was Sir Matt's final game in
charge of his beloved United.

I was getting to nearly all United's matches by this time. In two
seasons I had missed only Southampton away in November 1970.
Not bad for a school kid! I would save any money I was given and
put it towards my football trips. Sometimes to get to the furthest
away games I would sell part of my record collection or board
games. Other times I had to be a bit more devious. Most nights my
dad would give me a few bob to buy myself supper at the local chip
shop. I would leave the house, wait in the back entry for half an hour,
then come back in and tell him I had eaten the supper on the way
home. Every little helped. The pennies soon turned into pounds.

The lads I knocked about with, Dave Kirk, Geoff Milloy,
Dave Stockton and Ian McEwan, went to every home game and
about fifteen to twenty away. It wasn't a competition between
us but I used to keep a record of each game we had attended.
Nothing too strange about that for a lad of 15, we love making
lists don't we? But I also recorded how many miles we travelled,
the average miles travelled, the score of each match, the competition, the colour United played in, the different scorelines I had
seen, how many United games I had seen in which months etc.
You get the picture.

At the end of each season I would summarise the detail, study
it and dream of the coming season's away trips. I couldn't get
enough of it. As well as statistics I collected memorabilia; match
programmes, books, magazines such as *Charles Buchan's Football
Monthly*, *Goal*, *Inside Football* and *Shoot*, cigarette cards, ticket
stubs, pennants, badges, Football Pinks and any paper with a
United midweek match report in it. Basically, anything with
United's name on it.

Perhaps the most perverse was my United soil. In the late
1960s and early 1970s United supporters were allowed on the
pitch after the last home game of the season to salute their heroes.
It was a tradition and all good natured. I used to dig my heel into
the pitch and pull up a small sod or two. I took the turf home
in my pockets, put it in a clean, sealed coffee jar and labelled it

by season. As I got older I couldn't bring myself to throw out any of the items I had collected. When I was eight or nine I can remember my uncles telling me they used to have lots of United and City memorabilia including papers and programmes from the Busby Babes era. When I asked if I could come round to see the souvenirs they all said they had thrown them out, usually when they got married. I couldn't believe it – sacrilege!

This disappointment left me very determined on two counts. Never get rid of your football mementos and be very wary of this thing called marriage! Now well into my fifties, I've still got these treasures in a purpose-built storeroom including my jars of soil. Pride of place is my 1968/69 Old Trafford turf. The contents of the jar now resemble freeze-dried coffee beans and don't smell too good. But they still mean the world to me. Best, Law, Charlton and other European champions played on those beans.

I had completed my O Levels in the summer of 1970 and stayed on to do A Level languages. I had no idea what I wanted to do in life; I was drifting. Dave Kirk had left Stand Grammar to join Norweb, the local electricity company. He was working in the offices and loving it. I had thought of applying but there was a big obstacle – you had to work one in six Saturdays. That was enough to put me off. I had just escaped from the shackles of Saturday cross-country which restricted my free time to watch the Reds. In the spring of 1971, Dave told me Saturday working had been stopped and Norweb were advertising for new recruits. I applied, got taken on and stayed for thirty-six years. I started work on 16 August 1971 in the Frederick Road offices in Salford. Two days later United played away at Chelsea and I missed the game. It really rankled but I couldn't skive off three days into my working life. Later that week, a nice lady from Personnel gave me a holiday card and told me I was entitled to nine days leave. It came a bit late for the Chelsea game but it would be enough for me to get to all the remaining matches.

That Chelsea fixture on 18 August 1971 was the last time I would miss a United first team match for nine years and three months. I saw every competitive game United played until Brighton away on 22 November 1980. This sequence also included friendlies and testimonials bar one. The only United game I missed anywhere on the UK mainland in that period was at Aberdeen on a Monday night in October 1972.

I was now 17 and had the money and freedom to follow United wherever I wanted. I no longer needed my dad's financial support to travel although he still kept a close interest in what I was up to. When I received my first pay packet I opened a post office account to save for trips abroad to watch United play in Europe. Ever since I had seen that 1968 photograph of the supporter celebrating on the pitch with Kidd and Charlton in Madrid, I had dreamed of following United abroad. I only got paid £9 per week, but £2 to £3 went in the savings account. I did this religiously, firmly believing our return to European competition was imminent. I worried I might not have enough saved in time. Sadly, it would be a long five years before the Reds qualified again. I ended up earning quite a bit of interest on those savings!

Dave, Mac, Stocky, Geoff and I used to travel to away games by coach. We enjoyed the delights of J.W. Fieldsend Coach Tours from The Height in Salford. Fieldsends had a special talent for employing drivers who had difficulty finding most First Division football grounds. I lost count of the times half way through the outbound journey the driver would turn and ask the passengers if anyone had been to this ground before and did they know the way? Invariably we would park up at the last minute, run to the ground and get through the turnstiles just in time for kick-off. Their drivers were more familiar with transporting old 'biddies' to Blackpool and Morecambe than taking lively Reds on away trips.

In October 1970 we set off for a match at Newcastle. Lo and behold we made great time, didn't get lost, and arrived around midday. At last, a clued-up coach driver, he would get a decent collection on the trip home for sure. As our bus crossed the Tyne Bridge we saw a huge gang of Newcastle fans, all skinheads, all in black and white, booted up and looking particularly mean. Driving past them we exchanged the obligatory two-fingered salutes, mouthed words through the back window that the Stretford End was here and we would have them on the run later that afternoon. All of which had the desired effect of infuriating the monochrome natives. They started to give chase but gave up pretty quickly as the coach drove on.

A few hundred yards down the road the driver took a left turn and drove up a very steep road. Halfway up he pulled over, parked up and said, 'Right lads, see you here after the game.' As we got off the coach, I looked back down the road and saw the ugly mob we had just encountered walking past the bottom of the hill. They didn't see us at first so we jumped back on the coach and quickly explained to the driver he needed to park the coach somewhere else. He was having none of it, this was where he had planned to park and this is where we were going to park! I was just thinking how he had blown that chance of a great tip when a shout came from the back of the coach that the Geordies had seen us. I got off again to see the mob of eighty to 100 charging up the hill. This time they wanted an encounter of a slightly closer kind.

I had been to Newcastle before and knew it was a rough place. Two years earlier I went in their Leazes End with about 1,000 Reds and it was a non-stop battle all afternoon with bottles, belts and chains as their chosen weapons. So, here we had the classic fight or flee moment. There were fifty-two on the coach including girls and middle-aged supporters. There were also a few lads who didn't relish a skirmish. In seconds I had decided we would lose a fight so fleeing was the answer. We had a start of about 400 yards on them and ran up the hill leading to Leazes Park. It was the only way we could go but it was taking us away from the more populated city centre.

On a cold, damp October lunchtime there was hardly a soul about and certainly no police. The irony wasn't lost on me that normally we had the undivided attention of the boys in blue whenever we arrived at away matches. As we approached the park I was up with the leading pack and looked backed for the first time. Most of the people on our coach were behind us, and while I couldn't see our pursuers, I could hear their terrifying shouts. Surrounding the park was a wall about four feet high. Directly in front of me as we approached it was a lad called 'Fatdog', an affectionate nickname he had acquired for his slightly rotund shape. He wasn't a close mate but he was a good lad and a feature of most away matches with Fieldsends. Going over that wall was like the first fence in the Grand National; we were packed in and shoulder to shoulder. Sheer adrenalin got most Reds over the wall as if it wasn't there. But not Fatdog. Too many crisp butties had caught up with Fatdog from Salford, to give him his full title, and he struggled. He had three goes in what seemed a lifetime while I stood there watching in disbelief. Finally, I picked him up by his jacket collar and jeans and threw him over the bloody thing. The fall was a bit higher on the other side but he did thank me. Well, eventually he did.

My cross-country skills were kicking in and once in the park I ran like Forrest Gump. I was out in front and happy to be there. I was concerned for my mates and the others but, hey, this was survival at its rawest. It was terrifying and the noise of the chasing pack sent a chill down the spine. We must have run round that park for fifteen minutes. Every time I looked back our group seemed slightly fewer in number. When the opportunity arose one or two would 'deck-off' and hide in bushes or behind walls. It was risky but it worked for them because the Newcastle lads carried on chasing the leading pack. I didn't want to take that risk so I kept on running. From the park I saw the floodlights of St James' Park. Trying to think logically through the mounting fear, I headed for the ground where there would be police or officials or someone that could help. Unfortunately, it was still two and a half hours to kick-off. The gates weren't open and the nearest thing to any officialdom were a couple of hotdog sellers. I looked round again, there was now only a handful of us and all my mates had disappeared.

As the Newcastle fans closed in, I darted down a cobbled alley that ran down the side of the ground. It was long and straight, and as I got halfway along I realised the noise from behind had stopped. I looked round again and the mob had gone. Had they got tired, or just given up or were they pummelling the few sad souls I had just left behind? All I knew was I had to get out of that place as fast as I could, so I carried on running. When I reached the end of the alley I instinctively turned right but within seconds I stopped in my tracks. The black and white horde came spilling out of a parallel alley and the leaders were facing me about thirty yards away. I couldn't quite see the whites of their eyes but I could see the look on their faces and for a couple of seconds I froze. I thought I was history but something inside made me turn on my heels and run for my life.

I headed towards the town. The bemused shoppers provided a little bit more cover but the Geordies still had my scent. I had to try something, so after turning a corner I decked into a tobacconist's shop. I crouched down and pretended to tie my shoelace so I couldn't be seen through the shop window. Seconds later the pavement outside reverberated to the sound of thundering boots as the pack passed by. I held my breath and prayed none of them would choose this moment to stop for twenty Benson & Hedges.

As the noise of the rabble disappeared, I looked up to see an old fella leaning over the counter. 'Are you ok, son?' he enquired. 'Yes thanks,' I said, red-faced and exhausted. I wanted to hug this man and tell him his little shop had saved my life but I just muttered something about having rubbish laces and left.

I laid low for an hour trying to blend in with the shoppers but in reality I was still in shock from the ordeal and people probably saw a wild-eyed youth who seemed high on something. I didn't know what had happened to my mates or the other Reds on the coach. I made my way to the ground. United always took a huge following wherever we played which was more than capable of looking after itself. But the stories on the street were of Newcastle fans running amok and seeing off Reds at the station, the coach parks and outside the ground.

Once inside, I eventually found my mates who were all okay. They had managed to find refuge in the park and hid there until they could mingle with other fans going to the match. They thanked me for acting as a decoy up front! We stood at the back of the open Gallowgate end and throughout the match there were around twenty or thirty Newcastle lads just waiting outside on the forecourt for a scrap at full time. United lost a poor game 1-0 and at the final whistle the Geordies decided to follow the Reds heading for the old Manors Train Station and we sneaked back to our coach.

Everyone had a horror story of the afternoon's events. Amazingly nobody got badly injured but it had been a close call. Most had been chased all over Newcastle. There was a lad in his late twenties who had been wearing a big red jacket. I remember seeing him when we first got off the coach and thinking, 'Mmmmm … not a good choice.' Understandably he had found it hard to shake off our friends from the north so ran into Debenhams to hide but a few Newcastle lads followed him. On the second floor he ditched the red jacket in a bin, grabbed a suit off the peg and ran into the changing rooms where he sat until the coast was clear. Still petrified, he put the suit on and decided to buy it in an attempt to get out of there alive. He watched the whole game in his new outfit and travelled back home in it. He looked really smart, just a bit out of place.

On 9 June 1971 United unveiled Frank O'Farrell as the new manager. He had just led Leicester back to the top flight and prior to that he had three successful years at Torquay United. As a player he had been a talented midfielder at West Ham and Preston. Frank O'Farrell was 43 when appointed United's supremo. Sir Matt Busby moved onto the board as a director. The roles of club manager and chief coach disappeared and to all intents and purposes O'Farrell was the manager of Manchester United. He even had his own column in *United Review*. The 1971/72 season brought a fresh start all round. I had left school, was all grown up and had a job. United introduced a smart new red shirt which contained a white filled-in V at the front and white collar. On the terraces, combat jackets and denims were giving way to penny-rounder shirts, tank top jumpers, two-tone trousers and brands such as Ben Sherman, Brutus, and Jaytex.

Young lads started having their hair 'styled' instead of just trimmed and 'feather cuts' became all the rage. Straight men began wearing strongly scented aftershave and for a year or two the whole world seemed to smell of Faberge's Brut 33 Splash-On Lotion. Silk scarves, with your team's name on it, replaced woollen ones and were worn tied round the wrist rather than the neck. Boots were still essential footwear though, usually Doc Marten's.

Once again United were in the Watney Cup and Halifax Town's small ground was the venue for O'Farrell's first match. The omens weren't good as the Shaymen beat United 2-1. Worse still, we had to play our first two home matches away from Old Trafford after the ground was closed as punishment for a knife-throwing incident the previous February. This meant we started the league season with six consecutive away matches. Those two 'home' games were played at Anfield (against Arsenal, won 3-1) and Stoke (West Brom, 3-1). The Anfield game was on a Friday night and more than 20,000 Reds headed west. Entrance was by payment at the turnstile, so the big question was where to stand, Anfield Road or Kop? For me it had to be the Kop – it was too good an opportunity to miss.

As we got onto the terraces a big 'Liverpool!' chant went up. Fighting broke out and we found ourselves surrounded by Scousers in one corner. Some United fans spilled on to the pitch and legged it to the safety of the other end. I waited a short time but the situation in that corner of the Kop was getting worse so off I went across Anfield's lush turf. Unfortunately, the kick-off was imminent and the players were warming-up on the pitch. As I reached the halfway line there was an Arsenal player in my path. I diverted my

run but he moved across to block me. 'What's this tosser doing?'
I thought. 'Does he not realise it's just gone off back there.' As I got
within touching distance I realised it was Peter Storey, Arsenal's
renowned hatchet man. Just as I was thinking I should have taken
my chance on the Kop, he smiled, winked and moved out of the
way. Seconds later I reached the safety of the Anfield Road end.
Storey had just been having a laugh but I told my mates he bottled
it because he didn't want to risk losing his hardman tag!

Despite the handicap of all the away games the Reds got off
to their best league start for eight years. O'Farrell moved Willie
Morgan and Alan Gowling into midfield and it worked a treat. In
a superb first half to the season United led the the league by five
points in early December. The run to the top included some classic
matches. Sheffield United were early front-runners when they came
to Old Trafford on 2 October. George Best went on that famous
diagonal run past countless white-shirted defenders then fired the
ball into the far corner of the Scoreboard End net. At Maine Road
on 6 November, 17-year-old Sammy McIlroy made his debut and
scored the opener in a pulsating 3–3 draw which kept United top.
Reds, though out-numbered, out-sang City's faithful in their new
North Stand home. Just after United went 2–0 up, one fan next to
me was on his mate's shoulders knocking back a tin of Watney's
Party Seven. These were massive cans of beer that held seven pints
of bitter. They were cumbersome forerunners to six packs and normally taken to house parties rather than footie matches. Somehow,
he had smuggled it into the ground and perfectly captured the
celebratory atmosphere. United ruled the First Division again!

On 27 November I was lucky to see United beat Southampton
5–2 at the Dell when Bestie scored a hat-trick. This was my first
trip to Southampton and the big concern was getting in. It was
a tight little ground holding just over 30,000 and with United
riding high I knew it would be a full house. I travelled on the BR
special train and after a five-hour journey arrived at Southampton
at 2 p.m. I ran all the way to the ground, and just as I got through
the turnstile a bell rang out telling the operator that the stadium
was full. I must have been one of the last United supporters to
squeeze in that day; on the return journey there were hundreds
of disappointed Reds who had got locked out.

After three barren seasons it was great to have United in the
title race again and top of the league for the first time since

April 1968. Just as important, the team was playing in the United
style. Kidd, Charlton, Law and Best were scoring for fun, especially Bestie. He bagged seventeen goals in the first twenty-five
games, including two hat-tricks and several vital winners. There
seemed much to thank O'Farrell for. On New Year's Day 1972
we lost 3-0 at West Ham and, unbeknown to us, it would set
the tone for that year. George Best didn't turn up for training
the following week but the story didn't break until Thursday's
Manchester Evening News carried the front-page headline 'Best
Dropped'. Twelve months earlier George had disappeared to
London for a week, preferring the company of stunning actress
Sinead Cusack to that of the squad. This time it was London
again but Miss Great Britain Carolyn Moore was the attraction.
Within days everything was patched up. George apologised, was
fined and 'ordered' to move back into digs.

United's bubble had burst. We lost seven league games on the trot
including a 5-1 mauling at Elland Road. We fell from top to ninth
in two months. O'Farrell decided to strengthen the side and on
29 February bought Martin Buchan from Aberdeen for £125,000
– a club record. A week later the record was smashed again when
Ian Storey-Moore signed from Nottingham Forest for £200,000.
To put this expenditure into perspective, the previous club record
had stood for four years since Willie Morgan signed for £118,000 in
1968 and prior to that Denis Law for £115,000 in July 1962. United
meant business and the imports excited us. Buchan was a young but
classy defender while Moore had been a top winger in the English
game for six years. Their arrival stopped the rot but couldn't lift us
up the table. For the third season in a row we finished eighth. Stoke
put us out of both cup competitions, so once again no trophies and
no European football to look forward to.

We had all got carried away with United's apparent return to
greatness only to be badly disappointed. In later years, journalist
Jim White aptly described United's splendid pre-Christmas form in
1971 as 'the last twitch of a dying corpse'. We couldn't see that then
and many Reds hoped against hope the good form would return
the following season. As thoughts turned to summer holidays a
new bombshell hit United's faithful. On 21 May we picked up the
Sunday papers to read the front-page headline, 'Best: I Quit!' On the
eve of his twenty-sixth birthday George took off to Marbella and
announced that he was tired of football and Manchester United.

At the time it felt like the end of the world. What was once a mutual love affair between player and club now appeared broken and contemptuous. Worse still it was being played out in public via the world's press. George Best was my hero just as he was to thousands of United supporters. While his behaviour was disappointing, we would forgive him anything. He lit up our lives, our team, our city. Enough has been written elsewhere about the demons George faced throughout his adult life. We didn't understand it fully then; we just wanted George Best at Old Trafford playing like Georgie Best can. Remarkably, the episode blew over and he was back for the start of 1972/73.

United must have turned down the invitation for that season's Watney Cup. We met the entry criteria as only European qualifiers Leeds and City had scored more goals. Instead we opted for pre-season friendlies at Torquay and Bournemouth. Fine for me though, I had not been to either ground. The lads I knocked about with didn't fancy friendlies so I went on my own. I got the midnight Yelloway's coach from Chorlton Street, Manchester, travelled through the night and arrived in Torquay at 7am Saturday 29 July. The match didn't kick off until that evening so it was a while before other Reds started arriving. Through away trips with Fieldsends I had met a couple of girls who followed United all over, Denise from Salford and Liz from Stretford. Both were a great laugh, they wore big fashionable Crombie overcoats and two-tone strides and they knew their football. I met up with them in Torquay and we had a great summer's day just chilling out among the palm trees on the English Riviera. I had a crush on Liz but was still pretty shy around girls then. I was at ease chatting about general topics with them but any hint of making a romantic move rendered me tongue-tied and cumbersome. So we all just stayed good friends much to my frustration. The game at Plainmoor was watched by 17,000 on a balmy July evening in this picturesque south-coast town. United put a strong team out but a tame affair ended 0-0 despite Torquay being in the Fourth Division.

I had told dad I would get a room in Torquay but everywhere was full so after a few beers dozens of Reds settled down for the night in shelters on the promenade. Eventually we fell asleep only to be rudely awakened around 2 a.m. by the police and their dogs. The local council didn't take kindly to vagrants and anyone dossing was 'encouraged' to move on. The next six hours were spent finding any little nooks and crannies to get our head down but no sooner had we got settled than the police would find us and we would be moved on again. It was a bit of a laugh at first but the fun wore off as the night wore on. Next day we caught up on our sleep on the beach.

Denise and Liz were going back to Manchester as were most of the others who shared our disturbed night. I was going onto Bournemouth for the Monday night game. I decided to hitch-hike. You'll probably gather by now this wasn't a meticulously planned trip but that's the way I like it, it makes for a better adventure. One lift was from a soldier on his way back to Salisbury barracks. He had a red two-seater convertible sports car and it tore up those Dorset country roads. Later that Sunday afternoon I fell lucky when a van full of Ellesmere Port Reds pulled up in an old, converted ambulance. I opened the back doors and there, like modern-day illegal immigrants, were ten or twelve of the Stretford End's finest welcoming me with a rousing 'hello, hello we are the Busby Boys'. We hit it off right away.

After arriving in Bournemouth we got a bite to eat, had a few drinks and a great sing song. We encountered a few hostile natives on the way back to the van but the Ellesmere Port Reds and guest soon chased them off. They let me kip in the van overnight which was just as well because the summer sun had given way to heavy rain that stayed over the south coast for the next twenty-four hours. On the Monday three to four thousands Reds, mainly cockneys, descended on Bournemouth for the evening friendly, or 'Public Practice Match' as it was billed on the programme. Dean Court was a wet and windy venue that night but another 17,000 hardy souls watched United get a 3-1 thumping from their Third Division hosts. Bournemouth's striker Ted McDougall was the star of the show with two goals. United's manager would remember that performance and be back.

We dossed in the van again that night and took all Tuesday to make our way back up to the north-west. The lads dropped me at Warrington and I got home late that night to recount my great adventure to my dad. He didn't fully approve but he was happy I was back in one piece. I will always be grateful to those lads from the Port, they were a terrific bunch and I saw them regularly at away games over the next twenty years.

When the 1972/73 league season began it was another disaster. Our record after nine games was four draws and five defeats.

We were bottom of the table having scored just four times. In late September Frank O'Farrell went back into the transfer market and bought Wyn Davies from Manchester City for £60,000. Davies was a 30-year-old centre-forward renowned for his heading ability. Wily old Frank also remembered Ted McDougal's brace and handed Bournemouth £200,000 for his services. Both started scoring immediately but results didn't improve.

That autumn, Third Division Bristol Rovers knocked us out of the League Cup at Old Trafford, Spurs pasted us 4-1 at home and City whacked us 3-0 at Maine Road. We scraped a couple of wins but on Saturday, 16 December United were torn apart 5-0 by fellow strugglers Crystal Palace deep in south London. The result was our worst since March 1964 but the manner of the performance was the biggest embarrassment. We were out-classed; the heart had gone out of the team. Even Bert Head, the Palace manager, said he felt saddened to see a great club like United in such a sorry state.

For many United fans it was one embarrassment too many. Hundreds went on a wrecking spree on the train from Selhurst Park to Euston. Seats, tables, luggage racks and even toilet pedestals were ripped out and hurled through the windows. Extra police and dogs were brought in along the route to control the riot. The Sunday press enjoyed a feeding-frenzy with stories of United's demise on and off the pitch covering front and back pages. Four days later the board relieved Frank O'Farrell of his duties.

The Irishman was cruelly dubbed 'Frank O'Failure' in some circles, but let's deal with the facts. United's playing record during his time in charge was:

Played	W	D	L	F	A	W%	D%	L%
81	30	24	27	115	111	37	30	33

This performance puts the Irishman twelfth out of seventeen United managers based on win percentage. His reign was the third shortest in the club's history, beaten only by two men who stood in as caretakers – Murphy in 1958 and Hilditch in 1926. The record is very similar to that of his predecessor Wilf McGuinness. However, fourteen of O'Farrell's wins came in the first three months of his reign during that autumn surge to the top. Unlike McGuinness, O'Farrell was given big money to transform the team and the £585,000 outlay on four players in 1972 was colossal by any standards. He wasn't given the time to fulfil his rebuilding but when results are going so badly there is one eternal question – how long do you give the manager? In December 1972, United were rooted to the foot of the table and looked to be heading for the Second Division after thirty-five glorious years in the top flight and only four years since ruling Europe.

Perhaps with hindsight Frank O'Farrell would have been better advised focusing on the defensive frailties of the squad. He spent £460,000 on strikers yet the attack was still prolific, as our qualification for three Watney Cup tournaments proved. The real problem was in the back four, particularly the centre. United supporters knew we had not had a quality centre-half since Bill Foulkes peaked in the mid-1960s. I believe if O'Farrell had brought in a top-class stopper to play alongside Buchan he may have stopped the rot and bought himself more time. Teams struggle badly without a strong centre-back partnership. Trawl through the players who played in United's back four between late 1968 and 1972. Few loom large in the club's history.

Sadly, the biggest challenge during O'Farrell's reign was the 'enemy within'. The manager was battling against more deep-routed issues affecting the club. When he tried to establish himself and make the necessary tactical or personnel changes, some senior players covertly resisted. I believe Sir Matt deliberately and genuinely tried to distance himself from O'Farrell from the outset to give the new manager his own space. But there's an old saying in business, 'Be aware of the shadow you cast.' Sometimes people in authority don't always appreciate the impact they have on others around them. Just by his presence Sir Matt was a constant reminder of the glorious past. Once more, that prevented the shift of power, command and respect to pass to the new manager. I don't blame Sir Matt or United's board; it was a very delicate situation. How do you plan the succession of a legend, without offending the legend, while giving the new man full authority?

Frank O'Farrell also had the specific problem of dealing with George Best at a critical time. With hindsight we now know our beloved George was spiralling towards the end of his career with United. His off-field excesses were causing problems on it. In the weeks preceding the Palace debacle Bestie had gone AWOL for the fourth time in eighteen months. Frequently absent from training, this caused resentment within the squad and sapped morale. It was a huge distraction for a manager who already had a mammoth task on his hands. George was still the best player at Old Trafford and in the British Isles if not Europe. The manager couldn't let him go with the possibility of him turning out for City, Leeds or Liverpool. It was unthinkable. O'Farrell tried to coax the Ulsterman in an attempt to nurture a sense of responsibility out of the errant genius. One might draw a comparison with Alex Ferguson's handling of Cantona in the mid-1990s, but while Fergie's gamble paid handsome dividends O'Farrell's blew up in his face.

Fate had already pressed the self-destruct button for George and he couldn't respond to the challenge. As the main parties within the club realised failure was imminent there was an undignified race to disown the problem. In a sad couple of days in mid-December 1972, O'Farrell recommended to the board that Best be transfer listed, Best wrote a letter to the board stating he wanted to quit United and the board in turn sacked both O'Farrell and Best.

O'Farrell ran out of time mainly because of results. Should he have acted sooner? Should he have been more ruthless sorting out the Best situation and removing some of the other 'elder statesmen' in the squad and build his own team? Well, 'ruthless' wasn't his way of doing things and he paid the price. Like McGuinness, O'Farrell bitterly resented the lack of time and support from the United board and carried it with him for a long time. Also, like McGuinness, he never managed at the top in English football after his spell at Old Trafford. So once again the question has to be, 'Was he the right man for the job in the first place?'

There is no doubt that the enormous weight of expectation from United's own supporters was playing its part in the managerial merry-go-round at the club. Then, as now, we didn't simply expect success, we demanded it. I don't mean a guaranteed trophy every season, that would be arrogant, but as a minimum we wanted a team playing football the United way and up there competing with the top teams in England and Europe with a realistic chance of a trophy. That's the yardstick Sir Matt's successors would be measured against but it was coupled with an impatience that was probably unhealthy. For three seasons we had believed our team would return to the top within weeks. Events were proving otherwise and by December 1972 many supporters were starting to realise that a quick fix wasn't going to happen. United needed major surgery. Call The Doc …

6

EVERYWHERE I HEAR THE
SOUND OF MARCHING,
CHARGING FEET BOY ...

On Saturday, 23 December 1972 Tommy Docherty was paraded before the Old Trafford crowd as the new manager of Manchester United. If there had been uncertainty around what type of manager United would get with McGuinness and O'Farrell, there was little we didn't know about 'The Doc'. A feared but respected wing-half in his playing days with Celtic, Preston and Arsenal, he won twenty-five Scottish caps. In February 1961, he was appointed coach at Chelsea and a year later became their manager when only 33. He assembled an exciting young team at Stamford Bridge which for five years running was in contention for domestic honours. After a misconduct charge on a club tour, Chelsea sacked Docherty in October 1967. In the next four years he managed six clubs with mixed success but plenty of controversy. He was regularly in the papers.

In November 1971, his country came calling after Scotland failed to qualify for consecutive World Cups and European Championships. In thirteen months he restored Scotland's pride and set them on the road for qualification to the 1974 World Cup. Tommy Doc was an able coach, though not a great one. His predominant skills were motivating players and spotting latent talent. He was a wheeler–dealer in the transfer market and had a one-liner for any occasion. The Doc was flamboyant, enthusiastic, and ebullient; he was forthright, fearless and instantly roused United supporters who could readily relate to him. He was 44 when he became United's manager.

The Doc moved quickly to sort out the playing side. He had to, United were bottom of the table. Pat Crerand was appointed assistant manager and Tommy Cavanagh joined as coach. Within a month we had signed five new players; George Graham, Alex Forsyth, Jim Holton, Lou Macari, and Mick Martin. All bar Martin were Scots and when they lined up with Law, Morgan, Buchan and McDougall against West Ham on 20 January 1973 the press dubbed us 'Mac United'. Doc's tartan revolution gripped the Stretford End and thousands of us donned a variety of chequered scarves, tam o'shanters, trousers and even kilts. One guy somehow got a set of bagpipes into the Stretford End and treated us to a rendition of 'Scotland the Brave' at an early match under The Doc. It would take the arrival of the Bay City Rollers and Rollermania a couple of years later to make us realise we may have got carried away a bit with the tartan theme. But, hey, the previous couple of years had been such a bummer – we needed a bit of fun and Docherty's arrival provided it.

In that West Ham game we went 2-0 down but the team showed tremendous fighting spirit to pull back to 2-2 with a late Macari equaliser. The crowd loved it, almost overnight we had new heroes to celebrate and something to believe in. Macari, a £200,000 buy from Celtic, had endeared himself to United fans by choosing us over Liverpool. When Macari signed they were top of the league, we were bottom. It was a great coup by Docherty. Macari's debut goal shot him to cult status and 'who put the ball in West Ham net, skip to my Lou Macari' became a United anthem for the next twelve years. Then there was big Jim Holton, a tall, rugged, muscular centre-half picked-up from Shrewsbury for a snip at £80,000. He made his debut in the same game as Macari and instantly looked the part. He was the powerful centre-half we had needed for six years and was the perfect foil for Martin Buchan's more subtle defensive skills.

Bowie's 'Jean Genie' was riding high in the charts and Reds adapted the chorus to 'Jim Holton' but as the weeks went on and the big man entered United folklore the classic 'six foot two eyes of blue, big Jim Holton's after you' was born. On Saturday nights I used to go to a disco at Sedgley Park. The DJ played Jeff Beck's 'Hi Ho Silver Lining' around this time which got hijacked by younger Reds on the dance floor jumping around to the rocking chorus singing 'Man United's made another signing!' It perfectly captured the changing times down at Old Trafford.

If United were going to avoid relegation it would be a dogfight but now we had an impetus. Three defeats were followed by three battling draws which got us out of the bottom two. On 10 February, United won their first league game under Docherty, 2-1 against Wolves. We struggled to win away but scraped another couple of home wins to keep hopes alive. It wasn't pretty though and United were getting criticised in some quarters for rough play and sacrificing our traditions. But from mid-March The Doc's magic really started to work and a run of five wins and three draws lifted United to safety. A settled side had turned United's fortunes, for the last three months of the season the team was usually: Stepney, T. Young, James, Graham, Holton, Buchan, Morgan, Kidd, Charlton, Macari, Martin.

United finished in eighteenth place, seven points clear of relegation. Given our predicament in December, Docherty was a hero just for keeping us in the top flight. Most of his new signings had settled in quickly and were doing a decent job. The defence was a lot tighter, conceding nineteen goals in the last seventeen games compared to forty-one in the first twenty-five matches. Goalscoring was the problem. During the 1972/73 season only once did we score more than two in a league game, back in September when we beat Derby 3-0. The deficiency would come back to haunt us.

United accepted an invitation to play in the 1972/73 Anglo-Italian Cup competition. The contest was conceived in 1969 after third tier Swindon Town won the League Cup but were prevented by UEFA's rules from entering the UEFA Cup. The English and Italian leagues decided to arrange an annual tournament for their teams who had not qualified for UEFA's competitions. It appeased Swindon who then won the inaugural trophy. The Anglo-Italian Cup was promoted as a vehicle for bringing greater harmony between players and supporters of the two nations. The competition lasted just four years and witnessed trouble on and off the pitch in less than exotic Latin and English towns. It was a bit like the Watney Cup only with passports.

For this starry-eyed 18-year-old though it was a golden opportunity to realise his dream of seeing United play abroad. I had imagined it being in the European Cup but this would do. United were drawn in Group One with Verona, Fiorentina, AS Bari and Lazio. The English teams in our group were Crystal

Palace, Luton and Hull. Each English team would play one match against each Italian team – two at home, two away. Our schedule was Fiorentina and Bari at Old Trafford and Verona and Lazio away. The top English and top Italian team in the group would progress to the semi-final and play their foreign counterparts from Group Two. Still with it? Good. The games were played in midweek between February and May.

One tie stood out – Lazio away on 21 March 1973. The Rome club wasn't as well known in this country then but a trip to the Eternal City and a chance to see United in the Olympic Stadium with its 100,000 capacity was too good to miss. Wilpar Travel Agency had organised a two-day trip for £32. I was up for it and so were Geoff Milloy and Ian McEwan. I raided my virgin Post Office savings and the three of us booked on the trip. I sorted my time off from work and in the weeks running up to the game I could think of nothing else. I was like a little kid waiting for his first proper Christmas to arrive.

On the Monday before the game I got a postcard from Wilpar asking me to phone them urgently. The call was to advise me the trip had been cancelled due to lack of demand. The man at Wilpar was very apologetic and promised to refund our money in full. His words were kind but no consolation; gutted doesn't even start to describe it. I know it's not life or death but it felt like it to me. I rang the lads to tell them. We drowned our sorrows with a few pints in the local on the night of the game. Even news of a drab 0-0 draw couldn't lessen the hurt. People in the pub thought they were offering comforting words when they said we had missed nothing and think of the money we had saved. I just looked at them blankly – what planet were they on?

The remaining away tie was Verona on 2 May. We pressed Wilpar to run a trip but they felt there wouldn't be the demand. We searched round other travel agents but drew a blank each time. There was to be no semi-final either; United came second to Crystal Palace and were eliminated at the group stage. I would have to wait a while longer for my first Euro-away. The Anglo-Italian Cup for Football League teams was aborted after that season mainly due to supporters' lack of interest. United's home crowds against Fiorentina and Bari were around 24,000 and 14,000 respectively. The competition would return in years to come but for non-league teams. I got my refund from Wilpar but it was like getting your pound back in exchange for the lottery ticket that had won the jackpot.

However, it was springtime, the sap was rising and a man's thoughts can turn to other things. For eighteen months I had been going out with a beautiful girl from Prestwich called Gail. It was my first serious romance and at the tender age of 19 I believed it would be my last. We got on great and had talked about settling down sometime. Shortly after the crushing disappointment of the Rome trip that never was, I proposed to Gail. She accepted, we got engaged and off we went to Manchester to buy a diamond ring with my refunded £32. From then on I started putting a little more money in my Post Office account; now I was saving for a house as well as trips to watch United in Europe – such joy!

Doc's rebuilding meant it was time for some players to move on. The manager lost Ian Storey-Moore to an injury that cruelly curtailed the winger's career at his peak. Docherty decided Ted McDougall and Wyn Davies weren't part of our future and in February 1973 the classy Tony Dunne played the last of his 535 games for United. The great team of 1968 was fading away. On 16 April, Bobby Charlton held a news conference at Old Trafford to announce his retirement at the end of the season. Shy and a little embarrassed, he opened the proceedings by saying, 'I always thought press conferences were for Prime Ministers and other such people, certainly not professional footballers.' Apparently Charlton had wanted to hand out a statement to a few journalists at the end of training but was persuaded this was a big announcement and the football world would want to hear and see it. Hard to imagine in the news-hungry era we enjoy today?

When I started watching United, Bobby Charlton was already an established player, England international and legend. His trademark skills were his explosive shooting from great distance and his forty- to fifty-yard pinpoint passes. He didn't attract the fanatical following like Best and Law but he was the respected midfield general who, with Crerand, seemed to start 90 per cent of United's attacks in the mid to late 1960s. Bobby Charlton's career is unparalleled in English football and deserves a few volumes of its own but here are a few snippets of what he achieved in his Old Trafford career:

- World Cup winner with England 1966
- European Cup winner with United 1968
- Three league championships 1957, 1965, 1967
- FA Cup winner 1963
- FA Youth Cup winner three times 1954–56
- European Footballer of the Year 1966
- Runner-up twice 1967, 1968
- English Footballer of the Year 1966
- Manchester United all-time top goalscorer, 249
- Set a club record of 758 appearances that stood for thirty-seven years
- England all-time top goalscorer, forty-nine
- Twenty years as a player for Manchester United
- Awarded OBE 1969
- Awarded CBE 1974
- Knighted by his country 1994

Despite this success he remained unspoilt. His sportsmanship was second to none; he was never sent off in over 800 games for club and country. Charlton was loved and respected by football fans throughout Britain and across the world. Aged 20 he survived the crash at Munich. In the match programme for Bobby's testimonial against Celtic in September 1972 Sir Matt Busby bestowed this glowing tribute on one of his favoured sons:

> And when things looked blackest after the accident, and there were times when I felt a great despair, I was cheered enormously to think that Bobby Charlton was there. He was one of the foundation stones and his presence was a great source of inspiration to keep working for the restoration of Manchester United.

Bobby Charlton's last game at Old Trafford was an emotional affair against Sheffield United on Easter Monday, 23 April 1973. Five days later Geoff Milloy and I were at Stamford Bridge to see Charlton's last match on English soil. When we reached the ground the turnstiles at the United end were already shut so we went in the infamous Shed, normally a no-go area for away fans. We stood there quietly for ninety minutes and ignored the bile directed at United's players by the Chelsea faithful. At full time the mood changed completely. As the final whistle blew the whole ground started chanting Bobby Charlton's name and he was encouraged to do a lap of honour. When he came round to the Shed End the applause and cheering reached a crescendo. It was a rare show of appreciation for an opposing player from a particularly partisan crowd. Geoff and I looked around in amazement. We couldn't believe the reaction but we were proud to witness it and say our farewell to one of United's true greats.

By now our chosen form of transport to away matches was the 'Football Special' trains. Coach travel had become a little too tame for our lads. Gone were the days when half the Stretford End would pour off the coaches at the motorway service areas, pile into the restaurant and discreetly pinch sandwiches or sneak their full English breakfast past the cashier without paying. Sadly, the challenge to 'steal a meal at Keele' was consigned to history. The coaches were okay for the younger supporters or those who wanted a quiet trip to watch the Reds, it's just that we wanted something a bit livelier and the Football Special provided it.

The specials came of age in the 1970s when thousands of football fans up and down the country used them every Saturday to follow their team to away matches. Branded as Soccerail and run by British Railways, trips from Manchester went wherever United played. Officially termed '2nd Class Cheap Day Return' outings, the emphasis was on cheap. For only £2.50 British Rail would get you to a game in London compared to £2.15 on the coach. They used old, redundant railway carriages and attracted the hordes from England's roughest terraces. The idea was to keep travelling football fans away from the rest of BR's passengers who paid good money to travel in peace and comfort. United supporters often filled two or three specials with 500 on each train.

British Rail had run these trips since the 1950s and manned them with its own staff. Around 1963 there was an outbreak of vandalism on football trains, usually on return journeys when one of the big city teams had lost. I remember one of the first incidents involved Everton fans and got a lot of coverage on national TV. After that British Rail put police on the trains as a matter of course. The appeal of the specials certainly wasn't in the décor of the coaches which were one step away from the knacker's yard. Wobbly tables, smashed arm-rests, ripped seats, leaking windows, broken heaters and blocked toilets were all key features. Refreshments on the journey brought a new meaning to the expression 'bare minimum'. Often sold from the mail cage in the carriage at the rear of the train, there were ham or cheese rolls, Mars bars, crisps, tea, coffee and orange juice. Actually, it was okay. Well, okay for the palate of the average football fan. The big problem was there was never enough of it. The food and drink would run out an hour or so into the outward and inbound journeys and on a ten-hour round trip to Norwich, Ipswich or Southampton you would be left feeling weak with hunger. Taking your own sandwiches just wasn't cool, so necessity being the mother of invention, we looked for other opportunities.

On these long treks the special would make at least one unofficial stop at a station en route, usually where we had caught up with a local train and had to wait until there was a safe distance before we could continue our journey. An announcement on the public address system always advised supporters to stay on the train as it could pull out at any moment. Often the station's refreshment kiosk was tantalisingly in sight and a few Reds would dive off, and try to buy food before the special set off again. Only a few at the front of the queue would succeed in getting food before the train started moving. That triggered a mad dash to jump back on board quickly. Most made it because the train was so long but there were always a couple of lads who hung on a just a little too long in the food queue and were left chasing the train down the platform while juggling their pie and drink.

It was hilarious to see their expression as it dawned on them they would have to sacrifice either the food they coveted or getting to the match or home. For some, particularly the more rotund, the choice was just too hard to make. They clung on to their snack, carried on running but failed by a few feet to reach the moving carriage door that their mates had held open for them. They cut a forlorn figure as the train picked up speed and left them standing there on a remote platform, arms outstretched with a look of disbelief on their face. There was little sympathy for the stranded sole from their companions on the train, just a chorus of belly laughs, jeers and good-natured two-fingered salutes. Occasionally, you would see some daft lad left behind hurl their food to the floor in disgust. There they stood; no food, no train and miles from their destination. Priceless entertainment.

Another sideshow was the ubiquitous 'jibber' – the supporter whose conscience just wouldn't allow him to boost British Rail's profits by paying the fare. As the inspector came round checking tickets various cunning, and not so cunning, plans slipped into operation. The most common jib was to hide in the toilet; in the early days inspectors wouldn't bother passengers who were indisposed. Later they cottoned on, so two lads would squeeze into the toilet with one ticket between them. When the inspector knocked on the door one lad would stick their smiling head, hand and ticket round the slightly opened door. The ticket clipped, the inspector would carry on satisfied he had done a thorough job.

Other lads would climb into the luggage racks above the seats, a mate would wrap a couple of coats over them, and the inspector would be oblivious to the ruse as he moved through the carriage. Obviously this trick was restricted to the slimmer, lighter supporter. Some lads used a scam whereby they just came clean and admitted they hadn't bought a ticket. The inspector took their name and address and explained British Rail would send a bill to the house. Then they were allowed to continue the journey. Of course, the lads gave false details so the invoice would find itself in the 'return to sender' pile. No doubt there were more ingenious jibs but those smart enough to get away with them were also smart enough to keep their secrets under wraps. Some lads travelled thousands of miles over several seasons without ever buying a ticket, like latter-day artful dodgers.

The real attraction for United supporters travelling on the football special came into play as the train approached its destination. This is what we had all come for. The journey was over and the Manchester Boys were here. Before the train enters the station all the windows are open, there's a head sticking out of each one and chants of 'Manchester la la la la, Manchester la la la la' ring out to the tune of the Banana Splits classic. Before the train pulls to a halt dozens of carriage doors swing open and the first thuds of Doc Marten's hitting the stone platform are heard. Within a couple of minutes up to 600 fanatical Reds are off the train and moving through the station forecourt to a deafening rendition of 'MU … MUF … MUFC OK!' or the ubiquitous and enduring 'Hello! Hello! We are the Busby Boys!'

Any lethargy from an early morning rise or last night's beer fest is left behind. Everyone is up for it, everyone is on their mettle, everyone is focused. Now it's about sticking together, letting the locals know who we are, protecting ourselves against any attack and getting into the ground. The police were always outside the station to welcome the Red Army, their dogs barking, Reds singing and a nice officer on a megaphone asking us to stay on the pavement and follow the escort provided by his colleagues in blue. It is difficult to describe how it felt being part of this boisterous, vociferous, invading army but I guess the best word is exhilarating. It always gave me a thrill and was an integral part of following United.

The journey to the ground usually took us through the city centre. Sometimes there was no trouble and the locals would watch us from behind the police escort with looks of wonderment, fear, disgust or just plain indifference. In the bigger towns and the cities there would invariably be an ambush or full on attack by the home supporters. It would start with an opposing chant or someone at the front of our massed ranks shouting, 'Here they are! Come on!' We would all set off running towards our unseen enemy. That in turn would start the police and canine friends running too and for ten minutes or so it was urban mayhem until the local insurgents retreated to think again or the coppers managed to corral the Manchester boys and regain some order.

Through the 1960s to the 1980s United would take so many supporters away that we ruled the roost in most places but visits to Leeds, Newcastle, Merseyside and parts of London were a different kettle of fish. It was odds on that the United special would be met somewhere along the way from the station to the ground by a home 'mob' with significant numbers and serious intent. These fixtures were always heavily policed, with dogs and horses being widely deployed. Sometimes the police managed to keep order with United's lads on one side of the road and the opposition on the other but more often than not the two warring factions would have running battles with each other along the route. We would chase them, they would chase us and in between there was some old-fashioned fisticuffs before the coppers caught up.

Now when I say 'we' would chase them, I mean I was a part of the 600-strong mob that ran backwards and forwards trying to see off the opposing fans and get to the ground in one piece. It was a case of safety in numbers. The thrill of running with the United pack was exciting but I was never a fighter. I don't declare this with any great virtue; I was just no good at it and didn't have the stomach or bottle for the real nasty stuff. To be honest I didn't see the need for it, we were defending United's name but for me the singing and the show of strength was enough.

That said, I didn't condemn the confrontations either. Sometimes it was really hairy stuff. I remember going to Liverpool in September 1971 when I was 17. We were on the first of three United specials that pulled into Lime Street that day. There were 100 or so Cockney Reds who had come up separately so it was a big crew that came out of the station singing and chanting. We had arrived earlier than expected and there was no police escort, a rare treat. The Red Army was unopposed all the way through Liverpool city centre, down the notorious Scottie Road and through Everton Valley. United supporters were giving the locals plenty of verbal stick and going through the whole gambit of anti-Scouse songs. Liverpool had a hard reputation but it looked like they just weren't up for it.

We felt majestic and confidence was flowing through the ranks. 'Let's head for the Kop!' someone shouted. As we marched up a long, steep road that leads towards Anfield, Liverpool fans appeared at the top of the hill. They saw us, charged down the hill and we ran towards them. Like most non-fighters I used to stay somewhere around the middle of the pack just so I could weigh up what was going on. This time I found myself near the front. No problem with that, I thought, with this lot behind me we'll be alright. Anyway, more and more Scousers kept coming over the top of the bloody hill. It was beginning to resemble that scene from the film *Zulu* where the Welsh soldiers are outnumbered by thousands of native warriors at Rorke's Drift. Suddenly, most of the lads in front of me decided to turn and retreat to safer ground. Right next to me was a really big lad, probably in his mid-20s. He just stood there facing the oncoming enemy like a latter-day William Wallace, his long scruffy hair blowing in the wind, and bellowed, 'Don't run, stand your ground, United! Let's get the bastards!'

I looked at him with awe and thought, 'Bloody hell! What a guy! What a leader! What a Red!' I looked round expecting to see the rest of our group heed this rallying call to arms and charge at the Scousers. But no, most Reds had decided to live to fight another day and carried on back down the hill. I took one quick look at the hundreds of Liverpool supporters heading our way, then turned to the big lad and said 'sorry mate, time to go' and down the hill I went. I never found out what happened to him. The police arrived in numbers, got in between the two sets of supporters and escorted us to the ground.

Over the years there were other similar confrontations and there would always be some guy who would stand his ground to try and rally the troops with mixed results. Without wishing to glorify these encounters, I couldn't help but have the utmost respect for the 'bottle' those guys showed in such situations. Secretly, part of me yearned for that sort of role in the United's Red Army but I would like to have known the mortality rate first.

As the 1970s progressed, the trouble associated with fans travelling by train escalated. My mate Tezzer dubbed the football special the 'Hoolie Express'. The worst of the trouble took place after the match, often coinciding with a bad defeat. United fans would go on the rampage and it wouldn't just be a fight with rival supporters, it would be a wrecking spree with windows being smashed, cars overturned, shops looted and innocent bystanders threatened or attacked. In areas where there were high levels of recent immigration, such as the tight terrace streets around Derby's Baseball Ground, it had a darker side with racist taunts directed at any brown face. When the mob got out of control it was a dangerous beast and anybody could be seen as the enemy. It was ugly, dangerous and vicious. The police were relatively powerless to prevent these riots.

When I look back, all the ingredients were there for civil unrest. Every week you had thousands of 15- to 25-year olds from the backstreets and high-rise flats across the country being transported to a 'rival' city centre. Entrance to most matches was cash payment at the turnstiles on a first come first served basis so away fans could turn up in force. Of course, the majority didn't go seeking conflict but it would only take a spark to light the powder keg. Many times I witnessed how a handful of troublemakers could transform a loud but fairly good spirited group into a frenzied mob. There wasn't the police intelligence network to identify and isolate known ringleaders in those days. Hand-held video cameras hadn't been invented to capture criminal behaviour and CCTV in town centres was extremely rare. The best the police could do was to try to contain the trouble. That was a challenge on the way to the ground and almost impossible after the match as several thousand away fans tumbled off the terraces at twenty to five each Saturday.

Football hooliganism was a regular feature in the media for two decades from 1965 to 1985. A bi-product was a new national pastime whereby people offered their opinion on why so many young men were attracted to following their team in such numbers. Hooliganism and fanaticism came joined at the hip in some people's minds. During those years, I had read countless articles in the broadsheets by pseudo-intellectuals who concluded that people joined such 'gangs' because it brightened up their otherwise dull existence which was governed by dead-end jobs or life on the dole. The consensus was individuals joined in to give their lives some meaning and sense of belonging.

Now, I've no doubt that did apply to some characters but most of the United lads I knew had varied lives outside of football, many had decent and interesting jobs. In fact, they were doing okay. The point many commentators missed in judging from a distance was that the buzz created by these away trips was so great it enriched our lives rather than lighting-up one dark corner. If I choose to ride the Big One at Blackpool Pleasure Beach it's because the experience is so awesome, so thrilling, so breathtaking. It is not because I've got a boring life and need some excitement. Well the away day trip on the special provided that sort of thrill and it lasted throughout the whole of Saturday and well beyond.

I ran with the pack and while I didn't directly join in with the violence and vandalism around me, I didn't distance myself either. That leads me to an unpalatable and inconvenient truth – rioting is fun. Well, for those doing the rioting anyway. I am not an advocate for civil disobedience but I do know it provides a powerful adrenaline rush and it's not just a football thing. Separate studies were undertaken following the violent anti-Vietnam War protests in London's Grosvenor Square in 1968 and the anarchic Poll Tax demonstrations of 1990. A common feature was that many rioters were respectable, well-heeled, educated people. They didn't come from impoverished, dysfunctional backgrounds, they hadn't been abused or neglected and they weren't a disaffected generation.

When later reflecting on their actions several individuals shared a recurring view. They had embarked on a protest showing solidarity for a noble cause, then an incident by the police or other demonstrators lit the blue touchpaper and within a relatively short time a full-blown riot was under way. Rather than turn away from the unfolding lawlessness, they got caught up in the intoxicating atmosphere and became part of the disturbances which was feeding on its own frenzy. These people conceded afterwards that they joined in because they got a buzz from the rioting.

That's just how it was with United supporters on those specials to away games. Our cause was following Manchester United and showing we were the most fanatical supporters. When that spiralled into clashes with police or rival fans the buzz kicked in. I knew some of the antics were wrong. I also knew those wrong-doings brought shame on the club itself. Yet for many young football fans in the 1970s that's how life was. It was part of the scene and when we weighed up the pros and cons the positives always made it worthwhile.

In 1973 there were a couple of well-intentioned initiatives to stem the trouble caused by fans travelling by train. Firstly, the Football League introduced the 'League Liner' – its very own commissioned football special. It cost £250,000 and had £15,000 of special equipment designed to improve the lot of the roving supporter. To put a perspective on that outlay, the record British transfer fee at the time was £225,000 for David Nish. The super train had a discotheque (people still used the full word in those days) coach with garishly painted walls, a four-screen forty-two-seat cinema compartment and two music carriages where you could use headphones to listen to your favourite artists. It sounds quite tame now but in 1973 such creature comforts were way ahead of their time.

To be fair to the Football League it was a good idea; the concept being if you treat supporters like animals they'll act like animals, but treat them like human beings they'll behave responsibly. Clubs could apply to the League to hire the Liner and that club was then responsible for organising the sale of tickets to supporters, their security on the trip and their refreshments. Burnley were the first to use it when they played QPR in London and they had a trouble-free journey despite losing 2-0. The fans liked it because it was more relaxed and there was plenty to occupy them. Remember there were no mobile phones, iPods or internet connections to while away the boredom

United's turn came a couple of months later when we hired the train for the fixture at Spurs on 24 March. The trip cost £3.50, a pound dearer than British Rail, Season ticket holders and 'ordinary' supporters needed a full set of 27 tokens from that season's programmes to guarantee a place on the train; it was like getting tickets for a Cup Final. Nevertheless, Kirky, Geoff Milloy, Phil Lockett and myself were part of the 500 fans on the new train as it snaked out of Piccadilly, fourteen carriages long and quarter of a mile in length. The journey was the height of luxury compared to what we had been used to, like travelling first-class but with the added extras of music and films. We were all given reserved seats and everyone behaved themselves. There was no police presence on the train – this really was revolutionary stuff!

The journey down was quiet and uneventful with most supporters taking time to check out the facilities on offer. United got a valuable point at Tottenham, halting a string of away defeats and moving us further from the relegation zone. That felt like a win and we were ready to boogie the night away in our sumptuous new inter-city surroundings on the return. After a couple of beers we ventured down to the disco coach to see what was happening. There were a few more girls on the train than usual and some of the lads had high hopes. We needn't have got excited; the disco carriage was the most surreal part of the League Liner. As you know, it's not easy to stand up and walk along a train while it's hurtling along the tracks, so imagine how tricky it is to dance in a completely open plan but dimly lit carriage that's travelling at 100mph. The disco coach ended up with supporters lining its walls, desperately trying to stay upright, hold a drink and look cool all at the same time. Few succeeded.

The day out on the League Liner was brilliant but mainly because of the novelty value. It was a bit too good, too nice. Football supporters just weren't ready for that in the early 1970s. We wanted a bit more 'grit' with our football. The League Liner lasted a year before quietly fading away. I don't remember there being any bad incidents so I can only assume it became too expensive or the demand wasn't there. Anyway, we all went back to life on the British Rail specials.

Later that year, Dave Smith, the chairman of the United Supporters' Club, got together with British Railways to try another initiative. He convinced BR to let the club's official Supporters' Club charter specials for United away matches. The deal was that Smithy would organise the trips, sell tickets, provide refreshments and keep some of the profit for the Supporters' Club. If there was any damage to the train his Supporters' Club would have to pay to fix it. Dave's idea was that he would have very low policing on the train, brand it as United's train and hope the lads would respond favourably. If you wanted to travel on the United specials you had to apply for a travel card which included a photograph and acted as a 'passport'. It was a big risk given the climate at the time but it worked very well with few incidents on the outbound or inbound journeys.

Dave couldn't prevent trouble happening once United supporters got off the train or while in the visiting town but that wasn't his responsibility. I am sure the first rail trip he ran was to Ipswich in September 1973. I was standing near him in the United end at Portman Road and at half-time he told us he was leaving to go back to the station. Leave a match halfway through? Was there a serious problem? Dave explained that all the food for both legs of the journey had sold out just before we arrived at Ipswich. He didn't want his train to be like the BR specials where fans went hours without refreshments. So credit to the lad, off he went, bought a load of bread, ham, cheese, crisps and cartons of juice and loaded them on to the train for the return journey. I must admit I thought he was mad, I couldn't have done it. The thought of missing even part of a United match was abhorrent, let alone when you've travelled 225 miles and six hours to watch your team. At the same time I couldn't help respecting his commitment to making the United specials a bit more pleasant for the travelling faithful. It was quite a sacrifice and a nice touch, and just one reason why Smithy's Specials became so successful in the mid-1970s.

7

DON'T PUSH
YOUR LOVE TOO FAR,
YOUR WOUNDS WON'T
LEAVE A SCAR

In stark contrast to the celebrated, high-profile send-off for Bobby Charlton another of Old Trafford's gifted sons slipped quietly out of the back door during the summer of 1973. Denis Law was given a free transfer by Tommy Docherty and snapped up by our City neighbours. The writing had been on the wall. Law was 33 and carrying a knee injury picked up several years earlier. He played only four league games after Christmas 1972. His last goal for United was against AC Bari in the Anglo-Italian Cup tie in front of 14,303 hardy souls at Old Trafford on 4 April 1973. Three days later he made his final appearance for the Reds in a 1-0 home win over Norwich. In a shoddy episode Tommy Docherty reneged on a promise to find Law a job at United when his playing days ended. Law's exit was hasty and no way to treat a living legend.

But let's roll back the years briefly to give Denis Law due homage. King Denis was adored by United fans. His goalscoring record alone is incredible. During eleven years at United he scored 237 goals in 404 appearances. He is the second highest goalscorer in United's history, only twelve less than Bobby Charlton who played 354 games more. In 1963/64 he played forty-two matches and netted an incredible forty-six goals, including a goal a game in thirty league appearances and ten FA Cup goals in six outings. No United player has ever scored more than that forty-six in one season. In fifty-five games for Scotland he scored thirty times, a joint record held with

Kenny Dalglish. In 1964, he became the only Scottish player to be crowned European Footballer of the Year and helped United win the league in 1965 and 1967. In 1963, he won an FA Cup winner's medal and played a starring role in the defeat of Leicester City.

Denis Law was a goal-machine, but unlike other great poachers such as Allan Clarke, Ian Rush, Gary Lineker or Alan Shearer, the Lawman had a bagful of tricks. He scored from close range, long range, overhead kicks, flicks and back-heels. He scored from chances other players didn't even see, his reflexes were like lightning. Goalkeepers dreaded spilling the ball because they knew the predatory Scot would make them pay. His heading ability was phenomenal, soaring way above any height a 5ft 9in man deserved to then hang in the air until his head connected with the ball. The power and accuracy of his heading would leave even the best goalkeepers flat-footed.

Above all this, Denis Law had a charisma that the fans related to. He fought tooth and nail for United's cause and though not a burly forward he was fearless, determined never to come off second-best. He had an impish quality, a deadly assassin with a cheeky grin. His iconic goal scoring salute of a raised arm with fingers gripping his shirt cuff was copied on playing fields all across Britain. Law was a hero because he possessed one vital ingredient – he was heroic every time he stepped onto the pitch for United. Over time, United would right the wrong of 1973 and nowadays two statues of Law adorn Old Trafford.

So United started 1973/74 without the Holy Trinity of Best, Law and Charlton. The curtain had fallen on a golden era. The trio never played together under Docherty. Sadly, their final fling was in a 4-1 home defeat to Spurs on 28 October 1972. Their first had been a 4-1 victory at West Brom in January 1965 when each of them scored. Now only Stepney and Kidd remained from that triumphant night at Wembley five years earlier. The Doc had moved United on but could he move us up? He openly announced that he wanted to bring in a top name but failed to attract his target. He did, however, have Sammy McIlroy back after seven months out following a serious car crash.

We won two of the first three matches but it was a false dawn. The team failed to build on the progress made in avoiding relegation the previous season. A dire shortage of goals was the problem. In the opening fourteen games we scored just ten times.

Embarrassingly, our top scorer was goalkeeper Alex Stepney. In an early season game against Leicester, United were awarded a penalty and Stepney became a reluctant hero when he stepped forward and converted it. Seven games later against Birmingham he did the same. This goal put him joint top scorer with Kiddo and Sammy Mac – all with two goals and it stayed that way until after Christmas when McIlroy and Macari hauled themselves on to three each.

United were hitting hit rock bottom. The Doc had cleared out many of the players from the previous regimes and was giving youth a chance alongside the Scottish stars he had brought in. Unfortunately, it just didn't gel. In a desperate attempt to galvanise his team, Docherty gave George Best another chance at resurrecting his United career. From late October to New Year the bearded and slightly heavier Bestie battled to spark a revival. United arranged a series of midweek friendlies to accelerate George's fitness routine. Despite a couple of goals and flashes of his legendary footwork it wasn't to be. On 1 January 1974 I saw George Best play his final game for United in a 3-0 thrashing at QPR. The next week he turned up late for a cup match with Plymouth and Tommy Docherty showed him the door for the final time. His legacy would live on as a beacon for those who came after but for now there were more pressing matters.

The winter of 1973/74 was dismal for United followers. Between late October and the start of March we won just one league match out of seventeen. The football was workmanlike and defensive. Players battled hard and kept the respect of the supporters but ordinary teams were beating us. Our rivals City, Liverpool and Leeds loved it. They were chasing league and cup honours while Manchester United, the great but loathed Manchester United, were likely to be relegated. They lapped it up. The mickey-taking was the worst part of this period and it became relentless week in, week out. Monday mornings at work were torture. Having been reared on a diet of stirring European Cup encounters, league championships and epic FA Cup runs I was now seeing United's empire crumbling and all within five years. Not only did we not compete at that level anymore, we were down among the dead men at the foot of the table and regularly coming off second-best. Yet I never wavered an inch in my support for United. Like thousands of other Reds I became even more fiercely loyal and defensive of the team I love.

By the end of that winter United's plight looked pretty bleak. Mind you, the country's future looked gloomy too. Britain was in dire straits as long-running industrial action by coal miners really started to bite. Emergency power restrictions brought in by the Government saw offices, shops and commercial premises restricted to opening for business on only three allocated days in seven. The economy was in tatters, inflation was well into double figures and there were serious questions as to whether the unions or the Government ran the country. Many families feared for their future and some believed Armageddon was upon us. As a 19-year-old United supporter my concern was of a more selfish nature – where would my team's demise end? Relegation? Years confined to the Second Division? Or worse still, a full-scale plummet through the four leagues? I needed to get a grip of myself but whenever I got my hopes up, the next fixture would bring them crashing down with another defeat. We hit the bottom of the league on 9 February 1974 after a home defeat to Leeds United.

During life's darkest times all we have left is hope; yet hope is all we need. In the spring of 1974, United supporters witnessed a mini-revival that saved our sanity. It started with a trip to Bramall Lane on 2 March when the Reds won away for the first time that season. The team played with a confidence that had been missing since August. The defence was settling into a unit that would serve United well for the next three years – Stepney, Forsyth, Holton, Buchan and Houston. In his debut season Brian Greenhoff was now looking comfortable in midfield but he needed support. For that game at Sheffield United Tommy Doc brought in a young Irishman named Gerry Daly and we saw the first signs of United's recovery. Daly had joined United soon after Docherty arrived but in his first few games appeared lightweight. Now he looked ready to take on the challenge.

In mid-March, The Doc signed Jim McCalliog from Wolves. They knew one another from their days at Chelsea in the mid-1960s when McCalliog was a teenage prodigy. Now he was experienced at club and international level and a wise head to guide the youngsters. Brian Kidd became a casualty of these changes. Docherty had used the former European Cup winner throughout the winter but lost faith when the striker returned only two goals in twenty-three matches.

United went to Chelsea at the end of March and put on another great display. The football was superb as United sprayed passes all over Stamford Bridge and ran out 3-1 winners. It was like a breath of fresh air. We were seven points from safety with eight games to go, still in the days of two points for a win. A 3-3 draw at home to high-flying Burnley increased confidence followed by a 2-0 win at fellow strugglers Norwich. Eleven months without an away win, now three in five weeks. Home victories against Newcastle and Everton followed. Dare we hope?

Terry Jacks' 'Seasons in the Sun' sold over 10 million records worldwide and was being played everywhere you went in Britain. In spring 1974, the weather was glorious every time United played and the rousing sentimental chorus perfectly reflected the moment. Nine points out of ten, twelve goals for and only four against, this late-season burst meant the sun had finally started to shine for United supporters. The win over Everton left us third from bottom, just two points and one place from safety. Southampton occupied that safe spot and United's next match was at The Dell on 20 April 1974. United had four games left, Southampton three.

I don't know how many United supporters travelled to Southampton that day but it must have been close to 10,000. A show of strength, a call to arms for our great club. Fifteen of our lads wanted to go so we hired a big van, and I mean a big van. It had a cabin with three seats at the front, you couldn't see into the back, you had to get out and roll up a shutter at the rear to get to our live cargo. There were no seats just a floor! It was a bit uncomfortable but a good laugh. The main thing was being there to cheer United when they needed us most.

Knowing it would be a full house at the smallest ground in the division we set off around 4 a.m. The game was pay at the turnstile, no tickets were issued. I wasn't driving so had to settle for the 'comfort' of the back. We took turns sitting on the wheel arches inside the van which acted as seats and provided a bit of welcome relief to the backside. Three hours into the journey somewhere around Bristol (it used to be M6-M5-M4 to Southampton in those days) we heard grinding noises coming from outside. At first we thought it was a passing vehicle but it got steadily worse and ten minutes later our driver stopped the van, opened the back and announced the clutch was knackered. We rang the van hire company who said a breakdown truck would be with us sometime in the next four hours. Waiting for the repair probably meant missing the match. Missing the match was never an option. I had not missed a game for nearly three years and certainly wanted to see this crucial one. Mind you, I would have felt the same if it was a friendly against Accrington Stanley.

Not being able to get into a match was my worst nightmare – literally. Ever since I was a kid I used to have two recurring dreams about getting to watch United. In the first one I would be at the top of Cross Lane in Salford walking down towards Old Trafford. Everything was okay at first, then I would see Trafford Bridge was closed and would be for several hours. So I tried to find another way round through Salford Docks but to no avail. Then I tried another route over Barton Bridge at Eccles but that was blocked too. In my dream the harder I tried, the further I found myself away from United's ground and the clock was ticking towards kick-off time … I never found out what happened, I just woke up in a cold sweat each time. It was one of those very vivid dreams where even after you've been awake for a while you still believe it really happened. In the last twenty years with the development of Salford Quays a couple of new bridges have been built. Funnily enough, I've never had that dream since!

A second nightmare was trying to get into Highbury. I don't know why Highbury, these dreams started before I had even been there. This time I've got to the ground but I'm too late and the turnstiles are shut. I find some railings at one corner of the ground and peer through trying to get a glimpse of my heroes. But I can't see the pitch, only the backs of figures in the crowd and their cheers as the match ebbs and flows. Again the dream ends there with no happy ending – agony! When I finally went to watch United at Arsenal in 1970 I walked all round the ground to check if those railings existed. I never found them.

Now, at the side of the M4, my nightmare was in danger of becoming reality. Luckily the two lads who hired the van volunteered to stay with it while the rest of us headed on to Southampton. Once the clutch was fixed they would drive to Southampton and we would meet up after the match outside the United end. The two lads knew they would probably miss the match but didn't mention it. What a tremendous sacrifice, right up there with Captain Oates walking out of Scott's tent at the South Pole in 1912. We thumbed lifts into Bristol and jumped on the first train from Temple Meads station to Southampton.

We got to The Dell as the gates opened but the queues were massive. An hour later we were in. The game belied the lowly position of both sides. United continued with their new-found passing game and Southampton matched us all the way. Docherty called United's support 'overwhelming' that day. But despite that and a great attacking performance on the pitch we couldn't get the win we needed, drawing 1-1 thanks to a McCalliog penalty. There was some consolation when we met up with our mates outside with a new van. They had only been able to get into the game for the last twenty minutes when the gates were opened.

The draw allowed Southampton to keep some daylight between them and us. United went second-bottom behind Birmingham who had won that day. A win would probably have provided the momentum for United's young braves to get points in their last three games whereas our draw felt like a defeat. In the return game with Everton the following Tuesday we lost 1-0 while Southampton and Birmingham both won. For United to escape relegation Birmingham and Southampton both had to draw or lose their last game and we had to win both of ours. The Reds' penultimate game was a Manchester derby at Old Trafford on 27 April 1974. It would be a fateful day for Manchester United.

The half-time score against City was 0-0, the tension making for a scrappy game. Birmingham led Norwich 2-1. The picture remained the same until nine minutes from time, it was looking bleak but we desperately clung to hope. That hope was snatched from us sixty seconds later when a City attack ended with Denis Law back-heeling a goal past Alex Stepney. For a few seconds there was a stunned silence around the ground, then City fans in the Scoreboard Paddock started celebrating like there was no tomorrow and the sickening, gut-wrenching reality hit us.

That was it, we were down. Relegation had been mentioned in hushed terms during the preceding months. We had tried to prepare ourselves for the worst but when it happened it was a shot through the heart. People reacted in different ways. Most United supporters just sat or stood still, others were angry and decided to vent their frustration. I stood on the Stretford End that afternoon. As Law scored a small number of United fans in the Scoreboard End took to the pitch, some trying to abandon the game others wanting to confront the celebrating Blues. The referee stopped play and took the players to the side of the field while the police cleared the playing area. The fans left the pitch heading where they wanted to go, into the Paddock where City were.

As play resumed on the field, the battle commenced on the terraces. Three minutes later hundreds from the Stretford End decided they wanted a piece of the action. They streamed over the small wooden fences and charged towards the other end. The police tried to intervene but were woefully outnumbered.

The referee and players realised it was getting ugly and made their way to the tunnel through the rampaging Red Army. Mike Doyle, the self-confessed Red-hating City captain, came in for particular attention and there is TV footage of him squaring up to taunting United supporters as other City players run for cover. He soon gauged the mood and left the pitch pretty quickly. Police and fans were now battling all over the field. The referee abandoned the game from the safety of the dressing room. Eighty-six minutes had been played. City supporters fought their way to the exits. The Reds who went on the pitch stayed there for about an hour, singing and chanting before dispersing into the Manchester evening. The City fans had been routed and the streets of Salford and Manchester reverberated to a new chorus of the Terry Jacks' hit that provided some short-term comfort, 'We had joy, we had fun, we had City on the run. But the joy did not last cos those b★★★ards ran too fast.'

Although I used to go on the pitch at the last home game I decided to stay put while all this unfolded. Again, I don't say this to claim any moral advantage – I was still shell-shocked about United going down. As I surveyed the chaos around me I couldn't help thinking that the sad climax of relegation and riot had an inevitable feel about it. Inextricably linked, United's poor form, the boardroom turmoil and the terrace violence had all escalated in the previous eighteen months. Our fate had been mixed in the devil's crucible and now all hell was let loose. United fans had rallied round in vast numbers over the previous two years providing unbelievable support to the team. We had taken so much crap from the press, radio, newspapers, other fans and managers that this dénouement was the final straw. Our biggest rivals confirming our relegation in our own back yard was just too humiliating.

The events at Old Trafford that day received worldwide coverage. The inquest went on for weeks about the team and the fans, particularly the latter. The anarchic scenes at the end of the game might have been the same whoever we had played that day. The fact it was City created the perfect storm. Aside from the usual rivalry, many Reds were desperate to exact revenge on City fans. An obscure factor helped fuel the events of 27 April 1974.

Six weeks earlier, Tommy Doc filled a vacant FA Cup date by arranging a friendly against Glasgow Rangers who had suffered an early exit from the Scottish Cup. The game was at Old Trafford and for those United fans in attendance the meaningless friendly would live long in the memory. On the Thursday evening before the game there were reports on the local news of extensive fighting in Bury and Chorlton involving Scottish football fans. One fight had taken place in a pub, the other in a chip shop, in both cases a few people were seriously hurt. Bury and Chorlton are seventeen miles apart and at first it seemed a strange coincidence.

Over the next twenty-four hours there were similar outbreaks of trouble across Greater Manchester. On the day of the match, Geoff Milloy and I made our way to Old Trafford as usual. We always got there early to get in the Stretford End as soon as the gates opened at 1.30 p.m. Like many of United's younger supporters we had taken an interest in anything Scottish after Tommy Doc transplanted half that nation's football team into our own club eighteen months earlier. When we got to Old Trafford we decided not to go in straight away, we wanted to have a nosey around – soak up the atmosphere as I call it.

Approaching the ground we had noticed there were hardly any United fans, just thousands of Scots. They were everywhere; many carried Union Jacks with a Rangers slogan on it. They had all had a good drink and were belting out songs about their Celtic rivals. We soon noticed raw hostility towards us – snarls, menacing glares and the occasional curse that was difficult to decipher. We walked to the top of Warwick Road and passed a group who told us where to go in no uncertain terms and then kicked out at us. This never happened at Old Trafford, United always ruled the roost. Geoff and I were well out-numbered and backed off. We decided to get in the ground quick, we'd soaked up enough atmosphere!

Outside the Stretford End there was a huge piece of fresh graffiti on the wall proclaiming 'No Popery!' 'What's that got to do with anything?' I said to Geoff. Before he could answer a Rangers fan went past shouting 'Fenian bastards!' at us. We knew about the sectarian divide that dominated Glasgow football but thought it was confined to Celtic and Rangers matches. In the past we had heard rumours that Rangers regarded us as a Catholic club because of Matt Busby but because religion played no part in English football we had dismissed it. We were wrong.

Rangers despised us because of that Busby connection and the signing of Celtic players such as Pat Crerand in the past. Eighteen months earlier Celtic had brought 15,000 fans down for Bobby Charlton's testimonial and the two sets of supporters had got on superbly. Apparently, word of this got back to Rangers supporters and it embedded their bigotry towards Manchester United. To them we were Catholic sympathisers, the sworn enemy!

Never has a friendly match been such a misnomer. Inside the ground the atmosphere was hostile. Rangers had fans on three sides of the ground and regularly throughout the match there were outbreaks of fighting. The police in K Stand often found themselves in fist fights as they tried to arrest or eject Rangers supporters. Many older United supporters had stayed away (did they know something we didn't?) so the crowd of 23,000 was split fifty/fifty.

At half-time the Rangers fans in the Scoreboard End decided three sides of the ground wasn't enough and invaded the pitch in an attempt to get to the Stretford End. We had to defend the Stretford End – no visiting fans had come in en masse since Everton in August 1966 – so we moved down to the front of the terraces ready to protect our sacred territory. When the Rangers fans crossed the halfway line it looked like there was going to be an almighty battle. Suddenly they stopped and there was a stand-off with both sets of fans hurling abuse at each other. This gave the police time to restore some order and shepherd the invading army back from whence they came. Rangers won 3-2 which probably helped us get away from the ground in one piece.

During that weekend there was trouble all over Manchester involving Rangers supporters. One policeman was attacked with an axe and sustained a fractured skull, many more were injured. When the dust had settled, Greater Manchester Police announced that Glasgow Rangers would never be allowed to play a friendly in the city again.

On the Wednesday after the Rangers game, United played a league fixture against City at Maine Road. The match ended 0-0 but it was a night when tempers ran high on and off the pitch. A dour game littered with fouls erupted in the second half when Macari and Doyle squared up to each other. Both were given a red card but neither would leave the field. Referee Clive Thompson took all the players off the pitch to calm tempers and leave the dismissed pair to accept their punishment in the dressing rooms.

Manchester derbies, particularly in the 1970s, were always a hot-bed of tribal rivalry whether you were a supporter or a player but that night there was something different in the air. The fighting on Kippax Street was more intense and prolonged than usual and spilled out into the neighbouring Moss Side streets after the game. Both sets of fans fought a running battle all the way back to the city centre and well into the night. Dozens of cars were overturned and hundreds of shop windows smashed. The following day the *Manchester Evening News* ran several pages about the trouble including the front-page headline 'Manchester's Night of Shame'.

At the time I put it down to events on the pitch and the backdrop of United's fierce relegation battle. Some years later I learned from two different sources that several hardcore Rangers fans had stayed down in Manchester from the previous weekend and teamed up with City to form a 'Light Blues' pact to have a go at United.

Most seasons there would be a three- to four-month cooling off period before the return fixture but the mid-March game had been postponed from the previous December. The match at Old Trafford took place only six weeks later. Events at Maine Road were fresh in the minds of United supporters and revenge was on the menu. Old Trafford was a powder keg and Law's back-heel simply lit the blue touchpaper.

The night United were relegated I went to a disco at Stand Cricket Club Whitefield, had few beers, a bop and put on a brave face. My girlfriend Gail remarked how surprisingly well I was taking the crushing blow of relegation. The truth is I didn't really know how I felt other than a surreal numbness. I was functioning on all levels but in an anaesthetised state. On Sunday morning

I bought several newspapers and in a masochistic act read all the gory details. They made depressing, yet somehow compelling, reading. Graphic pictures of the pitch invasion were splashed across the front and back pages accompanied by stories of United's demise on and off the pitch. All the papers called for a big punishment and talked of points being deducted next season or the ground being closed again. Some called for both. Those articles were bad enough but *The News of the World* and *Sunday Mirror* also ran front-page exclusives about George Best's hedonistic escapades with former Miss World Marjorie Wallace on some sun-kissed beach.

As a schoolboy I dreamed of being old enough to travel and watch United win trophies home and abroad. I imagined glorious times where we would dominate Europe and dazzle millions worldwide with our brilliant football. The reality that Sunday morning hit hard. United relegated to the Second Division, the fans in disgrace and my hero Bestie forever lost to the glitz of celebrity when at 28 he should have been leading United to European triumphs in Rome, Paris or Madrid. I was 19 and those schoolboy dreams were shattered.

On the Monday night, United played at Stoke in their final match of the season. Another huge following filled the away end. It could have been a sombre occasion but a special spirit was born on the terraces that warm spring evening. With the uncertainty of relegation lifted, there was an overwhelming feeling of defiance among United supporters. We sang all through the 1-0 defeat. Old and new songs were adapted to proclaim that we'd be back. In particular, the renditions of 'We'll keep the Red flag flying high, cos Man United will never die!' had more significance and emotion than in recent times.

The Stoke game set the tone for Reds everywhere; we wouldn't sulk or pity ourselves despite the trauma of relegation. We would get behind the club, behind the team and battle on. We would take all the scorn others poured on us but we would stand tall in the knowledge that we'd overcome, because we were Manchester United. It drew a line under relegation and the slow, painful demise of the previous four years. We were in the Second Division but the Red Army would carry United back. That was our job. My numbness lifted and I started to look forward to the challenge of getting out of the Second Division at the first attempt.

8

DON'T YOU LOVE FARCE?
MY FAULT I FEAR

In late July 1974, my dad took a call from Dave Smith at the Supporters' Club asking if I would interested in a trip to United's pre-season friendly in Ostend. Interested?! I couldn't phone him back quick enough. Moments later I was booked on my first trip to see United play abroad. Well, just about abroad, I guess you would struggle to find a foreign fixture nearer to these shores but I didn't care, I had waited six years for this opportunity. Better still, it wouldn't put a big dent in my 'European' savings as the total trip cost just £10! That seems cheap now but it was cheap then too and hundreds of Reds snapped up the offer. For many United supporters of that generation, AS Oostende on 3 August was our first taste of a Euro-away and it would be a baptism of fire.

Four other mates decided to go – Ian McEwan, Pete Ward, and the Manifold brothers, Derek and John. Several coaches departed from Old Trafford late on Friday evening and travelled through the night to Dover. There we met a few hundred more Reds and caught the early ferry across the Channel. When we docked in Ostend most United fans made a dash for the exits. We decided to take our time, it was around 6 a.m. and we had plenty of time until the evening kick-off. We walked towards the town centre. The only noise that broke the early morning calm was the sound of a siren in the distance.

We thought it must be an ambulance but the din continued. We reached the outskirts of the town when suddenly a car screeched to a halt right beside us. The doors flew open and three guys in raincoats and hats got out and raced towards us. A man in the passenger seat pointed at Derek who was then bundled into the car, the doors were banged shut and off it sped along the deserted streets. It was all over in seconds and we were dumb-struck. In fact we were crapping it. We didn't have a clue who these men were, why they had taken our mate or where he had gone. We convinced ourselves it was underworld criminals and they could come back for us. This wasn't just my first United match abroad, it was my first trip outside of the UK. We decided to keep out of sight in the back alleys of Ostend and skulked around there for an hour until the town centre got busier.

We came across some other Reds who had a similar experience. They were with the first group of United fans coming off the ferry and witnessed what happened. The main posse of supporters had charged off the boat like they would a football special back in England, chanting, running and generally high-spirited. They ran through the shopping district where all the shops were closed. On the continent in those days shop owners would leave their goods displayed in glass cabinets in the walkways of the precinct for people to admire after close of business. Many designer items were on view including jewellery, sportswear and clothing. These proved too much of a temptation for some Reds and dozens of shopkeepers woke to the sound of breaking glass. Items worth thousands of pounds had been looted. Belgian culture had trust at its core and the local residents were horrified by the actions of the visiting English.

By the time the police arrived the offenders had fled, so they got a fleet of cars and drove some shopkeepers round the town to see if they could identify anyone involved. Now, in the mid-1970s, while not everyone dressed identically, their many male United fans under 25 looked very similar with long hair, flares, scarves round wrists and a smattering of denim jackets. Accurate identification was mission impossible but the shop owners decided any Red was fair game. Once picked out you had no chance, the police rounded you up, there was no discussion.

We knew our mate was innocent and headed for the police HQ, ready to right this injustice. We genuinely believed that after a brief explanation he would be released and we would be able to enjoy the rest of the day. How wrong. The police station was besieged with United supporters all with a similar tale to tell. Inside were dozens who had been arrested. We couldn't even get into the station because of Reds congregating outside. Eventually, the posse were allowed a meeting on the doorstep with a senior officer. To be fair he did listen to us but simply explained that a lot of crime had been committed, that it was an affront to the people of Ostend and the victims had managed to identify many of those involved. He confirmed they were processing each case and through the day the innocent ones would be released and the guilty charged. The officer seemed reasonable and asked us to leave the area around the station while they got on with their investigations.

We left in hope but around 5 p.m., unknown to us, the police deported all but six of the supporters they had rounded up. The remaining half-dozen were charged with theft-related offences and detained. We only learned this news when we arrived back in the UK on the Sunday. The rest of Saturday afternoon we spent on Ostend beach, soaking up the sun, playing football, taking the odd drink and hoping to see our mate Derek. United won 2-1 with both goals from debutant Stuart Pearson. AS Oostende were in the Belgian Second Division but they were a tough little team who battled hard even though it was a friendly. None more so than their right back, Willy Desmit, who turned out to be the town's chief of police. I guess he'd had a bellyful of Manchester United that day!

When we arrived back in the UK the media coverage was huge, especially in light of the aggro at the end of the previous season. The story ran for a week while the Belgian authorities traipsed the detained lads through their legal system. In the end they too were deported and refused access to Belgium in future. The rioting in Ostend was a forerunner to many European trips by English teams over the next decade. Coincidentally, it would take an appalling disaster in Belgium for UEFA to properly address the problem and for supporters of English clubs to realise we don't have to go to war every time we go abroad.

As this story moves through the 1970s you will notice a recurring reference to trouble involving United fans. The idea behind this book was to provide an insight into five fascinating decades following United and share some anecdotes along the way. The focus wasn't football hooliganism, that's not my scene. I prefer to leave those tales to the real hard men who can call on practical experience. However, I do want to portray an accurate picture of life as a supporter through the years and during the 1970s and 1980s aggro was an integral part of the football landscape. Even if you didn't seek it, it often came looking for you particularly at away matches. You always had to have your wits about you once you arrived in the city or town you were visiting. Maybe if you were over 50 you would be safe from it, but not always.

For twenty years professional football became a vehicle for tribal warfare to be played out on the streets of Britain. Once hooliganism had got a foothold it acted like a magnet for any rebel with or without a cause. The attractions that make football great – the passion, the large terraces, the huge crowds, the tension of the game, the travel, the camaraderie – also appealed to the hooligans. Add to this the relatively naive policing of football matches, inadequate segregation within the grounds, the mass migration of fans every week and the general liberalisation within British society and you had a recipe for anti-social behaviour that successive governments failed to eradicate.

Football had experienced outbreaks of hooliganism right back to the late 1800s, but it was during the mid-1960s that the problem became widespread. The 'teenage' culture had taken hold with rock and roll in the late 1950s and the troublesome 'Teddy Boys'. By 1964, Mods and Rockers were battling every Bank Holiday at a seaside resort near you. Soon the kids on the terraces wanted to join in. Each club claimed its own 'end' – a terrace where the home fans congregated to sing their songs and cheer their team on. The Stretford End, Kop, Gwladys Street, Shed, North Bank, Leazes etc. all became parochial hotbeds for local fanatics. United supporters travelled away in their thousands and invariably tried to take over the home end. This led to an afternoon of running skirmishes, usually with United coming out on top. United, Liverpool and Everton had the biggest away support but generally they kept out of each other's home territory.

By the start of the 1970s most police forces insisted on segregation and away fans were prevented from going into the home end. Trouble would erupt outside the ground but inside it was generally peaceful. A year or so later came a new phenomenon when home fans starting going into the away end looking for aggro. I remember going to West Ham in April 1971 for a league game. I got into the South Bank around 2 p.m. and the United support was coming in steadily. I chose a spot right behind the goal about halfway up the terraces. About 2.30 p.m. I noticed there were seven or eight lads stood behind me wearing white T-shirts with West Ham's logo blazoned across the chest. I remember thinking they were taking a risk given United's boisterous following.

They minded their own business until just after kick-off when they broke into a chant of 'West Ham! West Ham!' It was a deliberate attempt to evoke a response from United's contingent who duly obliged. Considering these guys were out-numbered they put up a fierce resistance until the police escorted them round to the home end. Rather than being crestfallen they celebrated their exit with chants about The Mile End, one of West Ham's top gangs before the Inter-City Firm. Prior to this, home fans might come round to the away end ten minutes before the end when the gates opened and try to steam in for a fight. However, Upton Park was the first time I saw hardcore home fans pay to go into the away end to have a go. Within a year most of the big clubs had a 'crew' that would do the same. This escalated the violence within grounds with attacks by home fans countered by revenge attacks when they visited their rival's ground.

Over the next decade and a half the police and authorities lost the battle against football-related violence and the carnage between rival supporters became increasingly worse. Across Britain each Saturday afternoon's final score would be as much about arrests, hospital cases and damage to property as it was about football results. Fences and pens scarred our football grounds and crowds started to dwindle. Football matches were not a safe place especially for kids and families and while the trouble was caused by a minority it was sizeable enough to inflict widescale damage.

Unfortunately, all football fans were tarred with the same brush. Labour tried various initiatives through the 1970s; Maggie Thatcher later threatened to introduce identity cards but fate, rather than politics, would intervene. On 15 April 1989, the caging of supporters and the authorities' failure to control large crowds at football matches led to the deaths of ninety-six Liverpool fans. The tragic events at Hillsborough, hosting the FA Cup semi-final between Nottingham Forest and Liverpool, brought about the

Taylor Report. Lord Taylor's inquiry would lead to the most dramatic change in how we watched our national game and, more importantly, who would watch it.

By the summer of 1974 United's following had a dreadful reputation, not just in football circles or domestically. There had been incidents throughout the previous season but the April riot at the City match received worldwide coverage. Now we had exported it to the continent. The truth is, United's support home and away was superb in terms of numbers and vocal support. The club's history and heritage inspire a fanatical and loyal following. Sometimes our sheer numbers and the extreme devotion resulted in conflict with police and rival supporters.

This provided club officials with a real headache. They welcomed, and needed, the passionate support but not the trouble that accompanied it. In the mid-1970s it was impossible to separate the two. Relegation to the Second Division galvanised the Red Army even further. It was our Dunkirk moment. There were record attendances at almost every ground we visited, often with thousands locked out. Clubs had their attendances doubled or trebled for the visit of the mighty Reds and our support equalled that of the home team at the smaller grounds. During the season in the Second Division we still retained the best average home attendance in English football, a staggering 48,388. But with a tainted reputation already, Doc's Red Army attracted the attention of a hungry media looking for stories and pictures of the next rampage.

Despite the outer confidence that United would win the Second Division title, many Reds were apprehensive about what the season would bring. Although it hurt to admit it, during the previous two years we had got used to seeing United lose more often than win. The second tier that year contained a number of big clubs trying to recapture former glories – Aston Villa, Sunderland, Nottingham Forest, Sheffield Wednesday, Southampton and West Brom. Tommy Doc admitted he had expected the sack following the relegation, conceding that for most of 1973/74 he turned United into a defensive team. A cardinal sin at Old Trafford. The board backed him, probably due to the inspired performances in the last two months of the campaign when we returned to passing the ball through midfield and playing a more attacking game.

The Doc had survived that difficult eighteen-month hurdle that saw McGuinness and O'Farrell stumble. In turn, he kept faith with his players and added only striker Stuart Pearson to his squad. In our descent to the Second Division we had equalled a seventy-two-year-old club record for the lowest number of league goals scored in a season – a miserly thirty-eight. Our top scorers in each of the previous two seasons found the net just six times. Firepower was needed up front and Pearson, with forty-four goals in 129 appearances for Hull City, was bought to provide it. On 17 August 1974, on a sun-drenched afternoon in east London, United played their first match outside the top flight since May 1938. A comfortable 2-0 win over Leyton Orient helped settle the nerves. Our line-up that day would feature in the majority of the league games that season: Stepney, Forsyth, Houston, Greenhoff, Holton, Buchan, Morgan, Macari, Pearson, McCalliog, Daly. Sub: McIlroy.

United sprinted out of the starting blocks with seven wins and two draws in the first nine games. We went top on the last day of August and stayed there. Stuart Pearson led the line superbly. His skill in holding up the ball with immaculate first touches as we broke from defence, coupled with his gift for finding a man in a red shirt, brought United alive as an attacking force. He could finish too; Pearson scored seventeen league goals that season while Macari and Daly weighed in with eleven each. Life felt great. United were winning regularly again and the football had flair and excitement.

That autumn United also had an thrilling League Cup run and Old Trafford witnessed some classic games. In early October we were paired with City. With no league fixture that season it was our only crack at putting one over on them. In a stirring cup tie United mastered the Blues, winning 1-0 thanks to a Gerry Daly penalty. We might have been in the Second Division but we gave City something to think about until we got back up. The next round brought First Division Burnley to Manchester. Another rousing game saw United win 3-2 with Willie Morgan hitting a sublime angled strike from twenty-five yards right into the top corner at the Scoreboard End.

On 30 November came the match of the season when United entertained second-placed Sunderland in a league clash. United had built up a four-point lead over the Wearsiders and they were desperate to peg us back. A crowd of 60,585, the biggest for a

Second Division match for fifteen years, packed Old Trafford. Pearson opened the scoring with a magnificent left-foot drive from the edge of the penalty area. Two strikes by Billy Hughes put Sunderland in front, only for Sammy Mac and Willie Morgan to restore United's lead. All through the match it was relentless attack and counter-attack and it left the fans breathless. We won 3-2 to maintain our lead at the top but the real winner was football. The game was featured on that night's *Match of the Day* and the football world got a sneak preview that United were on the way back.

A week later United featured in a bizarre game at Sheffield Wednesday. The Owls were languishing at the foot of the table but the gate was swelled to 35,000 by 20,000 United fans. This is the biggest ever United following I've seen at an away league game. At kick-off there were Reds everywhere around the ground and it was bouncing. Stewart Houston gave United an early lead but fifteen minutes in, terrace hero Jim Holton broke his leg in a fifty/fifty tackle. The supporters knew it was bad and the team seemed to be affected as well. Wednesday scored three times in ten minutes. In the second half, Macari pulled one back but Wednesday went up the other end to make it 4-2. Doc's team was starting to show its true mettle and goals from Pearson and Macari salvaged a 4-4 draw.

Little did we know but we had seen the last of Jim Holton in a United shirt. The leg healed slowly and during a comeback game against Bury reserves the following August he broke it again. In October 1976 Jim moved to Sunderland and, later, Coventry. Sadly he passed away in 1993, at the age of just 42. Big Jim was one of those special players who won the hearts of football supporters within minutes of their first appearance. Cantona had it, Whiteside, Rooney, Ronaldo, Van Persie all had it. The Stretford End idolised Jim Holton. He plugged a gap in our defence when we needed it badly; more importantly he provided us with a red-shirted hero when they were in very short supply at Old Trafford. For me he embodied the spirit of the time – the team and club were in a mess but we would give everything to get ourselves out of it.

In the League Cup United saw off Middlesbrough, another top flight club, to reach the semi-finals. Seven years had passed since we had graced Wembley but it seemed like an eternity.

Unfortunately our only blip during 1974/75 came early in the New Year. Between 4 January and 22 February we were dumped out of the FA Cup by Third Division Walsall at Fellows Park, Norwich ended our Wembley dream and we suffered league defeats to Oxford, Bristol City and Villa. Leading scorer Pearson had joined Holton in the sick bay for six weeks and United wobbled. Fortunately, none of United's title rivals could make up ground and we started March still four points in front.

During a 4-0 win over Cardiff, The Doc substituted Willie Morgan for a young lad he had just bought from Tranmere called Steve Coppell. The manager had been seeking a right-winger who could come through from midfield and he unearthed a gem. Coppell would become a fixture in United's team for the next eight years and serve up some inspired wing play. Sadly, it was the end of the road for Morgan. The Doc had made him United captain and resurrected his Scotland career in the first half of the 1970s, but the two had their differences early in 1975 and there was only going to be one winner. Morgan's stylish play was well appreciated by the Old Trafford faithful. Having joined a team that were champions of Europe he was a shining star through the six year decline that followed and a cornerstone of the revival.

The last eleven games of the season brought eight wins and three draws. Promotion was clinched on 5 April with a 1-0 win at Southampton. Top spot was guaranteed two weeks later with a point at Notts. County. 'United are back! United are back!' echoed throughout the land to the tune of Gary Glitter's 'Good To Be Back'. The trophy was presented at Old Trafford after the final match against Blackpool. A glorious May day with over 60,000 inside the ground, thousands locked out and a lad on the Scoreboard Paddock roof who stripped down to his underpants for some reason.

United's season in the Second Division turned despair into delight for the supporters. The matches were a thrill-a-minute roller-coaster ride and away trips to places like York, Cardiff, Bristol Rovers, Leyton Orient and Blackpool with an unbeliev-able following were one-offs that we would cherish forever. The key to our success was the settled side. Eight players made at least thirty-five league appearances out of forty-two and another two made over thirty. Tommy Doc had now assembled his team, his squad and they were playing in the mould of their manager – exciting, cavalier and proud.

There was one exception during that campaign when United didn't take a huge following to an away match. On Monday, 16 September 1974, United played at Millwall. I went with Geoff Milloy on the Football Special, Kirky was staying in London with family and we arranged to meet up at the match. For some reason Geoff and I only bought our train tickets on the day of the game. Oddly, our ticket numbers were 151 and 152. Usually when you booked that late the train would be nearly full and ticket numbers nearer 500–600. We were delighted and thought British Rail must be running a second train to cope with demand.

At the platform it was obvious there was no second train as just over 100 United fans waited for the train. Nowadays, everyone knows about Millwall. In fact, nowadays everyone knows about everyone else thanks to search engines. Back then your information came from the grapevine, newspapers or reference books. We had heard stories about Millwall being a hard area and knew their ground was closed a couple of times way back when for crowd trouble. But Millwall struggled to get 5,000–6,000 crowds in 1974, how were they going to pose United's following a problem? I remember saying to Geoff that most of the Millwall stories were probably myths anyway.

I bought a copy of the *London Evening Standard* as we boarded the train at Manchester. The front page headline screamed 'Red Army on march; 10,000 United fans heading for London'. That's what I had been expecting until I bought my train ticket. Something didn't add up. When we got on the train it was eerie with a handful of supporters in each coach – we were almost outnumbered by the police. The special stopped at Stockport and a few more Reds got on board but then I witnessed something I had never seen before. Around fifteen to twenty lads got off the train. I can only assume they decided the trip wasn't worth it if United fans weren't out in force.

At Euston we were met by the Cockney Reds as usual. The word went round to watch ourselves as Millwall were planning a welcoming party. United hadn't played at Millwall in a competitive match since 1953 so it was new territory for all of us.

We got the Tube to New Cross and walked to the ground with no sign of trouble. Most of us were wearing United colours and as we queued at the turnstiles a copper said, 'You might want to take your scarves off, lads.' I was about to laugh it off when I realised he was serious. I held my scarf in my hand as we went through the turnstile, just in case. Once inside I asked another copper, 'Which end are the United fans at, mate?' He looked blank, shook his head, and said, 'I've not seen any United fans tonight, I don't know, sorry.' 'What a plonker, what's the matter with these Met boys?' I thought.

Geoff and I were making our way up the steps to the terraces when a chant of 'United! United!' rang out around the old Den. I turned to Geoff and smiled, 'That's more like it, come on!' As we got to the top of the steps we were caught up in a stampede of young lads who were also heading for the end where the chant came from. We quickly realised these weren't United supporters. There was no segregation, in fact you could walk round three sides of the ground, so we hung back a little to sus out what was going on. Thank God we did. The small group of United fans who had gathered behind one goal were chased off the terraces by hundreds of Millwall fans and took refuge in the only seated area in the ground. Even at that stage Geoff and I thought it was only a matter of time before Reds arrived in numbers and United would fill an end. Well, we waited and waited but no Reds gathered on the terraces. As the teams came out there was a subdued chant from the routed Reds in the stand, the rest were cheers for Millwall.

The game, like the atmosphere, was tense but halfway through the first half Macari was upended in the area and the ref awarded United a penalty. Normally that would have brought a delirious response from thousands of travelling Reds. That night there was a small cheer, again from the United enclave in the stand. I took a look around at that point and there were no other Reds cheering in the ground. What I did notice was hundreds of lads with no colours. Some had pin badges but they weren't just Millwall emblems, I saw Chelsea, West Ham, Spurs and Charlton. 'Whatever you do, Geoff, if this goes in don't cheer or show any sign of celebration!' I whispered. 'Don't worry, I've clocked it,' he said like a master ventriloquist.

As Gerry Daly stroked home the spot-kick we stood there absolutely impassive on the outside. Inside I felt the same thrill

as whenever United score but I daren't let it show. Since that day,
particularly with advent of all-seater stadia, I've sat with home
fans when United play away because it's the only way of seeing
the game. I have mastered the art of sitting on my hands when
we score to avoid a beating or getting thrown out. But in Doc's
Red Army days it just didn't happen. I felt odd, a bit disloyal to
my team and club for not cheering even though I knew it would
have been suicidal. I am sure there were several hundred Reds
that did the same that night.

We watched the remainder of the half in silence. At the break
we checked out the situation. The crowd was nearly 17,000 –
inflated that night with gangs of lads from all over London who
had come down to have a go at United. Our reputation had
gone before us and a Monday night down Cold Blow Lane
provided an ideal opportunity for a bit of Cockney payback. As
I gazed around I couldn't help thinking back to those lads who
had got off the train at Stockport. Did they know something
we didn't? Then I spotted Dave Kirk in the crowd behind us.
He was quite a few steps back. I gave him a manly wave but he
just stared back, gently shaking his head and moving his eyes
from side to side indicating danger was all around. I just gave
him a thumbs-up sign and turned back to face the pitch. It was
every man for himself.

United won 1-0. Throughout the second half Millwall fans
became increasingly frustrated by the lack of action on the terraces. They felt cheated. During the last twenty minutes their
songs were all about 'where's your famous Cockney Reds' and
'it's a long way back to Euston'. They knew we were there somewhere in the ground. We decided against leaving early, too many
people were watching for absconders. Leaving at the end would
allow us to blend in with the crowd. On a day when we had
underestimated much of what was going on, we got it wrong
again. The crowd in the streets around the ground was like a
lynchmob. There were hundreds of lads our age just hell-bent
on seeking out United fans. Our colours were tucked away and
our mouths shut but the hostility around us was so fearsome we
daren't risk being identified as the enemy.

The police tried to control matters but that just sparked more
fury and the Millwall collective turned on them. Just in front of
us a police motorcyclist had his bike kicked from under him; a

copper on horseback came to his rescue but had to battle hard not to be pulled from his mount. Neither Geoff nor I fancied getting on the Tube with this lot so we took a detour down a side street away from the main crowd. The road was full of the big Victorian houses for which London is famous. It was quieter but there were still a lot of dodgy characters about. We decided to take refuge in a front garden, crouching down behind a privet hedge we felt safe for the first time all evening. There we sat for about forty-five minutes while the streets cleared.

We made our way to New Cross Station which was still swarming with Millwall fans, police and ambulances. We hung back another half-hour, knowing this meant missing our train back to Manchester, but survival was the over-riding emotion. Around 11 p.m. we finally ventured to the Tube station. Thankfully the mob had disappeared for the night and we made it back to Euston. As we checked out the train times a BR official told us we had just missed the special back to Manchester. That couldn't be right, it was approaching midnight and the special was scheduled to leave Euston at 11.15 p.m. He told us that the departure time had been put back twice because so few Reds made it back by then. Apparently it had really kicked off at New Cross and a supporter had been stabbed. Sitting in that garden might have saved our skin.

British Rail let us travel home on the mail train which arrived in Manchester at 6 a.m. I grabbed a couple of hours' sleep then went into work. Geoff and I had survived to tell the tale of a very strange night for the Red Army. I often think about that Millwall game when I hear Fergie talk about 'squeaky bum time'. The great man coined the phrase to illustrate anxiety levels at the business end of the season. Well, believe me, the term was never more aptly used than to describe the walk to New Cross Station that night!

As United's following increased through the Docherty years, so did our dedicated band of men who travelled away. As well as the six or seven lads from Salford that I've mentioned already we had also got to know Pete Ward and the Manifold brothers from Bury, John Scholic from Chorlton and Jeff and Steve Fanning from Longsight plus their mate Frank. We also knocked about with Lindsay, Jane and Anne from Runcorn who followed United everywhere on Barry Cooper coach trips. From early 1975 we started hiring vans to go to away matches. It was a cheap way to travel but the big attraction was the independence and the camaraderie. Twelve to fifteen of us could travel together and, unlike the coach or the train, we could go where we wanted when we wanted.

We didn't travel in comfort. Minibuses with seats were dearer to hire and guzzled the petrol. Simple transit vans were the vehicle of choice and we would pile at least ten in the back and three in the cab. I took it on myself to hire and drive the vans. This was a time when self-drive van hire was just taking off in the UK. Salford Van Hire was our local supplier which wasn't ideal because they had their name in huge letters across all their vehicles. In the 1970s you didn't want that sort of clue on display to rival fans in the big cities. We tried firms with more discreet livery but many introduced a mileage charge which made trips to London, the South Coast and East Anglia very costly. So we became very good customers of SVH over a three-year period.

We travelled the length and breadth of England in those vans during the Red Army's most colourful period. Around dawn I would pick up the lads in Salford, Bury, Longsight and Chorlton which took the best part of two hours before we even set off for our destination. The Bury lads often came straight from the 103 Club, a drinking den on Manchester Road near Gigg Lane. Last Orders didn't exist at the 103 so I often found them in a heap outside the club and I would simply lift them into the back of the van still cradling a bottle of vodka. That's them, not me, of course.

The first few hours on the road were always peaceful as the lads caught up on lost sleep. You would think the passengers would appreciate the running around and chauffeuring, but no. As they stirred, the driver became the butt of countless moans. We were going too fast, too slow, it was too bumpy, why haven't we stopped yet? Why have we stopped here? How much for petrol?! And so on. I quickly grew a thick skin.

After breaking the back of the journey we would stop at a pub where a hair of the dog was the order of the day. That got everyone in the mood for the game and as we approached our destination the sides of the van would be banging to United's top tunes. After the match the aim was to get as far north as possible, then find a decent watering hole, park the van, have a few drinks, a sing-song, back to the van to sleep it off before leaving early enough to return the van Sunday morning.

Invariably, we dropped in on some unsuspecting town around the south Midlands. As much as our lads liked a drink none of them went looking for trouble. Occasionally, as a large group, we would attract the attention of the local males but often ended up chatting to them to find the best pubs for a night out. On one trip we somehow got invited to a wedding reception being held upstairs in the pub we were drinking at. I don't know how or why but it was great night. Sometimes, where there was live entertainment a couple of our lads would provide a song or two, usually from the United repertoire.

Things didn't always go as planned though. After a really good night in Lutterworth, we called at a chip shop. Some local was having an argument with the owners, it got out of hand and on his way out he smashed the shop window. We didn't get involved but the police came tearing in ten minutes later ready for a battle. Seeing a gang of Manchester United supporters they put two and two together and started to round us up for a visit to the station. The shop owner explained it had nothing to do with us. The police accepted his explanation but still wanted us off their patch.

We explained we had all had a drink and were going to sleep in our van until morning. Well, they didn't like that, so I asked the lads to head for the van while I reasoned with the sergeant. He was having none of it, he had made his decision that we had to leave and wasn't for backing down. I explained I was the driver but that I would be over the alcohol limit. He said that was my problem. I made my way to the van which was parked on waste ground away from the main road. I told the lads to get inside, lock all the doors and we would just sit it out. As the sergeant realised what was happening he started barking orders at me through the glass, 'Drive this van! Drive this van now!'

I told him again I'd had a drink and wasn't legally fit to drive but he was like a rabid dog. He had about ten officers with him and things were starting to get pretty heated. I couldn't win. Drive the van and I could be arrested or have an accident; don't drive and risk the wrath of Leicestershire Constabulary's finest.

'Open the door!' snarled the sergeant.

'Just sit tight lads, they can't do anything,' I reassured our boys, most of whom just wanted to get some kip. The sergeant tugged angrily at my door but it didn't budge. He went round to the back of the van and found the same there. He came round to the passenger side where Dave Kirk was sitting and started giving him grief through the glass.

'Don't worry, Dave, he can't get us, just sit tight,' I said.

The sergeant pressed the passenger door handle and the door flew open. In seconds he had me by the throat and dragged me across the two passengers in the front seats ready to deliver a right bollocking. I could just about breathe. Kirky was sat bolt upright with me draped across his lap. I glanced up to him and said in a calm voice, 'I thought I told you to lock the door Dave?'

Luckily the sergeant saw the funny side. I took the verbal bashing, got out of the van and put a proposal to him. If all he wanted was us off his patch, why not let one of his men drive us to the 'border' where we could pitch the van overnight to sleep. It worked a treat. An obliging officer took the wheel and, escorted by an armada of police cars, we were taken to a field somewhere north of Lutterworth and left in peace.

The worst part of the van trips was always the Sunday morning. We had been on the go for twenty-four hours, the van stunk, we probably stunk, our mouths were as dry as an Arab's flip-flop, heads were banging and we still had to travel eighty to 100 miles. I used to drop the lads off, fill the van with petrol, sweep out the rear, bag up the rubbish then drive to the depot by 9 a.m. to collect my £75 deposit. I would get the bus home or ring my dad to collect me, have a light breakfast and grab a few hours' sleep. They were long days and long trips but full of fantastic adventures and hundreds of happy memories to last a lifetime.

It was after one such trip that I was faced with a really thorny dilemma, one of those times in life when you find yourselves at an important crossroad. In April 1975, United would seal promotion back to the First Division at the first attempt if we won at Southampton. We hired a van and, anticipating a celebration, decided to leave on the Friday night and make a weekend of it. Lou Macari's seventy-sixth-minute goal secured a 1-0 win and the party started – United were back! After the recent barren years, this was a shindig to savour.

We partied all Saturday night and most of the following day, arriving back in Manchester late Sunday afternoon. I was still going out with Gail and to be fair she tolerated these away trips with little complaint. We used to see each other once in midweek and every weekend but since the van trips had come on the scene sometimes I would only get to see her for a few hours when I got back on a Sunday. After the Southampton trip it was too late even for that. We chatted on the phone and she suggested getting together on the Monday night instead.

Now, this is where I cringe because what happened next makes me sound like a real selfish so-and-so. On Mondays I used to go to my local, the Brittania Pub on The Height, with Geoff Milloy, Dave Kirk and a couple of others. It was a regular practice and even though I had spent most of the weekend with these guys, I was looking forward to carrying on the celebration on the Monday night. Well, she saw red, I dug my heels in and we had an almighty fall-out.

I went to the local that Monday night. Over the next couple of weeks we patched things up but the incident highlighted an underlying issue for us both. Gail felt I was becoming too embroiled in my love of United and saw that as a threat to our relationship. At the same time, I had begun to realise that I wanted my freedom. I was still only 20 and felt there was so much I wanted to do with my life before settling down. Not just freedom to follow United, although that was a key element at the time, but the freedom to meet other girls, travel the world, carve out a career. The freedom to live life to the full. I had been hurtling towards marriage and it wasn't for me – not yet.

Gail was a warm, beautiful girl with a fantastic personality. We shared some wonderful times together, she was my first love and I couldn't have asked for a better partner – if I had been looking for one. The argument about that Monday night out brought into focus the desires that separated rather than connected us. By mid-May we had split. We had been together almost three years and telling her parents wasn't easy. Marjorie and Walter had always treated me like a son and there was no easy way of breaking the news to them. Walter asked me to stay in touch which I was happy to do.

Gail had a sister called Lindsey who was much younger. She had been born with a hole in her heart which needed surgery when she was older and stronger. Outwardly, she was a normal healthy child and lots of fun, we got on great. A few weeks after Gail and I parted, Lindsey finally received the green light for the operation to repair her heart. She was 8 years old and although intricate the procedure was considered routine. One evening I got a phone call from Gail to tell me that Lindsey hadn't made it through the operation. A few days later I went round to see Walter and Marjorie. I tried to offer some support, but their loss was immense. I couldn't help feeling I had let them down even though the split from Gail wasn't connected to what had happened to Lindsey. I had my freedom, it was time to move on, but the timing was dreadful.

9

I NEED EXCITEMENT
OH I NEED IT BAD,
AND IT'S THE BEST
I'VE EVER HAD

The sweltering summer of 1975 held one special moment for United followers – the new season's fixtures. Back on the agenda were excursions to Anfield, Maine Road, Highbury and Elland Road. To whet the appetite even more, the Supporters' Club decided to run a trip to Denmark for United's pre-season tour. Chairman Dave Smith had successfully managed the travel club for three years, organising coach and train travel to domestic away matches. Football clubs didn't do supporters' trips to pre-season tours in those days but Smithy saw a gap in the market – some fans wanted to watch their team wherever they played. Ostend had been the forerunner and despite the trouble, Dave decided to carry on regardless.

I was approaching my twenty-first birthday and dad asked if I wanted a 'do'. I said I would prefer to go to Denmark so he gave me some money towards it. The seven-night stay in Copenhagen cost £79.50; more than double the price of a full season ticket. I went with two mates, Pete Ward and Phil Lockett, along with seventy-four other Reds from around the UK. The flight was my first experience of flying. Arriving in the Danish capital we headed to our base for the week, the Hotel Centrum. I knew a few other lads from Salford on the trip and after dumping the cases we set off to explore our new surroundings. We didn't get far.

Right next to the hotel was a shop with windows filled with pictures of explicit sex scenes and a big sign enticing visitors inside to watch some 8mm films. We almost fell through the doorway, paid a nice man a relatively small fee and followed him to a back room where twenty of us watched an assortment of blue movies for a couple of hours. Now, let me put this into perspective, this was 1975 and sex had only just been invented in Britain. Porn videos, DVDs and websites were light years away. Back home, *Confessions of a Window Cleaner* at the cinema was the nearest we got to hardcore. The stuff in Copenhagen was the real thing and there it was on our doorstep.

We surfaced back into the daylight like a collective dog on heat and touring the surrounding streets came across several similar shops. We soon realised our temporary home was in the heart of the red-light district. The next day we passed a shop with a very attractive girl sat behind a desk, who smiled and waved. One of the lads decided he would pop in and chat her up. We laughed it off and carried on walking. We didn't see him again until tea time when he turned up at the hotel and explained that this beautiful girl was in fact a prostitute and that shop was her business premises. Nothing odd about that except she was 21, looked like a film star and provided her 'services' right next to the bakers and a greengrocers. He told us prostitution in Denmark was legal, well organised and run by a regulatory body. The profession was seen as a respectable 'career'. Of course, it had been a bit of a shock when our mate discovered her trade but it didn't deter him from trying to get a date.

He was taken aback though when the girl's parents popped in with some sandwiches for their daughter's lunch. The four of them sat around chatting interrupted only by phone calls to book future 'appointments'. All quite surreal and a million miles from the seedy world of prostitution we knew in the UK. Sorry, that should read 'knew of'! Despite this, the two did strike up a genuine holiday romance for the week.

At the end of the second day we bumped into Jim Holton, Lou Macari and Gerry Daly taking a stroll. We had a good chat and it turned out their hotel was just round the corner in another part of the red-light area. The first game on 3 August was in Korsor, a two-hour coach journey from Copenhagen, against Halskov. In a tiny stadium United won 3-0. There had been fears that United fans might cause trouble but the 250 Reds behaved impeccably. The hosts organised a naval band to entertain the crowd before the game. Security was so low-key it was like a kick-about in the park. The band played a couple of numbers marching up and down the pitch when a few dozen Reds ran onto the playing area. They lined up behind the band and marched in time, playing imaginary instruments to the stirring tunes. It looked hilarious and the Danes loved it. United aggro? Not a hint of it.

The party atmosphere continued back in Copenhagen the following Tuesday when United played Hvidovre to commemorate the hosts' fiftieth year as a football club. United coasted to a 3-1 victory and a half-time streaker from Manchester provided the 10,000 crowd with more impromptu entertainment with only a red and white scarf to cover his embarrassment. The final game of the tour was 200 miles away in Holstebro, north-west Denmark. It was a six-hour journey each way including a ferry trip. We were getting to see plenty of the Danish countryside but most young bucks on the trip would have settled for three matches in Copenhagen, close to our new best mate who owned the shop showing blue movies. The 1975 tour was an unforgettable birthday present, a true coming of age. I met loyal Reds from all over the UK who became good mates for many years.

United's return to the First Division kicked off with Midlands trips to Wolves and Birmingham. We won both 2-0 then hammered Sheffield United 5-1. Any doubts about United holding their own back in the big league were dismissed as the team stormed to the top of the table by mid-October. Doc's team played with the innocence of youth, going at opponents in wave after wave of attacking football. The Old Trafford crowd loved it, the media acclaimed it and football pundits extolled it. We were a breath of fresh air; the spell in the Second Division Two had given the young players time to gain confidence.

The Doc solved the centre-half problem by moving midfielder Brian Greenhoff alongside Martin Buchan. Initially, a stopgap solution Greenhoff formed a superb partnership with the Scottish captain. A defeat at title rivals West Ham on 25 October ushered in a November wobble. Veteran keeper Alex Stepney was dropped and Paddy Roche given a run in the team. Over the next five games we lost ground in the league, losing at Liverpool and Arsenal plus a 4-0 pummelling by City to end our interest in the League Cup. Roche looked nervous, indecisive and fumbled a couple of crosses which led directly to goals. He seemed to physically shrink with each game. Docherty tried to play him through it but supporters were angry that the title challenge was needlessly slipping away.

Docherty recalled Stepney and dipped into the transfer market to buy Gordon Hill from Millwall. Hill, a mercurial left-winger, gave United more firepower up front. The moves were a touch of Docherty genius, United lost only one of the next twenty-four league and cup games.

The key was a settled team. Out of fifty-two possible appearances in 1975/76, Buchan and Houston played in every match, Daly and McIlroy fifty-one, Greenhoff fifty, Coppell and Pearson forty-nine each, Stepney forty-seven and Macari forty-five.

From November, United played with two classic wingers in Coppell and Hill, giving us width and attacking options. A great FA Cup run featured two legendary ties. In the sixth round we drew 1-1 with Wolves at Old Trafford. The following Tuesday 10,000 Reds made their way to Molineux. The gates were locked thirty minutes before kick-off and there was a real buzz around the ground. Wolves raced into a 2-0 lead but we kept playing football and goals from Greenhoff, McIlroy and Pearson turned the tie round. 'Two-nil down, three-two up, now we're gonna win the cup!' bellowed the Red Army.

The semi-final pitched us against Derby County, the reigning champions and joint second with United in the title race. Hillsborough had been an unlucky ground for United during the 1960s but not this time as Gordon Hill, playing the game of his life, netted both goals in a 2-0 win. The strikes deserved the stage they were played out on; the first a direct free-kick from 25 yards, the second an exquisite chip from almost the same distance.

My dad had long since given up away matches but I managed to talk him into going to the Derby semi-final. We travelled together just like eleven years earlier when he took me to see United play Leeds at the same venue. I was 10 then, my first away match, and even though it ended 0-0 it was the biggest adventure of my life at that time. In the intervening years I had battled for my independence to go to matches under my own steam but I still loved catching up with my dad at home and talking about the matches and football in general. After

I deserted him for the Stretford End, he had bought a season ticket in K Stand when it opened in August 1972 and attended almost every home match.

As we made our way to the Leppings Lane turnstiles in April 1976, my dad said he was going to stand on the far right-hand side of the goal. Normally, I would have headed to find my mates somewhere directly behind the nets, but I decided to stay and watch the match with him. The terraces were absolutely packed even in the corner and we got tossed around in a sea of Red humanity for ninety minutes. But Hill's goals made it all worthwhile and my old fella at the age of 64 celebrated like a teenager as United finally made it through to another Wembley final. I didn't know it then, as we leapt around on those Sheffield steps, but it would be the last time we watched a United away match together. I couldn't tempt him to the final or future semis, he would tell me he was getting too old and preferred to watch it on the telly.

As spring arrived United stood on the cusp of the English double. Given our plight two years earlier we were in dreamland. Our Wembley opponents would be Second Division Southampton and the league table dated 3 April shows the title was ours for the taking:

	Played	Points
QPR	38	53
Liverpool	37	51
United	36	50
Derby	37	50

Note: 42-game season, two points for a win.

United were in their best form for a decade and just seven games from becoming only the fourth side to win the double. A week after reaching Wembley thousands of us made the long journey to Ipswich to support the lads in the final push. The Red Army turned out in force but the team didn't. In our poorest display of the season Ipswich scored three without reply.

We feared the Cup Final might prove a distraction. A backlog of fixtures meant United had to play four of our five remaining league games within one week. We beat Everton and Burnley over Easter to keep the pressure on Liverpool and QPR. The following Wednesday twelfth-placed Stoke visited Old Trafford. We had lost just once in two seasons on home turf. That night the whole season seemed to catch up with us. Stoke edged a 1-0 win with a late goal that dealt a fatal blow to our title dreams. United finished third. Liverpool claimed their ninth league title, winning eight of their last nine games, a finale that would become all too familiar over the next fifteen years.

The week before Wembley, United played at Leicester. The title had gone but the supporters turned the occasion into a celebration ahead of our first FA Cup Final since 1963. A generation of young Reds eagerly anticipated their first trip to the hallowed stadium. That day the classic, 'Que sera sera, whatever will be will be; We're going to Wemb-er-lee' was born on the terraces at Filbert Street. The song reverberated around the ground all through the second half and became United's anthem for future cup campaigns.

I managed to get a ticket for the final okay because I had been to all the matches plus several reserve or youth team games. So did most of the others in our gang. Twenty of us booked into a central London hotel for two nights and travelled down together on the Friday. I had longed to see United play in an FA Cup Final ever since the Leicester game in 1963. The whole day had a magic of its own. As football supporters we had all grown up watching the Cup Finals down the years and the build up on TV on the morning of the match. I remember in 1970 going to my uncle Albert's house to watch the game in colour for the first time as we still had a black and white set like millions of others.

This year I wouldn't be watching it on television – I would be there! But that brought with it another worry. What if I lost my ticket or had it pinched? The £2.50 tickets were changing hands for £25 and the police were warning fans to be careful of pickpockets. There was only one solution, before leaving home I put my ticket in the front of my Lybro Seadog jeans and stitched up the pocket. Those jeans stayed with me night and day for thirty-six hours.

Outside the stadium when turnstile H was in touching distance, I quickly unpicked the cotton and got the ticket out. Seconds later I was inside Wembley. In the years to come such trips became commonplace and not only does the novelty wear off but familiarity breeds its own contempt and you see the stadium stripped of its romance. But in 1976 at the age of 21, I was in awe of the place. Not just the bricks and mortar but the history and tradition. The walk down Wembley Way, the twin towers, the banners, flags, daft hats, hand-painted rattles, the friendly banter between fans and the stadium itself, there was no occasion to compare.

Inside I made my way up two flights of stairs to entrance fifty-eight in the West Standing Enclosure. Approaching the opening to the terraces I was trembling with excitement. I climbed the final few steps and the hairs on the back of my neck stood on end as I took in the spectacle; the huge, sweeping terraces, the giant scoreboards, the Royal Box, the Marine Band in gleaming white uniforms, the sounds and colours of the supporters and the pitch, so green and perfect on a sunny May day. It didn't seem real; dreams don't when they become reality.

I was at the other end from where I had stood in 1968 and I tried to relate what I remembered to what I was seeing now. Much of it fell into place but I was seeing it through adult eyes. I was a big tough Stretford Ender here to see the team that I had followed all over the country lift the Cup. While it was great to be with my mates a small part of me wished my dad had come too and we could have watched an FA Cup Final together. When the band played the eternal Cup Final hymn, 'Abide with Me', the emotion was incredible and many a big, tough Stretford Ender struggled to sing the words as they fought back a tear or two.

Tommy Doc could boast an injury-free line-up to face Southampton on 1 May 1976: Stepney, Forsyth, Houston, McIlroy, B. Greenhoff, Buchan, Coppell, Daly, Pearson, Macari, Hill.

United's fresh-faced side was expected to run rings around Lawrie McMenemy's veterans including Peter Osgood, Jim McCalliog, Mick Channon and Peter Rodrigues. The Saints had finished sixth in the second tier. As it turned out, our young lads were overcome with the occasion and never really got into gear. We had more of the play and the chances but as the game went into the latter stages Southampton looked more dangerous. In the eighty-third minute, McCalliog side-footed a thirty-yard lob over United's defence for Bobby Stokes to run on to and drive past Stepney. There was a hint of offside but the scoreboard showed 1-0. Southampton won the Cup for the only time in their history. We were absolutely stunned, hardly able to believe what we had just witnessed.

Despite the disappointment we had a good drink that night and headed back to Manchester to give the team a rousing return in Albert Square. Tommy Doc, ever the optimist, gave a great speech from the balcony saying he was sorry he couldn't bring the Cup home to the greatest supporters in the world but that he would next season. Brave words. A 2-0 victory over City in the final league game lifted our spirits. There is no doubt that in August 1975, United fans would have snatched at an offer of finishing third and reaching the FA Cup Final. In reality, when you get so close to winning the double and end up with nothing the disappointment is devastating.

Over the summer we came to appreciate what a thrill-packed season we had experienced. United were back, not just in the top flight but back in European competition and back to the brink of greatness. Doc's young braves would only get better; the future looked bright.

My own future looked anything but bright in the February of that momentous season. Doc's Red Army contained what the media coined a 'lunatic fringe' and trouble had become commonplace on United's travels. The Government imposed an entry by ticket only law for away matches in an attempt to control the numbers turning up on the day. If you read United's programmes during this period there is constant reference to hooliganism and pleas from the directors for the troublemakers to stop bringing shame on Manchester United. Throughout the season the programme carried a full-page advert showing a pointing finger (like the Kitchener poster in the First World War) with the words 'Manchester United: Our good name depends on you!' This message struck a chord with many Reds who were passionate in their support and defence of United but didn't want to tarnish the club's reputation. Conversely, there was an element among the Red Army who relished a good punch-up and a slice of civil disorder. The truth is, there was little the individual supporter could do when trouble erupted. In the 1970s it would quickly escalate into fighting with hundreds involved.

On 21 February 1976 I hired a van for the away match at Aston Villa as lots of our mates wanted to go and we didn't have enough cars between us. By the time we had collected the usual suspects we were running a bit late. There were no places to park anywhere near the United coaches and minibuses, but we found a petrol station forecourt with spaces and left it there. We only just got in for the kick-off. United lost 2-1, our first defeat in fourteen games. As thousands of Reds poured out of the ground the mood was ugly. You could tell trouble was brewing.

Our van was parked in the opposite direction to the coaches and train station. We all wore colours in those days and as we got further from the ground it was predominantly Villa supporters walking our way. They gave us a bit of verbal but we made it back to the van okay. Everyone was there except the two youngest lads, Keith Livesey and Steve Fanning. As we waited, like sitting ducks with 'Salford Van Hire' plastered on all four sides of the van, we attracted abuse from the triumphant Villa fans.

I persuaded the lads to stay in the vehicle and not retaliate, arguing that we were well outnumbered and it was best to lie low. My main concern was for the safety of the lads but I had also paid a £75 deposit to hire the van. Any damage and it was big money down the drain. Eventually the two lads turned up but Keith had been roughed up by some Villa fans and his face was cut. His older brother, Ged, burst out of the van doors to have a go at the villains (sorry!) responsible. A few of us restrained him and I ushered everyone back inside. 'Thank God for that, now let's get out of here!' I thought to myself.

I always took a Krooklok on these trips to immobilise the steering wheel and stop the van being stolen while we were parked up. A gang of Villa fans had spotted Ged's little out-burst and were now looking for aggro. I had just released the Krooklok and was ready to drive away when a brick hit the van. Having been the peace-keeper and voice of reason for the last twenty minutes I suddenly saw red. That brick could have cost me a fortnight's wages! I was out of the cab in a shot and ran straight at the Villa fans. There was about a dozen of them, at the front was a skinhead shouting abuse and leaping around like a Maori warrior performing The Haka. I still had the Krooklok in my hand. Without thinking, I swung it in his direction with all my might. He ducked, I missed, lost my balance and fell over.

As I quickly got up to have another go, I felt a hand on my shoulder. It was the biggest copper in Birmingham and I was nicked, caught red-handed. The Villa lads legged it. What the officer had seen was me attacking another group of supporters

with an offensive weapon. For that I won a free ride to Aston
Police Station. The 'oh shit!' factor kicks in pretty quickly at
times like this. A million thoughts scurried through my mind.
What would my dad say? What about the lads who were attack-
ing us, will they be arrested? Will any of our lads be implicated?
How will I get home? Will I lose my job? Thank God he ducked,
I could be facing a murder charge. Where is my Krooklok?

The police station was bursting at the seams; they were
bringing in fans every few minutes. I joined a long queue
to be booked in, finger-printed and charged. Then I was put
in a cell with two or three other lads. These guys had stayed
with the main group of Reds coming out of the ground and
explained how hundreds had gone on the rampage, running
through the local streets smashing windows, over-turning cars
and threatening anyone in their wake. Dozens of United fans
were arrested that day. The violence made national news not
just that weekend but all through the week. At United's home
game the following Saturday, several residents of Aston came to
Old Trafford with collection buckets for United fans to make a
donation to the cost of repairs to their properties.

Anyway, back in my cell, it got to 8 p.m. and my fellow
prisoners from Gloucester, Coventry and London had all
been released on bail. I asked why I couldn't go and an officer
explained it depended on how soon the Salford police could
call at my home and verify the address I had given. My heart
sank as I imagined my dad opening the door to a policeman to
hear I had been a bad lad. I would rather have told him myself.
Just after 10 p.m. I was released with my charge papers and
told to report to Birmingham Magistrates' Court on Monday
morning. The charge was 'threatening words and behaviour'.
I argued that I had not said anything as I ran at the lad, but
the arresting officer claimed I shouted 'come on, let's get the
bastards!' I didn't, but they weren't going to change it.

As I came through the police station to the public reception
area, I spotted our lads scattered around on chairs and cheap sofas.
I was really moved. 'Oh God lads, thanks for waiting for me,'
I blurted. 'We had no choice, Molly, the police impounded the
van!' came a rather less than sympathetic response from Longsight
Frank who was peeved because he was due on a late shift at the
Daily Mirror that night. The rest asked if I was okay and whether

the police had roughed me up – well it was the 1970s! I assured them I was fine. Throughout the two-hour drive up the M6 I couldn't stop thinking about what I would say to my dad when I got home. Just like when I nicked that scarf at Salford in 1968, I had let him down. Worse still, no matter what had happened with the attack on the van I would be tarred as a football hooligan, a United yob.

Long after midnight, after dropping off the lads, I put my key in the door and went in to face the music. My dad was still up and acted as if nothing had happened. I was a bit mystified. I asked him if the police had been round. 'No, why?' he said. 'Sit down, dad, I've got something to tell you,' I sighed. It is funny how when you think you are in for the biggest bollocking of your life, parents are pure gold. They realise you're in a mess and give you the support you need. Do something relatively minor and they can come down on you like a ton of bricks. My dad said it was just unfortunate and all I could do was take the punishment and move on. His biggest concern was me hiring the vans. He never liked it simply because of the responsibility I was taking on in terms of the passengers and the vehicle.

On the Sunday I started working on my defence for court. I thought if I explain exactly what happened I might escape with just a ticking off. I wrote down what I wanted to say and learned my lines well. Early Monday morning I put on my smartest outfit and drove back to Birmingham. The courtroom was a conveyer belt of sorry-looking individuals. Each one trudged into the dock, pleaded guilty to various public order offences, had a fine slapped on them and trudged out again.

The senior magistrate had opened proceedings with a sermon about the events of Saturday afternoon and how the people of Aston had been plagued by mindless morons who were a like cancer within society. Sympathy for the perpetrators was in short supply. Appearing near the end of this cast list I realised I would be wasting my breath, and the court's time, with my statement of innocence. I decided to plead guilty and get it done with. I was fined £75, ironically the amount I would have lost if the van had got damaged. I should have stayed in the vehicle. That week my name was in the Salford and Manchester papers which listed a rogues' gallery of those appearing in court in Birmingham.

Joking apart, I felt ashamed. Not because of what I had done but the fact it branded me as part of the hooligan element. I loved Manchester United and even though I portrayed myself as a bit of a lad, I hated the thought that I was now officially a lout. I felt it undermined my loyalty to United. If other Reds wanted to fight that was their business, but causing trouble wasn't my bag. I talked it through with my boss at Norweb, Alec Greenhowe, a wily old Scot who had shaped my career so far. He was brilliant. Knowing I wasn't really a bad egg, he assured me there would be no repercussions from the company and that it wouldn't affect my progress provided I carried on working hard. Most importantly, he told me not to beat myself up too much as the whole thing would be a seven-day wonder before people moved onto something else. Thankfully, he was right.

The only lasting damage was the mickey-taking from people who knew me. For the next few years wherever I went my mates would welcome me with, 'Here he is, The Krooklok Kid!'

10

THROUGH THE COLDEST WINTER IN ALMOST FOURTEEN YEARS, I COULDN'T BELIEVE YOU KEPT A SMILE

By August 1976 I had gone five years without missing a competitive United game home or away but that wasn't enough. I wanted to get to any game the Reds played. Long-haul trips to Australia and Iran were out of my reach, not even the Supporters' Club ventured that far in those days. But any game in the UK was on my radar. So I travelled to watch friendlies at Fulham, Portsmouth, Ross County, Torquay, Bournemouth and Hull; testimonials at Plymouth, Stoke, West Ham, Chelsea, Partick Thistle and Celtic; even a fundraising game at Cardiff against a South Wales XI to help save Newport County from extinction.

Often I travelled on my own to the friendlies and testimonials which were midweek evening fixtures that required a day off work. I always met up with fellow Reds at the game who shared the same crazy devotion. The real challenge was to find out what friendly matches were being played and when. Nowadays the games would be advertised well in advance and probably shown live on Sky or MUTV. In the early 1970s only information about competitive matches was issued. Details of friendly games were very sparse, you had to seek out any snippet of information from papers and magazines and keep a note of dates and times. Sometimes I would write to Les Olive, United's secretary, to ask if any matches were planned or to confirm rumours I had heard. He was really helpful, I always got a courteous reply and the details proved invaluable.

As Dylan prophesied, the times they were a-changing. Soon after I split with Gail, my two best mates Dave Kirk and Geoff Milloy were seriously bitten by the love bug. Not for each other, thankfully, that would have been a bit too scary. For over three years we had been to every United league match together. Dave, who I had known since my first day at primary school, married Elaine and moved to Hastings to further his career prospects. I wouldn't see him again until a chance meeting in a Milan bar twenty-nine years later. Geoff fell madly for a girl named Sue.

I remember stopping at some services on the way back from QPR in September 1975. Getting back in the van, Geoff was nervously holding a gift. When I asked what he had bought he sheepishly confessed it was a little keepsake for his new girlfriend. Geoff didn't really do gifts for girls and certainly not on a football trip. I knew in that moment our van would be one lighter sooner rather than later. So my two amigos rode off into the sunset on the trail of wedded bliss. Almost forty years later they're still with the same partners, so good luck to them. Geoff and Dave were, and still are, top Reds and great lads. Memories of the fantastic adventures we had in those teenage years often return to make me smile today.

Ian McEwen and I signed up for another of Dave Smith's pre-season tours, this time Germany and Holland in August 1976. Coach journeys in excess of ten hours between Rotterdam, Nuremburg and Hamburg enhanced our knowledge of German geography, while overnight visits to Hamburg's Reeperbahn and Amsterdam central furthered our education of Europe's fleshpots. Sure enough, the team was staying close by again! United won all three matches and we returned to England on the overnight ferry from Rotterdam to Hull.

After the late bar closed, Mac, me and a couple of others were starving but all the shops on board were shut. We thought we might find some food in the boat's kitchens. Sneaking below deck we could hear the faint sound of music coming from the restaurant area so we followed it with interest. The noise got louder. We crept up to the closed doors and peered through. Inside we could see fifteen to twenty men and women having a party, dressed up in very bright costumes like something out of a Broadway musical. Just then, we were swept into the room by a large woman who came up behind us. 'Come and join us, boys, the crew are having a bit of a knees-up,' she said. We explained we were just looking for something to eat and she told us to help ourselves to the buffet in the corner of the room.

The party was in full swing, the room looked nothing like a restaurant on a ferry. There was a DJ, the ceiling was decked out in bunting, balloons festooned the place and subdued lighting gave a romantic feel to the proceedings. As the four of us tucked in to our midnight feast we began to notice things weren't quite what it seemed. The girls all looked fantastic – great figures, beautiful hair, lovely long legs and sexy high heels – until you peered closer and noticed the dark hairs beneath their stockings.

'Jesus, lads! These are all f★★kin' fellas!' shouted Mac, almost choking on his baguette. Now, remember, this was 1976. Rod Stewart's 'The Killing of Georgie' was the nearest most heterosexual men got to anything remotely gay. Our hosts realised we had clocked the situation, the nice 'lady' who'd ushered us in came over and said we were welcome to stay, reassuring us with a smile that sodomy was only an optional extra. There was plenty of beer and food and a great atmosphere so we decided to party on and had a good laugh. Next morning at the breakfast table a familiar face leaned over and said, 'Tea or coffee, sir?' The big burly waiter looked so different without his make-up, tight hooped top and pencil skirt!

After a steady start in the league campaign United went top in early October with consecutive away wins at arch-rivals City and Leeds. The team was in great form until Martin Buchan tore his thigh muscle playing for Scotland. He would miss eleven United matches. This was a rare spell of absence for United's captain and it rocked the team. We won only two games without him and went out of the UEFA Cup and League Cup.

United's return to European competition for the first time since 1969 pitched us against the famous Ajax of Amsterdam. The Dutch club had won the European Cup three years running from 1971 to 1973 and though Johan Cruyff had departed, their side still contained many from that treble run. The first leg was away and thousands wanted to go. Our lads opted for another coach and ferry trip with the Supporters' Club. We set off from Manchester's Chorlton Street Bus Station at 10 p.m. on Tuesday and caught the 7 a.m. ferry from Dover to Zeebrugge. Most of the afternoon was spent on the coach travelling to Amsterdam. The authorities on both sides of the channel were very wary of potential trouble and United supporters were directed straight to the Olympic Stadium, a crumbling ground that had seen better days.

The route from the coach to the turnstile was wall to wall riot police with huge round shields backed up by rifles and guns. There was little chance of sneaking off for a quick pint. Despite the fears and a 1-0 defeat for United, the 3,000 Reds behaved themselves and gave the lads tremendous support. Tomislav Ivic, the Ajax manager, commented, 'I am worried what all the noise in Manchester will do to my young players.' Prophetic words. On 29 September, 59,000 witnessed a night to remember as Macari and McIlroy goals saw United through.

Seven years on from the last European game against AC Milan, many wondered if the atmosphere from the 1950s and 1960s could be matched. Well it was. The Stretford and Scoreboard Ends were in tremendous voice but, as the excitement grew, the adjoining paddocks joined in and then the whole ground sang United home. At last I had seen United play away in European competition but what seemed like an endless wait had certainly lived up to expectations. I was bitten by the Euro bug and wanted more.

More came in the shape of Juventus. Jeez! Ajax and Juventus! Somebody up there was taking the mick, surely? We had drawn two of Europe's giants and this wasn't even the European Cup. Juve's side contained six Italian internationals and in the first leg at Old Trafford their defensive mastery ruled the day. Only a piece of Gordon Hill magic divided the teams so United took a tenuous lead to Turin. The flight to Italy was 7.30 a.m. on Wednesday 3 November. I soaked up all the pre-match analysis in the papers and the hairs on my arms stood on end as I kept thinking, 'And I'll be there!'

This trip felt more like the European matches I had dreamed of. Ajax was great, but flying to a game adds another dimension. We had the afternoon free; some fans took in the famous Turin Motor Show but most settled for a few beers. As dusk descended we were shepherded to the ground by a small army of police. Before moving to the pristine Stadio delle Alpi in 1990, Juve shared an old ground with rivals Torino. The Stadio Comunale was in a shabby, run-down district of the city. Large numbers of foreign fans travelling abroad was still very new then and the welcome we received was hot and hostile. Inside the ground we were segregated by a flimsy twelve-foot high wire mesh fence held up by wooden stakes every few yards.

As the teams took the field, 66,000 Italians went berserk and the stadium erupted with cheers, screams, whistles, klaxons, and firecrackers. The terrifying din continued throughout the match with staccato drums beating loud in the winter night. This was far more intense than anything I had experienced at English grounds. I remember giant black and white striped flags being waved on the Juve terraces. They swayed on huge poles giving the effect of a titanic advancing army. The whole atmosphere was intimidating and the noise just enveloped us. Yet it was breathtaking and 1,000 Reds did our best to make sure United's name rang out. After one particular chant an Italian fan tried to scale the flimsy fence to get at us. He was mid-thirties, wore a wild-eyed expression and yelled 'Bastardos! Bastardos!' as he swayed at the top of the barrier. If that had come down there would have been mayhem. Fortunately, he lost his balance and fell back into the arms of his countrymen. That night Juventus were formidable and blew United away. We battled hard but badly missed captain Buchan's calm in a pressure-cooker atmosphere. Juventus won 3-0 and went on to lift the UEFA Cup.

Autumn 1976 saw United tumble from early leaders to seventeenth in mid-December. The Doc swooped to buy Jimmy Greenhoff from Stoke for £120,000. The signing was inspired. Jimmy was 30 with a keen football brain, similar to Teddy Sheringham twenty years later. A clever target man, he became the perfect partner for Pearson and another Old Trafford hero. After losing at Arsenal on 18 December United's good form returned, winning fourteen of the next eighteen league and cup matches, losing only to Ipswich Town on 3 January 1977.

The game at Portman Road was on a Bank Holiday Monday as New Year's Day fell on a Saturday. All the van hire companies were closed so we decided to take two cars for the ten lads who wanted to go. Despite the run of bad results United were still playing good attacking football and the fans stuck by them. There was never a problem filling vans or cars. Even when some of the 'old guard' didn't fancy a trip there were always young Reds waiting in the wings.

Over the New Year weekend the weather took a turn for the worse, snow covered much of Britain and temperatures fell well below freezing. My dad was nervous about me driving 230 miles to Ipswich in the conditions and tried to talk me out of it. I understood his concern but I just didn't miss United matches and certainly not because of a snowfall. Pete Ward and I decided he would take the Bury lads plus Jeff Fanning and John Scholic. In my car I would take the Salford lads – Brian Foy, Mike Horseman, Keith 'Beef' Livesey and Robert Gregan. I had known Bri from work for a couple of years and he had introduced me to Mike and Robert. We would regularly see one another on the fifty-eight bus going to home matches and lately they had come with us on the van trips. Keith had also become a regular in the vans, joining his older brother Ged.

On the Sunday night before the game I went to the 'Wellie' (Wellington Inn) on Irlams o' th' Height, my local and the centre of my universe. I was enjoying a quiet pint when a young lad called Andy Towler came over to ask if there was any chance of a lift to Ipswich. Andy had come with us to Arsenal just before Christmas, and despite the 3-1 defeat we had a great trip ending up at a lively pub in Birmingham. It had a resident three-piece band that was trapped in a 1950s time warp, punters were invited to get up and entertain fellow drinkers provided they sang rock and roll. This was pre-karaoke so it took some balls. Andy, clad in denim and with his black hair swept back, performed an unforgettable rendition of Elvis Presley's 'Teddy Bear' which brought the house down.

I explained to Andy that the car was full for the Ipswich trip. Over the next couple of hours he must have asked me a dozen times if I would somehow squeeze him in, even offering to travel in the boot at one stage. Each time I told him the car could only carry five and I couldn't take any chances given the length of the journey. He still wouldn't take no for an answer. I finally got him off my back by promising to call for him the following morning in the unlikely event that any of the others pulled out in the meantime.

Around 6.30 a.m. on a very, very cold Monday morning I went out to defrost the car. Wedged in the driver's door was a piece of paper with a note that read, 'Really sorry to let you down but I'm skint. Can't go today. Beef.' Okay, young Towler, time to call your bluff. I collected the other lads who directed me to Andy's house. When his mum answered the door I half expected her to ask who the bloody hell I was waking her up this early. But she just smiled and said, 'You must be Molly, Andy said you might call.' Before I could reply Andy shouted down from upstairs, 'Tell him I'm nearly ready!' Within seconds he was dressed and getting in the car. I was impressed.

The roads were tricky but passable with care. All the way there I could hear my dad's voice in my head reminding me to be careful. The early morning journey through the Derbyshire and East Midlands countryside was like a picture postcard with snow covering hill and dale. Our only entertainment was an old radio I had fixed up in the car. Fitted car radios were still for the elite. This was a portable transistor perched on the rear parcel shelf with a plug-in aerial which clipped onto the side window. Sounds primitive I know but for early 1977 it was hi-tech.

We met up with Wardy's car a couple of times on the way down and six hours later arrived at Portman Road. The long journey was worth it when Stuart Pearson fired a volley high into the Ipswich net after only twenty-five seconds. Second-placed Ipswich had gone thirteen games unbeaten and pushed hard for an equaliser but it was United who looked like table-toppers as McIlroy and Macari created several chances. It was a cracking game but the rutted pitch began to freeze as the sun went down and defending became a lottery. The Suffolk side piled on the pressure and just when it seemed we would keep them out Ipswich scored twice in the last ten minutes to win 2-1. What a sickener and a six-hour journey back to mull it over.

Leaving the ground we talked about heading straight home as the weather was getting worse. When I tried to start the car the battery was flat, the four lads got out to push and we just about managed to jump-start it. That made up our minds, we daren't risk getting stranded, so next stop would be Salford. The flat, straight roads from Suffolk to Nottinghamshire were well gritted. Fresh snow had fallen in the Derbyshire hills but the ploughs had shifted the worst to the side of the road. I had done the run from Chesterfield to Stockport many times on previous away trips in the vans. It was a tricky route of bending, winding roads with steep climbs and descents. My dad's lectures stood me in good stead and taking it easy we got through okay.

We had made good progress and reached Ardwick, on the outskirts of Manchester, just before 11 p.m. One of the lads remembered The Wellie was open until midnight, we were fifteen minutes from home and ready for a pint after a long day. We took the Mancunian Way heading towards Salford and climbed steadily until we reached the elevated section that carries you over the main roads coming out of Manchester city centre.

I remember noticing the road surface glistening and suddenly the car started to slide. I couldn't control the steering. We were in a skid. The car spun around, we went over a bump and seconds later there was the piercing crash of metal and breaking glass. Then silence. Just silence. I don't think I passed out, I remember sitting there in the driver's seat but I had been thrown at angle. My legs were against the door, I had banged my left side against the steering wheel and there was glass from the windscreen in my hair. My forehead was bleeding.

I clambered out of the car through the broken windscreen and staggered around in the road. I was badly winded and dazed. There were no other cars around. The first sound that broke the silence was a woman's voice. 'We've phoned for an ambulance, it's on its way, don't worry!' she shouted from a window in the flats that overlooked the road.

In what seemed like seconds a fire engine arrived at the scene. One fireman sat me down by the side of the road while his colleagues rushed over to the car. While I was sitting there a second fire engine arrived. As the driver applied the brakes it slid into the back of the first engine. It was surreal. No one was hurt in that collision but it showed how icy the road was.

Soon there were ambulances and police cars all around and Mancunian Way was closed. I stayed at the scene but was kept away from the car; the police asked me lots of questions which I think I answered. They told me the other lads were being taken to hospital. After about half an hour, Mike and Brian went in separate ambulances to Manchester Royal Infirmary and Salford Royal respectively. Soon after, I went in the ambulance with Andy to Ancoats Hospital. It was after midnight now. I knew Andy had leg injuries and they took him straight into theatre when we arrived. I sat in a cubicle in A & E.

My cuts were superficial, but my side was hurting. I was told a doctor would see me soon. My mind was in turmoil, everything around me seemed unreal. I just couldn't take in what was happening. Then my dad walked in. I had never been more relieved to see him. He asked me if I was okay, I said I was. He put his arms around me; I put my head on his chest and just broke down. I was 22 years old and I sobbed like a child. A short time later, a doctor examined me and was ready to let me go home subject to a urine sample. However, my wee was the colour of Ribena and they decided to keep me in for observation. My dad left and I was wheeled to a medical ward where I finally dozed off in the early hours.

Hospital wards come to life at a notoriously early hour. Shortly after 6 a.m., I woke to the sound of nurses going about their business. One came to check on me and I asked how I could find out about how my friends were. She said the duty manager was coming to talk to me soon. As I waited, a boy came round the ward selling newspapers. I beckoned him over to buy one but a nurse intervened, she paid for the paper but said she'd put it to one side for me as the manager was due any minute. I waited another half hour but no one came.

The man in the next bed was listening to the radio. I heard the broadcaster say, 'Piccadilly News, it's 7 a.m. One Manchester United fan has been killed and four others seriously injured in a car crash while travelling back from the club's game at Ipswich Town.' A nurse heard the bulletin too and hurried to turn it off. She was very apologetic and assured me somebody would come and speak to me right away.

A few moments later, a tall man in a suit came to my bed and pulled the curtain round for privacy. He briefly told me the reason for his delayed arrival, apologised and said he had to tell me some bad news. He spoke softly, clearly and firmly. He explained that the car I had been driving had skidded on black ice, mounted the central reservation, collided with a lamppost and come to rest against the crash barrier on the other side of Mancunian Way. The lamppost had fallen onto the car. Robert Gregan had been killed, Andy Towler had lost both legs, Mike Horseman and Brian Foy had both sustained serious leg fractures. At that point he paused, realising I just couldn't absorb any more information. He stayed with me for quite a while, trying to comfort me and answer all sorts of questions that were racing through my mind.

After he left, I saw the newspaper; the story of the crash was on the front page. I couldn't read it. The ward sister and her staff were very understanding and did their best to help but what could they do? Eventually I just needed time on my own. Time

to think. Time to make some sense of what had happened. I had
walked away from the crash virtually unscathed and for that
reason I assumed the lads were okay too. I knew they had been
taken to hospitals around Manchester but thought that was to
treat fairly minor injuries. The truth was they had been taken to
different hospitals to ensure they each got the emergency treatment they needed. This just couldn't be happening, surely?

Over the next couple of days I had lots of visitors and everybody was so helpful offering to do anything that was needed.
I desperately wanted to visit the other lads right away but the
doctors ordered complete bed rest. There were long periods
alone with my thoughts and the same ones kept coming back to
haunt me, 'Why did it happen? Why did we crash just three miles
from home when we had travelled over 450 miles through dreadful conditions? How were the other lads doing? Why was I able
to walk away unharmed?'

I knew I had done nothing wrong. I hadn't had any alcohol
and wasn't speeding or messing about at the wheel. But that
wasn't enough to stop these nagging, gnawing thoughts swirl-
ing round my brain every second I was awake. I wasn't feeling
sorry for myself. I realised I had been very lucky, but emotionally
I was in a very dark place. Nowadays they would recognise it as
survivor's guilt and I'd probably receive counselling, but in those
days you just had to get on with it. For forty-eight hours it drove
me crazy thinking about what had happened. I became obsessed
looking for answers to those questions. It was consuming me.
Then I began to think more and more about the conversations
with Andy in the pub last Sunday and Beef pulling out of the trip
at the last minute. Gradually, I began to think maybe there doesn't
have to be a reason. Maybe it was simply a set of circumstances.
My thoughts got clearer and focused on doing what I wanted to
do – see the other lads and visit Robert's parents.

I knew Andy was in a nursing ward on the floor above me at
Ancoats Hospital. I spoke to a nurse whose friend worked on
his ward and asked if she could arrange for me to see Andy, if he
wanted to see me. It was fixed up for Wednesday afternoon, just two
days after the accident. I was very nervous. I didn't know Andy very
well, he was 18 and knocked about with a younger crowd but we
had got on really well during the two trips we had been on. I didn't
know how he would be in himself and I was unsure how he would

respond to me. But I had to do it. I walked into his ward and there he was sitting on his bed messing with some playing cards.

'Hi Andy, how you doing?' I asked.

'I'm doing alright, Molly, I'm doing alright. How are you?' he replied, a big smile lit up his face, 'Sit down here, I'm just trying to sort these out.' It was as if nothing had changed.

I knew in that second we would be okay. We chatted for the rest of the afternoon, Andy was really bubbly. I knew he was being brave but he was also just being himself. He talked about how he felt, how the operations had gone and what the doctors would do next plus a thousand other things. We laughed and we joked. Many, many months would pass before life got back to anything like normal but that long journey started that afternoon in Ancoats Hospital.

The following evening Andy's parents, Molly and Harold, called in to see me just after visiting time finished. They wanted to know if I was okay and reassure me that they didn't blame me for what had happened. It must have taken tremendous courage in the circumstances, they didn't have to do that, but it meant a great deal to me. I found it difficult to find the right words to say back to his mum but she lightened the moment by joking about us both being called Molly.

She told me that when Andy got in from the pub on Sunday night, he had told her if Molly called for him tomorrow morning to wake him up no matter what. She had asked him why a girl would be calling so early and he explained 'Molly' was a nickname for Pete Molyneux. We laughed. It was good to see her.

Towards the end of that first week in hospital I was feeling fine physically and was itching to go and see Mike and Bri. However, an X-ray showed a narrowing in the passage leading into one of my kidneys. They might have to operate, I had to drink lots of fruit squash and have a daily check. When the doctor came round on the Friday I expected to be discharged but he decided to keep me in over the weekend as a precaution. That set my mind off in a different direction.

What I'm about to share with you now might seem thoughtless, selfish, stupid or all three. I don't know. But it's what happened. United were at home to Walsall in the FA Cup third round the following day and my thoughts turned to being there. My logical head told me not to be so ridiculous. I was lucky just to be alive, three friends were still recovering in hospital, one had lost his life and I was thinking about going to the match?! My football head told me I needed to be there, I went to every game. Following United had become an addiction by now. Common sense was no longer the main driver.

Wanting to go to the match didn't reflect how I felt about my mates. They were two entirely different issues. That Friday afternoon I confided in one of the nurses that I needed to get out tomorrow for the match. She thought I was delirious but I finally convinced her I knew what I was doing. She told me I would have to sign myself out and re-admit myself after the game but the hospital might refuse the latter. At visiting time I told my dad and he went berserk. We had words in the corridor, in the end he said he would leave it up to my conscience. When I woke the next day I knew I had to be at Old Trafford. I discharged myself around noon.

As I got into the cold daylight for the first time in five days I felt light-headed. I also realised I didn't know where the bloody hell I was. I had never been to Ancoats before and had to ask directions to the centre of Manchester. I caught a bus from Aytoun Street which was packed with Reds singing and shouting but I just sat there quietly. I didn't tell anyone else I was going to the game and I didn't go and stand with the rest of the lads on the terraces. I bought a seat in the stands and watched on my own.

When the teams came out and chants went up from the Stretford End the emotion of the last six days welled up inside me. I was shivering and tears rolled slowly down my face but I knew I had done the right thing. In an unreal time, I was clinging onto my reality. United won 1-0 but that felt incidental. The ward sister had told me if I wasn't back by 6 p.m. there would be no re-admission. She took a stern view but I think a couple of the nurses had softened her up a bit. I caught a taxi to the hospital and returned to the ward at 5.30 p.m. The sister re-admitted me.

Later that evening Tommy Docherty, Tommy Cavanagh and Laurie Brown visited Andy and me in Ancoats. They brought us scarves and souvenirs from the club and chatted for an hour or so. They had been round to see the lads in the other hospitals too. This was the first of many kind gestures by the club to help the lads involved in the accident. I felt more of a cheat than a loyal supporter and kept quiet about having bunked off for the afternoon. It was very odd indeed.

I didn't need an operation in the end, the problem cleared itself thanks to Mr Robinson's Barley Water. I was discharged on Tuesday 11 January. Later that day I visited Brian and Mike in their separate hospitals. Again, I was apprehensive about how they would react to seeing me, but just as with Andy, they made me very welcome. Their broken legs were on the mend but they would be in hospital for a couple of months.

The same day I phoned Mrs Gregan and asked if it would be okay to call round sometime. The following week I visited Robert's parents at their home. I wanted to pay my respects but I was frightened. Not of any physical reaction but what do you say to a mum and dad who have just lost their 18-year-old son? I was 22, I didn't know how to handle such a delicate situation. But again, I knew I had to do it. I knew it was the right thing. I needn't have worried, Jim and Alice couldn't have made me more welcome and put me at ease right from the start. Annette, his sister, joined us. They were kind, gentle people just like Robert. Their faith was helping them come to terms with the tragedy and it left a deep impression on me.

We talked about the trip to Ipswich and what had happened throughout that day. We talked about how the other lads were doing. We talked about Robert. I learned that he had died from an injury to his spleen and his parents shared with me some details the police had given them about that fateful night. In the hour before midnight on Monday 3 January the temperatures across the UK had dropped rapidly. The gritting lorries were due out shortly after midnight when the council workmen returned after Bank Holiday. That delay of an hour was critical. The Mancunian Way quickly freezes on the elevated section because the cold winds pass over and under the road and accelerate the process. This resulted in large patches of black ice. Every so many metres along the road were manholes which carry warmer air and it was the wheels going over an unfrozen manhole cover that sent the car into a skid. The police confirmed that when a car goes into a skid it actually picks up speed. This is why the impact with the lamppost did so much damage. Robert had been in the front passenger seat and that side of the car took the brunt of the collision.

Andy Towler never changed from that first visit to his ward in Ancoats Hospital. He was always cheerful, always joking, always wanting to join in anything that was going on. While he was in hospital he would get to hear about parties in the nurses' accommodation because these lodgings were connected to the main hospital by a discreet door. With the help of a couple of the staff we would smuggle him off the ward late at night, in his wheelchair, to join the party then back again later. These absences were unauthorised of course but nobody in charge ever found out so no harm was done.

Towards the end of January the doctors felt Andy was fit enough to attend United home games. These trips were sanctioned. United issued Andy with a pass for the disabled area next to the old tunnel, near where Fergie spent his years in charge. The first match was the FA Cup fourth round tie against QPR. Beef and I took Andy to the game. Access to the allotted area was via the players' tunnel. As we arrived the United team had just come out of the dressing room minutes before running out on the pitch. Several players came over for a quick chat with Andy.

Martin Buchan told us he had read about the accident and wanted to know how we were all doing. I know the United captain was impressed by Andy's attitude and they struck up a friendship that would last quite a few years. That May, when Buchan stepped off the coach in Albert Square after beating Liverpool in the Cup Final, he made a beeline for Andy, passed him the famous trophy and waited while the press took their photos and Andy's details. The next day his smiling face made all the papers.

Several local pubs and clubs organised fundraising nights for Andy during the early part of 1977. Tommy Doc made a guest appearance at our local, The Wellie, where he confided in us that Gerry Daly was being transferred to Derby the next day! Folk really rallied round and as dreadful as the accident had been, we learned a lot about human kindness as the lads began to put their lives together again. Andy was a little embarrassed by the fundraising and the fuss but really grateful for the trouble people had gone to.

By early March, Brian, Mike and Andy had all been discharged from hospital and we met up with the rest of our crowd almost nightly in one of the local pubs. Andy made several trips to Withington Hospital to be fixed up with his new 'legs'. He made rapid progress and by July was walking again, initially with the aid of sticks, then completely unaided. Everyone he came in contact with was touched by his determination and cheerful outlook. I will always remember the courage Andy showed in those difficult months after the accident; he was an inspiration to us all.

The whole experience bonded the four of us in a way that went beyond just friendship. We knocked about together for many years after the accident and though time has moved on that bond remains. Andy bought Mike, Bri and me a present soon after he came out of hospital. It was a silver chain and pendant with a simple inscription 'Keep United'. We have and we will.

The winter of 1977 was Britain's coldest since the Big Freeze of 1963 but we were warmed by United's return to form. The football was scintillating and the goals returned. We finished sixth in the league, and without the mid-season blip we would have mounted a serious assault on the title. The recovery was just in time for the FA Cup. After Walsall and QPR we got revenge against Southampton by beating them in a replay at Old Trafford. The sixth round was also at home, United seeing off Aston Villa 2-1 in a thrilling tie with a superb atmosphere. Towards the end of that game the Stretford End unleashed a new song, 'Wember-lee, Wember-lee, we're the famous Man United and we're going to Wember-lee!' Later that night you could hear the song being sung around Manchester no matter where you were in the city. United were on a mission.

Leeds stood in our way with another Hillsborough semi-final and it proved to be third time lucky for the Red Rose of Lancashire, United winning 2-1. The final would be a first ever between Liverpool and United. The Stretford End versus The Kop at Wembley! The Scousers had just won their tenth title overall and third in five years. Worse still, they had reached the European Cup Final. Four days after playing us they were off to Rome to meet Borussia Mönchengladbach.

All that mattered to us was United winning the FA Cup. Doc's team on Saturday, 21 May 1977 was the one that had played most of the season plus a very young Arthur Albiston in for the injured Stewart Houston: Stepney, Nicholl, Albiston, McIlroy, B. Greenhoff, Buchan, Coppell, J. Greenhoff, Pearson, Macari, Hill.

The United end was awash with banners and flags of all shapes, sizes and wit. The eventful but goalless first half gave way to an explosion of action after the break. On fifty minutes Jimmy Greenhoff back-headed a through ball to Pearson who was on it in a flash and hit a low drive past Clemence from twenty yards. Jimmy Case equalised two minutes later but within three minutes United were in front again. This time Macari headed through to Greenhoff who got in a tangle for possession with Tommy Smith inside the penalty area. The ball ran loose and Macari swept a shot goalwards which hit Greenhoff's chest on the way into the net. Bizarre but brilliant.

Hitting back so soon stopped Liverpool settling and taking control of the game. The remaining thirty-five minutes felt like thirty-five years but nothing could stop United winning the FA Cup for the fourth time in their history. The scenes of celebration were unforgettable and when Martin Buchan lifted that silver trophy it was the best day in my life up to that point. It meant so much, the nine long years starved of success, the semi-final defeats, the managerial upheavals, the despair of relegation.

On a personal level, the trauma of that season made the success taste even sweeter but the tears of joy were tinged with sadness as I thought of Robert Gregan and the tragic events of that night in January.

11

DON'T NEED NO POLITICIANS TO TELL ME THINGS I SHOULDN'T BE, NEITHER NO OPTICIANS TO TELL ME WHAT I OUGHTA SEE

Tommy Docherty had delivered on his promise, returning to a hero's welcome in Albert Square with the FA Cup. He had transformed the club in just over four years. The team was playing great football, winning trophies and qualifying for European competitions again. The perfect recipe for Old Trafford devotees. In late June a newspaper broke the story that United's manager was in an extramarital relationship with the wife of club physiotherapist Laurie Brown. After initially supporting their manager, the directors called a press conference on Tuesday 5 July to announce that Docherty had been sacked.

I was devastated. Just when we had found a man who was capable of managing Manchester United we score a colossal own goal. Most United supporters weren't bothered about the manager's private life; we just wanted a good winning team. I felt sorry for Laurie Brown and his family but I didn't want anything to jeopardise United's return to glory. In the weeks that followed, stories circulated that The Doc's sacking was not just about the affair with Mrs Brown. His managerial wheeler-dealing was clever but unscrupulous at times. In changing United's fortunes he had made enemies with the old guard at Old Trafford, the people Doc called the 'Junior Board' – influential season ticket holders who had the ear of the directors.

When I went to those matches with Andy towards the end of 1976/77 we sat just in front of the Main Stand which housed

United's season ticket holders. I often heard shouts of discontent towards Docherty. It was on a fairly small scale, just individuals with veiled barbed comments but nothing that seemed to carry any momentum. I heard one middle-aged guy shout, 'We know what you're doing Docherty, you're a disgrace!' Other comments referred to the treatment of players. I remember thinking it was odd. United were playing well, results were good, we were on our way to another Cup Final, so why the abuse? I just dismissed it as the work of the odd 'nutter'.

With hindsight perhaps the Manchester Mafia got their man in the end. Perhaps The Doc's treatment of Denis Law, Willie Morgan, Paddy Crerand and a few others had upset some to the point where they wanted him out no matter what. The scandal involving Docherty and Mary Brown was the coup de grace they sought. On the terraces Docherty was adored, he was a Stretford Ender in the manager's chair. His sacking was a sickener and took some gloss off the cup triumph. For me, it put uncertainty back on the club's agenda. United's playing record under Tommy Docherty was:

Played	W	D	L	F	A	W%	D%	L%
228	107	56	65	333	252	47	25	28

The statistics make him United's fifth best manager out of seventeen, based on win percentage. Given the turmoil The Doc inherited it's a pretty impressive record over four and a half seasons. Tommy Docherty rescued United at a time when we had lost direction and almost our soul. The club's prospects looked grim indeed in December 1972. United's history carries a thread of triumph over adversity. John H. Davies paying off our debts in 1902 and converting the club from Newton Heath to Manchester United, James Gibson rescuing us from bankruptcy in 1931, the ground being bombed in 1941 and the tragedy at Munich in 1958 are all woven into the tapestry of United's glorious heritage. In my opinion, the job Tommy Docherty did in reversing United's fortunes deserves its rightful recognition in the club's history.

I loved the Docherty era. It was such an exciting time and there was never a dull moment. I was 18 when he arrived and nearly 23 when he left; his reign coincided with my formative years. I was experiencing the freedom and pleasures that go hand in glove with

moving from boy to man. I have tried to divorce that nostalgia from reality and still come to the conclusion that the Docherty years are among the best I have experienced as a United supporter.

The football from 1974 to 1977 was a joy to watch, packed with swashbuckling and cavalier matches. United's home support was awesome and matched that of the 1960s. Away from home, the following was enormous at almost every game and in excess of 10,000 on occasions. This made every away match an unpredictable adventure and led to some unforgettable experiences. Of course, it didn't last long enough. The Doc never got the chance to build on the foundations he laid, so his time at Old Trafford cannot be compared to that of Sir Matt or Sir Alex. History shows us that Tommy Doc managed several clubs who were in crisis. He often brought stability, even a taste of glory, but never won any long-service awards. If he had been a Prime Minister he would have been Churchill, who won the war but struggled to win the peace. Nevertheless, it's intriguing to speculate whether Docherty's United would have wrestled the title from Liverpool's grasp if he hadn't been sacked for a personal indiscretion. He certainly had the Scousers in his sights in 1977.

As Tommy Docherty adorned the front pages with his arm around Mary Brown, the back-page columnists speculated on his successor. Prospective candidates included Lawrie McMenemy, Ian Greaves, Don Revie, Noel Cantwell, Brian Clough, Johnny Giles and Jack Charlton. The bookies' favourite from the outset was Dave Sexton and on Thursday, 14 July 1977 his appointment was confirmed, United's fourth manager in the eight years since Sir Matt stepped down. Sexton was 47 when he took on the best job in football. His playing days as an inside-forward took him to West Ham, Luton, Brighton, Leyton Orient and Crystal Palace making a total of 187 appearances with an impressive return of sixty-nine goals. A knee injury finished his playing career at 32 after which he went into coaching roles at Chelsea and Arsenal.

In 1967, Sexton followed Docherty into the manager's chair at Stamford Bridge and three years later guided a star-studded side to Chelsea's first ever FA Cup success. He followed that by winning the European Cup Winners' Cup in 1971. Sexton moved to QPR in 1974 and made them London's top team. In 1976 they finished runners-up to Liverpool and were pipped for the title by just one point.

The newspapers reported his track record and coaching abilities but many focused heavily on Sexton's personal reputation. There were several references to his 'rigid principles' and his 'integrity'. The *Manchester Evening News* sports editorial led with an article saying, 'Sexton's arrival will restore the dignity to one of the world's greatest clubs. He is a man of unwavering principles who will put the club before any personal considerations.' The article went on to draw comparisons with Matt Busby's strong character, toughness of mind, love of flair football and being a family man. It felt like we were appointing a new Pope rather than a football manager! Nevertheless, his record with Chelsea and QPR was impressive.

We opened the league campaign with three wins out of five but lost in the League Cup to Arsenal at the first hurdle. Once again the focus was Europe. United drew St Etienne in the Cup Winners' Cup. They had dominated French football for a few years and lost to Bayern Munich in the European Cup Final just twelve months earlier. Another tough draw, another mouth-watering tie.

I used to go to the Students' Union disco at Manchester Poly on a Friday night with a couple of mates, Keith Scriven and Steve Tilzey. Both are keen Reds and Steve's dad held a licence to pilot small planes. One Friday the lads turned up at the Poly very excited with the news that Mr Tilzey senior had offered to fly us to St Etienne in a four-seat Cessna. It sounded like a great adventure, and I do like great adventures, but I hate heights. I am okay in a big plane but all the way to southern France with a single engine between me and my maker felt a little too risky. I might have been able to do it with my eyes shut but where's the fun in that? Luckily, the offer came to nothing without me having to declare my cowardice. I opted for the safety of four wheels on tarmac and booked on the Supporters' Club coach trip.

A week before the fixture I got a call from Dave Smith asking if I could help him out. He explained the Supporters' Club was taking nine coaches to the game but they were under enormous pressure from the Government and the football authorities to minimise the threat of trouble. During the previous season, Doc's Red Army had continued to run amok across England. In April 1977, a BBC TV crew filmed a documentary about United's trip to Norwich. The focus was the fans' behaviour. Nothing was undercover; it was just ordinary cameras on the

trains and coaches travelling to the game and shots around the ground before and after the match. United lost for the first time in three months and United's 5,000 following made sure the BBC got something worth reporting.

A normally docile away fixture turned into a full-scale riot with Reds battling with police and locals and almost demolishing the roof of the Barclay Stand. The weekend papers were full of the troubles and at 6 p.m. on the Monday the BBC aired the documentary on their network programme *Nationwide*. It wasn't pretty viewing and brought a huge backlash from the FA, the Football League, the Labour Government of the day and the general public. The consensus was that United had been given enough warnings and the country had also had enough of United. The Government banned United supporters from the three remaining away matches at Bristol City, Liverpool and West Ham. I managed to get tickets for each game by various contacts and watched like a Trappist monk for ninety minutes.

At the start of 1977/78 the Government ban was lifted but future away matches were strictly ticket-only for the travelling fans. The home clubs had discretion over whether any tickets would be offered to United at all.

The restrictions could only apply in Britain as the Government had no jurisdiction over games abroad. With the draw taking United to nearby France, the authorities were naturally worried. Talks were held at the highest level and a master plan drafted to ensure an *entente cordiale*. United fans would be strictly segregated inside the stadium, no alcohol would be allowed on transport carrying our supporters, no tickets would be sold in the days leading up to the match and the coaches would arrive in St Etienne no more than an hour before kick-off. The *piece de resistance* was that United would appoint a number of their own fans as stewards. They would wear special armbands, stand in the gangways of the segregated terraces and act as a mediator between the police and the Red Army. If there was any sign of trouble the police would ask the United stewards to talk to the supporters involved to try and prevent any escalation. It was felt that might avoid any misunderstandings with the language.

United handed responsibility to Dave Smith to make the necessary arrangements. Smithy decided he would have one steward per coach to enforce the alcohol ban and those nine

supporters would also be on duty in the ground. Travelling on
the coaches were three fans who were coppers from Stretford
Police. Chairman Smith put them in charge of a coach each and
set about choosing another six stalwarts he could trust. Hence
the telephone call. I listened to his plan and was flattered that he
had picked me but trying to supervise United's Red Army was
bordering on the perilous. The Cessna flight was starting to look
the safe option!

Smithy sensed my unease and said, 'I know it could be tricky
so we're offering the stewards a discount of 25 per cent on the
cost of the trip …'

'Dave, of course I'd be delighted to help!' I interrupted. 'What
do you want me to do?'

'Oh? Good. Come down to the office Sunday morning at
10 a.m. for a full briefing,' said Dave, closing the deal.

I told my dad about the plan and he was quite impressed
with my newly acquired responsibility. It assured him that my
Krooklok capers twelve months earlier hadn't blackened my
name too much. I was travelling to France with Pete Ward and Jeff
Fanning so I rang them to explain what was happening and took
a fair bit of mickey-taking. Nevertheless, at 6 p.m. on Tuesday
13 September around 500 Reds set off from Chorlton Street Bus
Station for another great European adventure.

The long coach and ferry journeys were quite uneventful; all
I had to do was a headcount whenever we got back on the bus.
Arriving in St Etienne on time, most Reds went straight to the
ground. There was a tremendous atmosphere as we joined with
a thousand or so other Reds who had made their way over. We
moved onto the terraces at one end of the Stade Geoffroy-Guichard
only to find there was no segregation, French and English supporters mixed at will. There was no hassle and I thought the police
would soon come in and divide the terraces into two sections. In
the meantime we got on with having a good sing-song. Both sets
of supporters were in great voice and the banter was good.

The teams came out and still there was no attempt to segregate
the fans. In fact, there were no police on the terraces at all, they
were all stood at the front next to the pitch behind a big metal
fence. I put my hand in my pocket and pulled out the plastic
steward's armband that Smithy had issued to his nine trusted men.
I shrugged, I guess I wouldn't be needing that tonight.

Just before kick-off the French lads started throwing bread rolls at us. They were taking the proverbial because there was a bakers' strike in Britain and our Gallic friends thought the prank was hilarious. We just threw them back. For five minutes or so all kinds of confectionary was hurled around the terraces. Suddenly there was some pushing from the back as a few dozen Reds came in late. The French pelted them with bread too but the mood changed in a moment. The late-comers thought they had walked into a fight and fought back. The French thought United were trying to take over their territory and scuffles broke out. The police just stayed behind the fence and watched.

The fighting could have been nipped in the bud by a handful of coppers but it escalated with bottles and cans accompanying the bread. Five minutes later a platoon of police emerged from the players' tunnel, marched at double time towards our terraces, opened the metal gates, drew their batons and came charging into the ranks of United supporters. Anyone wearing red and white was targeted whether they were involved in the fighting or not. It was mayhem. Older men, women and children all got caught up in the sustained attack.

The master plan in tatters, it was time for plan B – everyone for themselves. The police opened a side gate and tried to run United fans out of the ground. Desperate to watch the game I needed to hide my colours. I climbed from the terraces on to a toilet roof, then clambered down inside. For a few minutes I was safe but I could hear the pandemonium close by outside. I had a scarf and a large red and white banner, I managed to tie them round my legs under my jeans. Thank God for big 1970s flares!

I ventured out, the police had retreated back behind the fence leaving several supporters nursing cuts and bruises or ejected from the ground. That was my first introduction to the CRS, the French military police established to deal with civil unrest. They specialise in the art of asking no questions when carrying out their duties. The game was delayed for ten minutes and the first half was played out in a very tense atmosphere. United fans had been dispersed into small pockets around the ground and didn't regroup until half-time when people were still coming to terms with the ferocity of the attack by the police.

On the pitch United put on one of their best displays in Europe. The French team had never lost at home to foreign opposition but St Etienne struggled to deal with the torrent of attacks from United's 4-2-4 formation. Pearson led the line intelligently and United had the ball in the French net five times, sadly four were disallowed but it was a measure of our superiority. Hill finally breached St Etienne's defence in the seventy-seventh minute with a brilliant angled shot. Within three minutes a defensive error let the French back in for a 1-1 draw.

That night on British TV, *News at Ten* opened with footage of the fighting in the stadium and the police with raised batons charging United supporters. The story was the main item on all radio and TV channels in the UK. The morning papers had pictures resembling a battle scene splashed across their front pages. I didn't know any of this at the time. We were travelling back through the night. There were no mobile phones then and no opportunity to call home on a landline even if we had known how. So when my dad settled down to watch TV he was horrified by the images he saw. The plan for his son to act as mediator between fans and police had obviously gone badly wrong and he didn't know what state I was in.

Early media bulletins grossly exaggerated the situation with reports of 500 fans arrested, fifty badly injured and a fleet of twenty-five ambulances ferrying the wounded to hospital throughout the match. It wasn't until David Meek's report was published in the following day's *Manchester Evening News* that a more accurate view of events was in the public domain. Another sleepless night for my poor old fella, I'm afraid.

We arrived back in Manchester around 11 p.m. on the Thursday and my dad came to meet me. I could see the relief in his face as I stepped down from the coach in one piece. As a parent now, I can appreciate the heartache he had gone through in the previous twenty-four hours but at the time it didn't seem a big deal. Only when I got home and saw the papers did I realise the extent of the coverage. Over a late-night coffee I explained what happened at the ground and we had a good laugh about the best laid plans of mice and men.

The following Monday, UEFA held a summit in Berne and announced that they had thrown United out of the Cup Winners' Cup because of the actions of their fans. The second leg at Old Trafford on 28 September was scrapped and St Etienne were given a bye into the next round.

Much of the British media turned on United and felt we were getting our come-uppance after ten years of fans rampaging at home and abroad. United's board kept cool and appealed on two main counts, one that the French authorities reneged on their responsibility to segregate fans inside the stadium, and secondly that the punishment was too severe. Fortunately there were a number of independent witnesses prepared to give evidence to support United's case including two of the coppers who had travelled with the Supporters Club. Sir Matt presented the case in person to UEFA on 26 September. They were swayed by the great man's argument and reinstated United.

There was talk of playing the return leg behind closed doors, a horrendous prospect for Reds who went to every game. In the end, UEFA stipulated that the match must take place on a neutral ground at least 125 miles (200km) from Old Trafford. Many British venues were considered but in the end United opted for Plymouth Argyle's Home Park. The club beamed the match live to Old Trafford on giant screens to deter fans from travelling. A crowd around 27,000 turned up.

I chose to join the 31,634 at Plymouth to watch the Reds see off St Etienne 2-0. Despite all the distractions, United picked up where they left off in France, taking the game to St Etienne who once again struggled to contain our forwards. United fans weren't banned but the club asked supporters not to travel in a desperate attempt to avoid trouble. Around 3,000 to 4,000 Reds were at Home Park that night but everyone behaved impeccably. There was no damage, no fighting, no arrests. After the game UEFA confirmed United could play at home in the next round and the fans could travel to the away leg. Our opponents would be FC Porto.

Dave Sexton had kept virtually the same team as the previous season, but league form was patchy. By mid-October we were ninth. Jimmy Greenhoff was injured for several weeks and as he returned his strike partner Stuart Pearson picked up a knock. Both missed the trip to Portugal for the first leg against Porto. That night in front of 70,000, Porto put on a super show, beating United 4-0, the Brazilian Duda scoring a dazzling hat-trick. With little in our attack we had to combat wave after wave of Portuguese raids.

United took two plane-loads of supporters and we were watched like hawks everywhere we went. In the ground we

weren't just segregated, we were isolated like lepers in the corner
of an otherwise unused stand. Again, there was no trouble but the
bad news this time was confined to the pitch. Nobody comes
back from a 4-0 first leg defeat but on 2 November United went
as close as possible. On a night when the Stretford End scared the
pants off the visitors United raced into a 3-1 half-time lead. We
needed another three and after the first-half mauling of Porto the
unbelievable seemed possible.

On sixty-five minutes Coppell got his second of the night to
make it 4-1. The roar from all around the ground was ear-splitting; United's faithful were in a frenzy. The wingers and forwards
poured forth, creating at least a dozen great chances, but eight
minutes from time Porto broke away and scored a killer second.
United made it 5-2 with the final kick. Everyone was exhausted,
players and supporters alike. We had given everything. It was a
glorious failure but an unforgettable Old Trafford night.

Getting to every game was becoming harder. After the melee at
St Etienne the Government tightened the restrictions on United
supporters following their team. Tickets could only be allocated to
United if they were in seated areas. No tickets were to be sold on the
day of the match. At most grounds in those days all the seats were
taken by home season ticket holders. The number of spare seats was
very small. Most clubs didn't want United fans in the stands mixing
with their best customers and opted to give us no tickets at all.

In a war of attrition you have to get smart. I managed to get
tickets from some clubs by writing to the their secretary and
enclosing a cheque. Many took the view that if you could draft a
letter and had a bank account you wouldn't be a hooligan. Failing
that I would ask people I knew if they had any relatives, friends
or contacts in the place where United were playing. If they did
I asked if they could pop down to the local ground for tickets
that were on open sale to home fans. When both these strate-
gies failed I would just turn up early at the away ground on the
day and 'sniff out' a ticket. Once you were there in person it was
surprising just how many clubs flouted the ruling and sold tickets
discreetly on match days. The measures stopped United's mass
support travelling and in turn the trouble that went with it, but
they were draconian. Imagine a British Government imposing
such sanctions now? We would be at the Court of Human Rights
before you could say UKIP!

So Reds had to do the best we could and it became a lonely business. Sometimes I travelled on my own or sometimes with one or two keen mates. There was always the chance of not getting in so it was hard to find enough lads to fill a car and take that risk. The ban hit the vocal support United got at away grounds and results deteriorated. A lonely business also became a scary business. At places like West Ham, Liverpool, and Chelsea the ban gave home supporters a chance to pick out Reds in small numbers and dish out a bit of revenge for earlier years when the Red Army ruled the roost. Even if you didn't wear United colours you still stood out from the home fans.

At Upton Park in December 1977, Mick Horseman and I managed to buy tickets for the paddock, usually a safer place than the two ends. But the atmosphere was evil with Hammers fans walking around trying to flush out Mancs by asking for the time. We sweated through the first half but it felt like there was no hiding place. At half time we bottled it and bought cheap satin West Ham scarves on sale in the ground. Shameful I know, but you had to be there to understand. We watched the second half in relative safety. The measures affected attendances and revenue for the home clubs. Without United's vast support the West Ham game attracted a meagre 20,000 crowd compared to over 38,000 the season before. There were no winners under this clampdown.

Despite these severe restrictions, I still managed to get in to every United game. I had gone more than six years without missing a competitive match. Nothing could deter me but I was about to face my biggest challenge. In early 1977 my sister Michelle announced she was getting married. I was really pleased for her. The wedding would be Saturday 29 October that year. Bloody hell! A Saturday in October? Alarm bells started to ring, it was bound to clash with a United fixture.

Now, call me narrow-minded, but wouldn't it be a far better world if weddings were limited to June and July each year? You know, a bit like a football transfer window? That way, the weather would be ideal for the photos and millions of football fans could enjoy the season without having to dress up in a suit and pretend they are interested in someone else's nuptials, or even their own!

At first I went into denial, it was months off and anything could happen. When the fixtures came out, instead of looking for the Manchester derby or the Liverpool matches, I went straight to 29 October. There it was … Aston Villa away.

I didn't discuss the matter with anyone, including Michelle. As the day got nearer I knew I would have to declare my intentions. In my heart I wanted to go to the match but my head told me to go to the wedding. By now though, I was hooked on United. As bad as any crack-head and not for the first time I put my allegiance to the Reds ahead of anything else. I decided I would go to the game.

I still couldn't pluck up the courage to talk to Michelle. All joking apart, even though I was besotted with my team, I love my sister and I desperately didn't want to upset her or spoil her special day. I was trapped. Whenever any family members asked if I would be there I just changed the subject. For weeks, I couldn't relax around the house when dad and Michelle were at home in case they confronted me with the dilemma. About two weeks before the big day I was in our living room watching TV with Michelle when she asked in a soft voice, 'So what are you going to do about the wedding then?'

I froze. I knew this was it, but still bottled it. With a pathetic look on my face I just shrugged my shoulders. Michelle knew the mess I was in and simply said, 'Look, I'd rather you go to the match and be happy than come to the wedding and be miserable. Just make sure you get back in time for the reception.'

With that she gave me her blessing to go to Villa. At first it was like having the weight of the world taken off me. That's how much even the thought of missing a game had become. Over the next fortnight I felt bad about what had happened and what I had put Michelle through. Once again, my father was disgusted and in one of his rare shows of anger gave me a right dressing-down about priorities and finished with something I'll never forget, 'This bloody football lark has become an obsession with you! When I first took you to a match I never thought it would turn into such a monster!' With that he stormed out.

I tried to dismiss it at first, but the words stayed with me and I had to concede he was right. United had become the biggest thing in my life. My dad had had enough and I couldn't blame him. In the previous eighteen months he had seen his son arrested, almost killed in a car crash, sign himself out of hospital, get embroiled in a riot overseas and now miss his sister's wedding

– all in the name of following Manchester United! While I understood his feelings, I couldn't change anything. I loved the whole United scene. It was what I wanted to do.

I went to Villa and even got stick from the lads I travelled down with. Mike Horseman and Brian Foy couldn't believe I was missing my own sister's wedding for an away game and they were loyal Reds. They didn't let me forget it for a long time. In fact, whenever Mike introduced me to anyone over the next ten years or so he would always grin and say, 'Have you met Pete Moly? He missed his sister's wedding for a football match yer know!' I gave up trying to explain.

Anyway, United lost 2-1 at Villa. I got to the reception early, Michelle and Stuart were fine and my dad had calmed down by then but the older relatives were a bit frosty with me. Without anything being said, I knew they didn't approve of what I had done. Feeling as welcome as a porcupine in a condom factory I went over to the buffet where I was joined by my auntie Edith. Now aunt Edith wasn't really my aunt Edith, she was just a good friend of the family but she was always very good to Michelle and me, especially after our mum died. She was a very kind, polite, mild mannered lady in her seventies.

Her face lit up as she approached me, just like it always did. 'How are you Peter?' she said, grabbing a few vol-au-vents.

'I'm fine thanks auntie Edith,' I replied, glad to hear a friendly greeting.

'How did United go on today, then?' she inquired.

'Oh they lost 2-1,' I said sheepishly.

'Good!!' she replied. 'I'm bloody glad!' and gave me a steely look right in the eye before turning to go back to her table.

I had never heard her swear before, I was shocked. It was like seeing Father Christmas eating venison. Point made auntie Edith, point made.

From mid-October United's league results fell away badly. Three days after the drubbing at Porto we went down by the same score at West Brom then lost six out of the next nine matches. A week before Christmas, Nottingham Forest visited Old Trafford. This was their first season back in the top flight and Forest led the table with a team of fairly unknown players. Brian Clough's boys gave us a footballing lesson in yet another 4-0 defeat, our biggest at home since August 1968.

Our next game was away to second-placed Everton on Boxing Day. Expecting the worst, we murdered them 6-2 with the same side as the week before except for young debutant Andy Ritchie. Gross inconsistency was the problem and Dave Sexton decided he had seen enough. He started to break up the team that had played together for the best part of four years.

His signings would shock the football world, let alone United supporters. In the first week of 1978 he took battling striker Joe Jordan from Leeds for a club record £350,000. Four weeks later he popped back over the Pennines to steal centre-half Gordon McQueen from Elland Road for an incredible £500,000. These were two players right at the height of their game. It seemed too good to be true, and from Leeds as well! We already had a very good team, these signings would make us unbeatable, surely? I was convinced the Football League would step in and stop the transfers because it was so unfair on the other teams in the First Division. Their first appearance in the same United side was at Anfield on 25 February. Expectations of a golden future for United were huge and it would all start at the home of the reigning league and European champions. For the first time in ten years we were going there with a team likely to batter the Scousers. Learning to live with setbacks is a special talent that all football supporters possess. However, there are some that just leave you gut-wrenchingly crushed.

Our oozing confidence simply tweaked the lion's tail. Liverpool rose to the occasion and gave us a sound 3-1 beating. How the Kop gloated. I have never heard 'what a waste of money' sung so loudly or with such relish. The following week Leeds visited Old Trafford with a point to prove to, and prove it they did by winning 1-0. There would be no instant cloak of invincibility for this United side.

Joe Jordan played eleven matches before he earned a win bonus. West Brom put an end to our reign as cup holders in the fourth round, and the season faded away disappointingly. We finished tenth on forty-two points, twenty-two behind new boys Forest who walked away with the First Division title. That baffled many United fans. How could a relatively small club come through from the Second Division to win what the mighty Manchester United had been chasing for eleven years?

Our world became one hero lighter from early April when the manager decided Gordon Hill was surplus stock. The winger was sold to Derby, welcomed with open arms by his former mentor The Doc. Hill played 134 games for United and scored fifty-one goals. Millwall fans nicknamed him 'Merlin' and he continued to weave his magic at the highest level at Old Trafford.

Hill always played football with a grin and a swagger. He excited and delighted the United faithful with his exquisite dribbling and shooting skills, scoring vital goals and great goals. His brace in the 1976 FA Cup semi-final will live forever in the memory of any Red who saw the game. Hill was 24 when Dave Sexton sold him, not even close to his peak. He was United's top scorer in his last two seasons. There were reports that the manager didn't think Hill displayed enough discipline to warrant his place, that didn't sit comfortably with many fans and sowed seeds of doubt about the direction Sexton was taking us.

12

ONE MAN ON A LONELY PLATFORM, ONE CASE SITTING BY HIS SIDE

If the previous five years had been a ride on The Big One we were now coasting on a Blackpool tram. Very safe, extremely efficient but no wow factor. The 1978/79 season began with too many drawn games. Three months in, we hovered around seventh place, effectively out of the title race before winter arrived. Worse still, the football was becoming dour – the worst of crimes at Old Trafford.

In early November, we drew 1-1 at home to Southampton. The game was dire and some fans wrote open letters to the press questioning Dave Sexton's tactics. A week later we lost 5-1 to a Birmingham team bottom of the league and without a win. Even the press were getting bored by the football we served up.

Mike Dempsey, sports editor of the *Daily Express*, captured the mood on the terraces when he wrote on, 14 November 1978, 'Sexton's standing as a coach is indisputable, but what he has brought to United is not magic; it is the grey reality that you can see on most other football grounds.'

In response the manager snapped up Mickey Thomas from Wrexham for £330,000, a left-sided midfield dynamo. Sexton finally realised that Paddy Roche was never going to be a top-class goalkeeper, something United supporters had concluded three years earlier. He tried to sign Jim Blyth from Coventry for £444,000 but the player failed a medical. As a temporary measure he blooded young reserve keeper Gary Bailey. On his debut against Ipswich Bailey played a blinder, stayed in the team and played 375 matches for United over the next nine years.

The poor form continued and we ended the year with three awful defeats over Christmas, 3-0 at Bolton, 3-0 at home to Liverpool and 5-3 at home to West Brom. The New Year brought consistency and United became hard to be beat but we continued to draw too many games. One notable exception was the derby match against City on 10 February 1979. On a frozen pitch United made a mockery of the conditions as we waltzed to a 3-0 win. We left Maine Road with a chorus of, 'Oh dear what can the matter be, Manchester City got hammered on Saturday!' to the old nursery rhyme of 'Johnnie's So Long at the Fair'.

The celebrations carried on into the evening and to a night out with the lads at a Bier Kellar in Manchester. I loved the atmosphere in there but the combination of the strong beer, the night air and a dazzling victory in City's backyard dulled my sense of self-preservation. Waiting for the all night bus back to Salford, I thought it would be fun to climb up the traffic lights in Piccadilly Bus Station and give Manchester an impromptu rendition of our new 'what can the matter be' ditty. My mates tried to get me down but I wasn't for listening and only the bus driver getting into his cab finally moved me from my perch.

As I stepped down to the pavement I felt a heavy blow to the side of my head. I fell on my back and saw Mike Horseman running towards me asking if I was okay. Apparently, some guy had emerged from a group of lads, hit me with a bottle and ran off. My head was bleeding and my jaw hurt like hell. I know singing isn't one of my strengths, so it could be that someone took exception to the racket I was making. Or perhaps it was a bitter Blue who had suffered enough mickey-taking for one day. I will never know. Mike walked me to Ancoats Hospital where they confirmed my jaw was fractured and stitched up the cut to my head. We caught a later bus and I woke up next morning with the mother-and-father of all headaches. But hey, we had whooped City – it was all worthwhile.

A run to the FA Cup Final salvaged our season. We beat Chelsea, Fulham, Colchester and Spurs before meeting Liverpool in the semi-finals. United always went the extra mile against the Scousers. We were regularly their nemesis throughout the 1970s and 1980s when they ruled English football. In a 2-2 draw at Maine Road the Reds of Manchester were unlucky, Liverpool grabbing an equaliser eight minutes from time, but many believed United's chance had gone. With the Goodison replay at stalemate, after seventy-seven minutes came one of the most iconic goals of the era. Breaking down the left, Mickey Thomas delivered a wicked, low cross that curled away from the keeper. It bounced right in front of the goal eight yards out and Jimmy Greenhoff stooped slightly to head the ball past Clemence. United were in their third final in four seasons and a first ever meeting with Arsenal at Wembley.

The Gunners were never serious contenders for the title between 1972 and 1988 but were a decent cup team and in 1979 had a strong line-up including Pat Jennings, Pat Rice, David O'Leary, Graham Rix, Frank Stapleton, and the excellent Liam Brady. United's team on 12 May 1979 was: Bailey, Nichol, Albiston, McIlroy, McQueen, Buchan, Coppell, Greenhoff, Jordan, Macari, Thomas.

This final has been given more hype than it ever deserved, even achieving 'classic' status in some quarters. A truly unremarkable game had a truly remarkable finale. Losing 2-0 after eighty-six minutes, United had been pale shadows and needed a miracle. McQueen ventured forward and swept home a Jordan cross, then two minutes later Sammy Mac tiptoed his way through the Arsenal penalty area to equalise. The goal led to the wildest scenes of celebration I had ever experienced at a United match and would only be surpassed in Spain twenty years later.

The momentum was with United. Surely we would win it in extra time? As we tumbled about on those steep Wembley terraces, Brady raced to the other end fed a pass to Rix who crossed for Alan Sunderland to win it for Arsenal. I have never experienced so much pleasure and pain inside ninety seconds.

I was high up on the United terraces that day. For most of the second half the atmosphere was subdued, a reflection of Arsenal's dominance and United's poor performance. Twenty minutes from the end, about five yards in front of us, a United supporter climbed on to a crash barrier to address the Red throng around him. I knew him by sight, he was a United 'face' from Stretford going back to the 1960s. With his mates holding him in place, he bawled, 'Come on lads, for f*ck's sake! Let's get behind 'em!' With that he started singing, 'Oh when the Reds, go marching in, oh when the Reds go marching in, I wanna be in that number when the Reds go marching in.' A handful of us joined in but it was a slow burner. Most hearts were heavy and hope forlorn; but we persevered for a good ten minutes.

Finally the chants picked up and spread throughout the whole United end. Defiance kicked in. If we were going lose we would go down singing. The team's performance improved almost instantly. Heads were high once more, shoulders back, chests out proud, passes more purposeful. The players believed. The combination sparked an incredible revival and one of the best climaxes in the 107-year history of the FA Cup. Respect to that supporter who got up and sang when all seemed lost. If only he had started five minutes earlier we would have beaten those bloody Gunners!

The cup run papered over serious cracks in our league form. We finished ninth, twenty-three points behind champions Liverpool and this was still the era of two points for a win. Sexton's first two seasons brought mid-table positions despite a record outlay of £1.2 million on three new players.

There was an undercurrent of disenchantment among United supporters that went beyond the results. At the end of February 1979, United played QPR at Old Trafford, only 36,085 turned up and at half-time the team was booed-off despite leading 1-0. I have never agreed with booing the team, that's heresy, but the mood was very despondent.

The Winter of Discontent had descended on Old Trafford and the following night, David Meek opened his report in the *Manchester Evening News*:

> After following the triumphs and tragedies at Old Trafford for over 21 years it hurts to acknowledge United's magic bubble has burst. The halcyon days are finally over. United no longer walk with the soccer Gods. Great names, great deeds, the right to belong in the top echelon are things of the past.

British football transfer fees went crazy in 1979. In the previous seven years, the record had been broken three times: in August 1972 when David Nish moved from Leicester City to Derby County for £225,000; February 1974 when Bob

Latchford joined Everton from Birmingham City for £350,000; and June 1977 when Kevin Keegan left Liverpool for Hamburg for £500,000.

In January 1979, striker David Mills switched from Middlesbrough to West Brom for £516,000, and the following month Trevor Francis became the first £1 million British footballer when Brian Clough took him to Forest from Birmingham. In September, Manchester City paid Wolves £1.45 million for Steve Daley but before the month was out the Molineux club handed Aston Villa £1.469 million for Andy Gray.

Against this backdrop United broke their transfer record and paid Chelsea £825,000 for Ray Wilkins. Expectations rose again, United were top by mid-September and jostled for the leadership with Liverpool until Christmas. The team settled into an effective unit, well balanced with a strong defence. Though not playing scintillating football, we achieved consistency and the results were good.

On Boxing Day, United played Liverpool at Anfield. Both teams were locked at the top on thirty points though we had played a game more. This fixture wouldn't decide the title but it was a chance to prove we were serious contenders. The history books show we lost 2-0, in reality we were buried under an avalanche of Liverpool attacks all afternoon. Only brilliant defending kept the score this side of respectable. Alan Hansen opened the scoring on fourteen minutes but the reigning champions didn't seal the game until the last ten minutes. In between they gave us a footballing lesson. The closest United came to scoring was an enormous punt downfield by goalkeeper Gary Bailey which got carried by the wind, bounced over Clemence and hit the angle of the woodwork. That was in the seventy-second minute.

Despite this embarrassing setback, United recovered, Liverpool wobbled and by 1 March the two giants were level on forty points at the top. That weekend marked the next pivotal point in the league title race. United were away at Ipswich, while Liverpool had a tricky derby at Everton. Ipswich, fourteenth at Christmas, had put in a storming run to reach third spot, five points behind the joint leaders. I remember getting on to the terraces just before kick-off, it was a bright sunny day and the pitch looked immaculate like green baize. I felt really confident about United's chances and sensed an upset at Goodison. I shared my vision with the lads, boldly predicting this will be the day we put some daylight between us and Liverpool in pursuit of that elusive title.

In a frightening repeat of the game at Anfield, Ipswich tore into United and we offered little resistance. This time though the goals went in, six to be precise, all to Ipswich. Gary Bailey managed to save two penalties otherwise we would have been re-writing the record books. It is the biggest United defeat I've witnessed and one of our most lacklustre performances. The scoreline came through from Merseyside, Liverpool had won 2-1 to go two points clear with a game in hand. Our daylight had been robbed!

The supporters felt let down and the mood was hostile coming out of the ground. The animosity wasn't directed at rival fans or the police but towards the manager. A posse headed for the players' entrance and I was ready to join them when I saw Brian Foy get hit by a piece of flying metal. It had been boarding up a small window near an exit when a frustrated Red booted it. The metal flew out and a sharp corner hit Bri on his cheek, causing a nasty cut. We rushed him to the first aid station at the side of the ground. Before the medics would stitch the wound they wanted to consult a dental surgeon. We had to wait while one was called out.

In the meantime we watched the police quell the protest around the player's lounge next door. Eventually, despondent Reds melted away into the night. We had hung around the medical room for the best part of an hour when I noticed the players outside walking to the team bus. Close behind strode a very sullen Dave Sexton. I raced to the door shouting to my mates I was going to give him a piece of my mind. I wasn't aggressive, just gutted by the way we had capitulated again in a crunch fixture. Keith Livesey ran after me, pulled me back and said it was the wrong time and place. We needed to get Brian sorted. He was right. I walked away from Sexton, but my belief in him as a United manager faded dramatically that day, just like our title chances.

Brian was transferred to Ipswich Hospital for X-rays. Fortunately there was no serious damage so he was patched up and discharged around 8 p.m. Half a dozen of us had travelled down on the football special train which was somewhere around Birmingham by then. Using Bri's bandaged head and blood-stained clothes to get sympathy, we jibbed our way on service trains across to London then up to Manchester without paying a penny. We knew it would be the early hours of Sunday before we arrived home so we phoned to explain what had happened. Bri couldn't talk, so Keith spoke to Mrs Foy. This was Bri's first visit back to Ipswich since the car crash three years earlier, it was a difficult phone call to explain he had been involved in another accident.

Dave Sexton's response to the 6-0 drubbing was to tighten the defence. Consequently, we drew the next two matches 0-0, against sixteenth-placed Brighton and nineteenth-placed Everton. Liverpool opened up a six-point lead with twelve games left. A bolder manager would have seized the initiative knowing that if we didn't succeed we would have given all we had and retained our pride and reputation. A late rally reduced the gap but Liverpool steamed ahead to claim a twelfth league title, their fifth in eight years. The second-place finish was United's highest since 1968. Life should have felt good, but it didn't. Most United regulars knew in their hearts we hadn't played like champions. More importantly, as the 1980s dawned, we weren't playing like Manchester United.

I find it difficult to describe how badly the 1980/81 season started for United supporters. There was no great disaster, terrible tragedy or humiliating defeats. There was just ordinariness. More ordinariness than the previous two seasons but now it was mind-numbing, mundane, ordinariness. The football was consistently poor, defensive and very much safety-first tactics. The side still contained great players but we played without flair.

By mid-November, we had drawn eleven of our eighteen league matches and fell at the first hurdle in the League Cup and UEFA Cup. A lack of goals was the problem. United didn't score away from home until 4 October, a run of seven matches. The attack lacked bite, top scorer Joe Jordan missed ten matches through injury, Jimmy Greenhoff was past his best at 33 and Andy Ritchie needed more experience.

In late October, Dave Sexton smashed United's transfer record again by signing Garry Birtles from Nottingham Forest for £1.25 million. Under Brian Clough, Birtles had been transformed from a non-league, part-time carpet fitter to a double European Cup winner. He made his United debut in a 2-1 win at Stoke and looked useful. The signing should have been Sexton's last piece in the jigsaw to make United genuine title contenders. It would backfire badly.

Despite our poor form the UEFA Cup draw provided an exciting prospect. United drew the Polish team Widzew Lodz. This was another dream come true, seeing United play in Eastern Europe or behind the 'Iron Curtain' as it was known then. There was added spice when, a month before we played there, Russia's leaders got twitchy about Poland's loyalty to the Communist cause. The recently formed Solidarity trade union movement, started by Gdansk Shipyard workers seeking better pay and conditions, was trying to emasculate their Communist government. Poland was strategically critical to the Soviet bloc and the response from Moscow was predictable. They placed tanks along the Polish border as a gentle reminder of what happened to Hungary and Czechoslovakia when they failed to toe the party line in the 1950s and 1960s. For three months the threat of a military invasion was very real; in the end it was sorted politically rather than by force. A first for post-war Russia.

We were warned that the trip to Lodz might be cancelled if there was an invasion, although the match would go ahead. I am sure that wouldn't have stopped most Reds. We could have had the ultimate face-off, the Red Army versus the Red Army. At least it would have livened up the bloody season. The trip cost £180 including the obligatory visa. To put that in some perspective, the dearest season ticket at Old Trafford that year cost £63.

Brian Foy and I were up for it. Like me, he didn't bother with holidays in the sun in those days. This was our Torremolinos, following United. Travelling supporters each received a nice letter from United chairman Martin Edwards, who had succeeded his late father Louis earlier that year. We were advised that as well as Russian invaders, we should be on our guard for black market traders selling currency illegally, customs officials with no sense of humour, cold water with black specks of dirt and very cloudy hot water. The letter thanked us for making the difficult trip to support the team and reminded us not to cause trouble. Suitably advised, we set off from Old Trafford at 4.30 a.m. on Tuesday 30 September on a coach for London Heathrow to catch the 10.30 a.m. flight to Warsaw Okecie Airport.

By mid-afternoon we were checking into the Hotel Polonia in central Warsaw. The day was grey and very dull, it captured the feel of the city. There was little colour around and the people seemed very serious. The mood got heavier as trench-coated men in trilby hats discreetly approached anyone who ventured outside the hotel that evening. They were offering to change Zlotys, the Polish currency, but they looked more like secret government agents setting up a sting. We gave them a wide berth.

Lodz is eighty-four miles from Warsaw but the journey took well over three hours as the last third was on tiny roads through Polish farmland. The ground was pretty impressive with an all-seater capacity of 35,000. We were segregated from the Lodz supporters on one side of the ground but there was no hint of trouble. Having drawn the home leg 1-1 we had to score, something we had yet to do on our travels. United went straight on the attack and Sammy Mac blasted a good chance over the bar just three minutes in. Our defence was solid all night but the nearest we came to a goal was Stevie Coppell hitting the post in the thirty-fifth minute. The 0-0 draw put the Poles through.

I remember the players disappearing straight down the tunnel, there was no attempt to acknowledge the fans who had spent a fortune making the long journey. As disappointed as the players were, it was a missed opportunity to show a bit of empathy with the club's most loyal supporters. Ironically, the Polish fans gave us plenty of attention after the game. They invaded the pitch to mob their heroes then charged towards us on the terraces. The situation looked ominous but they were just interested in exchanging scarves, badges and flags.

That night it was a long, long journey back to the hotel. As the coach made its way through winding country lanes, I had plenty of time to think. For the first time in my life I felt disillusioned about United. Not the club or my devotion to it, but the standard of football we were watching each week. It had been woeful for such a long time and there was no sign of improvement. I felt I was staring into a void. I started to question whether following United across the UK and Europe was worth it. We arrived back at the hotel well after midnight. Our hosts had laid on a special Polish meal with some ethnic entertainment. I dismissed my doubts as tiredness and the frustration of defeat and tucked into my sour cabbage soup.

The numbers travelling to United away games had reduced significantly during the previous three seasons. Initially this was due to the Government restrictions but when the sanctions were lifted many Reds chose to stay away rather than suffer the tedium. Home gates dropped to the low 40,000-mark. I had always felt it was a joy and a privilege to watch United, whether we won or lost, now it had become a chore. I never thought I'd feel that way. Ninety-minute games seemed to last three hours. Instead of being enthralled by the action on the pitch you found yourself wondering what you would do that evening or asking your mate next to you what he was having tea! It was dire. I found it particularly difficult because I was still hooked on getting to every game, trapped by my craving. I had gone more than nine years without missing a match. The trouble is, I was no longer getting the kicks from my addiction.

Curiously, the 1980s started as they would finish. I decided action was required – a protest to let the manager know my feelings. I considered running on to the pitch at the start of a home game, handcuffing myself to a goalpost, then holding up a placard with some suitable words of dissent. I wish I had gone ahead with that idea because it would have made a great story now. But when I thought it through I didn't have the bottle.

Tamely, by comparison, I decided to write a letter to Dave Sexton. I briefly explained who I was, then outlined my grievance saying that our play had become predictable and was crying out for flair and incisiveness. I commented that we didn't need new players as the squad was one of the best in the country, the problem lay in tactics of slow, controlled play. I explained that many United supporters felt the same way and had started to vote with their feet. I reminded him that United's reputation had been built on adventurous football over many years. I invited Mr Sexton to either explain how he justified his tactics or better still abandon them and return to the 'United way' of playing football. On 13 November 1980 I posted the letter addressed to Dave Sexton marked 'personal'.

The good news is I got a speedy reply. On 18 November I received a letter typed on official club paper, signed personally by the manager. It read:

> I acknowledge receipt of your letter and have read the contents carefully. Thank you for taking the time and trouble to write to me, which is much appreciated. Yours sincerely, Dave Sexton.

I was disgusted. I hadn't expected him to commandeer a spot on prime-time television to renounce his whole approach because Pete Molyneux from Salford had written to him and now he had seen the light. I did, however, hope for some acknowledgement that he understood how loyal Reds were feeling and outline what he was trying to achieve without giving away any trade secrets. No, he basically chose to ignore my comments and in doing so treated them with contempt.

Herein lay Dave Sexton's main problem at Old Trafford. He wasn't in tune with the supporters and that's a dangerous place for a United manager to be. I kept thinking back to the opportunity I had at Ipswich in March to give him a piece of my mind. I deeply regretted not doing that. I mulled over the situation for a couple of days and made a very difficult decision. United's next game was at Brighton and I decided not to go. As tough a choice as it was, the letter from Sexton made it easier. I wasn't about to turn my back on United, I would still attend every home game and decide on each away match as it came along.

I told my mates I wouldn't be going to the Brighton match. A couple of them bought train tickets on the back of it, saying they just had to be at a match I was missing! Others tried to talk me out of it. They felt the sequence of unmissed games was too good to break. No one tried harder than Brian Foy. We had followed United everywhere in the previous five years and he felt I should give Sexton more time. He even phoned me around midnight on the Friday and for the next hour tried to convince me to join him on the special at 9 a.m. the next day. I was flattered by these genuine attempts to change my mind but I knew I would only be going to maintain the sequence and that was the wrong reason. The next morning, Brian and Beef spent the first hour walking up and down the Football Special still convinced they would find me somewhere.

Mike Horseman wasn't going to the game so he suggested we go to Manchester that afternoon. He needed a few things and felt I needed a distraction. Throughout the Saturday I was remarkably relaxed, now I had made up my mind I felt a lot better. Nevertheless, Mike kept asking if I was okay. It was like being on suicide watch. I did feel strange as 3 p.m. approached and I thought about United kicking off some 230 miles away, but once that milestone had passed I was fine.

We beetled around Manchester, deliberately trying to avoid any score flashes until full time. At twenty to five we went into a clothes shop on Bridge Street, and a local radio station was reporting from the grounds. The anchorman announced a report was coming in from the Goldstone Ground that Manchester United had beaten Brighton by four goals to one. Mike and I looked at each other in amazement then burst out laughing. I said, '4-1 Mike! Four f★★king one! We've not been able to score for toffee, the football's been shite, I write to Sexton to moan about the negative tactics, I miss me first match in over nine years and United go and win 4-1! Jesus Christ!' Delighted as I was about the result, I did feel a bit cheated.

Over the next few weeks the pattern of drawn games returned, sprinkled with the odd wins or defeats. The Brighton result had been a one-off. Nottingham Forest ended our season with a defeat in the FA Cup fourth round. There wasn't one game worthy of note throughout that winter. Perhaps the most telling statistic is that in the first forty games we played in 1980/81 we failed to score in nineteen of them.

Then came a remarkable flourish. United won all the last seven league games including victories at Everton and Liverpool. Despite this run, five days after the final game Dave Sexton was sacked. I heard the news around lunchtime at work. I was delighted, it was the right decision for the good of the club. Bri and I worked at the same location and I remember breaking the news to him. He was gutted, feeling United had been hasty and Sexton should have been given more time. We begged to differ on that one.

I have always felt Dave Sexton's reign at Old Trafford never really ignited. He failed to seize the initiative with his style of play and his relationship with the supporters. Even during the cup run of 1979 or the title tilt in 1980 there wasn't a conviction about the team. Sexton's final season was a catalogue of underachievement given the cost of assembling the side – eighth in the league and out of the three cups by the second stage. Record signing Garry Birtles didn't bag a single goal in his twenty-five leagues games. Given the final flurry though, it took a brave decision by the United board to sack their manager but the club statement on 30 April was spot on:

In spite of recent results the team's performance has failed to live up to
the high standard of football entertainment expected of Manchester
United … The decision was reached after taking into consideration
the discontent among a predominant percentage of regular supporters. This is reflected in the hundreds of letters received by the club,
adverse comment from our nationwide supports' clubs and a significant drop in recent attendances.

United's playing record under Dave Sexton was:

Played	W	D	L	F	A	W%	D%	L%
201	81	64	56	290	240	40	32	28

Sexton ranks eighth out of seventeen United managers based on
win percentage. The only remarkable statistic is the high percentage of drawn matches. Only the McGuinness reign produced a
higher proportion of draws. Successful football managers need
two key factors – time and resources. Sexton had four full seasons
at Old Trafford and given the FA Cup-winning team he inherited that should have been sufficient time to deliver a trophy and
close in on that elusive title.

During those four years Sexton broke United's transfer record
four times in recruiting Jordan, McQueen, Wilkins and Birtles.
In addition, Mickey Thomas cost £330,000 and Nikki Jovanovi
£300,000. United's board backed their manager when he wanted
to strengthen the squad but the team failed to win one trophy.

However, Sexton's biggest 'crime' was to strip United of their
magic. I am sure he didn't intend to do that, but when the going
got tough he reverted to type – caution rather than adventure.
Bobby Charlton recalled in his autobiography that the great
Sir Matt had talked of a professional footballer's duty to provide a
little colour for the people who came to watch United at the end
of a working week. Busby understood that those people didn't
want more of the humdrum grind of their working lives, they
wanted something else to carry them through the drab days of
winter; they wanted excitement. That's the visionary genius that
should be in the DNA of every Manchester United manager
who follows Busby.

If Sexton didn't possess that quality initially, he had the chance
to discover it during his tenure as manager. The aura and history

around Old Trafford would seep into most people's conscience. United supporters and the media also tried to help the manager to understand that he was tampering with a sacred tradition. He chose to ignore the advice.

There is a great song by The Eagles called 'Already Gone' which contains the line, 'When you look up in the sky, you can see the stars and still not see the light.' Whenever I hear that song I can't help but feel it is a fitting epitaph to Sexton's time as manager of Manchester United.

Sexton did recover his career after United, building a tremendous reputation behind the scenes coaching for the FA. He was admired and respected throughout football. On 25 November 2012 he passed away, aged 82.

13

THIS INDECISION'S BUGGING ME

If United needed an injection of calm and respectability after Tommy Docherty left in 1972, we were desperate for a shot of glamour, glitz and excitement when Dave Sexton departed. Enter Big Ron. On 9 June 1981, Ron Atkinson became United's fifth manager in eleven years.

The larger than life character had built an excellent side at West Brom that played with flair and panache. Atkinson was captain of unfashionable Oxford United when they went from the old Southern League to the second tier of English football between 1962 and 1968. He cut his managerial teeth at Kettering before guiding Cambridge United into the Third Division in 1977. The U's were on the verge of a second consecutive promotion when Albion came calling.

Atkinson was 42 when he accepted the United job. His first challenge was to try and keep Joe Jordan at Old Trafford. Twenty years after Italian clubs first came shopping for English strikers they returned and AC Milan targeted Big Joe. The lure of the lira won the day and Jordan's four-year reign as the hero of the Stretford End was over. Atkinson moved quickly to tempt the unsettled Frank Stapleton from Highbury. Mickey Thomas and Andy Ritchie left the club that summer while full-back John Gidman joined Stapleton on the newcomers list.

Before the league campaign began there was a tasty adventure to be had north of the border. United took part in a four-team tournament at Pittodrie at the start of August. Fairly tame by today's glamorous curtain-raisers, the remaining line-up was West Ham, Southampton and hosts, Aberdeen. Not Rome or Mandalay but we had to be there. Keith Livesey and myself persuaded Brian Foy to take his beloved Ford Escort on the road trip and on Friday afternoon we headed north. Margaret Thatcher's policies were starting to bite and money was in short supply. Keith wasn't working, I had bought the house from dad when he re-married, so this trip had to be low budget. Staying in hotels was out of the question so we packed up our camping gear, Keith's camping gear to be precise, plus a few pots and pans and a bit of food.

I had first met Keith about five years earlier, through his older brother Ged who travelled with us in the vans to watch United. Ged's family lived near me on the Duchy Estate in Salford and I became good friends with them over the next twenty years. In February 1976, Ged brought along his kid brother Keith for the van trip to Leicester. He was only 16 but Ged promised to keep an eye on him. Keith was introduced to us as Beef, as apparently when his younger sisters were growing up they couldn't pro-nounce his name properly; it would come out as Keef. At school, Keef became Beef and the name stuck.

At the Leicester game Beef was last back to the van. Under his coat he had a full frozen chicken which he claimed had fallen off one of the market stalls we had passed in the city centre. Ged gave him a right bollocking but decided it would come in handy for the family lunch the next day. I realised then we had a bit of a character in our midst. Beef was a good lad but in those days he was a feisty young buck and desperate to prove he was nobody's fool.

A week after the Leicester trip we played Aston Villa away, scene of the Krooklok incident. It was Beef who had a spat with a few of their lads. So on my first two trips with him, he had nicked a chicken and got embroiled in a bit of fisticuffs. Despite that we went on to become good mates, you just needed to expect the unexpected when he was around. Beef always had an eye for an opportunity.

Back to the 1981 pre-season trip, and we drove as far as we could on the Friday before crashing out in the car somewhere north of Montrose before pressing on to Aberdeen the next morning. United took the biggest following of the three English clubs but the tournament was poorly attended with crowds of 10,000–11,000 on both days. United played Southampton on

the Saturday tea time after Aberdeen had seen off West Ham 3-0.
A Saints team containing Kevin Keegan, Charlie George and
Mick Channon coasted to 3-1 victory.

United's performance was that bad we headed straight for
the pub after the game. The atmosphere was good and a few
became many before we remembered we hadn't pitched the
tent for the night. By the time we got back to the car it was
dark. We got the camping gear out and headed for the nearest
bit of flat grass we could find. Now I must confess, my ability to
erect a tent even when I'm sober and in broad daylight leaves
a lot to be desired. I was never in the Cubs or Scouts so it was
all alien to me. We battled with that tent for at least an hour
against a wild wind coming in off the North Sea. Finally we got
enough pegs in to hold it down, laid out our sleeping bags and
crashed out. Early next morning we awoke to brilliant sunshine,
the sounds of waves crashing against rocks and seagulls squawk-
ing overhead. Bleary eyed we clambered outside and found to
our horror we had pitched the tent just yards from the edge of a
cliff face. Thank God none of us wandered out in the middle of
the night for a wee.

The Reds' poor form continued into Sunday when we
played West Ham for third place. The Hammers won 1-0.
Aberdeen won the tournament by thrashing Southampton 5-1
with many of the team who would go on to win the European
Cup Winners' Cup under Fergie the following season. We
decided to stay in Aberdeen that night and found another cosy
pub to put the world to right. Beef got chatting to a local girl
and was doing well until her boyfriend turned up. Not to be
deterred, Beef flitted between our table and theirs throughout
the evening. We weren't sure what he was playing at but when
it was time to leave Beef announced he wasn't coming with us.
He had been invited back to the couple's house for a drink and
said he would meet us later at the tent. Neither Bri nor I were
completely surprised, Beef often befriended people at home or
on his travels.

The next morning there was no sign of Beef and we started to
get worried. We hadn't moved the tent so the first thing we did
was look over the cliff! Nothing there, thankfully, so we started to
wonder if the friendly couple might have a darker side and was
Beef imprisoned at their house? We knew nothing about them

or where they lived. All we could do was wait. As we packed up
the tent a smiling Beef appeared. Apparently he'd had a good
drink with his new buddies and they were so worried about
him finding his way to the tent they let him sleep in the spare
bedroom. Then he stayed for a full Scottish breakfast before ven-
turing to see how we were. You had to admire him. Bri and I had
managed to grab a few hours' sleep in a cold tent and were so
hungry we could eat a scabby cat. Meanwhile, Mr Livesey turned
a failed chat-up attempt into free booze, a warm bed and a king's
breakfast. He wasn't daft that Beef.

Big Ron's reign began with a jolt. After four games we
were bottom of the league with two draws and two defeats.
Then we witnessed a minor miracle. In the home game against
Swansea on 19 September 1981 Garry Birtles scored his first
league goal for United. Though eleven months and thirty-three
appearances in the making, it proved to be the winner and a
change of fortune for club and player. More importantly it put
an end to the stream of jokes about his scoring drought that
were churned out every Monday morning in offices, shops and
factories across Manchester. The Swansea game also marked the
debut of Remi Moses after Atkinson went back to West Brom
to snap up the midfielder.

Results improved but even with Moses, the midfield of
Wilkins, Coppell, McIlroy or Macari lacked real bite. Big Ron
knew it and in early October returned to the Hawthorns to land
one of United's best ever signings. Breaking the British transfer
record he paid £1.5 million for Bryan Robson. The Albion
skipper wasn't a star name and some considered it a huge gamble
but Robson added the steel we had lacked and the powerhouse
engine any successful side needs. United climbed the table, on
24 October we went to Anfield with a team that was really starting to shine: Bailey, Gidman, Albiston, Wilkins, Moran, Buchan,
Robson, Birtles, Stapleton, Moses, Coppell.

Liverpool had won their third European Cup earlier that year
and the Kop was lauding it. Packed like sardines in the corner
of Anfield Road, the Red Army held their own. Robson looked
stylish and composed in midfield. A couple of his early tackles
let the opposition know they were in for a battle in their own
backyard. United went in front when Frank Stapleton's header
hit a post and Moran poked home the rebound. Liverpool

equalised with a penalty. We had been used to Liverpool pegging us back in the last fifteen minutes of matches at Anfield but this time it was United pressing hard for a winner. With minutes remaining, Arthur Albiston went on a sortie down the left wing, did a neat one-two with Frank Stapleton and slid the ball into the Liverpool net. Game over.

Our delight intensified as results came in from the other grounds and we realised United had gone top of the table with this late win. How sweet that victory tasted, our second in six months at Anfield after twelve barren years and how we let those crestfallen Scousers know it as we left the ground.

Bottom to top in six weeks, Ron Atkinson's magic seemed to be working. Southampton, City, Swansea, and Ipswich were the other contenders that winter. Up to New Year, Liverpool were conspicuous by their absence as they laboured in mid-table. This was the season when three points for a win was introduced which made draws, let alone defeats, costly. The top four were taking points off each other and no team was able to break away.

Just two wins in nine games between mid-February and April saw United lose ground. The loss of form at such a crucial stage was as mystifying as it was disappointing. Europe and the domestic cups weren't a distraction nor did we have an injury crisis or mounting suspensions. The loss of form, with hindsight, was a question of bottle. When the going got tough we were found wanting. It would become a feature of the early 1980s. United regained their composure to win seven of the remaining nine games but Liverpool had caught the pack and moved into overdrive winning thirteen of their last sixteen league fixtures. They became champions for the thirteenth time while United finished third, nine points adrift of top spot.

Though disappointed, the majority of Reds were satisfied with Atkinson's first season. The team was playing attractive football again, the balance was good, we were strong in every department and we had qualified for Europe. Big Ron had endeared himself to United supporters. His Champagne Charlie image was a little irksome but most of us saw through it as his way of dealing with the media and it worked for him. His Docherty-esque quips and one-liners connected with the supporters, he was a big character for a big job.

Bryan Robson signed for United in a stage-managed ceremony on the Old Trafford pitch prior to a game against Wolves. Sammy

McIlroy scored a hat-trick in a 5-0 victory that afternoon, one of his finest displays in an eleven-year career of fine displays for United.

Ironically, Robson's arrival would herald the end for Sammy Mac. In February 1982 he joined Stoke having played 419 games and scored seventy-one goals. In a memorable debut in November 1971, 17-year-old Sammy swept to stardom putting United 1-0 up against City. But it was his sterling performances in midfield as we came storming back out of the Second Division and reached two Cup Finals in the mid-1970s that Reds of a certain age will cherish. From 1975 to 1980 he averaged fifty games per season for United and was twice voted Player of The Year. He was idolised by the fans. If you were on one of those coaches or ferries travelling through the night in September 1976 to our first game back in Europe for seven years, the strains of 'Que Sera Sera, with Gerry and Super Sam, we're going to Amsterdam!' will warm your heart forever.

Ron Atkinson realised the urgency to deliver the league title to Old Trafford. His priority was the first team, not building for the future. Yet ironically, he inherited one of United's best youth teams for almost twenty years. Eric Harrison was beginning to weave his magic with a side that included Norman Whiteside, Mark Hughes, Clayton Blackmore, Billy Garton and Graeme Hogg.

The star of the pack was Whiteside. After starring for Northern Ireland in the 1982 World Cup, Big Ron knew the boy was ready. He started the new season in the first team and played as though he had been born to a role on the biggest stage.

Whiteside's rise may have triggered the decision to sell Birtles before the season began. Atkinson signed Ipswich playmaker Arnold Muhren who at 31 brought one of the most cultured left feet to Old Trafford and added sheer class to our midfield. Ron's team was starting to take shape. United looked strong and exciting.

Elton John's Watford with Graham Taylor in charge were on an incredible journey from the fourth tier of English football to the first in five seasons. Their top flight debut in 1982/83 saw the climb continue as they challenged United and Liverpool for the title. All three stayed out in front until mid-December when Liverpool went on a winning spree that opened up a ten-point gap. That lead would prove unassailable. The Liverpool machine was well-oiled at this stage and didn't need to rely on title rivals capitulating, they just powered on regardless.

We found solace in domestic cup runs that season. Since 1977 United had been notorious cup failures and it looked liked the sequence would continue when Valencia CF beat us in the first round of the UEFA Cup. I had decided to miss the away leg, saving my money for the later, more glamorous rounds instead. A month later I was on a League Cup trip to exotic Bournemouth with the money I had saved, followed a few weeks later by a Wednesday night sojourn to Bradford. Ah, well, as the Dalek said climbing off the dustbin, we all make mistakes!

Although our sights had been lowered, the League Cup was still a coveted trophy and one United hadn't won. We triumphed in the two-legged tie against Bournemouth but the home leg was notable in that United's number ten was a certain Peter Beardsley. That is the same Peter Beardsley who would go on to win fame, fortune and medals for Liverpool, Everton and Newcastle over the next fifteen years.

In 1982 he was trying to get back into English football after a spell in Canada. Big Ron, seeking cover for Stapleton and Whiteside, signed him from Vancouver Whitecaps after the striker scored twice against us in a friendly. However, the game against Bournemouth would be Beardsley's only appearance for United. It wasn't a big deal when he left a few months later because we had only seen a glimpse of his ability. Only when he became a prolific scorer on the banks of the Mersey and the Tyne did Ron's judgement appear questionable.

United progressed in the League Cup and beat Southampton to reach the quarter-final. Shortly after that tie, Brian Foy called round to my house unexpectedly and brought his girlfriend Janet. After a general chat and a cup of tea, he broke the news that they were going to get married in the spring. I was pleased as both had become good friends, but wedding announcements still made me nervous. Trying to disguise my true motive, I pressed them for a date.

'It's March 26,' Brian proudly confirmed. 'We'll send out invitations in the post but we just wanted to tell you the news face to face.'

'Oh, right, er … good. Yeah, thanks for that I appreciate it,' I mumbled through a worried smile. I joked with Bri, 'March eh? Hope you checked the fixture list?' It wasn't a joke really, it was dead serious but I thought it inappropriate to let it show. Anyway

Bri was a true Red; he wouldn't let it clash with anything that really mattered. Well, not intentionally.

'Yes, we're away at Tottenham in the league. No harm in missing that one,'' laughed Bri.

'Oh, right, fine. No, no problem at all,' I replied, the relief seeping out.

Since I had stopped going to every United game nearly two years earlier, I now went to about two-thirds of the away league matches plus all the domestic cup games. Home matches were sacrosanct – they were not for missing. So Spurs away at the end of March wasn't a big deal.

As I waved farewell to the happy couple, I still had a nagging worry about the date, 'The end of March? Isn't that when they normally play the League Cup Final?' I had to check it. Sure enough in the United programme against 26 March it showed Tottenham away, but right next to it in brackets it said 'Milk Cup Final'. The final wasn't played on a Sunday in those days so it would be Saturday at 3 p.m.

I went into a cold sweat, it was 1977 all over again and the turmoil I went through over Michelle's wedding came flooding back. I wanted to ring Brian there and then. He might want to change it. I knew that wouldn't be right and we weren't even in the bloody final yet! I calmed down and decided to leave it to providence. At the next home game I told Brian what I knew and he took the same fatalistic view.

In mid-January we beat Nottingham Forest 4-0 to set up a two-legged semi against Arsenal. After the turn of the year United were in great form, with only one defeat in seventeen league and cup games and goals aplenty. On 15 February, Brian, Beef and I travelled down to Highbury for the League Cup semi. It was a surreal build-up to the game for the three of us. We were all very good mates and shared a passionate love of United. Yet we knew that if United reached Wembley two of us would have a very difficult decision to make. Not life or death, but it would feel mighty close.

But hey, we were up against Arsenal – a real force in the game – this was a very tough tie. Well, no it wasn't. Leading 2-0 at the break, United powered into a four-goal advantage after sixty-seven minutes during one of the finest spells of football I have ever seen. Robson and Moses won all the midfield battles for Stapleton, Whiteside and Coppell to tear Arsenal to shreds in our first win at Highbury in fifteen years. In the last ten minutes Arsenal pulled two goals back to salvage a little pride but the tie was effectively over.

On the way back we joked how fate had left us in no doubt about where United would be on 26 March 1983. We knew where Brian had to be. The big question was – where would Beef and I be? The three of us agreed that Bri should send out the invitations and we would take it from there. I was deferring the decision, just like I had done in 1977, hoping against hope that some global catastrophe might occur that would mean the match was postponed – or the wedding! United won the return leg 2-1 and Liverpool beat Burnley to set up a mouth-watering Wembley final. A few days later the invitation to the full wedding dropped on my doorstep.

Squeezed in between the two Arsenal ties, United had an FA Cup fifth round tie at the Baseball Ground. We had seen off West Ham and Luton and suddenly the FA Cup took on even more importance than usual. I was beginning to think that if I did go to the wedding, having an FA Cup Final to look forward to would soften the blow. I was clutching at straws and trying to square a circle. Nothing could compensate for missing a United cup final. A late goal from Whiteside beat Derby and an even later one from Stapleton knocked Everton out in the sixth round just two weeks before the League Cup Final.

That victory made up my mind for me. It had been a very tough decision but I would go to the wedding out of respect for Brian and Janet. Hopefully I would be rewarded with a date at Wembley in May. When I told my dad I had opted to attend the wedding he nodded approvingly. 'Well done, son. Well done,' he said quietly with a smile he used to give me when I had done something right as a child. I think it convinced him that perhaps his son hadn't completely let football rule his life as seemed the case a few years earlier.

Beef chose to go to the wedding too and on the Saturday morning the two of us went round Salford Market to take our minds off what we were missing. It didn't work. Every stall had a Manchester United Wembley 1983 flag flying proudly in the breeze. It felt really strange, more so than missing the Brighton game after that nine-year run. The wedding was in Stockport and there we joined up with Mike Horseman who was Brian's best man. We all wanted to be there for Bri, that was important, but our minds were 200 miles away.

As the ceremony finished we heard Whiteside had given United the lead. On the coach to the reception we stayed in tune with the unfolding drama at Wembley. United's centre-backs Moran and McQueen were injured. A brave United battled on but Liverpool equalised to take the game to extra time where Ronnie Whelan won the cup for them. We were gutted as we tucked into the meal but put on a smiling face for the married couple.

The evening wore on, lads arrived who had been and we got blow-by-blow accounts. We all had a good drink and I knew I had made the right decision for a good friend. It is still the only United cup final I've missed in 50 years watching the Reds.

In the FA Cup semi-final the Gunners were desperate for revenge after their annihilation at Highbury. On a gloriously sunny day and with a contingent of Reds on all four sides of the famous Villa Park ground, United once again proved too good for their North London rivals. Norman Whiteside struck an unforgettable left-footed volley from just inside the corner of the Arsenal penalty area to win the tie. In a fairytale debut season the young Irishman was proving to be a revelation, Robson too was imperious as United marched on to Wembley again.

The game marked the beginning of a tradition whereby United used Villa Park to break other teams' hearts at the semi-final stage, invariably by scoring memorable goals. The victory was all the sweeter for Bri, Beef and myself. The three amigos would have a Cup Final trip after all.

Managers need luck and though we picked up injuries in other positions in 1982/83 the two main strikers stayed free of knocks, suspension and loss of form. Stapleton and Whiteside played in fifty-nine and fifty-seven games respectively out of a possible sixty and delivered thirty-three goals between them. Throughout the winter, Big Ron tried hard to get suitable cover for the only department without strength in depth. Reluctant to give Beardsley another chance, the manager tracked Alan Brazil. The Ipswich striker had made a big impact during their five-year golden period with seventy goals in 154 outings. Ipswich initially set a fee of £750,000 which scared off even the big spenders.

United's overdraft was still substantial after five years of big-money signings so with Whiteside playing well, the club played a waiting game. We lost. After four months Spurs nipped in and signed Brazil for £450,000.

In April 1983, Atkinson explored another avenue bringing in Laurie Cunningham on loan from Real Madrid. The 'Black Flash' had played for Big Ron in a slick West Brom side between 1977 and 1979. With Madrid he won the Spanish double in his first season and reached the 1981 European Cup Final, losing 1-0 to Liverpool in Paris. Serious knee ligament damage put Cunningham out of the game for a year before Atkinson gave him a chance to resurrect his career.

The striker played five matches for United, scoring on his home debut. Steve Coppell had picked up an injury and Atkinson was planning on playing Cunningham in the FA Cup Final against Brighton. Sadly, he also got injured on the eve of the game giving young reserve Alan Davies his chance of glory. Cunningham was released by United soon after.

We drove to Wembley on 21 May 1983, confident of another United triumph. Our form was good; Brighton had just been relegated from the top flight. A formidable United lined up: Bailey, Duxbury, Albiston, Wilkins, Moran, McQueen, Robson, Muhren, Stapleton, Whiteside, Davies.

Wembley wasn't the sun-drenched nirvana of previous finals and the rain-soaked pitch seemed to hamper United. Gordon Smith gave Brighton a shock lead on fourteen minutes which they held until Stapleton equalised ten minutes into the second half. Wilkins' exquisite seventy-second-minute curler seemed to have won it for the Reds before Gary Stevens sneaked an equaliser three minutes from time.

Extra time brought few thrills until the final seconds when Mick Robinson bulldozed his way past both our centre backs and squared the ball to Smith, ten yards from goal and only Bailey between him and Wembley folklore. Smith took a split second too long to control the ball allowing Bailey to advance and smother the shot. The line between success and failure was never finer than in those few seconds and Brighton would never forget it. United lived to fight another day and achieve more cup glory while the South Coast club plummeted to years of lower league anonymity.

United's first replayed final the following Thursday had a more familiar feel as the Reds strode to a 4-0 victory. We were 3-0 up at half-time thanks to a brace from captain Robson and one from Stormin' Norman. After sixty-three minutes, Muhren caressed a penalty into the net. It was a night of records. The biggest win in a Wembley final (which we equalled in the drubbing of Chelsea eleven years later), Whiteside becoming the youngest player to score in an FA Cup Final and the first to score in both the League Cup and FA Cup Finals. The 4-0 victory was the biggest FA Cup Final winning margin for eighty years since Bury beat Derby 6-0 in 1903.

Another long-standing record could have been broken if Bryan Robson had been more selfish. Pulled down for the penalty decision, he got up and handed the ball to Muhren who was the team's penalty-taker. Only Stan Mortensen, in 1953, has scored a hat-trick in a Wembley FA Cup Final and no Red would have begrudged Robbo re-writing history.

I travelled to both games by car with Bri, Colin Green, Tezzer Lomax and Beef. We had taken a bottle of champagne with us on the Saturday – well it was the Atkinson era – but it stayed in the cool bag. On the Thursday, in the back streets of Wembley Borough, we raised a glass to Big Ron for delivering us our fifth FA Cup success and his first major trophy at Old Trafford. Liverpool won the league by eleven points with Watford pipping us for the runners-up spot. Nevertheless, third place, a League Cup Final appearance and FA Cup winners tasted sweet enough.

United were undefeated at home in all competitions in 1982/83 for the only time since 1896/97 and would be back in Europe the following season. Big Ron's side was ready for a full assault on Liverpool's title supremacy.

14

SO DON'T YIELD
TO THE FORTUNES
YOU SOMETIMES
SEE AS FATE

Ron Atkinson had given Manchester United its glamour back. Not just the guy himself as he beamed at us from United's match day programme with a golden tan, immaculate pale grey suit and elegant cream shoes. Top three finishes, Wembley finals, entertaining football home and away and packed terraces – this felt like Manchester United again.

There was just one blot on the landscape – Liverpool. Not the city itself, although now I think about it … no, I mean the football team. As much as we despised their success you looked on with envy as they continued to pile up the trophies at home and abroad. We desperately wanted the league title that would make us champions of England and provide entry into the European Cup. By the summer of 1983, Liverpool had won fourteen titles, seven in the previous eleven seasons. United had gone sixteen seasons without that crown and it was really beginning to hurt. The three European Cups that Liverpool had won rubbed salt in those wounds.

When Bill Shankly left Anfield in 1974 I thought that would signal the end to Liverpool's renaissance that swept in with the Beatles in the early 1960s. Bob Paisley was anonymous to most football followers so how could he possibly fill the shoes of the enigmatic Scot and at the age of 55? How wrong we were. Paisley took Liverpool to even greater heights becoming the first and only manager to win the European Cup three times. But now he had retired and in came 62-year-old Joe Fagan. Surely this was a golden opportunity to halt Liverpool's dominance?

United scored only fifty-six goals in forty-two league games during 1982/83. Big Ron's year-long search for a striker continued. Celtic star Charlie Nicholas was the main target for Liverpool, United and Arsenal that summer. He had scored fifty goals the previous season and was crowned Scottish Footballer of the Year. Surprisingly, he opted for the bright lights of London rather than the North West. Arsenal paid £800,000. Big Ron signed 30-year-old Arthur Graham for £50,000 from Leeds instead.

The 1983/84 season heralded two significant innovations for the top tier of English football. Firstly, ITV and BBC were allowed to show league matches live on Friday nights or Sunday afternoons. Nowadays, it's difficult to imagine the impact that had for football fans. Only FA Cup Finals and international tournaments had been broadcast live. The second innovation was the sponsorship of the English First Division. It was renamed The Canon First Division after the company delivering leading edge imaging technologies. That is cameras and photocopiers to me and you. So, after ninety-five years, the Football League decided to sell its soul to corporate patronage. Since 1983 we've had Canon, Carling, Today and Barclays incorporated into the name of our top flight.

Despite losing our eighteen-month unbeaten home record to Nottingham Forest in the second game United got off to a good start. By mid-October we were top and had beaten Liverpool in the league and Charity Shield. Progress was made in the League Cup and European Cup Winners' Cup. Tricky ties against Dukla Prague and Spartak Varna were overcome to put United into the March quarter-finals.

Throughout that winter it was nip and tuck between Liverpool and United with both sides dropping points to teams in the lower half of the table. We stayed in Liverpool's slipstream, just lacking that impetus to set the pace. A lot was being expected of 18-year-old Whiteside. Atkinson dipped into the transfer market to freshen up his strike force but it wasn't the big signing United supporters felt was necessary.

Garth Crooks came on loan from Spurs. We were shopping in the bargain basement again. Crooks had been a regular scorer for Stoke and at White Hart Lane, winning two FA Cups, but the goals had dried up and he had been pushed out by Alan Brazil. That is the Alan Brazil we tried to sign but lost out when we wouldn't pay the fee. Crooks stayed for two months, playing seven times and scoring twice, but he didn't inspire confidence and returned to London. United's manager settled on giving 20-year-old reserve Mark Hughes a run in the first team.

As spring arrived United's title hopes were very much alive after an undefeated run stretching back to early December. We just needed Fagan's men to slip. On Friday 16 March, the BBC broadcast Liverpool's game live from Southampton and thousands of Reds watched with delight as the Saints won 2-0. United had a chance to go top with only ten games left. The following day we destroyed Arsenal 4-0, Charlie Nicholas *et al.*, and the cacophony of noise from the Stretford End captured a confidence inside Old Trafford that the title was a very real possibility.

Four days later that confidence was reinforced when we played the second leg of the European Cup Winners' Cup quarter-final against Barcelona. In Spain we had been unlucky to lose 2-0 with the Catalonians scoring the second in ninetieth minute. The return game on 21 March has gone down in United folklore and rightly so. An all-ticket crowd of 58,547 raised the roof as two-goal Bryan Robson led United to a 3-0 victory in one of the finest comebacks in the club's history. The great Spanish club, with Maradona and Schuster in their ranks, were humbled that night as United reached the semi-finals.

The run-in for the title was on and the Red Army descended on Nottingham the following Saturday only for a freak storm to flood the pitch an hour or so before kick-off. We were driving into the city centre when it came on the radio that the game was off. We couldn't believe our luck, March 24 and a match postponed due to bad weather. Liverpool were playing in the League Cup Final that weekend so our postponement was a lost opportunity to keep the momentum going and put pressure on the Scousers.

There was no rain at West Brom a week later, but our spirits were dampened by a 2-0 defeat. Liverpool beat Watford to regain top spot by two points. What happened next was bizarre on two counts. Firstly, both teams stumbled badly, each winning two, losing one and drawing three of their next six games. Secondly, their sequence of results matched exactly – won, lost, drew, won, drew, drew. So the two-point gap remained throughout April.

The pain was excruciating for United supporters. With the Holy Grail within touching distance and our great rivals displaying uncharacteristic vulnerability, we faltered against sides outside the top six. The defeat was at relegated Notts County.

We simply needed to string a couple of wins together but it proved too much. The matching sequence of results was broken on Monday 7 May when we lost at Ipswich and Liverpool beat Coventry. A point the following week brought Liverpool their fifteenth league title. They equalled Huddersfield and Arsenal's record of winning the First Division three times in a row. Later that month they would win their fourth European Cup, beating Roma on penalties in Rome. Three trophies in Joe Fagan's first year as manager. We could only despair.

Our capitulation over the last lap let in Southampton and Nottingham Forest to finish second and third respectively. All season the pundits had talked up this great two-horse race because the Reds of Manchester and Merseyside were so far out in front. Not content with their own success, the Scousers mocked our misery all summer by reminding us that we had finished fourth in a two-horse race.

In the Cup Winners' Cup semi-final we met a Juventus side containing Platini, Boniek, Paulo Rossi and Gentile. A 1-1 draw in Manchester was always going to make the away leg an uphill battle but United put on an exceptional performance. A goal down at half-time, United tore at Juventus in their own back yard, something we had failed to do in 1976. Substitute Whiteside continued his love affair with the big occasion to equalise and as the clock ticked away, United pressed for a winner. Fortune didn't favour the brave on this occasion as Rossi netted ninety seconds from time to take Juve to the final in Switzerland.

The wretched emptiness we felt at the end of 1983/84 was overwhelming. Some blamed injuries to key players as Coppell had missed the whole season while Robson, Muhren and Moses missed important games in that final stretch. Others pointed to the limited striking options and lack of strength in depth. Big Ron had played at the edge of the transfer market for the last two years when we should have been in there with the big boys. However, there was a bigger factor in our downfall. A characteristic all champions need, particularly during the run-in. This fine United side could mix it with the best on most days but the stuttering finale raised serious doubts about holding our nerve when it mattered most. Privately, most Reds knew we had bottled our best chance in sixteen years to be champions of England.

Around this time United lost three players who provided me and thousands of United supporters with some unforgettable moments. Steve Coppell's career was cut short by a bad knee injury at 28. For eight years he thrilled us, firstly as an electrifying winger who beat opponents at ease with pace or sublime dribbling skills then as an attacking midfield maestro. Coppell still holds the record for the most consecutive appearances for an outfield United player – 207 from 1977 to 1981 – and graced the famous number seven shirt.

Martin Buchan and Lou Macari were awarded testimonials against their former clubs Aberdeen and Celtic then quietly disappeared from the Old Trafford stage. Buchan, a stylish left-half in old parlance, was United's Beckenbauer. Great players always seem to have plenty of time on the ball, when Buchan had possession time stood still. In the dark days of the early 1970s, when United's galaxy of stars was dimmed one by one, Buchan shone like a beacon. Often playing with colleagues much less able, he held the defence together like a button. His pure class adorned Old Trafford for eleven years and 456 appearances, none as a substitute.

Shortly after Macari joined United, the Stretford End had a little ditty that went, 'Five-foot five and dynamite, skip to my Lou Macari.' The line summed him up perfectly. When a half-chance came along, he was explosive. Macari switched from dynamite to dynamo when his skills were needed in midfield. He would run all day for the United cause and scored some vital goals. My fondest memory was when he was thrown into a sixth round FA Cup tie against Everton in 1983. Both sides had battered the defences with chance after chance but the score remained 0-0 and we were all planning a midweek trip to Goodison for the replay. Big Ron gambled by bringing Macari on in the eighty-ninth minute and pushing him up front. In the next attack, Macari, with his back to the Stretford End goal and on the corner of the six-yard box, rose to knock a header down into Stapleton's path. Big Frank volleyed it into the far top corner and the 'End' went ballistic. The ensuing rendition of 'We're on the march with Big Ron's army, we're all going to Wembley' with 20,000 voices in unison was orgasmic.

Away from football, I had to say a sad farewell of my own when my dad passed away in December 1983. After my mum died in 1965, dad devoted nearly all his spare time to Michelle and me. He didn't get involved with another partner until we had grown up. Then he started referring to a 'friend' at work called Kath. He started visiting her regularly and in February 1979 they married and set up home in Stretford.

Whenever United played at home I would call round for a meal, watch *Football Focus* then walked round to the game with dad. He had a seat in K Stand but I still preferred standing on the Stretford End. Occasionally, for cup matches he would let his seat go and come and stand with me. We had always shared the passion for United, but now the conversations were free of the father/son angst that dominated our exchanges in my teenage years.

I called round one day in July 1983. He was sitting in his armchair but seemed a bit listless. When I mentioned it, he complained of feeling sluggish in the mornings but laughed it off. The situation didn't improve and after a few hospital visits a consultant confirmed he had a shadow on his lung that needed treatment. Four years earlier, just after he remarried, he had successfully fought throat cancer with radiotherapy at The Christie Hospital in Manchester. He was prepared for another fight and scheduled for admission on 8 November.

When I phoned Kath that night, she told me dad was there with her. The consultant had decided to abandon the treatment, send dad home and prescribe a course of tablets. The doctors had sent him home to die; there was nothing they could do to treat the cancer. Unfortunately they didn't tell Kath that information. I arranged to meet my dad's GP and he confirmed the worst. Macmillan nurses attended dad through the nights and ensured his final days were as free from pain as possible. In the early hours of 14 December, he quietly passed away.

In the weeks leading up to his death, I carried on with life as normal but I was going through the motions. My passion for work, friends, and hobbies was blunted. I remember sitting with my dad after I had watched a vital home game against Everton in early December. The morphine made him drift in and out of consciousness and in a rare moment of clarity he asked me the score. I told him we had lost 1-0 and he showed his disappointment by shaking his head gently from side to side and tutting.

I knew I was losing my dad – the score and the match didn't matter to me anymore. I desperately wanted to tell him how much he meant to me, but I couldn't find the words. He drifted into sleep again and I just sat and held his hand.

My dad's funeral was on Friday 16 December. That night United were playing at home in their first-ever live televised league match. By one of those strange quirks of fate the game was against Tottenham Hotspur, the team United had played when he took me to my first game in September 1964. I hadn't missed a home game for seventeen years and knew in my heart he wouldn't want me to miss this one. Out of respect I checked with Kath and she agreed I should go to the match. United won 4-2 in a great game reminiscent of the fixture two decades earlier. From the Stretford End I swear I could pick out my dad's empty seat at the other end, but I didn't feel sad, I knew he would be watching.

One can only imagine the meeting in the summer of 1984 between Ron Atkinson and United chairman Martin Edwards when they sat down to review the season. The financial review probably went well with United still the best supported club in England, four bumper attendances against Juve and Barcelona and more European football next season. The playing side, however, must have had both men shuffling uncomfortably in their chairs. Both knew that unless they delivered the league championship anything else they achieved would pale into insignificance. I would speculate that Big Ron advised his chairman that United had to splash out to attract the players he needed to win the league. Quite possibly the chairman reminded Ron of the board's generosity in backing the huge signings of Robson and Moses within weeks of his appointment. To which the 'Golden One' may have pointed out that that was now three years ago and he had tried to operate on a relative shoe-string budget since.

By the time the new season started United's squad had been significantly strengthened. A trio of top players came in – Gordon Strachan, Alan Brazil and Jesper Olsen. United supporters were delighted, we had expected a new striker but three international signings really was exceptional. To help finance these transfers Atkinson sold Ray Wilkins to AC Milan for £1.5 million. There was talk of Robson being courted by the Italians too but thank-fully that didn't materialise.

The new trio plus the emerging Mark Hughes meant we had quality cover in every outfield position. The challenge facing the United manager was knowing his best eleven. Frank Stapleton needed a pre-season operation and opportunity came knocking at Mark Hughes' door. Like Whiteside twelve months earlier he quickly made himself an indispensable member of the team and led United's goalscoring charts. Ron Atkinson rotated Hughes' partner, with Whiteside, Brazil and Stapleton jockeying for the position. Later in the season he moved Big Norm into midfield to replace the ageing Muhren. In defence, Graham Hogg had come through the ranks and established a centre-back berth with Kevin Moran, but faced stiff competition from Gordon McQueen and Paul McGrath.

After drawing the first four league games United got into a winning run with the team playing open, attacking football. Strachan and Olsen settled in quickly and provided great width. But a new force was emerging. Howard Kendall had brought Everton out of the doldrums. Having won the FA Cup the previous season they had their sights on the league title. Our good start was given a jolt twice in four days as October ended. Everton ripped us apart 5-0 at Goodison in the biggest defeat United suffered under Big Ron then knocked us out of the League Cup 2-1 at Old Trafford.

By the turn of the year United, Spurs and Everton battled for top spot. United's first two league fixtures of the New Year were Sheffield Wednesday and Coventry, both at Old Trafford. It was a great opportunity to push for that top spot. We lost both games. Although that didn't kill off our title chances it damaged United's credibility. Too often we still struggled against inferior opposition.

However, it wasn't our own shortcomings that lost the title. Everton's superb form from Boxing Day to early May saw them win sixteen and draw two of eighteen league games. The title was theirs with five matches to spare, amassing an incredible ninety points, twenty-three ahead of the field. They were unstoppable. United hung on to Everton's coat-tails until April but four games without a win saw us slip. Liverpool and Spurs overtook us and once again we finished fourth. The title loss wasn't quite as galling as the previous season because Everton won it rather than us blowing it. Nevertheless, given the team strengthening it was still a bitter disappointment.

Once more, our old friend the FA Cup provided our redemption. Bournemouth, Coventry, Blackburn and West Ham were comfortably despatched to reach the semi-finals where we met Liverpool again at Goodison. A thrilling 2-2 draw saw United leading twice and Liverpool clawing late equalisers in normal and extra time to force a replay at Maine Road.

The second game was even better as Liverpool pushed forward more, but United were on song right from the off with an intoxicating blend of powerful running and silky skills. First blood went to Liverpool when McGrath scored an own goal on thirty-eight minutes. United needed a pick-me-up and ninety seconds after the restart Bryan Robson delivered it. After harrying Liverpool into a mistake in midfield United's captain played a one-two with Stapleton, ran straight through the middle with the ball at his feet then unleashed a venomous left-footed shot into the top corner of Grobelaar's net from twenty-five yards.

United's young team came of age with their best performance of the season and on the hour Hughes raced on to a Strachan through-ball to blast the winner from outside the penalty area. United won 2-1 to reach Wembley. In almost identical scenes to the Barcelona game at Old Trafford twelve months earlier, Bryan Robson had to be rescued from exuberant fans who carried him shoulder high around the pitch in celebration.

Our FA Cup Final opponents were Everton, league champions and newly crowned winners of the European Cup Winners' Cup. They were favourites to make it a treble even though we were appearing in our sixth Wembley final in nine years.

Since the uninspiring days of Dave Sexton's reign the mates that watched matches with us had increased significantly. Beef and Bri were still around, as were those old warhorses Colin Green and Tezzer Lomax. In recent years I had become friends with two big families from The Height, the O'Malleys and the Branagans. Eddie O'Malley was a particularly good mate as was Christina Branagan whose father, Ken, starred for City in the 1950s. Also in the gang were Steve Heywood, a young Turk from Norweb, Mark Wileman and Fartin' Tony from Swinton who, despite his nickname, was great company. Most of us got tickets for the final and travelled to Wembley in a convoy of cars.

Harrow-on-the-Hill was our drinking hole and the King's Head with its many rooms and sprawling beer garden made us welcome for a pre-match loosener. The Wembley terraces seemed more packed than usual, uncomfortably so. Later, a scam emerged that gatemen had taken cash bribes from ticketless fans pushing the attendance beyond the 100,000 limit.

United's line-up on 18 May 1985 was: Bailey, Gidman, Albiston, Whiteside, McGrath, Moran, Robson, Strachan, Stapleton, Hughes, Olsen.

The teams showed too much respect for each other, which led to stalemate and few clear chances but on seventy-eight minutes the game exploded into life. Everton's Peter Reid capitalised on a rare McGrath error and raced towards United's penalty area. In his path stood Kevin Moran, a daunting prospect at any time but given the occasion Moran was not going to let anyone pass. Reid pushed the ball a little too far forward and Moran went in. The Everton midfielder almost somersaulted in the air, more to avoid injury rather than any cynical dive. Referee Peter Willis went for his pocket for what we thought would be a booking but red was the colour. Moran was off, the first dismissal in FA Cup Final history.

The injustice inspired United on the pitch and the terraces, our defiant chants rang out. Stapleton went to centre-half. Despite the man advantage, Everton seemed to tire. Twenty minutes into extra time United broke away. Mark Hughes, inside his own half, sprayed a pass with the outside of his boot to Norman Whiteside on the right wing. The boy wonder took the ball down the wing, edging his way along the touchline as Van Den Hauwe jockeyed him. His route to goal was blocked but he moved the ball onto his left foot, curled it round the defender and goalkeeper just inside the far post where it nestled in the net. The goal triggered wild celebrations among United's 30,000 followers as we triumphed against all odds.

The journey home was the sweetest feeling and The Wellie was rocking that night as we celebrated United winning the Cup for the sixth time. As I staggered home, I felt like the happiest man in the world. The fact that we weren't champions didn't matter for now; the Cup was ours. We had beaten both Merseyside teams on the way and stopped Everton winning a treble.

As I tottered down Minden Street where I lived I had a great idea. Outside the house was my cream-coloured Triumph Toledo car which I'd had for five years and cost me a shed load of money in repairs. I had run it into the ground and it was going to the scrap yard that week. So why not paint it with red slogans and take it on its penultimate journey to welcome United home tomorrow? I used to have lots of good ideas after a few pints of Joseph Holt's finest ales but most of them never saw the light of day. This one did.

Next morning I bought a can of pillar-box red paint from the local DIY shop. For the next two hours I scrambled all over the car daubing graffiti about our cup victory. Along one side I painted 'SCOUSEBUSTERS', along the other 'WHERE'S YOUR TREBLE GONE, HOWARD?' On the bonnet I wrote 'FA CUP WINNERS 1985' and on the boot 'THE REF'S A MORON NOT YOU KEVIN' – which seemed hilarious at the time! The *piece de resistance* would be the roof which I saved until last. There I would have 'GOD BLESS NORMAN' in reverence to our goalscoring hero.

When I was at school I was okay at Maths, English and a couple of languages but when it came to anything creative I was crap. Art, metalwork, engineering and drawing just weren't in my DNA and never have been. I knew this, so I tried very very carefully to get my rooftop artwork spot on. I kneeled precariously on the roof, desperate to write neatly with just the right spacing. I managed to get 'GOD' painted on centrally at the rear of the roof, then 'BLESS' in the middle below that, leaving one third of the space for 'NORMAN'.

I gently brush-stroked in the N, the O, the R, the M, the A then … shit, I had run out of roof! There was no room for the second 'N'. Bloody hell! I stood up and looked at my botched handiwork which read 'GOD BLESS NORMA'. What a prat! I sat there with my head in my hands, distraught. In the end, all I could do was paint over the 'A' and leave it as GOD BLESS NORM. It didn't look great with a big red blotch after his abbreviated name but it would have to do. I went to collect Mark Wileman who wanted to see the homecoming. I hadn't told him about the car.

'Bloody hell, Molly, what've yer done here?' he greeted me as he came out of his house.

'Oh, don't worry, I'm scrapping it next week,' I reassured him.

'I'm not bothered about that, it's being seen in it all the way along the A56 with thousands watching. We're going to look a right pair of tossers!' he replied and gave me a look somewhere between a smirk and a growl as he climbed into the passenger seat.

If there's a good laugh to be had I don't worry too much about detail but I could see he felt uncomfortable. Respectability in numbers, I thought, so we called for Chris Branagan and her mate Rebecca on the way. They were up for it as long as they could sit in the back and hide if necessary. We set off for Dunham Massey where the team's open-top bus was due to start its journey through the suburbs to Manchester Town Hall. We drove out of the city centre, along the route the bus would be coming but in the opposite direction. The plan was to turn the car round just before the bus set off, get right in front of it and escort the team all the way back into Manchester. There were thousands already lining the pavements and as we passed they cheered and laughed at our decorated vehicle. Even the policemen stationed at each set of traffic lights found it amusing.

'I told you it was a good idea Mark, people think it's great!' I said with a satisfied grin.

On the outbound journey through Sale, the Toledo seemed to be losing power. Reluctant to abort the plan I carried on, but I couldn't get more than twenty miles per hour from the car. Suddenly a dreadful grinding noise started. The reason I was scrapping the car was that the crankshaft was in a bad way. I couldn't risk going any further, we had to get home before it conked out altogether. So I turned the car round and headed back along the route the players' bus would take just minutes later.

The crowds had increased and they lined the road six-deep. We chugged along at about ten miles per hour with a horrible din coming from the engine and gaudy red lettering strewn across every surface on view. Kids looking on found it was hilarious, they must have thought clowns had been hired as a warm-up act for United's homecoming. As the crowds cheered and waved at us I kept smiling but felt increasingly uneasy. We travelled through Stretford with the car spluttering and back-firing – it was like a poor man's *Chitty Chitty Bang Bang*. By this time the crowd was in hysterics, Chris and Beccie in the back couldn't take the humiliation and hid under their coats. Mark looked at me and in his deadpan style said, 'Molly, is this thing safe?'

'Yeah, it's fine, don't worry,' I said with blind optimism.

Just then, smoke started rising from under the bonnet and beneath the dashboard, there was a terrible smell of burning.

'Jesus! Everyone out of the car, quick!' I screamed, switching the ignition off. The four doors flew open and we dashed to safety.

The car had come to a stop at the crossroads with Sir Matt Busby Way, or Warwick Road as it was then, right outside Lou Macari's chip shop. The packed crowd gave us a thunderous round of applause. By this time I was wishing I did have a big red nose, a stupid hat and a long jacket with a button-hole that squirted water – at least the disguise would hide my embarrassment.

Once the imminent danger of an explosion had passed, a policeman helped us push the car to the side of the road. We let it cool down, drove it slowly down the back streets and parked up near the Mancunian Way flyover. There we stood and watched the United team bus, FA Cup and all, go past in all its glory. Norman Whiteside looked over towards us, got the attention of a few of his team mates, pointed out our car and gave us a wave.

'There you go, Mark, it was worth it in the end!' I smiled

'Sure it was Molly' he replied, unconvinced. 'I'll go and phone me Dad to come and tow us home.'

He knew how to party that Mark Wileman!

15

IS A DREAM A LIE
IF IT DON'T COME TRUE,
OR IS IT
SOMETHING WORSE?

If 1966 was a great year for English football, then 1985 was its nadir. The stain of football hooliganism saw the game tarnished almost beyond repair. Late-season cup ties at Chelsea and Luton were marred by mass pitch invasions where fans fought running battles. The police were overwhelmed. At the European Cup Final on 29 May a dreadful disaster unfurled before the Liverpool and Juventus game at the Heysel Stadium, Belgium. Marauding Liverpool supporters charged at Juve fans and as the Italians fled there was severe crushing against a retaining wall at the side of the ground. Eventually the wall collapsed and thirty-nine people who had gone to see a football match never returned. Eighteen days earlier an old wooden stand at Bradford City's ground caught fire during their game with Lincoln. Many supporters were trapped by the flames and fifty-six lost their lives.

All were distressing but the live broadcasts from Heysel which clearly captured the cause and effect sent shockwaves throughout the civilised world. The truth is, it came as no great surprise to most football supporters, especially those who had travelled abroad with England or any club team. Since the early 1970s English fans invariably ran into trouble abroad. Hooliganism had gone relatively unchecked in Britain for two decades. In the first half of that period fans didn't travel abroad in numbers but as European excursions become affordable we simply exported the problem.

There was an eternal merry-go-round of blame in the UK. The FA and Football League blamed the clubs, the clubs blamed society, society blamed the fans, the fans blamed the police, the police blamed the Government and so on. Nobody took responsibility, everyone passed the buck. I heard a wise old saying many years ago, 'When all's said and done, there's more said than done.' When it came to tackling football hooliganism the saying was never more true. Following Heysel, the European and world football authorities took the decision out of the FA's hands. Enough was enough; English clubs received a five-year ban from all UEFA competitions. Liverpool were handed a further three-year embargo as punishment for their fans' direct involvement in the disaster. The British Government and police authorities began intense work tackling domestic hooliganism but it would take one more tragedy to force English football into radical action.

Ron Atkinson had brought the FA Cup back to Manchester twice in three years. Before Fergie's era of a trophy almost every season, this was no mean achievement. In the previous ninety-nine years we had won the cup just four times. Big Ron had assembled a formidable side, the seventy-seven league goals in 1984/85 was the highest since 1968. The defence looked solid, McGrath and Hogg forging a strong partnership with Moran there if needed. Mark Hughes had an incredible first full season, scoring twenty-four times in fifty-six appearances and collecting the PFA Young Player of the Year award. Whiteside was turning into a midfield maestro, while Strachan and Olsen provided width, skill and goals during their debut seasons at Old Trafford. Alan Brazil struggled, making twenty-one starts out of a possible sixty and scoring just nine times.

The colossus in Atkinson's team was Bryan Robson. I could fill this page with superlatives of his ability, leadership and bravery and still not do him justice. Robbo was the embodiment of every United die-hard and he carried that on to the pitch whenever he played. United began 1985/86 with a first eleven nearing its peak and more than capable of capturing the league title: Bailey, Gidman, Albiston, Whiteside, McGrath, Hogg, Robson, Strachan, Hughes, Stapleton, Olsen. A drab 2-0 defeat to Everton in the Charity Shield gave no indication of what came next. United re-wrote their own record books by winning the first ten league matches. The previous club record was six straight wins in 1905. In this book

I've tried to avoid getting too bogged-down in stacks of statistics, preferring to throw in some interesting titbits as we stroll through the seasons. However, 1985/86 does warrant closer scrutiny simply because of the amazing opening run and the dénouement that followed. Beware, though, it's not for the squeamish.

Thirty points in the bag before October gave United a nine-point lead over second-placed Liverpool. Aside from the results United's football was breathtakingly beautiful. Opponents weren't just beaten, they were blown away. For the first time since I started watching United, older supporters who had seen the 1948 side, the Babes or Best, Law and Charlton admitted that the current team was up there with the best. The 3-0 defeat of Newcastle on 4 September, in particular, had all corners of Old Trafford purring with delight. We were witnessing something very special.

United had the best home attendances even then, but the crowds came flooding back with gates regularly over 50,000. We couldn't get enough of it. United's souvenir shop starting selling videos of each match, not just highlights, the full ninety minutes. They cost £14.95, a princely sum, but sold like hot cakes. The football was that good. United supporters were ecstatic. Ron's planning was coming to fruition and at every opportunity we made a point of telling the Scousers our day had come. We lapped it up. This had to be our year for the league title.

During this run there was one small hiccup but it was quickly discarded as an irrelevance. The 1985 FA Cup triumph should have given United entry into the European Cup Winners' Cup but the post-Heysel ban scuppered our adventures abroad, as it did for Everton, Norwich, Spurs, Liverpool and Southampton. Those six teams were invited to play in a new competition called the Football League Super Cup. It was seen by fans for what it was – a desperate money-spinner to replace the revenue from UEFA. The six were split into two groups of three and each team played the other two home and away. The top two in each group progressed to a two-legged semi-final and then a Wembley final.

As you can imagine the public's appetite for this concoction was tepid at best. United were grouped with Everton and Norwich with games played between September and December. The Football League managed to get sponsorship and the competition was renamed the ScreenSport Super Cup

after the cable TV company. We lost home and away to Everton
and drew twice with Norwich to crash out of the inaugural
contest. Few tears were shed.

The record number of opening wins in English top flight football is eleven, a feat achieved by Spurs in 1960 on their way to the
first double of the twentieth century. The eyes of the world were
on United as 7,000 Reds travelled down to Luton on 5 October
to see if we could equal the record. When Hughes gave us the
lead in the second-half we were on cloud nine but Brian Stein's
late equaliser preserved Tottenham's record. Initially there was
a feeling of disappointment but Liverpool lost that day so we
extended our lead to ten points. Big Ron picked up Manager
of the Month awards for August and September while United
recovered from the Luton set-back by beating QPR, Chelsea and
Coventry and drawing with Liverpool. The table at the end of
October was the stuff of dreams:

	P	W	D	L	F	A	Pts
Man United	15	13	2	0	35	6	41
Liverpool	15	9	4	2	32	16	31
Sheff Wed	15	8	4	3	24	23	28

November saw us stumble with two away defeats and two home
draws. The goals dried up but more worrying were the injuries
we collected on a weekly basis. Gidman and Strachan missed
several games, but crucially Bryan Robson picked up calf and
hamstring injuries After starring in the opening twelve league
games he played only once more before the end of January.
United weren't a one-man team but Robson's impact was so
great we just weren't the same force without him. Ron Atkinson
moved centre back Paul McGrath to midfield, but it was a
holding role at best.

To address the goal famine, the manager shuffled the pack with
various combinations of Hughes, Stapleton and Brazil through the
winter. Alan Brazil never made his mark when given the opportunity. He reminded me very much of Garry Birtles, battling hard
but very little came off for him. His striker's luck deserted him,
chances would go just the wrong side of the post or the keeper
would pull off a brilliant save. Like Birtles, Brazil had made his
name by latching on to through-balls and beating the goalkeeper

one on one. He was brilliant in those situations but United didn't play that way and the striker struggled to adapt. By the spring of 1986, Atkinson had seen enough and off-loaded Brazil to Coventry for less than half the £650,000 he paid for him.

Liverpool put us out of the League Cup at Anfield but the focus for our supporters was 100 per cent on winning the league. United picked up a couple of wins before going into a Christmas double-header at home to Arsenal and away to Everton. There was little festive cheer around Old Trafford as we lost both games. Our lead at the top was down to four points and alarm bells were ringing. United's performances at home had become unconvincing. The players seemed to lose confidence playing on the stage that had been a fortress eighteen months earlier. The crowd in turn became very nervous and the atmosphere that used to intimidate the opposition simply evaporated.

Further injuries forced Atkinson into blooding reserves Clayton Blackmore, Billy Garton and Mark Dempsey then dipping into the transfer market to sign tenacious full-back Colin Gibson from Villa and Everton veteran Mark Higgins. Off the field a very black cloud was looming. In the run up to Christmas there were rumours that Barcelona were tracking Mark Hughes. The player had a clause in his contract that if any club came in with a £2 million bid United had to release him. The clause was instigated by United's board to protect the club's interests, believing nobody would bid so much.

The board under-estimated how highly rated Hughes had become during the previous season, especially in Spain where football fans had witnessed his remarkably acrobatic goal for Wales against their countrymen. The rumours persisted and by early January even David Meek was writing about it in United's programme. The prospect of losing Hughes riled United's faithful and the incessant press speculation became a massive distraction

United's form after the turn of the year was terribly inconsistent. From 11 January we didn't win two consecutive league games. Champions Everton had put together the best run of the trailing pack. On 2 November the Toffees were seventh in the table and seventeen points behind United. A sequence of ten wins and two draws closed the gap. On Saturday, 1 February 1986 the unthinkable happened. Everton knocked United off their perch at the top. The early season ten-point

lead had gone. There was a terrible feeling of desperation
setting in, certainly with the supporters and I suspect with the
players. Atkinson's response was to sign defender John Sivebæk
and diminutive striker Terry Gibson and throw them in at the
deep end. February also saw Bryan Robson return to the team.
Perhaps he could salvage our title challenge? The league table at
the end of February read:

	P	W	D	L	F	A	Pts
Everton	30	19	5	6	69	35	62
Man United	29	18	5	6	52	23	59
Liverpool	30	15	9	6	57	33	54

In any other season the table might have warmed our hearts, but
in this race we had been a lap in front. Tellingly, the club shop
had stopped selling the match videos! Our torment increased and
March opened with a surprise defeat at lowly Southampton. Four
days later in a drawn FA Cup tie at Upton Park, Robson broke his
collarbone for the second time in fifteen months. Most believed
his season was over. West Ham won the replay 2-0 at Old Trafford
and just 29,733 turned up to witness our drab performance.

Big Ron dipped into the transfer market again, buying Peter
Davenport from Forest to replace Stapleton. The striker made
no difference as United finished the month with one win in six
league matches. Liverpool joined Everton at the top:

	P	W	D	L	F	A	Pts
Liverpool	36	20	10	6	73	36	70
Everton	35	21	7	7	74	38	70
Man United	35	19	8	8	57	28	65

Bryan Robson returned to the side just twenty-four days after
the injury to his shoulder. It seemed far too soon but with the
support of a special brace he made it through to the end of the
season. I am no doctor and I've no evidence Robson was rushed
back but a similar injury the previous season sidelined him for
nine weeks. Robbo did his best but was carrying the shoulder
which prevented him being the all-action player we knew and
loved. In the Mexico World Cup that summer his collarbone
would go again.

By now United supporters were just hoping against hope that somehow we would recapture that autumn magic. A 3-1 win at Coventry on 5 April closed the gap to two points and inspired hope. Almost inevitably, that was dashed four days later when Chelsea came to Old Trafford and struck a mortal blow with a 2-1 win. Three days on, Sheffield Wednesday put us out of our misery by inflicting another home defeat. The dream was over. The marathon that started with a glorious sprint had slipped from our grasp. Liverpool won eleven of their last twelve games to pip Everton to the title. West Ham won six of the last seven to finish third – their highest league position ever. United, once again, came fourth. The final table made depressing reading:

	P	W	D	L	F	A	Pts
Liverpool	42	26	10	6	89	37	88
Everton	42	26	8	8	87	41	86
West Ham	42	26	6	10	74	40	84
Man United	42	22	10	10	70	36	76

Any Manchester United supporter who lived through this period won't need reminding how low we felt. Although on paper we were in the race for the title right up to the finale, our form from early November resembled a mid-table side at best. We played twenty-seven games, winning nine, drawing eight and losing ten. Also in November, United led rivals Liverpool and Everton by ten and seventeen points respectively yet they finished twelve and ten points ahead of us.

United's home form turned out to be our Achilles heel. After an opening run of seven wins and a draw, the remaining thirteen games served up five victories, four draws and four defeats and a ridiculously low return of seventeen goals.

While injuries are an occupational hazard in football, United did suffer more than most during the season. Key players were out for weeks rather than a couple of games. Injuries didn't affect our strikers, but loss of form did. The early flood of goals dried to a trickle. The magnificent Mark Hughes was top scorer with seventeen in the league, followed by an impressive eleven from Jesper Olsen, but Stapleton netted only seven, Whiteside just four and Brazil a meagre three. The emergency buys failed to deliver too.

Davenport netted one in eleven appearances and Terry Gibson
didn't get off the mark at all.

The handling of Mark Hughes' move to Barcelona was a terrible own goal. United's hands may have been tied but the board
should have kept the business under wraps until the end of the
season. In the summer of 2008, we saw how rumours of Cristiano
Ronaldo's move to Real Madrid sold millions of papers around
the world and had United's communications department working
round the clock. So imagine the effect of the Hughes transfer
saga running through several months of a season in which United
have the best chance of winning the league in almost twenty
years. Hughes moved to Barcelona in the 1986 close season.

Creeping desperation was another feature of the 1985/86 campaign. Big Ron had set out his stall with some astute buys and
blended them well with the existing squad to form a very useful
outfit. His good work really started to pay dividends with that
unbelievable opening run. When the wobble became a banana
skin the manager bought five new players and threw them straight
into the mix. That must have come across to the other players as
a sign of nerves. Buying two new strikers, Terry Gibson and Peter
Davenport, late in the season smacked of a last throw of the dice
rather than a carefully planned strategy. Likewise, Robson's return
in a shoulder brace. Teams just don't win championships like that.

When the gambles failed, I believe it did irreparable damage
to Big Ron's reputation. But perhaps the key weakness had been
around for some years. Atkinson's autumn 1985 team looked destined to out-shine the Old Trafford greats who had gone before.
But those sides possessed a strength that got them through the
more mundane fixtures and achieved results on days when the
football wasn't flowing. When a top player was injured an able
reserve would come in and cover that role seamlessly. The great
United teams had consistency and they had bottle. None of
Atkinson's exciting sides in the previous five years demonstrated
they had enough of either quality to win the title.

For United supporters who had been in search of the Holy
Grail since 1967, the 1985/86 season left us scarred. We weren't
just disappointed – we were traumatised. Looking back now, after
twenty-six years in Fergie's Promised Land, we can smile about it.
In 1986 it was difficult to see a funny side despite being the butt
of so many jokes especially from the Scousers. It hurt more than

anything in football had hurt before and shook our belief system to the very core. Would we ever be truly great again? Would we ever see United crowned champions of England once more? Would we ever walk among Europe's finest and hold that giant cup aloft like Charlton had done in 1968? The answer had always been an optimistic but confident yes! The winter of 1986 tested that conviction to the maximum.

In bringing the curtain down on this eventful season, I realise I must have stretched the reader's curiosity to the extreme in not revealing the outcome of the ScreenSport Super Cup. Well, Liverpool and Everton eventually won their semi-finals but the apathy that gripped the competition reached a climax as both clubs failed to agree on a suitable date for the final. It was carried over to the start of the following season when Everton fielded a reserve team and lost 7-2 on aggregate to their neighbours. Rumour has it that Ian Rush threw the trophy to an Everton ball boy as Liverpool left Goodison and suggested he keep it in his bedroom as a souvenir. There would be no second season for the Super Cup.

On a personal note, during that unbeaten winning start, I did something that was totally out of character – I went on holiday in mid-season and missed a home match. Worse still, the match I missed was against Liverpool. Even writing this, many years later, I feel a terrible glow of embarrassment coming over me. It was the first United home game I had missed since 18 March 1967, a run of more than eighteen years. I wish I could offer up some earth-shattering reason for not being there. The truth is, in the previous eighteen months I had got a couple of promotions at work, there had been a massive re-organisation and I had been working really long hours. I simply needed to get away for a break. Two mates, Mike Horseman and Frank Batty, were off to Crete for the last of the Mediterranean sun and I decided to join them.

I wouldn't blame you for chucking this book in the bin in disgust at this point, with a cursory 'tosser!' thrown in for good measure. What a lame excuse. Anyway, on Saturday, 19 October 1985 the three of us huddled around a small transistor radio at 5.20 p.m. Cretan (I think I've spelt that right!) time and tuned into the BBC World Service to catch the second half of the 1-1 draw. It's funny looking back how Mike Horseman is always there when I lapse badly from my United faith, like some modern day Beelzebub. Bless him.

After that Liverpool match and up to May 1988 I missed a further four home games until I came to my senses and embarked on another unbroken run. In the last twenty-five years I've missed just two home matches, Barnet in the League Cup in October 2005 and Fulham in the league in 2011. I hope you've followed that closely; there's a short test at the end of the book.

Throughout the summer of 1986 the inquests continued. David Meek, who had covered United's games for the *Manchester Evening News* since the Munich crash, wrote, 'United's failure to win the League Championship for 19 years has become something of a phobia. It makes life difficult for managers and players whose success, or lack of it, is measured instantly.' Ron Atkinson labelled it 'a maddening season' but in acknowledging the disappointments he still felt 'we are very very close to having something really exceptional at Old Trafford'. Hope springs eternal.

For 1986/87 Big Ron kept faith with the players who had served him for three years, with Davenport in for the departed Hughes and Chris Turner given his chance in goal. Bryan Robson missed the first four matches recovering from his shoulder injury and United lost three times in the opening week. The first home game attracted a disappointing 43,306 against West Ham. A draw and a win offered some hope to the faithful but three more defeats on the bounce left United joint bottom. Eight games played and six defeats. Big Ron needed a miracle, instead he got a mini revival with two wins and three draws in an undefeated October.

A 4-1 thrashing in a League Cup replay at Southampton sealed Ron Atkinson's fate. He was relieved of his duties on 5 November 1986. The last two home games had attracted gates of 23,639 and 36,946. Enough to convince the board the club needed a new impetus.

United's playing record under Ron Atkinson was:

Played	W	D	L	F	A	W%	D%	L%
292	146	79	67	461	266	50	27	23

Based on win percentage, the statistics place Big Ron a very respectable fourth out of seventeen United managers. Atkinson can take pride he has been beaten only by Ferguson, Mangnall and Busby and his games lost percentage of twenty-three is second only to Sir Alex's 18 per cent. An impressive record and one achieved by playing the United way. However, his draw percentage of twenty-seven is second only to Sexton's 32 per cent in United's top eleven managers. If only Ron could have turned some of those home draws into victories against lower placed teams we would have seen that elusive championship trophy at Old Trafford in the 1980s.

In appraising each United manager from the last fifty years I've considered three questions – Were they given enough time? Were they given enough resources? Did they deliver what was expected? Ron Atkinson occupied the hotseat for over five seasons – the longest serving manager in the era between Busby and Fergie. By any standards that was sufficient time. As regards to resources, well, within four months of his appointment Atkinson smashed the British transfer record to bring Bryan Robson to Old Trafford. He signed another twelve top names in five years excluding the loan players – an array of talent that didn't come cheap. The United board certainly backed the manager in the quest to return United to the top of English football and therein lays the crunch. Despite sufficient time and adequate funding we didn't win the league title. Incredibly, United never even came second under Big Ron.

For all his strengths and talent, I believe Atkinson's downfall hinged on three factors. I have touched on two already, the failure to instil consistency into his sides and the absence of real bottle in the white-hot furnace of the title run-in. The third factor was Big Ron's failure to bring a top striker to Old Trafford when we needed it most. To be fair, he signed a star in Frank Stapleton right at the start of his tenure then got lucky with Whiteside and Hughes coming through the ranks in 1982 and 1983. But Atkinson knew if United were to win the elusive title we needed another top scorer. The bargain buys fell well short, he bought poorly with Alan Brazil and panicked into signing Davenport and Terry Gibson as our 'unassailable' lead disappeared. By that time he was trying to mend the roof after the rain had started. I believe another top goal scorer in the squad around 1983 and 1984 would have brought us our most coveted prize and maybe more besides. Perhaps Ron simply lacked the eye for a top striker? He let Beardsley slip from under his nose.

Back in January 1979, when West Brom were chasing Liverpool for the league title, Atkinson broke the British transfer record and made centre-forward David Mills the first £500,000 footballer. Mills would score only six goals in fifty-nine appearances for Albion before being transferred for a mere £30,000 three years later. West Brom finished third in 1979. Food for thought, maybe?

Ron Atkinson did his best for United but couldn't take us beyond cup glory. That was the story of his managerial career. He also brought cup success to Aston Villa and Sheffield Wednesday but in a number of epic challenges for the league title with West Brom, United and Villa between 1979 and 1993 Big Ron's teams would fade as the finishing post came in sight. He never managed a team to the English championship.

In Atkinson's final week at Old Trafford, the club dismantled the thirty-year-old floodlight pylons and replaced them with huge spotlights attached to the perimeter of the stadium roof. The changes would herald a new luminary. One who would shine brighter than any manager in United's remarkable history, but not before a few fuses had blown.

'Pete, we need another striker, any ideas?'
'Have you looked at that Jimmy Greenhoff, Tommy?'

Ipswich 1976 – the Van Crowd. Reds from Salford, Manchester, Bury and Runcorn.

Porto Away, 1977. Pete Ward and Bri Foy are holding the flag.

Cup triumph! Car Triumph! Handiwork ... tragic.

Montpellier 1991, with Chris Livesey, Roger Woods and Pete Seymour. Chris is smiling – I've not told her we're hitchhiking back yet.

Dumbarton, 1991. Ok, kid, I'll ask you one more time, is this the man who held up that banner?!

Norwich Airport, 1993. Respect.

Turkish Delight, anyone? Hell, 1993.

Friendly match, 1995, with nephew Simon, niece Carly and their dad, Pete Seymour, just minutes before the fashion police took me (us) in for questioning.

Nou Camp, 26 May 1999 – a night to remember.

Barcelona, 1999 – a crowd to remember.

Manchester, 2008. European Capital of Trophies. From left to right: Col Green, me, Tez Lomax, Frank Cooper, Pete Seymour and Mike Stewart.

16

SWING FROM HIGH TO DEEP, EXTREMES OF SWEET AND SOUR

Nowadays, when you read articles about Fergie's reign at Old Trafford there is always a concise summary of those early years. The gist will be ... arrived 1986, had a troubled start, Mark Robins saved his skin in an FA Cup tie at Nottingham Forest, we won the cup in 1990 ... and everything since has been pure silver. Given the unprecedented success we've enjoyed over the last twenty-three years that's the way it should be, of course.

For those of us around at the time the revival wasn't that simple or instant. After I made my protest in December 1989, United's fortunes continued to plummet. We didn't win a league match between mid-November and mid-February, drawing five and losing six. Goals were at a premium with just five in that period. We sank to seventeenth in the league, one place above the relegation threshold. A couple of wins kept us hovering above the bottom three with just eight games left.

As we prepared for a battle to avoid the drop, United's form came good with four straight league victories. There was no silver bullet, the team simply settled down around the mainstays of the campaign – Leighton, Martin, Bruce, Phelan, Pallister, Ince, McClair, Hughes and Wallace. We finished in thirteenth place with forty-eight points. Now, here comes the inevitable, I'm afraid. Liverpool won the league. Seventy-nine points secured an eighteenth league title, their tenth in fifteen years, an unparalleled feat in the league's 102-year history up to that point. Here is the good news. I am delighted to announce that this is the last time in this book that I am obliged to report a league title success for the Anfield club. Hallelujah!

Salvation for United supporters, and Fergie, came in the FA Cup but few were predicting that when the third-round draw sent us to Cloughie's Nottingham Forest. Given the events of November and December, the match attracted special attention. The BBC chose it as their live match on the Sunday afternoon, the media could smell the blood of a sacking and talked the tie into a 'win or bust' situation for Fergie. The speculation wasn't without foundation. United supporters were watching each game with increasing anxiety as the results continued to go against us. The tension wasn't caused by the media; it was caused by what had been happening out on the pitch over several months. Yet there is something very special about United supporters and their loyalty to the club – particularly in times of adversity. The unique Manchester swagger kicks in, we come out fighting with a defiance that is unrivalled in British football and we rally round the team in numbers.

That Sunday afternoon, 7 January 1990, brought a show of strength that made you proud to follow Manchester United. We were given the lower tier of what is now the Brian Clough Stand, 7,000 seats which ran the full length of the pitch crammed with devoted Reds. Any concerns about the manager, chairman or league plight were put aside as we roared United on. The attendance was 23,072 so we had nearly one-third of the support but United's contingent sounded like 70,000 and being so close to the pitch it really lifted the players. The United team missing Robson, Ince and Wallace was: Leighton, Anderson, Martin, Bruce, Phelan, Pallister, Beardsmore, Blackmore, McClair, Hughes, Robins.

Forest were a strong and talented side with a good record in cup competitions. The FA Cup was the one trophy that had eluded Brian Clough and he knew the sands of time were running out. Led by captain Stuart Pearce his lads were breathing fire as the tie kicked off. Forest tore into United but we stood firm, defending superbly and attacking at every opportunity. Every United man was playing for the shirt. The first half ended goalless but on fifty-five minutes United engineered a brilliant move. Full-back Martin found Mark Hughes wide on the left just inside Forest's half. Hughes looked up, saw Mark Robins racing through the centre and played an exquisite curling ball with the outside of his right boot. The ball bounced once and as it rose up Robins nipped in front of Pearce to nod it home. The celebrations in the stand were worthy of a Wembley winner and I've never heard a louder rendition of 'We're on the march with Fergie's army'. For the remaining thirty-five minutes the City Ground reverberated to a repertoire of United anthems.

We will never really know if Mark Robins' strike saved Fergie's bacon but there's no doubt it was a vital victory. Defeat would have left United staring into an abyss whereas now we had something to build on. And build on it we did. Amid poor league results we carved out Cup wins at Hereford, Newcastle and Sheffield United to reach the semi-finals for the first time in five years. Oldham provided the unlikely opposition and by the time we met at Maine Road, United had started to win league matches.

One issue still causing real concern among United's faithful was goalkeeper Jim Leighton. Arriving from Aberdeen in the summer of 1988 he had an excellent first season, playing in all forty-eight fixtures and conceding only thirty-five league goals. He was Scotland's keeper and looked solid as a rock. The cracks started to appear as the team struggled during the winter of 1989/90. Each week you could see Leighton's confidence ebbing away. Silly mistakes became commonplace, he looked indecisive and was plagued with poor handling. Fergie persevered despite intense criticism of his keeper from United fanzines. The Cup semi-final against Oldham should have been straightforward for United but we leaked three goals as Leighton dithered. We drew 3-3 before finishing the job at the same venue the following Wednesday when another Robins winner sent United to Wembley with a 2-1 victory.

Our opponents were Crystal Palace who had gained revenge for their 9-0 league defeat at Anfield by beating the Scousers 4-3 in the other semi-final. United old-boy Stevie Coppell had steered them clear of relegation and to their first ever FA Cup Final. On Saturday 12 May, United looked regal in all white. To accommodate Robson and Webb's return to midfield, Fergie had moved Paul Ince to right-back. United lined up: Leighton, Ince, Martin, Bruce, Phelan, Pallister, Robson, Webb, McClair, Hughes, Wallace.

Our usual gang, Tezzer, Bri, Col, Beef and myself, drove down to Wembley and visited what had become our favoured Cup Final haunts, the King's Head at Harrow and J.J. Moon's in Wembley

High Road. After the customary walk down Wembley Way we went inside the ground. This was the first Cup Final where the famous old terraces had been replaced by seats in the wake of the Hillsborough disaster. The new seats behind the goals had been installed on top of the existing terraces and when you sat down in the first thirty-odd rows you were below pitch level. The view was atrocious.

Understandably, most fans decided to stand up. That is when we first encountered a dreadful new phenomenon – the over-zealous steward. Completely unsympathetic to the supporters' difficulties, the stewards were barking at people to sit down. The first twenty minutes of the match were pandemonium as United fans and officials argued the toss about standing to see the action. It didn't help the stewards' cause when Palace took the lead on eighteen minutes. Common sense prevailed and the yellow-clad menace backed off. We had paid a ridiculous price for the privilege of those seats, and they were a disgrace. The only consolation of being so low down was getting our picture in the *Mail on Sunday* as Bryan Robson headed a thirty-fifth-minute equaliser.

When Mark Hughes put us 2-1 ahead in the second half the final seemed to be going United's way. Twenty minutes from time Palace threw on a young striker hungry for glory. Within two minutes Ian Wright had pulled his team level and in the first period of extra time he volleyed home a second. United were looking tired and devoid of ideas but Hughes summoned up his trademark strength to save the tie with only seven minutes left. Another 3-3 draw, another replayed final for United.

Hughes had matured into a great player and an inspiration to his team-mates particularly in big games when nothing was ever a lost cause. Top scorer, his thirteen league goals had rescued United's season and now his brace at Wembley kept our hopes alive. The same couldn't be said of our back five who looked out of sorts as a collective unit. Once again Jim Leighton's confidence was called into question. During the six league games between the semi and the final Fergie rotated his goalkeepers, giving loan signing Les Sealey and youth-team player Mark Bosnich a chance to shine. Up to that point Leighton had gone nearly two full seasons without missing a first-team game. Sealey played well in a 2-1 debut win at QPR and stayed in the team for the home match against Villa the following Wednesday. In the opening fifteen minutes he coolly intercepted a couple of high crosses right in front of the Stretford End who responded with a spontaneous chant of 'Fergie, Fergie, sign him on'. They knew their stuff, Sealey exuded confidence and the back four were noticeably more steady as United recorded their second victory of the week. Sealey had made his mark.

Following the poor defensive showing at Wembley, Fergie decided to drop Leighton for the replay. The crowd only knew of the change just before the players came out of the tunnel when the teams were announced over the public address system. The United end roared their approval. Just at that moment Leighton, dressed in his suit, walked along the running track in front of us. The fans' reaction shook him visibly. He looked a broken man. Leighton never recovered from that setback, playing only one more time for United. Several years later Fergie said he would not have dropped Leighton if he had known what it would do to the keeper's career. No doubt the great man was showing humility but from a United supporter's viewpoint the manager had been overly loyal to his keeper in a season of poor performances. That sole act of choosing Sealey for the replay may have been the key to winning the Cup and to kick-starting Fergie's trophy haul at Old Trafford. However, it wouldn't be the last time Fergie persevered too long with a weak goalkeeper.

As United took the pitch for the replay, confidence levels seemed higher than on the Saturday and United's Red Army was in fine voice right from the start. Sealey was United's only change and the Reds started confidently. Palace, having put on a great performance in the first game, resorted to spoiling tactics for the replay. Fortunately the referee was strong and the Eagles had to curb the rash and heavy challenges. The cup was won in the fifty-ninth minute when full-back Lee Martin ran on to a superb cross-field pass from Neil Webb and volleyed it high into the Palace net.

The 1990 FA Cup campaign sticks in the memory for many reasons. It had its quirks – we were never drawn at home, every round was won by a single goal margin and we lifted the Cup without winning a game on a Saturday. It had its place in history as United equalled Aston Villa and Spurs' record haul of seven final victories. The 1990 Crystal Palace team was the last all-English team to play in an FA Cup Final. The run to the final had the sublime – United supporters giving it their all when their team needed it most at Forest. It also had the ridiculous when our mate Tezzer drove us to Newcastle and back, blasting out his new tape of Jive Bunny and the Mastermixers. Five hours of that tosh without any chemical substances was inhumane but we forgave him on two counts. Firstly, he was father to two kids under five and was enjoying that period where your brain goes mushy and you really do believe 'Bob the Builder' is a catchy tune. Secondly, by the time the final came round, the infuriating Bunny had been replaced by the sublime debut album from the Stones Roses. Some turnaround that, Tezzer!

The legacy from the 1990 Cup campaign shouldn't be under-valued in United's history. Staying in the competition kept Fergie in a job. There is no doubt in my mind that had we gone out of the Cup at any time before the semi-final stage, United's season would have imploded. The low league position, the threat of rel-egation, the falling crowds, the poor football and the vast outlay on players meant time was running out for United's manager. In the intervening years many individuals have lined up to say how secure Fergie's future was as we entered the 1990s. Despite the good foundations he was laying behind the scenes, supporters starved of league titles wanted jam today – not tomorrow. An early Cup exit would have had the Old Trafford faithful clamour-ing for Fergie's head and eventually the board may have been left with no choice but to change the manager.

The Cup run provided Fergie with a lifeline. Winning it gave him a foothold to take United on to greater heights. Success gives a manager authority and control over situations, such a foothold eluded McGuinness, O'Farrell and Sexton and it cost them dearly. Tommy Doc and Big Ron achieved the foothold but were unable to build on it. Fergie did. When United's entourage took their lap of honour at Wembley that night I applauded Alex Ferguson as fervently as any United supporter. I reflected on the irony that in five months, two games against Crystal Palace had served up the worst and best moments of his career to date. As Fergie disap-peared down the Wembley tunnel I wished him well in my heart. United's football still wasn't pretty and the league results were a worry but he had bought himself time and a second chance.

In the summer of 1990, UEFA lifted the ban on English clubs playing in European competition although Liverpool had to serve an extra year. The loss of allocated places during that five-year period meant only two English teams were eligible to play in Europe, Manchester United in the Cup Winners' Cup and Aston Villa in the UEFA Cup. It was fantastic news. The ban had cost some teams dearly. A total of seventeen English clubs had missed out on a chance to play in the UEFA competitions during the ban and eight suffered afterwards because of the reduced places. It wasn't until 1995 that English clubs earned back all the European places they had held before 1985.

There were few changes around Old Trafford despite talk of United signing a top keeper or striker, instead Fergie bought a full-back called Denis Irwin. In a mixed start to the season United were sixth in the league after ten games but a telling fourteen points behind Liverpool who got off to a flying start. We lost four games in that period then played City at Maine Road almost a year after the 5-1 thrashing. The signs were ominous as the Blues coasted into a 3-1 lead by seventy-eight minutes. As I stood on the Kippax terraces I winced at the thought of another hammering, we seemed to be slipping back into the dark days of the previous winter. With Blue Moon echoing round the ground, City substituted Peter Reid to rapturous applause – he had run the show.

Triumphalism was in the air but Reid's absence sparked a United revival with a McClair brace earning United a 3-3 draw. We had got out of jail and celebrated as if we had won, but as the euphoria wore off the realisation kicked in that once again we were out of the title race before the end of October. Those doubts about Fergie came creeping back, the league form was inconsistent and the team rotation was still baffling even the most tactically aware supporters.

In the cup competitions it was a different story. We beat Liverpool 3-1 in the League Cup with Mark Hughes having one of his best games. With his thigh heavily strapped he almost single-handedly led a United rampage. All throughout the game Liverpool's defenders had no answer to the Welshman's strength or skill. I am convinced Ridley Scott must have been in the Old Trafford crowd that night and got the idea for his classic film *Gladiator* where he cast Russell Crowe in the role of United's number ten. A week later we completed a two-legged victory over Wrexham in the Cup Winners' Cup having beaten Pecsi Munkas in the opening round. The quarter-finals beckoned in the spring.

United were starting to click. Les Sealey had added a degree
of reliability in goal, Hughes and McClair were scoring again
and so was centre-back Steve Bruce as well as establishing a solid
partnership with Gary Pallister. Teenager Lee Sharpe became the
first player in a while to come through United's ranks and star in
the first eleven.

Having eliminated undefeated league leaders Liverpool,
United were drawn against unbeaten second-placed Arsenal at
Highbury. Wednesday, 28 November 1990 would be an historic
day in London. Margaret Thatcher left Downing Street for the
last time, ousted in a coup by her own party after eleven years
as Prime Minister. The following day's front pages would carry
that iconic picture of her being driven away from No. 10 with
tears in her eyes. The back pages, however, would describe one
of the greatest displays in United's history. The mighty Reds took
Highbury by storm, thrashing Arsenal 6-2 in their biggest home
defeat in sixty-nine years.

Fergie dropped captain Neil Webb and paired Hughes and
Danny Wallace up front supported by Sharpe and McClair. It was
unbridled 4-2-4 and fortune favoured the brave as Blackmore put
United ahead after only seventy-seven seconds. In the final two
minutes of the first half Hughes doubled the lead then Sharpe
scored the goal of the night with a curling right-footed shot that
flew into Seaman's net from twenty yards. Arsenal rallied after
the break and pulled it back to 3-2 but United had them reeling
again with three stunning goals in seven minutes. Sharpe bagged
two to complete his hat-trick before Wallace put the finishing
touch to a remarkable tie.

To put the victory into some perspective, Arsenal would finish
the season as league champions with only one defeat in thirty-
eight games – the lowest number of defeats since the top league
was extended to twenty clubs in 1905. Arsenal's rearguard was
probably the best in their history – they would concede a mere
eighteen league goals that season. As those famous Highbury
stands emptied well before the final whistle, United's faithful sang
the lads home. 'We want seven' and 'Easy! Easy! Easy!' On the
coach trip back to Manchester, I realised we had witnessed something very special. Not simply a one-off magical performance,
but a United team finally starting to play with conviction. Fergie
had found a recipe that would serve him well in his quest to put

United back at the top, a fluid formation that could turn defence into attack in the blink of an eye and destroy teams with a series of rapier thrusts.

The win at Highbury sparked a sixteen-game unbeaten run that kept us in the top six and saw us progress to the League Cup Final at the expense of Southampton and Leeds. Bryan Robson returned at Christmas following an Achilles injury at Italia '90. Norwich ended our reign as FA Cup holders but there was little time to dwell on that as we entertained Montpellier Herault in the quarter-final of the Cup Winners' Cup. A disappointing 1-1 draw left us with an uphill battle in the south of France. This was the game when most travelling Reds decided to dust off their passports after the imposed five-year abstinence. A dedicated few had gone to Hungary for the first round, and a new generation of Reds lost their Euro-away virginity at Wrexham but Montpellier flushed out an army of old Reds who had followed United through the 1960s, 1970s and 1980s. I had not been abroad with United since Lodz nine years before. Between 1982 and 1985 I made a series of bad judgements where I chose to wait for the next round only for United to get knocked out.

I was really up for the Montpellier trip and I fancied a bit of an adventure but there was a bit of a problem. I was starting to suffer the 'Billy-no-mates' syndrome at away matches. I was 35, still a single fella and still trying to live life long and fast like Rod Stewart advocated in his 1976 'The Killing of Georgie' classic. My long-term footie mates were on their 'raising a family' sabbatical. These lads still went to the home games but only a big away game in the cups could tempt them from their paternal duties. A European trip was out of the question in terms of cost and maintaining domestic bliss.

Not to be deterred, I booked a week off work and decided to travel to France and back using a variety of transport. I didn't want a package trip, I just wanted to book travel and accommodation as I went along. A week before the game I bumped into Beef's sister, Chris Livesey. When I told her about the trip she said she had always wanted to see a United game in Europe. We had always got on well and she was great company, so we teamed up. On the Saturday we took the National Express coach to London, then over to Gatwick for a flight to Paris, stayed in the French capital on Saturday night before heading for Montpellier on the

TGV, France's new high-speed train. After a 475-mile journey through the French countryside Chris and I arrived at the Mediterranean resort just after dark on Sunday night.

The streets around Montpellier's St Roch railway station were deserted and most buildings closed. Eventually we found a 'vacancies' sign at the Strasbourg Hotel, a welcoming site on a rainy night in a strange city. When we went back into the town centre a couple of hours later the place was buzzing with small gatherings of Reds among the bars and restaurants. Like us, few had match tickets, United's allocation was only 500 and many Reds missed out especially if you didn't travel with the club. The word on the street was that there might be tickets on sale at the Montpellier ground the following morning. About 100 United fans hung around the ticket office most of Monday but there was nothing available, the game was a sell-out.

Later that evening Chris and I were having a drink in the town when we heard a whisper that a tout was selling tickets at the stadium. We headed down there right away. It was around 9 p.m., dark and the route to the ground looked a lot more menacing than it had in the morning sunlight. We walked through a very poor district that seemed solely inhabited by Moroccan immigrants, a ghetto with shadowy figures lurking among the buildings. We hurried on to the stadium, the concourse was in darkness and almost deserted. We circled the ground then saw a man with a couple of locals around him. They seemed to be exchanging tickets. When he finished with those punters we approached him. His English was good, he had tickets for sale and they looked genuine. The tout wanted double the face value and they were in the Montpellier end but it was our best chance given the lack of spares around town. We bought the tickets.

As we walked away two United lads approached the tout and went through the same process, checking the tickets just like we had done. Suddenly an argument broke out. I don't know if the lads tried to nick the tickets or if they felt the tout was trying to fleece them but it got pretty heated. Chris and I turned back to see if we could help, but as we tried to calm the situation someone came up behind us and sprayed an aerosol. I didn't know what was happening, but within seconds I couldn't see anything and was on my hands and knees coughing and spluttering. My throat felt like it was on fire, my eyes were streaming and my nose running uncontrollably. It felt I was choking. It was pretty scary stuff; we were disorientated and completely defenceless. We didn't know if we were being attacked or mugged or what.

It was several minutes before I could open my eyes. Chris and the other lads were okay but very groggy. The tout had disappeared, we checked our pockets and wallets and everything was there. We figured that the tout had an accomplice watching from a distance and when the argument started he decided to intervene with a can of CS gas. It was very effective! We beat a hasty retreat back into town, a little the worse for wear but mission accomplished. We had got our match tickets, time for a well-earned drink.

Tuesday was match day and from early morning you could hear Reds arriving in the town. Around midday we headed for the main square, the quirkily named the Place de la Comédie, which was awash with hundreds of United's faithful enjoying the Mediterranean sun and the odd glass of beer. Dozens of United banners and flags draped the buildings, balconies and street furniture around the square. Reds had travelled from all over the UK and the rest of Europe to get to this game.

The town square was surrounded by quaint, old-fashioned narrow streets; throughout that afternoon those streets echoed to United songs as more and more Reds swelled our ranks. When each new cluster of supporters marched into the square they were greeted with deafening cheers and applause by the burgeoning Red Army. The locals looked on bemused and tolerant, happy to welcome this boisterous throng. The afternoon was a colourful, poignant and peaceful reunion of United supporters who had been robbed of European adventures for almost six years.

We met up with my brother-in-law Pete Seymour and good mate Roger Woods who had come over with a group of Swinton lads on the Supporters' Club trip. They all had tickets but the touts were having a field day as 1,000 Reds turned up without any. Chris and I made our way to the terraces where the Montpellier faithful gathered. We didn't wear colours, I wore a discreet MUFC badge and we stood quietly in one corner of the ground. The home fans welcomed their team with fireworks, flares and several renditions of their favourite song – 'Montpellier Herault! Herault! Herault!' sung to the tune of The Beatles' 'Yellow Submarine' while twirling their scarves high above their heads. The Stade de la Mosson was packed on all four sides and the atmosphere electric, the perfect setting for a special European night.

United lined up on 19 March 1991: Sealey, Irwin, Blackmore, Bruce, Phelan, Pallister, Robson, Ince, McClair, Hughes, Sharpe. Sub: Martin. The main threat was Montpellier's Colombian Carlos Valderrama who had starred at Italia '90 but Pallister and Bruce were unbeatable that night. In midfield Ince and Robson won most of the challenges and led by example. Montpellier were happy to play a patient game and keep the match goalless which would take them through.

For forty-five minutes a young Laurent Blanc marshalled the home defence superbly, but in first-half injury time Clayton Blackmore fired home a thirty-yard swerving free kick to send the travelling Reds into raptures. The goal was scored at our end and all plans to keep a low profile were abandoned as we danced around with twenty or so other Reds. United's players made a bee-line for our small pocket of celebrating fans in the corner. It took the locals by surprise but there were no repercussions.

Within two minutes of the break United struck again when Steve Bruce converted a penalty after Blackmore was tripped. The tie was as good as over and United supporters gave two new songs an airing. One was 'Swing Low Sweet Chariot' before it was widely adopted by the rugby union hordes. The other was the more enduring 'Always Look on the Bright Side of Life'. United fans aimed it at the French initially then adopted it as a celebratory anthem of the fighting spirit the team had shown in southern France. United were in a European semi-final, Fergie's renaissance was taking shape and the victory at Montpellier was another landmark.

Chris and I spent the next day chilling on the beach and topping-up the Salford tan before heading homeward. We had only bought a one-way ticket on the train. The plan was not to make a plan. I have always had a fascination with hitch-hiking to and from football matches. I think it goes back to the 1960s when many cash-strapped young Reds found it was their only way to get to United away matches. It was a dying art by the early 1990s and I fancied giving it one last shot. I managed to persuade Chris it was a good idea and we made our way out of town in search of 'les autoroutes'. To cut a long story short I misjudged the generosity of the French drivers and how long it would take to thumb lifts for nearly 500 miles.

The aim was to get to Paris by nightfall for the Friday morning return flight to London. We waited nearly three hours for our first lift which took us only forty miles north. The next four lifts were all short-haul with significant waits in between. Finally we got a ride that took us a couple of hundred miles to a junction on the A6 just north of Auxerre. But it was now after midnight, we were still ninety miles from Paris and we were knackered. While grateful for the lifts we got, luck had not been on our side. None of them were in comfy, leather-seated saloon cars; all were in run-down vans or wagons that threw us around in the back. So there we were, miles from anywhere and no plan B. Chris's grin-and-bear-it approach was wearing thin.

As we wandered forlornly through the French countryside in the pitch black of night she chose to remind me what a great adventure I had promised her and how exciting hitch-hiking was meant to be. Any response would simply have provoked a full-on argument so I stayed silent and looked out on the horizon praying for some sort of miracle. In the distance I saw a neon light, we headed towards it. As the words 'MOTEL' came into focus our mood lifted. After a few hours' sleep we were on the road early as our flight left Paris at 10 a.m. and it would be touch and go. What a difference a day makes, within twenty minutes we had got a lift that took us all the way to Charles de Gaulle Airport and caught the plane with twenty minutes to spare.

What an epic adventure. I felt like Indiana Jones, this was great fun. The look on Chris's face told me she thought otherwise. A stress-free flight and coach journey had us laughing again as we arrived back at Manchester. We parted company amicably, each heading for the one luxury we craved after a week on the road. For Chris a fragrant bath, for me a pint in the local to recount the tale. *Plus ça change, plus c'est la même chose*, eh Rodney?

United drew Legia Warsaw in the semi-final – they were thirteenth in their league. So it was another trip to the Polish capital for the first leg on 10 April. This time I settled for the simplicity of a day trip with the club. Around 1,400 United supporters reached Warsaw and made their voices heard in a crowd of only 20,000 in the Wojska Polskiego Stadium. United began where they left off in southern France, confident and assured. Lee Sharpe tormented the Legia defence throughout the first half and Ince provided enough steel to win the midfield battle.

The Poles scored against the run of play but sixty seconds later McClair hooked in the equaliser. After the break United took command with Mark Hughes rifling in number two and Steve Bruce notching an incredible eighteenth goal of the season. We should have added to the scoreline, it was easy for the Reds but we settled for a 3-1 win and one foot in the final. The victory was the first time any United side had won the away leg in a European semi-final.

While we waited in Warsaw Airport for the return flight, the team arrived. There was no bevy of security guards or posse of stewards in those days, United supporters spontaneously broke into a round of applause and formed a guard of honour for the players and staff to walk through to their departure gate. I think the squad were taken aback a little, firstly because they were right in among the fans but mainly because of the genuine warmth and respect afforded to them for their performance. Remember, they had taken a lot of flack over the previous couple of years and this was an early sign that the good times were back again. On the flight home all the talk was about the final in Rotterdam. It took a while to soak in, United were on the brink of their first European final since the halcyon days of the great Sir Matt twenty-three years earlier and only the second in their history. Having already qualified for the League Cup Final it meant we would play in two finals that season, unbelievable after the pain of the previous five years.

The League Cup Final on 21 April pitched us against second tier Sheffield Wednesday and Ron Atkinson. Mike Phelan lost out to Neil Webb in midfield in a team that was almost picking itself now. We had never won this trophy in its thirty-year history so it was an ideal opportunity to right that wrong. To say we never got going seems a glib cop-out, but it was true. After a string of great results and performances to get to Wembley, United saved their worst display for the final. A spirited Wednesday won 1-0 thanks to an eighteen-yard volley from former Stretford Ender John Sheridan. Big Ron had given Fergie a bloody nose and Wednesday their only major trophy since the Second World War. The Owls are still the last team from outside the top tier to win a major English trophy.

A hangover from the defeat blunted United against Legia in the second leg three days later. A 1-1 draw saw us through and a date with Barcelona in Rotterdam. Before that, we had the harsh reality of getting tickets and jumping through all the hoops the authorities put in place to attend the match. United supporters had been ambassadors for club and country throughout that winter but the shadow of Heysel, the last time an English team contested a European final, loomed large. The prospect of thousands of Reds making the short Channel crossing filled parliamentary and football authorities with dread.

Making our own way over to Rotterdam was the preferred choice but it would put us way down the queue for match tickets so we opted for a one-day flight with the club. All the lads were up for it, Tezzer Lomax, Col Green, Steve Heywood, Pete Seymour, Mike Stewart and Brian Foy. Everyone but Bri had sufficient tokens, he was one short, but that wasn't his biggest problem. Two days before the tickets went on sale his wife gave birth to daughter Katherine. With two young sons at home already, a football trip to Holland wasn't going to get him nominated for Husband of the Year but this was United in a Euro final and desperate circumstances call for desperate measures.

The lads spared him a four-hour queue down at Old Trafford by phoning him when we were in sight of the ticket office. He rushed down to join us, explaining to the people behind us he had just popped out of the line for a burger. Brian had forged a duplicate token and was confident it wouldn't be spotted but as he stood there showing us his handiwork the blood drained from his face when he noticed his passport was out of date! Because of all the security fears, UEFA insisted that supporters present a valid passport when purchasing the match ticket. So now Bri had a forged token and an expired passport threatening his trip to Rotterdam.

Luckily the people who worked in the ticket office weren't the bright young things that staff the slick contact centre nowadays. They were elderly guys who had served the club since the days when the team were a bunch of railwaymen. You wouldn't doubt their commitment or loyalty, but their eyesight was a different matter. Distracted by some light-hearted banter from Bri, a pleasant chap signed off the documents as okay and handed our mate his match ticket. All Brian had to do now was explain to his wife why he was on his way to the Passport Office in Liverpool. God loves a trier, eh?

There was nothing glamorous about our trip to Rotterdam, we flew into Schiphol Airport in the early afternoon and went by coach to Rotterdam arriving around tea time. United's security guys were extremely nervous of anything that might be construed as supporters misbehaving. A church outing would have looked like a riot compared to our trip. Alcohol was taboo. But we were there and that was the main thing, so it was straight inside the ground to take up our seats in the top tier of the concrete tub that is the de Kuip Stadion. If the trip had been 'dry' the game certainly wasn't as the heavens opened over the vast uncovered terraces. It didn't matter, Red spirits were high as 25,000 roared the boys on.

On 15 May 1991, United played their most important match in twenty-three years and lined up: Sealey, Irwin, Blackmore, Bruce, Phelan, Pallister, Robson, Ince, McClair, Hughes, Sharpe. United were facing a formidable Barcelona side. They had won the Cup Winners' Cup three times in the previous thirteen seasons. More importantly they were on the brink of being crowned champions of Spain by ten clear points, the first of four consecutive La Liga titles. In 1992 they became champions of Europe for the first time in their history. Barca manager Johan Cruyff was assembling a dream team, but on that rainy 'Manchester' night in Rotterdam, Fergie outfoxed the Dutch master to win the tactical battle.

Firstly, he assigned top-scorer Brian McClair to man-mark the majestic Ronald Koeman, whose surging runs and long accurate passes to the front men had destroyed teams at home and abroad. McClair was the unsung hero that night, sticking rigorously to Fergie's game plan and snuffing out the threat. No one saw that coming, least of all Cruyff. Secondly, Fergie knew that Spanish teams were uncomfortable with the high balls that English teams play into the opposition's penalty area. United went on a series of 'air raids' to make good use of Bruce, Hughes and Robson's powerful heading. Fergie's emerging team came of age in that European final playing with belief, tactical awareness and flair. Hughes was unplayable, scoring both goals in a 2-1 victory. It capped a brilliant season where he finished joint top scorer and led United's front line fearlessly. Hughes became the first footballer to win the PFA Player of the Year award twice.

Winning the Cup Winners' Cup was incredible. A season and a half earlier we never dreamt we would see United win one of Europe's major competitions so soon. United had blazed a trail back into Europe for English clubs; how fitting given Sir Matt's foresight thirty-five years earlier. The celebrations on those wet Rotterdam terraces would have been memorable no matter what, but the club had taken its own DJ in case of victory. The guy played a blinder, pumping out anthem after anthem from the Manchester scene and a few 'adopted' numbers. The ground was rocking for an hour after Robbo had held the cup high and the song that stole the show and was James' classic 'Sit Down'.

The following night the team took part in one of the longest homecoming parades ever. After travelling the customary route from Altrincham to Manchester, the open-top bus carried on through Salford to Eccles. It was almost 10 p.m. on a mild May day when United's bus reached Salford Precinct. The crowds were thinner there and I was able to get right next to the road with nobody blocking my view. The trophy glistened as dusk descended. I was only feet away from it and the heroes who had performed so valiantly. There was a lump in my throat as I proudly applauded this Manchester United team and there towards the back of the bus was the man who had given us back our pride. Maybe, just maybe, Alex Ferguson could be the man to put us back where we belong. Dare we dream?

17

HE HAS SOUNDED FORTH
THE TRUMPET THAT SHALL
NEVER CALL RETREAT

As the curtain rose on the 1991/92 season, Fergie's programme notes sent a very clear message, 'This team's next objective is to win the league and end United's 24 year wait to be Champions of England again.'The manager backed his words with three signings that would prove pivotal. In came giant Danish goalkeeper Peter Schmeichel, England full-back Paul Parker and Ukrainian winger Andrei Kanchelskis. The newcomers cost under £3 million in total and all made an immediate impact as United came flying out of the traps. We went top after four matches and stayed there for most of that autumn. By Boxing Day we were sitting pretty as the league table below shows:

	P	W	D	L	F	A	Pts
Man United	20	14	5	1	41	13	47
Leeds	22	12	9	1	38	17	45
Sheff Wed	21	11	5	5	35	22	38

Reigning champions Arsenal languished in seventh, fifteen points behind United and Liverpool fifth, thirteen points adrift. A new world order seemed to be taking shape with United and Leeds locked in a two-horse race. Of course we had been here before and even the most optimistic Reds tried to keep a lid on their expectations but United's form up to Christmas was sensational. Schmeichel and Parker reinforced a sound defence that kept eleven clean sheets in the opening fourteen league and cup games. Paul Ince came of age in midfield, Hughes and McClair provided the goals again ably assisted by wingmen Kanchelskis and an 18-year-old Ryan Giggs who had made his debut towards the end of the previous season. Both men could play on either flank.

During the season Schmeichel developed a skill that became a trademark for United attacks in the 1990s. After catching the ball he would hurl it enormous distances, with unerring accuracy, to our wingers. Before the opposition could regroup we had four forwards hurtling towards their penalty area.

United were winning matches convincingly and comfort-ably. As well as the stunning league form we won the European Super Cup, beating Red Star Belgrade in a one-legged tie at Old Trafford. Since its inception in the mid-1970s the Super Cup had been played over two legs but the escalating war in Yugoslavia made it unsafe for United to travel there. The only blot on United's landscape that autumn was an early exit from the Cup Winners' Cup at the hands of Atletico Madrid.

Title rivals Leeds were a surprise package having returned to the top flight in 1990 after eight years in the wilderness. Howard Wilkinson had emulated Don Revie in the 1960s, taking over with Leeds at the bottom of the second tier and turning them into title chasers in only a couple of years. Wilkinson didn't want big stars and their egos; instead he bought decent players and harnessed them into a useful side with his technical know-how. The title race meant old rivalries were rekindled across the Pennines.

Just to spice up matters even further, United were drawn away to Leeds in the League Cup and FA Cup. Both matches took place in the first fortnight of 1992 and in a further twist of fate the two sides had met in the final league game of 1991. So Leeds played three consecutive home matches against United in three different competitions. Must be some kind of record?

The Revie era was long gone but the contempt we had for Leeds lived on. Our enmity wasn't borne out of jealousy or grudging respect for a team who won the top trophies, as it was with Liverpool. It was a genuine loathing of a club who had been the very antithesis of all that is good about the beautiful game. Nowadays, I try to avoid using the word 'hate' in relation to football, it's such a destructive emotion. But when I was a teenager I really did hate Leeds United and so did most of the Stretford End.

Around the summer of 1973 my mate, Ian McEwen, got a job at a sign-writers in Whitefield and was working with some new technology making signs out of white plastic or Perspex. One lunch break Mac made a rectangular lapel badge about three inches long and an inch high engraved with red letters on a white background saying 'Man United'. He proudly wore it to the next game. The badge looked smart and so different from the small enamel ones everybody else had. I asked if there was any chance he could make me one.

'Sure, what do you want on it?' he replied, thinking I would opt for George Best or Denis Law.

'Can you do "I Hate Leeds"?' I asked mischievously with a glint in my eye.

'Yeah, of course I can,' he laughed.

Next week the badge was ready and it looked superb. The bright red letters standing out against the white plastic; it took pride of place on my tartan scarf. I wore it to Leicester away and the badge attracted interest from fellow Reds desperate to know where I had bought it. The same happened at the next home game, I couldn't even go for a pee in peace. It really caught the imagination of the Red Army. At half-time I told Mac there was a market for his little creation and he might make a few bob if he wanted to work some more lunch times.

Mac made a dozen 'I Hate Leeds' badges and started selling them at the next home game for 10p under the tunnel in the Stretford End. The melee brought a new meaning to the expression about hot-cake sales. People were pushing 50p and even £1 notes into Mac's hand to get a badge. When they had all gone he had to promise to be back with some more in two weeks just so he could get out in one piece. He worked all his breaks plus an hour extra each night and produced thirty more badges. Despite raising the price to 20p, demand far out-stripped supply and dozens of disappointed Reds had Mac pinned in a corner begging him to bring some more.

The police thought trouble was brewing and came over to intervene. When they found he was selling merchandise they gave Mac a right bollocking because he didn't have a licence and he was on private property. They threatened him with arrest if they caught him again. Mac used this as an excuse to put an end to his brief entrepreneurial career; it was becoming too much hassle.

Looking back, I wish I'd had a bit more of a business head at the time. We could have set up a cottage industry to supply the badges by mail order as well as selling them from the back of a van outside Old Trafford on match days. Mac and I would have been sitting on a small fortune, we could have been Salford's Del Boy and Rodney but ten years ahead of our time. Within months the 'professional' badge sellers had cottoned on and you could buy metal pin badges exhibiting your hatred for any team, player or fans under the sun. They became the football fanatic's must-have accessory for over a decade. The posh nutters could even buy car stickers with similar slogans.

So a financial opportunity missed, but I had the street 'cred' of starting the craze and walking round with the original 'I Hate Leeds' badge. I was respected by my peers on the football specials and the terraces. There had been nothing like it before, the badge was daring, scandalous, confrontational and attracted attention from fans and the police up and down the country. For me it went perfectly with my chain-clad, felt-tip-daubed combat jacket. I looked even cooler and even harder, even though I was neither! For my dad, it was just another milestone down the road of despair.

Anyway back to 1991. Leeds had snatched a draw in the league game with a last minute penalty to stop United going five points clear at the top with two games in hand. United were still in the driving seat but it was in the two cup matches that we sent out a strong message to the football world. In the League Cup, goals from Blackmore, Giggs and Kanchelskis blew Leeds away in a 3-1 victory. Leeds were desperate for revenge in the FA Cup third round tie a week later. They had territorial advantage but United's defence stood strong and just before the break Giggs and Hughes combined for the latter to score the winning goal. In seven days we had put the title contenders out of both domestic cups, given them a footballing lesson and lauded it on the terraces.

Amid the Elland Road trilogy United had a surprise setback when fifteenth-placed QPR came to Old Trafford on New Year's Day and inflicted a 4-1 defeat with Dennis Bailey scoring a hat-trick. The cup victories suggested we had recovered from

our New Year hangover, but as January turned into February
the free-flowing football and goalscoring dried up. Nervousness
crept into our play and we drew five out of seven league games
whereas Leeds recovered their composure quickly. Had we made
it easier for them to focus on the title?

There was another irony. In the FA Cup game, Leeds' top
scorer Lee Chapman broke his wrist and was out for six weeks.
Wilkinson needed goals and gambled on two loan deals, Tony
Agana from Notts County and an unknown Frenchman who
was trying to get into the English league – Eric Cantona. By
mid-March the two Uniteds were still well out in front and it
was the Reds holding all the aces, two points behind with three
games in hand.

United reached the League Cup Final but it was played so late
in the season it felt like a distraction from the title race. Still, Fergie
went for his strongest team in an attempt to bring the trophy
to Old Trafford for the first time in its thirty-two year history.
The line-up against Nottingham Forest on 12 April 1992 read:
Schmeichel, Parker, Irwin, Bruce, Phelan, Pallister, Kanchelskis,
Ince, McClair, Hughes, Giggs. Sub: Sharpe

In a solid and determined display United made it third time
lucky in League Cup Finals. Brian McClair scored his 100th club
goal after a neat exchange with Giggsy in the fourteenth minute.
The strike was enough to win the cup. United's dashing young
winger was proving a man for the big occasion even though he
still played for United's FA Youth Cup team.

We were delighted with the League Cup but our eyes were
focused on the big prize. United's 'advantage' of games in hand
was the key but it would work against us. With England in the
European Championships that summer the Football League
insisted all league matches were completed by 2 May. United
would have to play five games in eleven days between 16 and
26 April. The sequence began with a Thursday night home
game against Southampton. A 1-0 win sent United back to the
top. On Easter Saturday both teams drew, United at Luton and
Leeds at Liverpool. As we travelled back up the M1 we overtook
United's team bus. Amid the honking of car horns, flashing lights
and cheering I couldn't help thinking how that coach was carrying the next champions of England and those champions would
be Manchester United. I felt a warm glow.

Easter Monday at Old Trafford saw our third meeting with Nottingham Forest in a month. United's display was flat and we lost 2-1. Leeds, playing later that evening, strolled to a 2-0 win over Coventry and regained the lead. Two days later United played their remaining game in hand, a midweek fixture at West Ham. The Hammers were bottom of the table with one win in thirteen, their relegation sealed the previous week. Thousands of United fans flocked to Upton Park to give the team that final push, but despite attacking West Ham all night we couldn't break them down. With sixty-six minutes played Kenny Brown scored the winning goal. Ironically, on the ground where United last won the title twenty-five years earlier our cherished dreams would fade and die.

The journey home that night was the longest and most painful I've experienced in fifty years watching United. Mathematically the title wasn't over but in our hearts we knew we had blown it again. I felt sick, it was an agonising re-run of the early 1980s when the prize kept slipping from our grasp in the season's finale. The league table read:

	P	W	D	L	F	A	Pts
Leeds	40	20	16	4	70	35	76
Man United	40	20	15	5	60	30	75

Everyone goes through bad times. Times when life drags you up a back alley, kicks the shit out of you and walks away. In April 1992, life did exactly that to Manchester United supporters. But just as 'life' was walking away it stopped, turned, slowly walked back up the alley and gave us a final crushing kick to the parts you treasure most. A few weeks earlier, we had been looking forward to United's first title in a quarter of a century and the mouth-watering prospect of winning it at Anfield in the penultimate fixture. A party to end all parties, we had been winding up the Scousers for weeks. They had been dreading it. Now the boot was on the other foot with a real possibility that our cherished hopes could bite the dust on Merseyside.

The games involving the two leaders were moved to Sunday for the benefit of TV. Leeds played first, a high-noon tough away derby against Sheffield United. Our hopes were raised when Alan Cork put the Blades in front. After that it was a case of

'send in the clowns' as both defences put on a slapstick performance reminiscent of the Chuckle Brothers. In first-half injury
time Leeds equalised when a defender's clearance bounced off
two Leeds strikers standing yards from each other and into the
net. Leeds went 2-1 up when Sheffield's keeper flapped at a
McAllister cross, only for the home club to equalise when Lee
Chapman deflected a cross into his own net.

But in the end, the Ronald McDonald of the Season Award
went to Sheffield's Brian Gayle for his antics in scoring one
of the craziest own goals ever. Running back towards his own
penalty area with Cantona and Wallace in hot pursuit, Gayle
played the ball high into the air with his right knee, neither
clearing the ball nor getting it back to his goalkeeper. So Gayle
carried on running, out-jumped his own keeper who came to
collect the ball and headed it into the net from fifteen yards.
Leeds couldn't believe their luck, a 3-2 win and the title served
up on a plate. The ITV commentator summed it up perfectly,
'Brian Gayle may as well have been wearing a yellow [Leeds]
shirt there!' Nowadays it would warrant a match-fixing investi-
gation by FIFA.

We had been listening to this fiasco unfold as we travelled
to Anfield, only a victory would keep our hopes alive now.
Liverpool sensed United were reeling and played like their lives
depended on it. Ian Rush gave them an early lead then late in
the second half a Mark Walters goal triggered scenes of delirium
across Anfield and West Yorkshire. The finale was played out to
sarcastic renditions of 'Always Look on the Bright Side of Life'
echoing round the ground. All we could do was stand there and
take it. We had lost three games in a week having lost only three
others all season. A Cantona-inspired Leeds took thirteen points
from the final five games compared to United's four. Leeds won
the last Football League title and Howard Wilkinson became the
last English manager to win the English league.

Just like a decade before, we had thrown it away. The fixture
congestion didn't help and injuries caught up with us but we
should have been big enough to overcome them. That is what
champions do. A familiar demon had returned to haunt us – we
didn't have the bottle to win the title! It had plagued Sexton,
Atkinson and now Ferguson. The pursuit of the league championship had become a wearisome burden for the club, the fans

and a succession of top players. Had that burden become too big? Was the expectation to return United to the top of English football creating a debilitating nervousness? Did we now fear fear itself? Naturally Fergie was gutted, he felt he had let the fans down. Though distraught and disappointed, the supporters didn't blame him. He had given it a good shot and we recognised that. I still wasn't sure if he was the man to deliver the league title but that was because I wasn't sure if we would ever win it again in my lifetime.

United's final home game against Spurs brought the curtain down on the original Stretford End. The Hillsborough disaster and the ensuing Taylor Report meant top grounds had to be full of seats. For United it was more economical to rebuild than refurbish the Stretford End. The closing of those terraces that I had loved since I was a boy left me with a heavy heart and was another twist of the knife after the title loss. By the summer of 1992, United supporters had become tormented, tortured souls putting on a brave face while privately wracked with anguish and doubt about the quest for the title. Time would reveal we were just like Charlie before he won the ticket to go into Willy Wonka's Chocolate Factory. We were the luckiest supporters in the world ... we just didn't know it yet!

The 1992/93 season brought a significant change to the football landscape and it wasn't just the big gap where the Stretford End used to be. The twenty clubs in England's top league broke away from the 104-year-old Football League and formed the FA Premier League. The driver behind the break-up was the income the top clubs could earn from television revenues which had rocketed in the previous five years. Most football supporters saw it as an administrative change initially, but it was a revolution that would have a significant impact on English football and its standing in the world game.

A radical step at the time was the decision to assign TV rights to the formed satellite television company BSkyB which customers could subscribe to. This would have a more instant impact on supporters with live football on Sunday afternoons and Monday nights a key feature. The deal between the Premier League and BSkyB was the bedrock of both company's success. From 1992 to 2008, BSkyB had the monopoly of live matches, outbidding the BBC and ITV every time the TV packages were auctioned. Setanta and ESPN broke this stranglehold but their allocation of live matches was small compared to BSkyB's ongoing contract. The Premier League is the most-watched football league in the world, broadcast in 212 territories to 643 million homes. Annual revenues from TV rights rose from £3.2 million in 1986 to £1 billion in 2010.

Despite the previous season's finale, Fergie kept faith with the team he had assembled, striker Dion Dublin being the only significant addition. That decision looked suspect as United got off to a dreadful start. We had the 'pleasure' of witnessing the first ever goal in the new Premier League when Brian Deane netted for Sheffield United after five minutes. We lost 2-1 but the real shock came in midweek when Everton slammed us 3-0 at Old Trafford. In the third game we managed a 1-1 home draw to newly promoted Ipswich. There was a distinct hangover and a crisis seemed to be looming.

In the fourth game of the season United played their first fixture on BSkyB, a tricky Monday night trip to Southampton. Fergie handed Dublin his debut and he popped up to grab an eighty-eighth-minute winner. Dublin's arrival gave the team options to the Hughes and McClair partnership and cover for the sidelined Lee Sharpe. But fate can deal cruel blows. In his third game Dublin suffered a broken leg and severe ankle ligament damage. He would be out until March and left Fergie scratching his head for a solution.

The victory at The Dell kick-started five straight wins which shot United to third in the table. The new Premier League table had a very unfamiliar look. The leading pack was Norwich, Blackburn, Coventry, QPR, Middlesbrough and Ipswich.

Perennial contenders Liverpool were well off the mark for the second season running. For twenty years I had craved the demise of Anfield's dynasty only to be frustrated as each new manager won more trophies. In the early 1960s, Bill Shankly found a recipe for success that became a way of life for future Liverpool managers selected from the inner sanctum of Anfield. When Kenny Dalglish resigned in February 1991, Graeme Souness took charge and introduced his own formula. To the delight of every Manc it proved to be a disaster and would cost them dearly. Liverpool never recaptured their domination of English football or even come close.

The end of their supremacy coincided with the Premier League 'goose' laying the golden egg, where habitual success brought untold riches as well as glory. Liverpool and their fans would have to look on as those riches and accolades went to their biggest rivals, leaving the Scousers trailing badly in terms of transfer funds and ground capacity. As a result they struggled to attract the world's best footballers who flocked to England in the first decade of the twenty-first century.

That scenario seemed light years away in the autumn of 1992. After the five consecutive wins, United embarked on a dreadful run of twelve matches which threatened to ruin the whole season and the manager's credibility. Between 16 September and 7 November United drew five and lost two of seven league matches, were knocked out of Europe by Torpedo Moscow and lost to Aston Villa in the League Cup. The league table on 7 November looked ominous for United's title hopes:

	P	W	D	L	F	A	Pts
Arsenal	15	9	2	4	22	13	29
Blackburn	15	7	6	2	24	11	27
Aston Villa	15	7	6	2	24	15	27
Norwich City	14	8	3	3	24	25	27
QPR	15	7	5	3	22	15	26
Coventry City	15	6	5	4	18	18	23
Man City	15	6	4	5	21	14	22
Chelsea	15	6	4	5	22	19	22
Ipswich Town	15	4	9	2	20	18	21
Man United	15	5	6	4	14	12	21

Tenth in the league, less than a goal per game, we were on the road to mediocrity yet again. Fergie knew goalscoring had been his team's weakness for most of 1992. In the summer he pursued Southampton's Alan Shearer but the player settled for Jack Walker's shilling at Blackburn. Fergie considered a couple of bargain buys, Mick Harford and David Hirst were mentioned in the press, but it all came to nothing. By November, in a chilling reprise of Ron Atkinson's dilemma in 1986, Fergie had to move quickly otherwise his good work would be buried under the avalanche of expectation that surrounds the club. United were still a collection of very good players waiting to be great. Even the greatest managers need a lucky break and Fergie was about to get the biggest of his career. In the short-term, it would answer the striking problem. More critically, it would provide that catalyst to take us from good to great.

Tea time, Friday, 27 November 1992, I'm sipping coffee and watching TV in Manchester's plush new YMCA building waiting for my girlfriend Louise to arrive from work. She walks into the café and as I stand up to greet her I hear the TV broadcaster announce that in a surprise move Manchester United have signed Eric Cantona from Leeds for £1.2 million. Sensing my distant look she asks if I'm okay. 'Yeah, fine. Bloody hell, United have signed Cantona! Bloody hell! Cantona!' I blurted. Credit to the girl, she knew who Cantona was, but didn't fully understand the impact of the news.

To be fair, neither did I at first. Like many Reds that evening I was shocked that we had managed to steal a star player from our main rivals. The more I thought about it, the more I got this warm glow inside. I did my best to get back to more earthly topics – finished my coffee, looked round the shiny new gym, signed-up for membership then went for a meal with the light of my life. But inside I kept chuckling to myself, 'Cantona, bloody hell! Well done Fergie.'

The story is now folklore of how the great man was in the office of United's chairman, when Martin Edwards received a call from the Leeds chairman. They were enquiring about the possibility of Denis Irwin being available. Edwards turned them down flat after a quick check with the manager. Fergie then asked Edwards to see if Leeds would release striker Lee Chapman. Leeds said no. Fergie scribbled a note advising Edwards to 'ask about Cantona'. It was a chance in a million. When the Leeds chairman replied 'go on, keep talking' the United pair knew the door was ajar. Within a few hours the pivotal deal was done.

Eric Cantona made only six starts for Leeds during their title run-in of spring 1992, netting three goals. However, his performances and the magic in his goals brought an uplifting, celebratory mood to the Leeds camp just when it was needed most. Compare this to the debilitating uncertainty that descended over Old Trafford at the same time. Since the start of the new season the Frenchman had scored twelve times including two hat-tricks but results weren't going Leeds' way. Wilkinson felt last season's stop-gap signing was surplus to requirements. God bless you, Mr Wilkinson.

With Cantona looking on from the Highbury stands the following day, United won at Arsenal. The next weekend was the Manchester derby at Old Trafford and, for the only time in

Cantona's career with United, Fergie played him as a substitute. Coming off the bench he added some delicate touches in a 2-1 United victory which lifted us into fifth. Next up was a home game against surprise leaders Norwich City. They were nine points ahead of United so it was crucial we pegged them back. As well as the Cantona impetus, we also had Lee Sharpe back after eighteen months interrupted by injuries and illness. The whole team looked more balanced and the rock-steady defence was now complimented by a creative midfield and dangerous attack. We beat Norwich 1-0 and followed it up by a 1-1 draw at third-placed Chelsea, Cantona scoring his first for the Reds.

Fittingly, it was during the Christmas period that United supporters witnessed the advent of their new Messiah. A Boxing Day fixture at Hillsborough found United 3-0 down to Sheffield Wednesday with sixty-two minutes gone. We weren't playing badly and battled valiantly for what seemed a lost cause. The Leppings Lane seats were bouncing as United's faithful responded to the team's fighting spirit. Brian McClair pulled one back on sixty-seven and the volume went up a few notches. Credit to Wednesday, who didn't sit back trying to defend their lead, they came at United looking to add to it. We now had the classic end to end game but it was painful for us as time after time our shots were saved or just went the wrong side of the woodwork. With ten minutes left McClair sneaked in a second and the atmosphere at the United end was white hot as a miracle seemed possible. More chances went begging, Sharpe alone could have had a second half hat-trick. With six minutes remaining, Cantona nudged a Sharpe cross over line for the equaliser. You can imagine the bedlam.

I had never seen United recover a three-goal deficit before that match. It was extraordinary. We had saved a valuable point but far more precious was the team spirit forged that afternoon in the Steel City. Two days later Coventry visited Old Trafford and we had first sight of the silk that would go with the steel in United's title pursuit. The team simply purred that day, winning 5-0. The football was sublime all over the pitch and throughout the ninety minutes. At the centre of this master class was Cantona with his deft flicks, mazy runs, precision passes and regal presence. A new King was born; a King at ease on the Old Trafford throne. Twelve days later United repeated the superb performance in a

4-1 victory over Spurs to go top. I remember telling friends later that night that I had seen something very special in United's play that day. Whisper it, but United were playing like champions.

United, Villa and Norwich broke away from the pack in the New Year to provide a three-cornered race with each team taking turns at the top. United had no cup distractions after mid-February, the focus was the league and maintaining consistency. The match at Anfield on Saturday 6 March was critical for United's team and supporters. Liverpool were well out of the title race, fifteenth in the table. The three points were vital but we also wanted revenge for the humiliation the previous April when Anfield revelled in our demise. Gems from Hughes and McClair gave us our first win there in six seasons. To complete the perfect day the victory sent United top of the league with eleven games left.

Recent history had found United wanting at this stage of the season and nerves started jangling again. The Anfield triumph would be our only win in March. Three days later we lost 1-0 to bottom placed Oldham and drew three consecutive league games, two at Old Trafford. No matter how much we tried to banish those fears it all had a familiar feel. The table on 31 March reflected a lost opportunity to forge ahead:

	P	W	D	L	F	A	Pts
Norwich	36	19	8	9	50	49	65
Aston Villa	35	18	10	7	51	33	64
Man United	35	17	12	6	51	27	63

United's next match was a Monday night clash with Norwich live on Sky. The trip to Carrow Road was always a long haul, especially for a night game. The Supporters' Club organised a flight for £90, a bit extravagant but what the hell. The choice was forty minutes in the air or a ten-hour round slog across the country. We dug deep in our pockets. By now the regular gang for away matches had whittled down to three, a question of quality rather than quantity. My two accomplices were brother-in-law Pete Seymour and Mike Stewart. I had known Mike since the late 1970s, but only as the younger brother of my mate Gary Stewart. Mike had got married around that time so we didn't knock about together. In 1990 he split from his wife so we teamed-up socially and for away matches. Since then Pete, Mike and I have followed United all over the UK and Europe.

On the mid-afternoon flight to Norwich there was just enough time to serve tea and biscuits before touching down in sunny Norfolk. Every Red knew this match was the crunch. Villa had won on the Sunday to open up a four-point gap over United. Lose tonight and we would be in another end-of-season tail-spin. Win and we were flying high. The stakes were enormous. United had Hughes suspended, so Fergie moved Giggs inside to play with Cantona and brought in Kanchelskis. The rest of the side had picked itself since Christmas. The full line-up on 5 April was: Schmeichel, Parker, Irwin, Bruce, Sharpe, Pallister, Cantona, Ince, McClair, Kanchelskis, Giggs.

Norwich were nobody's fools but United tore them apart in a blistering start. We were 3-0 up after just twenty-one minutes, all scored within an amazing eight-minute spell. Time after time Kanchelskis, Giggs, Sharpe and Cantona made rapier-like thrusts into the Norwich half. Carrow Road echoed to United chants as we strolled to a 3-1 victory and spirits were high as we boarded the plane for the return flight. Everyone who had flown down seemed to be aboard but the captain announced there would be a short delay while we waited for the remaining passengers.

Out of my window I saw Fergie, Bobby Charlton, Cantona, Hughes, McClair *et al.* walking across the tarmac to join us on the flight back to Manchester. The squad got a standing ovation as they boarded the plane and players mingled with fans before settling into their seats for take-off. The whole cabin had a special buzz as we flew home that night. At Manchester Airport the players and staff posed for pictures with supporters as we stepped off the plane. That ninety quid seemed dirt cheap now.

The Easter fixtures approached – the hurdle where we stumbled so badly the previous season. Norwich played on Good Friday and were savaged 5-1 at Spurs. They had gone. It would be United versus Villa, Fergie versus Atkinson, for the title. Was fate going to deal us another cruel, ironic blow? The top two were at home on the Saturday afternoon, United to Sheffield Wednesday, Villa to Coventry. Both games were 0-0 well into the second half when a significant event took place in the Old Trafford game. Referee Mike Peck suffered an achilles injury and was eventually carried from the field to be replaced by his senior linesman. The delay lasted seven minutes.

Shortly after play resumed, the replacement referee John Hilditch awarded Wednesday a penalty which Jon Sheridan converted. Full time arrived at all the other grounds and fans' radios confirmed Villa had scrambled a 0–0 draw. In those days, there were no officials with electronic boards to confirm the added time, nor a slick broadcaster to announce it. We knew the ref's injury had delayed proceedings but by how long? Could we possibly grab an equaliser?

What happened next passed into United folklore as Steve Bruce twice powered in headers to give the Reds a decisive 2–1 win. Those late, late goals put one hand on the trophy and provided the biggest confidence boost in a generation. The fixture at Hillsborough in December had ignited our self-belief; the return at Old Trafford bore the hallmark of champions.

United were top by a point with five games to go and held our nerve with wins over Coventry and Chelsea. Villa matched us with six points from their two fixtures. On Wednesday 21 April both teams were in action, Villa at Blackburn, United at Crystal Palace. At least 10,000 Reds were in a crowd of 30,000 at Selhurst Park that night. Many more were locked out and another 14,000 watched a live transmission on big screens back at Old Trafford. The atmosphere at Palace was the best I had known for a United league match, it was like a home game.

Our fixture kicked off fifteen minutes later than Villa's due to TV coverage and as the teams lined up news came through that Blackburn had taken a 2–0 lead at Ewood Park. The place erupted but there was still a job to do. United had the bit between their teeth but Palace fought hard. Mark Hughes, always the man for the big occasion, rifled in his 100th goal to break the deadlock on sixty-five minutes. We heard Blackburn had won 3–0 but it wasn't until a minute from time that Incey broke away to score a second and guarantee United victory. Fevered celebrations erupted around the stadium then came a chant that I had not heard from United supporters for almost twenty-five years, 'Just like a team that's going to win the Football League, we shall not be moved! We shall not, we shall not be moved!' The song rang out from all corners of those old stands in south London. The hairs on my arms and the back of my neck stood on end. I had dreamt of nights like this for a lifetime. The win at Palace was our fifth on the bounce, the nerves that crippled us in previous seasons had vanished. United had a four point-lead with two games to go.

Due to international fixtures United had a twelve-day break before playing Blackburn on Bank Holiday Monday, such a difference from the congestion twelve months earlier. Villa's penultimate game against third-bottom Oldham was twenty-four hours earlier and covered by Sky. It looked a formality for Villa but any slip would leave United champions so it was essential viewing. The lads, WAGs and kids descended on Pete Seymour's house on the afternoon of Sunday 2 May. The champagne was chilling in the ice-bucket on top of the telly ... just in case.

Oldham started well and on the half-hour Nick Henry gave them a shock lead. We expected Villa to hit back but as the clock ticked down during the second half, Reds all round the world were getting to grips with the reality of the occasion. Ten minutes before the end of the game I popped upstairs for a wee. On my way back down, sensing United's victory and realising I wasn't wearing any colours, I went to get a United scarf from my nephew's bed room. Simon was 10 years old and United-mad, I couldn't see his scarf but around his window were long red and white curtains. 'They'll do!' I thought and within seconds they were unhooked and draped round my back. Now I was ready.

Referee David Allison's full-time whistle at Villa Park ended twenty-six years of torment and kick-started the mother of all parties. Manchester United were champions of England! I couldn't contain myself. I just took off with the curtains held above my head and ran down the street screaming like a banshee, 'Champions! Champions! Champions!' My young nephew, niece and their friends thought it was great and came racing after me as we circled the block announcing to all and sundry that United had finally won the league. Back at the house the tears and the champagne flowed in equal measures.

The feeling was impossible to describe. The last time United were champions I was only 12, a starry-eyed kid bursting with pride that his team, his heroes were the best in the land. Now I was 38 and the feeling was magnified a thousand times. It was an emotion too potent to take in right away. Rarely in life do you spend twenty-six years yearning for something and then it comes to pass. Sometimes when a dream comes true there can be a tinge of disappointment as the euphoria doesn't match the expectation. Better to journey than to arrive, some say. Well, this wasn't one of those occasions. If anything, the elation, relief, and pride surpassed expectation. And it would last all summer.

After quaffing the champers it was off to Old Trafford, a Mecca for any Red who could get there. The forecourt was awash with United supporters, men, women, kids of all ages, dancing and singing without a care in the world. For thousands it was the happiest day of our lives. It was Bank Holiday Sunday, the weather was glorious and the party was going to last well into the early hours. From Old Trafford it was off for a few beers at the Farmer's Arms in Swinton. Their 'beer garden' located in an urban jungle isn't the most scenic but that evening it felt like the Garden of Eden. Most of the local lads and lassies who had followed United loyally for many a year, called in to savour the celebrations. Truly, a night of nights.

No United supporter wanted that day to end, but sleep merely put the party on hold as we relished the prospect of seeing United crowned champions the following day. There will be few occasions when supporters and players have to sober up on match day but that was the case on Monday, 3 May 1993. Alcohol was still in the bloodstream as Blackburn stole the lead, then adrenaline kicked in and the champions played like champions to win 3-1. It was important to win in style, especially with the world watching, but the presentation of the trophy was the main event for United's faithful who had been to hell and back during the previous two and a half decades.

Old Trafford, with its emerging new Stretford End, housed just over 40,000 but we were joined by the spirit of thousands more who couldn't get there or who had gone before. Truly magical nights like this don't happen often in a lifetime. As United were crowned champions of England and performed the lap of honour, the songs and anthems rang round Old Trafford like never before. I thought I was too old for public tears but as Fergie and the lads saluted our corner of the ground the emotion was too much. I thought of my old fella, I thought of the many people I had travelled with watching United over the years and I thought of the countless times I had dreamed of seeing what I was seeing. After twenty-six years the world was back on its axis and it felt just champion!

18

DON'T THESE TIMES
FILL YOUR EYES

The morning after United won the league title I sat down and wrote a letter to Alex Ferguson. I congratulated the United manager on winning the league. I explained I was responsible for the '3 Years of Excuses' banner four years earlier. I made no apology for that incident but explained that having criticised him when United's plight was so bad, I felt it only right to salute him now. I thanked him for making my team the best in the country again and said this feat alone would guarantee him immortality at Old Trafford and rightly so. Finally, I wished him well. Rather than pop the letter in the post to arrive with thousands of other celebratory messages heading his way, I decided to try and hand it to Fergie personally.

Early that hot Bank Holiday Monday afternoon, several hours before the Blackburn game, I drove down to Old Trafford on a mission. The place was heaving with fans making a full day's pilgrimage to the home of the new champions. I fought my way to the main entrance and found Norman Davies, United's kit man, chatting to some friends. I excused myself and asked if Alex Ferguson was around but was told he was busy with the directors. I asked Norman if he would pass my letter to Fergie and thrust the envelope marked 'personal' into his hand. I smiled and said, 'It's important, thanks.'

I didn't expect to get a reply from Fergie; none was necessary. The new season couldn't come soon enough and the day the postman drops that season ticket through the letter box you know it's nearly here. The trouble is he didn't seem to be delivering mine. It usually came through in late July but we were now well into August. I telephoned the ticket office a couple of times, they assured me the ticket application had been processed and the booklet dispatched. I gave it a few more days but nothing came. I started to suspect our postman – a keen Bolton fan and not beyond a bit of skulduggery!

With days to go to the first home game, I called in at the ticket office in person and threw myself on their mercy. A nice chap behind the counter checked the records and confirmed it had gone out. I explained I had been told that before but it still hadn't arrived. He said he would look in the 'query' pigeon-holes. About fifteen minutes later he tottered back, his face alight with good news, he had found my season ticket! It had fallen down a narrow gap at the back of the pigeon-holes. He seemed baffled and assured me it had never happened before. I thanked him profusely for his diligence and walked back to the car. Although relieved, I couldn't help wondering why my ticket should have a query against it anyway. Then a terrible thought entered my head. Had Fergie sabotaged the process as revenge for my role in his darkest hour in football? From the letter I had sent him it would be easy to trace my season ticket details. Surely not? Not Fergie?!

For the first time in a generation United supporters looked forward to the new season with accomplishment as well as expectation. We had worn our 'CHAMPIONS' T-shirts with pride all summer and now it was time for the next stage of the journey. Like many Reds I felt we had broken through a psychological barrier and learned how to win the league, with a bit of luck we could repeat it. The team Fergie had assembled was impressive, McClair's conversion to midfield and Ince's growing maturity gave us class and strength in the middle of the park, the three wingers provided flair and goals, Hughes majestically led the front line and Cantona's arrival added dimensions we could only fantasise about.

Sadly, Bryan Robson was fading out of the picture. He made fourteen appearances in the championship side but nine of those were as sub. At 36, our stalwart for over a decade could only manage a peripheral role. Fergie knew we needed a new Robbo and bust a gut to prise Roy Keane from Nottingham Forest for a record £3.75 million. Alongside Cantona and Schmeichel it would prove to be one of our best ever signings. The opening league game was at Norwich. No quick flight this time, it was back to the everlasting road trip but that was all worthwhile just to be standing at Carrow Road ten minutes before kick-off chanting, 'Bring on the champions! Bring on the champions!'

Keane fitted in immediately and the team just purred. United went top after the second league game and by the end of December 1993 had a fourteen-point lead over second-placed Blackburn Rovers. In the calendar year of 1993 United lost only three league matches, all away and each by a one-goal margin, to Ipswich, Oldham and Chelsea. Our overall league record for the full twelve months read:

	P	W	D	L	F	A	Pts
Man United	43	31	9	3	86	34	102

By any standards this sequence was remarkable but aside from the statistics, United played inspired football home and away, week in week out. Fifteen of the thirty-one victories were on opponents' grounds. Domestically the team was on a par with the great United side of the mid-1960s and possibly the Busby Babes between 1956 and 1958. After the comparatively barren years of the 1970s and 1980s it really felt like we had arrived in the Promised Land with our team at the forefront of English football once more.

Older Reds believed United's rightful place was at the forefront of Europe too. For the first time since May 1969, United were back in the European Cup. Entry to the competition was only for champions of a country or the holders. United were drawn against Hungarians Honved in the first round, winning 5-3 on aggregate. Although attracted by the historical nature of the tie, I didn't travel to Budapest, deciding to save my money for a later round when the competition hots up.

In round two we were paired with Turkish champions Galatasaray. Turkish teams were minnows of the competition but travelling to Istanbul appealed to my sense of adventure. For those Reds who made the trip, the European Cup was certainly about to hot-up. Five of our lads were up for it. Pete Seymour and Simon Rumsey from Macclesfield joined me on the club's one day trip. Dave Gabriel from Derby and Mike Stewart decided to have a week in Istanbul and travelled independently. In the first leg at Old Trafford United had raced into a 2-0 lead. The Turks were no mugs though, scoring three times to turn the game around. Only a late Cantona equaliser saved United's unbeaten European home record.

Today, so much more is known about Galatasaray, the foreboding Ali Sami Yen Stadium and the 'Welcome to Hell' mentality of their fans. YouTube provides some graphic footage. But in 1993 university boffins were still designing the worldwide web, so we didn't have access to detailed information about opponents or their supporters. There were reports prior to the second leg that the Turks were passionate supporters but that was fine, we were Stretford Enders – we do passionate. The evening before the game, ITV and BBC showed film of United's arrival at Istanbul airport. The club's players and officials were met by hordes of Galatasaray supporters who had worked themselves into a frenzy, spewing out a tirade of menacing gestures while those at the front held banners aloft proclaiming 'Welcome to Hell!' I thought, 'That looks a bit tasty!' and could hardly wait to get out there and give our lads some support.

The combination of anticipation and a 6 a.m. flight meant a restless night, but once up and dressed I was ready for it. Demand for the trip had been good and United chartered an Airbus instead of the planned Boeing 757. What a feeling, 300 Reds heading for historic Istanbul, the world's third largest city and the gateway to Asia, to watch Manchester United play in the European Cup. Fantastic! We didn't get the welcome the team had got; in fact the airport was very quiet. So it was straight on the coaches for an afternoon of culture, a Turkish banquet, an exhibition of belly dancing and a sight-seeing tour of old Istanbul. The city is a huge sprawling metropolis with a strong middle-eastern feel, a world away from the customary European trips with United.

As dusk fell our fleet of coaches snaked its way through the narrow streets of Istanbul's Sisli district to the Mecidiyeköy quarter where Galatasaray played. The pavements were bustling and several locals, realising who we were, took great delight in either holding up five fingers to denote their score or drawing a finger across their throat in mock execution. We took it in good spirit, it was nothing more than bravado.

Around 5 p.m. the coach reached the stadium and drove us into a dark side street cordoned off by police and the Turkish Army. They wanted to shepherd us straight to the turnstiles. Pete Seymour and I took one look at each other, we didn't want to be in the ground three hours before kick-off. It had been a good trip so far but we'd had enough of travelling 'under the control and protection of the club' to quote our itinerary. 'Fancy a pint, Mr Seymour?' I asked. 'I do, young man, yes!' he replied and with that we slipped into the shadows and tried to blend in with the locals.

As we walked round the outside of the stadium we were amazed by the thousands of Turks trying to get in so early, the queues for the turnstiles were chaotic and there were dozens trying to scale the high walls. At one end there was a human pyramid of twenty to thirty men leaning against the stadium wall letting fellow supporters climb up to gain entry to the ground. Pete and I shrugged our shoulders and headed for a bar. We met a few other Reds and struck up a great rapport with the bar owner who provided free snacks out of his respect for 'English Gentlemen – the finest in the world'. Over the next hour or so we availed ourselves of his generous hospitality. Welcome to hell my arse!

About an hour before kick-off Pete and I decided to head back to the ground. As we reached the street where the coaches had dropped us there was nobody about, just Turkish Army officials. They let us through the cordon but just looked at us and laughed. We walked down to the turnstiles only to find them closed with dozens of Reds banging on the door. We talked to the army guys who shrugged their shoulders and muttered something about the ground being full. I showed them our tickets but they just shrugged again. I felt sick. Reds were turning up in small groups, each one tried to barter with the Turks but to no avail.

Then we got a glimmer of hope, a smartly dressed local who spoke impeccable English and looked uncannily like George Graham asked us what the problem was. He explained that the custom in Turkey was to be inside the ground up to four hours before the match and that the officials had shut the turnstiles believing everyone was inside. He offered to take us to the main entrance and act as a translator. We followed our Pied Piper and initially hopes were high but there was much shaking of heads by our white knight and Galatasaray officials. He got no joy but insisted on another attempt at the United turnstiles.

We walked back round the ground and the well-dressed chap started talking to security stewards through the closed gates.

He was trying to gain access himself so he could discuss the situation face to face. The minutes ticked by but he was getting nowhere and a few Reds gave up in despair. Out of instinct Pete and I stayed close to him. Suddenly, a steward opened the gate a few inches to let the man in. The time for diplomacy was over, I grabbed Pete and we barged our way in followed by a small posse of Reds. Nobody tried to stop us in the confusion, the stewards were more concerned about closing the gate again and holding back a hundred or so United supporters still outside. The gate was open for no longer than ten seconds but we were in, thank God. The relief was tangible. Pete and I made our way up the terraces and found our mates. We explained what had happened and they told us the ground was packed even when they arrived over two hours earlier.

The noise inside the Ali Sami Yen Stadium was incredible. It held 35,000 but every one of their supporters joined in with the chants. Huge drums constantly beat out a rhythm for their songs which were more like mantras. The singing and whistling was incessant and ear-splitting. When the teams came on to the pitch the whole place erupted, flares were lit all around the ground. There was so much red and yellow smoke it looked like the stands were on fire. Some 30,000-plus Galatasaray fans were bouncing up and down in unison, like an enormous tribe preparing for war. We tried to start a United chant but it was like singing into a vacuum. I couldn't hear myself think, let alone sing. We were completely drowned out by the mayhem around us.

Segregating us from the home fans was a platoon of Turkish soldiers, behind the troops was a baying mob of home fans, with their 'hell' banners, cut-throat gestures and firecrackers. Now, I'm all for a bit of edge between fans at a footie match and I love a lively atmosphere but this was something different. It felt like we were in the midst of a political rally in the Gaza Strip rather than a European Cup match. In all the years I've followed United, Galatasaray is the loudest, most raucous and sinister atmosphere I've ever experienced.

One plucky Red stood up and beckoned the Galatasaray legions to bring on their homicidal threats. A soldier quickly got to his feet, lifted up the butt of his gun and held it aloft close to the fan's head. That kind of set the tone for the evening. The United supporter sat down quickly. To cap it all, as the game kicked off, the home fans held up a giant banner proclaiming, 'R.I.P. Man United'. We chuckled, then they started to pass a full-sized coffin, decked out in United's colours, up and down the terraces for all to see. They don't do anything by halves those Turks!

Needing only a draw to go through, Galatasaray played a very defensive game. United were hampered by UEFA's rule that teams could play no more than five foreigners and that included Welsh, Irish and Scots. Fergie's headache was who to leave out. Mark Hughes was dropped in a team that lined up: Schmeichel, Irwin, Phelan, Parker, Bruce, Robson, Keane, Ince, Sharpe, Cantona, Giggs.

United were well contained by the Turks, I felt the intimidating atmosphere affected the players as it had the fans. With hindsight the battling Hughes might have been a better selection than the youngsters Giggs or Sharpe who looked lost. We created only one clear chance all evening and the game ended goalless, giving Galatasaray victory. Our dreams of revisited glory in the European Cup were gone.

We landed at Manchester about 4 a.m., I was working the next day and there was no chance of sneaking in quietly. I was still with Norweb and based in large open-plan offices near Rusholme. Lots of Reds worked there plus a few Blues and the ubiquitous United-haters. For many years, McVitie's the biscuit makers produced a small snack called a 'United' bar, a biscuit base covered in chocolate and wrapped in blue and white striped paper like a football shirt. After we had won the FA Cup in 1990 I bought a couple of dozen, took them into work and handed them out around elevenses. I briefly announced it was to celebrate Manchester United winning the trophy for a record seventh time. The City fans hated it, but ate it, while Reds chuckled at the point made. It started a tradition.

I did the same for the Cup Winner's Cup and League Cup victories of the early nineties, each time bringing in more bars to spread the word. Winning the league in 1993 called for a big celebration so I bought 200 of the bloody things, went in on the Bank Holiday Monday and placed one on every desk on our floor. Next day I got in early. All I could hear that morning were the moans of Blues as they arrived at their desk, saw their little gift, then effed and jeffed about Pete Molyneux and his sodding United bars! Priceless.

City fans were desperate for revenge but they wouldn't be buying celebration chocolate bars for another eighteen years. They needed another way to hit back and the defeat at Galatasaray provided it. When I walked into work bleary-eyed the morning after the game, I found my desk covered with bars of Turkish Delight. You couldn't see any wood, just dozens and dozens of those famous dark red wrappers piled high. How the City fans loved it, giggling together in little groups as if they had won something!

Their euphoria carried on into the weekend when their beloved team met United in the derby at Maine Road. It was one of the last occasions the two sets of supporters stood next to each other on the Kippax Street terraces and the atmosphere was electric. City used the pre-match build up to taunt us about the shock exit to Turkish underdogs. 'Two-nil up and you f★★ked it up, United is your name' rang out continuously as they celebrated our European demise.

Worse followed. Niall Quinn scored twice in the opening thirty-two minutes to put City in the driving seat. United surfaced for the second half with their heads high and by the seventy-seventh minute Cantona had put United level. With four minutes remaining the turnaround was complete as Keane slid home the winner. Elation engulfed the Red side of the Kippax while it was desolation for our neighbours as we hit them with, 'Two-nil up and you f★★ked it up, City is your name. City is your name …' He who laughs last, eh? All in a week when we had been to hell and back.

Consolation for the early European exit was found in United's tremendous league form that winter. The fourteen-point lead was supplemented by great runs in both domestic cup competitions. United's squad was essentially just fourteen players – Schmeichel, Parker, Irwin, Bruce, Pallister, Ince, Keane, Hughes, Giggs, Cantona, Kanchelskis, Sharpe, Robson and McClair. No other player appeared more than five times in all competitions that season.

The excitement of another title bid was interrupted early in the New Year. On Thursday, 20 January 1994 Sir Matt Busby passed away. Anyone with a fleeting knowledge of football will understand what Sir Matt meant to Manchester United. It was time to pause and reflect. Two days after the news, United had a league game at home to Everton. The club had less than forty-eight hours to find an appropriate way to honour this great man. Engulfed with grief, it was a challenge to hit the right note. What the club arranged was a credit to Sir Matt, United and the fans.

At 2.50 p.m. a lone Scottish piper led the two teams from the players' tunnel to the centre circle playing the mournful lament, 'A Scottish Soldier'. The piper finished his piece and Old Trafford fell silent, 45,000 inside, thousands more outside. The minute's silence was impeccably observed. On the front row of the director's box the late club president's seat, number B122, had two black ribbons tied to the red armrests. The Everton supporters observed the proceedings with immense dignity and respect, a credit to their fine club. The match seemed strangely irrelevant but it was fittingly graced and won by an impish Ryan Giggs the embodiment of the spirit of the Busby Babes.

I took a day off work on Thursday 27 January and stood under the slate-grey skies on Warwick Road with 10,000 others to pay my respects to Sir Matt. At 12.06 p.m. the cortége came to a dignified halt opposite the Munich memorial, stopping for two minutes while the supporters said a silent farewell. The hearse contained a flower arrangement spelling out 'The Boss' while another was in the shape of Old Trafford. In the days that followed we came to appreciate what a blessing it was that Sir Matt lived long enough to see his beloved side lift the league title again.

Progress on three fronts started to take its toll on United's league form with several draws. Blackburn Rovers, galvanised by benefactor Jack Walker and manager Kenny Dalglish, put in a run of ten wins in twelve games. It was a two-horse race and both went neck and neck throughout the second half of the season with few stumbles. By March the bookies were offering odds of only 5/4 for United to win an unprecedented domestic treble. We were top of the league with only one defeat, an FA Cup semi-final date booked with Oldham, and a Wembley League Cup Final against Aston Villa.

But March was a tricky month. We had players sent off in four matches; Schmeichel against Charlton in the FA Cup, Kanchelskis in the League Cup Final and consecutive dismissals for Eric Cantona in drawn games at Swindon and Arsenal. Chelsea completed a league double over United and we were dropping points and picking up suspensions. We lost the League Cup Final to Ron Atkinson's Villa 3-1. The treble dream had gone and the double was in jeopardy. Cantona's dismissals brought him a five-match ban as we entered the run-in. The first game of his ban was the crunch match at Ewood Park on Easter Saturday. Since the New Year, Blackburn had reduced United's huge lead to just six points. The table on the morning of the titanic clash read:

	P	W	D	L	F	A	Pts
Man United	34	22	10	2	69	32	76
Blackburn	34	21	7	6	52	29	70

United were second-best to a strong Blackburn side and two-goal Alan Shearer won the game. We were beginning to look fragile, the majestic football had faltered, nerves gripped players and supporters alike. Easter Monday brought a much needed win at home to Oldham, Rovers won their fixture and remained three points behind. The following week United met Oldham again in the FA Cup semi-final at Wembley. A bizarre choice of venue that vexed both clubs but money was becoming king at FA head-quarters. Now missing Kanchelskis, Cantona and Keane, United struggled. Oldham took the lead in extra time after a goalless ninety minutes. The clock ticked by and we were pulling our hair out with frustration. With seconds left, Brian McClair lobbed a hopeful ball over his head into the Latics' penalty area and as it was falling to the ground Mark Hughes leant back and volleyed home a right-footed shot into the top corner of the net. Season saved!

In the replay at Maine Road a rejuvenated United walloped Oldham 4-1 to reach the FA Cup Final. We had our wake-up call. United won four of the next five league games while Blackburn won only one. Rovers' defeat at Coventry on Monday evening, 2 May, meant United sealed a second consecutive title while not playing and on the same date as the previous year. I had listened to the Coventry-Blackburn match on the radio at home, expecting Blackburn to win. The other lads had done the same. At the final whistle I phoned Pete Seymour and hastily arranged to meet him in the Farmer's Arms at Swinton. It was a lot quieter than twelve months earlier but the landlord, a man blessed with a sense of occasion, came round with a tray full of whisky measures and all those present toasted Manchester United, the champions of England!

Retaining the title was a fantastic feat but took some getting used to. After all those years of drought, a flood had arrived. Fergie had assembled a side that mastered the art of playing attractive and winning football. The whole team was a class act but Eric Cantona's impact was phenomenal. Aside from his twenty-five goals, the man's sheer presence electrified our performances. United lost only four league games, their best record since 1906, and Eric was missing for three of those. United wasn't a one-man team but with Cantona in the side we were virtually unbeatable.

United amassed an incredible ninety-two league points. The class of 1994 had matched the deeds of the Babes in 1957 with back-to-back titles. That pre-Munich side also had the chance to become the first winners of the English double in the twentieth century but a serious injury to goalkeeper Ray Wood in the FA Cup Final had robbed them.

Now United faced Glenn Hoddle's Chelsea in the final. Fergie could win the double for the first time in United's history but not before a few headaches over the team selection. Fourteen players had got United this far but only two substitutes were allowed. Fergie let his head rule his heart on 14 May 1994 and went with 'the dream team': Schmeichel, Parker, Irwin, Bruce, Pallister, Kanchelskis, Cantona, Ince, Keane, Hughes, Giggs. Subs: McClair, Sharpe.

There was no place for Bryan Robson who was leaving to manage Middlesbrough. His finale was lifting the league trophy with Steve Bruce the week before. Chelsea had inflicted two of our four league defeats and the thirst for revenge spurred United on. After a quiet and goalless first half we came alive on the hour with three goals in nine glorious minutes. Eric coolly slotted home two penalties and Hughes rattled in a third. Choccy McClair put the icing on the cake with a fourth. United had won the double!

Only a year earlier, most Reds would have paid a king's ransom and donated a kidney just to be champions – now we had witnessed United's best season ever in terms of trophies. Euphoric doesn't start to describe the feeling. With the club back at the pinnacle of English football Fergie dedicated the double to the memory of Sir Matt. On the coach journey home from Wembley when Fergie got a quiet moment to reflect on his work-in-progress he must have felt a warm glow inside. He had won six trophies in five years, delivered the Old Trafford faithful their coveted title, won the double and given us an unexpected taste of European glory. The supporters now worshipped Alex Ferguson and rightly so. Critically, the trophies brought him the 'control' he regarded as essential for any manager to succeed at any football club.

Fergie's contentment will have been magnified by the calibre of players coming through the ranks. Raw potential was turning into genuine talent. The nucleus of the 1992 FA Youth Cup winning team had stayed together and in 1994 won the reserve league title for the first time since 1960. But while the United supremo contemplated his wonderful world, I had an urgent task to perform. I spent most of the Sunday afternoon clearing Tesco's shelves of 200 Double Decker chocolate bars and putting one on each desk at work ready for Monday morning. I couldn't disappoint my public, could I?

During the summer of 1994 I married a wonderful girl called Louise. I was twelve days off my fortieth birthday but it was my first marriage. After splitting with Gail in 1975 I managed to stretch 'a couple of years being footloose and fancy free' into life as a serial bachelor. I had a place of my own, was fairly independent and enjoyed living life without too many constraints or commitments. I could never quite understand why others around me had wanted to get married so young or so quickly. While I held the sanctity of marriage in high esteem, I tended to take the long-term view and decided not to rush into wedded bliss.

I remember an old TV sketch where the great Benny Hill and his sidekick, Henry McGee, played two old Chinese philosophers. They were discussing the subject of matrimony when one asked the other, 'What do you think is the definition of a bachelor?' After careful consideration the second wise man replied, 'I would say it's a man who hasn't thought seriously about getting married. What do you think?' 'Mmmm, that's interesting,' said the first wise man, 'I'd say it's a man who has thought seriously about getting married!' A brilliant sketch, a great philosophy.

Of course, man cannot live by football alone. During those twenty-odd bachelor years I was fortunate enough to enjoy the company of some striking and remarkable women. Not wishing to mislead the reader, this wasn't a constant stream. As most lads know, on the carousel of love or lust you have your purple patches and you have your barren times. But overall I did okay and was happy.

That didn't stop the endless concern about my love life from aunties, uncles, mates' parents or the older generation at work. They could only see the downside of a single life and rarely failed to ask when I was going to settle down. Not wanting to offend I would invariably retort with a glib line like, 'The day after the Pope'. The line wore thin after a few years, I needed something equally dismissive but a bit more personalised. I fell into the habit of answering the question about marriage with, 'Not until United win the league again.' It was just a line. I never expected to use it for so long!

The odd thing is, I proposed to Louise in November 1993, just months after that elusive title win. Not planned, just serendipity. Louise and I met as a result of a blind date arranged by a mutual friend, Carolyn Heywood, wife of my good mate Steve. The first date, in June 1991, had been subject to several postponements by both parties. Throughout that spring, I was distracted by trips to France, Poland and Holland to see United cover themselves in glory while Louise kept getting cold feet about a blind date with an ageing bachelor who sported an out-of-date perm. Given these factors, it's amazing we got together at all let alone hit it off and get married. But, on 30 July 1994, marry we did, setting sail on a high sea for which no compass has yet been invented.

19

THEY CAN LIE TO MY FACE, BUT NOT TO MY HEART, IF WE ALL STAND TOGETHER, IT WILL JUST BE THE START

United's commercial arm was eager to capitalise on the team's new found success and souvenir shop sales rose sharply after the double triumph. The club wanted an official mascot to help promote their merchandise. During United's long history the role had been filled by a goose, a dog, a goat, a one-legged ex-soldier called 'Hoppy' and a chap with an umbrella called Jack Irons. That is the mascot, not the umbrella. In 1994 a red devil character more akin to Mickey Mouse was required for branding purposes and 'Fred the Red' was launched.

Normally such a marketing ploy wouldn't interest me let alone get a mention on these pages. However, if you followed United home and away during the 1970s and 1980s you were likely to know the real Fred the Red. Fred came from Stretford, although I think he later moved to Salford. Anyway, he followed United everywhere, usually on the Football Specials. Well over six feet tall with long, shaggy blond hair and always clad in denim jacket and jeans, Fred was renowned on the terraces for his witty, cutting banter and his ability to lead the singing. I never knew his full name or much about his background but I would bump into him at many away games and we would have a good chat about football-related topics. Fred wasn't a trouble-maker, though his fanaticism occasionally landed him in hot water. He was simply United daft.

In May 1976, United played Celtic at Parkhead in a testimonial for Bobby Lennox and Jimmy Johnstone. I hired a car and travelled up with Jeff Fanning, Pete Ward and Manny from Bury. We had heard terrifying tales of the Glasgow gangs, the Gorbals and fierce battling at Old Firm matches and were still getting over the shock of Rangers' visit two years earlier. So we headed north with some trepidation. United took 200–300 supporters up there but in dribs and drabs, there were no organised trains or coaches. It was every man for himself. Approaching Parkhead we got stuck in slow-moving traffic. Hordes of rowdy Celtic supporters making their way to the game on foot mingled with the vehicles. Inside the car we sat quietly, making sure we didn't make eye contact with anyone outside and hoping they wouldn't spot the sticker on the back window advertising the Manchester-based car hire company. We were sitting ducks if it turned nasty. I needed some fresh air so opened the window a little. Among the hubbub of the Celtic fans I heard a faint rendition of a familiar song, 'When the Reds go marching in, Oh when the Reds go marching in.'

It came from a lone voice, we looked at one another in amazement. Jeff laughed, 'There's some nutter out there singing United songs!' The voice got louder and louder. I wound the window right down, craning my neck to see this kamikaze guy. It was Fred the Red, United scarf round his neck, singing to his heart's content in this green and white mass. As he passed our car he spotted me. 'Molly, me ol' mate! How yer doing!!?' he shouted. Within seconds he had opened the car door, ushered me out on the street, put his arm round my shoulder and belted out another verse of his favoured song but this time with even more gusto. It would have been rude not to join in, so now both of us were standing in the middle of the road entertaining the locals. I prayed it would be a quick death, nothing drawn-out or unbelievably painful. But the Celtic supporters just gave us a cursory glance and carried on with their business. I hopped back in the car and Fred disappeared into the crowd again. As it turned out the Bhoys fans made us welcome all evening. We learned that night of the affinity towards United in that part of Glasgow. But did Fred know that? I doubt it.

Towards the end of the 1980s Fred didn't seem to be on the scene as much and we lost touch. In late 1994 I bumped into him again, we caught up on old times and had a good laugh. Suddenly, the laughter stopped and his brow became furrowed, something had come into his head that obviously caused him concern.

'D'yer know what those bastards have done Molly?' he asked forcefully.

I shook my head and shrugged my shoulders. I didn't even know which bastards he meant.

'They've only nicked me f★★cking name!' said Fred, poking my chest with his finger.

I was halfway though saying, 'How do you mean Fred?' when it hit me, United's new mascot was called Fred the Red! I wanted to laugh, not out of any disrespect for an old pal, but just because the idea of a cartoon character suddenly pinching someone's name was amusing. But Fred, the real Red, wasn't seeing it that way. He was well pissed off.

'Anyway, I've contacted the club and told them they can't use it. I'm Fred the Red and have been for years! You know that, Molly'

He was ready for a battle with United's lawyers if necessary. We parted company and I wished him well in his dealings with the club. I had visions of one day being summoned to court and asked to swear on oath if I recognised anyone in the room known as Fred the Red. Anyway I didn't see Fred for the next seventeen years and I often wondered how the dispute was resolved. I would have paid good money to watch Fred take on United's commercial manager face to face. I could only speculate as to the outcome. Maybe he's the guy inside the Fred the Red costume parading round Old Trafford every home game? I could understand him keeping that one quiet. Finally at an FA Youth Cup Final in 2011 I caught sight of Fred outside Old Trafford. It was only a brief encounter but I can at least rule out the hitman theory.

David May was a surprise signing from title rivals Blackburn Rovers and the only addition to the squad in summer 1994. United soon got into winning ways and looked a decent bet to defend their title again. Through that autumn Fergie gradually blooded his youngsters into league action, usually one at a time so as to minimise the impact on the team and results. He used the League Cup to play up to six of the 1992 youth team all together.

For a second consecutive campaign United were badly constrained in Europe by the limit on foreign players. The UEFA

Champions League now had group stages instead of knockout rounds and United were pitted against Barcelona, Gothenburg and Galatasaray again. With two teams qualifying United's chances looked good. The trip United supporters were relishing most was Barcelona away on 2 November. Every man and his perro were up for it, Barca gave us 7,500 tickets and at least a thousand more travelled without. Twenty of our lads opted for the club's one-day flight. We had a smashing day, no trouble, plenty of banter, a barrelful of laughs and a few scoops of ale – perfect. Night fell and we joined thousands of Reds serenading the locals with United ditties as we made our way to the magnificent Nou Camp stadium. United lined up: Walsh, Parker, Irwin, Bruce, Kanchelskis, Pallister, Butt, Ince, Keane, Hughes, Giggs. Sub: Scholes.

Our perfect day ended almost as soon as the match started, United out-classed by a slick-passing, fast moving and very skilful Barcelona. Their front men Stoichkov and Romario were out of this world. The Bulgarian scored after eight and fifty-two minutes with one from the Brazilian slotted in between. In the end United lost 4-0. As good as Barca were, United struggled all over the field. English football was still playing catch-up with the best in Europe. A 3-1 defeat to a Jesper Blomqvist-inspired IFK Gothenburg meant our European dream was over before the Christmas shopping had begun. Fergie knew his team was falling short on the highest stage and had to act.

Domestically it would be United and Blackburn challenging for the big prize again. As far as anybody knew then, UEFA's five-foreigner rule was here to stay. Fergie had to change the mix of the side to contain more Englishmen. On 10 January 1995, United shocked the football world by signing Andy Cole from Newcastle for a British record £7 million, almost double the fee for Roy Keane just eighteen months earlier. The Cole transfer should have been the biggest football story of the year, but as January unfolded it wouldn't even be the biggest that month. Cole made his debut in a top-of-the-table clash with Blackburn at Old Trafford. Rovers were on a great run having gone five points in front with a game in hand. United pegged them back, Cantona delivering the killer blow in a tight 1-0 victory. Fergie's strategy was for Cole and Cantona to forge a powerful strike force.

By the end of the pair's second game together, Fergie's plan lay in tatters. During the midweek match at Crystal Palace, Cantona received a red card after an altercation with Richard Shaw. The Palace defender had been marking him closely and Eric felt indignant that the ref hadn't afforded him appropriate protection. As he walked off the pitch, the great Frenchman was verbally abused by Palace fan Matthew Simmons. Deciding to exact his own retribution he launched himself Kung-fu style at the surprised Londoner.

The events of Wednesday 25 January have been well documented and there is nothing more I need to add in these pages. The outcome for United was the loss of our best player for the rest of the season and much soul-searching for the manager, chairman and club solicitor on how best to deal with the world-wide attention the incident brought.

Cantona's ban gave Mark Hughes a reprieve and he formed a decent partnership with Cole. United won five of the next six league games including an incredible 9-0 victory over Ipswich with Cole netting five. The run brought us level with Blackburn but we missed the magic of Cantona. In tight, nervous games Eric could open up opponents with thirty seconds of genius.

Home matches with Spurs, Leeds and Chelsea all ended 0-0 and Blackburn took advantage, with six games left they held an eight-point lead. But with the finishing line in sight Blackburn got jittery while United recovered ground to take the title race into the last day. The table read:

	P	W	D	L	F	A	Pts	GD
Blackburn	41	27	8	6	79	37	89	42
Man United	41	26	9	6	76	27	87	49

Sky Sports had got the finale they wanted and it made great TV for the watching millions. The top two were away in the final game, United at West Ham, Blackburn at Liverpool. United had to win to have a chance, if they did and Blackburn drew or lost we would win our third consecutive title. Fergie had lost Giggs and top scorer Kanchelskis to injury and surprisingly left Hughes on the bench, going with a line-up of: Schmeichel, G. Neville, Irwin, Bruce, Sharpe, Pallister, Cole, Ince, McClair, Keane, Butt.

For the thousands of us who ventured to Upton Park it was sheer agony. Shearer scored at Anfield after twenty minutes, twelve minutes later West Ham took the lead. At half-time Fergie threw Hughes into the fray and United immediately slipped into gear, bombarding the Hammers' goal. McClair pulled us level on fifty-two minutes; twelve minutes later news came through of a Liverpool equaliser. One goal would crown United champions but despite being camped in West Ham's penalty area we were denied by a super show from keeper Luděk Mikloško and some errant finishing from Andy Cole.

To rub salt in the wounds Liverpool scored an injury time winner to leave both sets of supporters dancing on the Anfield terraces. For the second time in four years the Boleyn Ground was the graveyard of our title hopes.

United had battled to the FA Cup Final despite Cole being cup-tied. Six days after surrendering the title a demoralised team succumbed to an ordinary Everton side 1-0. We were just three goals away from back-to-back doubles. There is no doubt in my mind United would have achieved that feat with Cantona. The season's finale was cruel and disappointing but Fergie had seen enough to know what he had to do.

> Let me make my position clear straight away. I am committed to the cause of Manchester United and I am not the slightest bit interested in anyone who can't match that commitment.

These were Alex Ferguson's opening lines from his programme notes at the start of 1995/96. The summer had been troublesome for the United manager. Having earned the respect and trust of United supporters with an array of glittering prizes and scintillating football, he found his authority being challenged in some quarters. United sold three top players, Hughes, Ince and Kanchelskis, all instrumental in taking United back to the top and immensely popular with the United faithful. While Hughsie was the wrong side of 30, Ince, 27, and Kanchelskis, 26, were at their peak. The Ukrainian winger was top scorer with fifteen goals in thirty-three starts.

The transfers worried Reds. The media and at least one fanzine tried to whip up a storm but there was more sizzle than sausage and the 'campaign' petered out. Most United

supporters, including the author, put their faith in Fergie's judgement. The manager had a vision and in keeping with United's
fine tradition was ready to give youth a chance. He believed the
time was right but his decision was still a brave one. He was dis-
banding a great team that had delivered for five consecutive years.

Furthermore, Cantona's ban didn't end until 1 October, eleven
games into the season. United supporters expected a couple of
top signings but Fergie didn't buy any replacements. Instead he
went straight in with the kids for the opening game at Aston Villa.
The youthful line-up read: Schmeichel, Parker, Irwin, G. Neville,
Pallister, Sharpe, Butt, Keane, McClair, Scholes, P. Neville. Subs:
Beckham, O'Kane.

Thirty-seven minutes into the new season our trepidation
turned to horror as United went 3-0 down. You could see the
expressions of disbelief among Reds at Villa Park. There was a
collective sinking feeling that bordered on panic. Fergie stemmed
the haemorrhage at half-time and we got a grip of ourselves.
A late Beckham goal gave the score some respectability but it
didn't make pretty viewing on *Match of the Day* that night. Pundit
Alan Hansen asked what a lot of people were thinking, was it
wise to put so many young players in at one go? Summing up his
piece to camera he said the now immortal line 'you'll never win
anything with kids'.

Fergie stayed calm, the kids battled hard and United won the
next five league games including a comprehensive 2-1 victory
over champions Blackburn at Ewood Park. Scholes and Butt
settled quickly into their midfield roles, Beckham shone on the
right, and Gary Neville made the right-back berth his own. Eric
returned in regal style against Liverpool, setting up a Nicky Butt
goal within two minutes then scoring in a 2-2 draw.

The improvement continued and by late November United sat
three points behind surprise leaders Newcastle but as a bitterly
cold winter set in the progress stalled. In nine league matches
we picked up a mere ten points. Injuries to Schmeichel, Keane,
Bruce, Pallister and May stretched the young team too far.
The centre-back crisis even forced Fergie to bring in a chap called
William Prunier on trial from Bordeaux for two games. A thoroughly miserable Christmas included comprehensive defeats at
Liverpool, Leeds and Spurs. Fortunately, one of two wins in that
period was against Newcastle otherwise the Geordies would have

been out of sight. The table on Saturday, 20 January 1996 showed
how far we had slipped:

	P	W	D	L	F	A	Pts
Newcastle	23	17	3	3	45	19	54
Liverpool	23	12	6	5	46	21	42
Man United	23	12	6	5	41	27	42

In just four years Kevin Keegan had taken Newcastle from the
foot of the second tier to a twelve-point lead in the top league.
The Geordies had waited even longer than United for a league
title having last been champions in 1927. They were desperate
for success and Keegan was revered for the revolution. United's
injuries cleared up, the team settled down and we embarked on a
remarkable run. In the remaining twenty league and cup games
United won eighteen, drew one and lost one. Newcastle didn't
fall apart but our fine form meant whenever they drew or lost we
chipped away at that huge lead.

On Monday 4 March we played Newcastle at St James'
Park, it was do or die for our title hopes. Pete Seymour,
Mike Stewart and I drove up to Tyneside and arrived in time
for a quiet pint in the city centre. It had to be a quiet pint,
the pubs were heaving with Geordies and they were already
in celebratory mood. Everybody decked in black and white
was totally convinced they would beat us and open up the
lead again. Thousands of singing and dancing Newcastle supporters filled the roads leading to St James' Park. Tyneside's
pathological affliction for inflated expectations was in overdrive. I have never known fans so hyped up before a match.

Newcastle threw everything at us that night and we rode
our luck. Peter Schmeichel had his best game in a United shirt,
making a handful of breathtaking saves, United dug in and the
score remained 0-0. In the fifty-first minute we broke away,
Cole fed Phil Neville whose cross was met at the far post with
a Cantona volley. For a few seconds there was stunned silence
from the packed Newcastle stands but in a small corner 3,000
of us celebrated like never before. Those last forty minutes were
as tense as any I've known but the joy at the final whistle was
almost unequalled. Fergie's exciting young team 'arrived' that
cold March evening in the North East and showed the world its

pedigree. That match is still the most memorable league game I've seen United play. The team that night warrants a mention: Schmeichel, Irwin, Bruce, G. Neville, Sharpe, P. Neville, Keane, Giggs, Butt, Cantona, Cole.

A massive psychological blow had been inflicted on Geordie confidence, Newcastle lost three of their next five matches and on March 20, United topped the league for the first time that season. By mid-April United and Newcastle were neck and neck:

	P	W	D	L	F	A	Pts	GD
Man United	35	22	7	6	64	35	73	29
Newcastle	34	22	4	8	62	35	70	27

Fergie decided to spice things up. Interviewed after Leeds had narrowly lost at Old Trafford, he suggested it mattered more to some of their players to stop United winning the league than anything else. Fergie hinted that they weren't being true to their manager if they couldn't show similar commitment when they played other teams. Newcastle's next opponents? Leeds United!

The remarks got a few column inches and we all moved on, well most of us did. United beat Nottingham Forest 5-0 and Newcastle won 1-0 at Elland Road. If Fergie's words were intended to galvanise Leeds they seemed to have failed. Three days later the Geordies played their game in hand but fluffed the chance to catch United by drawing 1-1 at Forest. In a post-match interview on Sky, Keegan delivered a rant that has become legend. Showing raw emotion he lambasted Fergie's comments about players' commitment as a slur on professional footballers. His *piece de résistance* was blurting out how he would 'love it, love it' if his team beat United to the title. Priceless!

Finally, United had the opportunity to win the league while playing a match and Reds were in buoyant mood heading up to the new Riverside Stadium. I was lucky enough to get a ticket but some of our lads went up without one. We got word of a pub where Middlesbrough fans were selling their tickets to United supporters to finance their season tickets for the following season. It was a rough pub in a Boro stronghold but we were desperate for tickets. Their lads turned out to be okay; they wanted United to win the league to stop their neighbours Newcastle, so they tolerated us.

They also had a golden opportunity to cash in, with asking prices around £100 per ticket. Some of our mates had to sit with the Boro fans but they would be there to witness United's triumph. The United end of the ground was rocking to two new anthems, 'We're gonna win the football league again, down by the Riverside' and the rousing, 'Cheer up Kevin Keegan'. Both have been adapted many times since, but they were perfect for that sunny day in May 1996. Some Reds displayed hastily made but topical banners. The best one proclaimed, 'Kevin Keegan eats British beef', a reference to Mad Cow Disease that was prevalent in Britain at the time. Others reminded Alan Hansen of his prophecy about kids and winning things.

David May headed United into a thirteenth-minute lead right in front of the Red legions and settled everybody's nerves. After fifty-two minutes Andy Cole put United two up to kick-start the celebrations. Giggsy sealed a 3-0 victory. The stage was set, literally, for United to receive their third league trophy in four years. The presentation took place at the United end of the ground with players and supporters only yards apart belting out our new and old songs together. It was a bit more intimate than the spacious backdrop of Old Trafford. We were home by nine o'clock and it was straight down to the Farmer's Arms to continue the party, another May Bank Holiday and another United title.

Just like 1994 the incredible form after Christmas also carried us to the FA Cup Final, our third in succession. Six teams had won the English double, none had won it twice. Opponents Liverpool were desperate to prevent our double double and we would relish achieving it against them just to further emphasise the shift of power.

I remember a BBC TV preview a few days before the final. The focus was on the young lads who had come through in both camps that season. The Beeb visited the respective training grounds and filmed an interview with each group. What stood out as I watched the programme was the total focus, respect and professionalism of Scholes, Butt, Giggs, Beckham and the Nevilles. In sharp contrast, Fowler, McManaman, McAteer and Redknapp were wise-cracking their way through the interview with that cocky Scouse attitude. You know what I mean – they think they're being dead funny; you would rather be removing your fingernails with a pair of pliers. I have no doubt the United youngsters got up to plenty of mischief off camera, but on it they were representing Manchester United and the serious business of winning trophies for the club and supporters. The next time I saw the Liverpool lads they were taking in the Wembley atmosphere dressed in white Armani suits. There could be only one winner that day and it wouldn't be the Spice Boys.

Strangely, Fergie left Steve Bruce out of the squad. He didn't even make the subs' bench despite being fit and having played in thirty-nine of the forty-nine competitive games that season. United's line-up on 12 May 1996 was: Schmeichel, Irwin, P. Neville, May, Pallister, Beckham, Butt, Keane, Cole, Cantona, Giggs. Subs: G. Neville, Scholes, Sharpe.

The anticipated thriller turned out to be a fairly sterile affair with neither goalkeeper being troubled. United's support was superb throughout but particularly during the second half as we pressed for a winner. The deadlock was broken with five minutes remaining by the newly crowned Football of the Year and captain, Eric Cantona. As David James punched away Beckham's corner it bounced into the path of the noble Frenchman on the edge of the area. Taking one step back to realign his body he threaded a volley through eight Liverpool defenders between him and the goal. The strike was the hallmark of a genius.

His form since returning in October had been peerless. Despite the ban, he finished top scorer with nineteen goals in thirty-eight games but it was the crucial goals during the run-in that made the difference for United. Single-goal victories against Liverpool, Spurs, Arsenal, West Ham, Coventry and Newcastle were all courtesy of Cantona strikes plus a last-minute equaliser at QPR. His behaviour and attitude on and off the pitch was exemplary and the extra time he dedicated to training was an inspiration to the young lads coming through. Eric Cantona was now a legend at Old Trafford.

For United supporters life was getting better with each passing season. Three titles in four seasons proved we had learned how to win the league while two doubles in three seasons was unbeliev-able and unprecedented. When it came to having bottle at the end of the season we had it in abundance. Perversely, old rivals such as Liverpool and Arsenal seemed to have lost the recipe.

Everyone connected with the club knew we had unfin-ished business on the European stage. United were back in the

European Cup and we needed to make our mark. All Fergie's kids distinguished themselves in that first big season and would continue to serve United well for many seasons. Stalwarts Keane, Cantona, Pallister, Schmeichel, Giggs and Irwin gave the team immense experience and ability but Fergie felt there were two areas that had to be strengthened. The centre of defence was creaking; it had almost cost United the title during Christmas. Similarly, the striking partnership of Cantona and Cole wasn't gelling and it was too soon to rely on the boy Scholes.

The biggest story of the summer was United's attempts to sign Alan Shearer. In the end the Geordie striker joined his beloved Newcastle for a world record fee of £15 million. This was the second time he had opted not to sign for United and inevitably he incurred the wrath of Reds for the rest of his career. The move to Blackburn in 1992 was predominantly driven by uncle Jack's money while the Tyneside transfer gave him the chance to play for his boyhood idols. I can understand both those motives and, biased as I am, I don't think every top star should want to join Manchester United. However, I think Shearer passing up the opportunity to play for United at that time showed a crass lack of ambition to play at the top and win medals. Let's be honest, even with all that money, Blackburn would always be a small town club. Similarly, despite Geordie optimism, there was little to suggest they were on the verge of becoming a dominant force in football. Perhaps Shearer thought he could make the difference?

I wonder whether he privately regrets his decision to reject United. I am convinced Alan Shearer would have been great for us, particularly in 1996 when our strike force needed bolstering. I believe we would have conquered Europe sooner with him in the team and for longer. United certainly would have been good for Shearer, bringing the stash of medals his ability deserved. If hero worship was his desire, United supporters would have outstripped that of the Geordies many times over. Anyway, Newcastle broke the bank and believed they could take away United's title. We signed a young Norwegian called Ole Gunnar Solskjaer for one tenth of Shearer's fee. Funny old world, isn't it?

After much speculation, Stevie Bruce left Old Trafford to join Birmingham City. It brought a sudden end to a distinguished nine-year career at Old Trafford where he made 414 appearances and scored fifty-one goals including an incredible nineteen in 1990/91.

Bruce was the foundation stone on which Fergie built the modern Manchester United. Truly fearless, he gave everything for the United cause and the supporters recognised that. He became the first English player in the twentieth century to captain a team to the double, but we'll always remember him for those two headed goals against Sheffield Wednesday in April 1993 which changed United's destiny.

Fergie also released another Old Trafford favourite, Lee Sharpe, who had struggled with injuries and lost his edge in the previous two seasons. Joining Ole Gunnar at Old Trafford were Ronnie Johnsen, Karel Poborsky and Jordi Cruyff. So why did Fergie buy four foreigners when his previous assaults on Europe had been thwarted by UEFA's restrictions? The 1995 Bosman ruling not only allowed players to move freely to another club at the end of their contract, it also banned any restrictions on EU members within the national leagues or UEFA competitions. From 1996/97 clubs could play any EU player in European competitions and overnight a stifling handicap was removed.

Fergie handed Cantona the club captaincy but it was Beckham who stole the headlines in the opening game against Wimbledon with his wonder goal from inside his own half. That was the moment the nation fell in love with David Beckham. A 3-0 win augured well but the first couple of months were littered with draws as Fergie experimented with his new purchases. In late October it looked like we had lost the plot completely with consecutive league defeats at Newcastle (5-0) and Southampton (6-3).

As pundits searched the records book, and Fergie searched his soul, our descent continued. We lost our forty-year unbeaten European home record to Fenerbahce (1-0), followed by a defeat to Chelsea which ended a twenty-three-month unbeaten run at Old Trafford. We scraped a 1-0 win over table-toppers Arsenal, only to lose at home again in the Champions League to Juventus. A week later, Leicester put us out of the League Cup. It was life Jim, but not as we knew it. People started writing us off but Fergie didn't panic. It would take time to find the right formula, especially at the back.

With hindsight we'd taken for granted the rock-solid partnership of Bruce and Pallister during the previous seven years. Now May, Johnsen and Pallister were rotated and sometimes it wasn't pretty. Giggs and Cole picked up long-term injuries. The young

Welsh genius had become an integral part of our strike force but calf and hamstring injuries caused him to miss ten games that autumn. Unlucky Cole missed six months, contracting pneumonia then breaking both legs on his return thanks to a clattering tackle by Neil Ruddock in a match against Liverpool reserves.

United's European campaign was stalling too. We had played five of our six group matches and lay outside the qualifying positions. The last game was Rapid Vienna on 4 December. We had to win in Austria and hope Fenerbahce failed to do the same in Turin. It was a must-see game and we fancied a bit of a treat so Pete Seymour, Mike Stewart, Simon Rumsey and myself booked a two-day trip with Independent Travel. Simon had broken his leg a few weeks earlier, though not in a tackle with Neil Ruddock. He was given the all-clear to fly but a week before the game contracted a dodgy infection which needed treating with rat poison. I kid you not. For those who know Simon quite well, it seemed a fitting remedy. Anyway, his medical team ruled him out of the trip.

With everything paid up, he was about to lose a couple of hundred quid. In a moment of madness/romance/softness (please delete if not applicable) I decided to take my wife. Louise isn't into football but takes a passing interest due to my obsession. However, she does enjoy travel, likes a drink and is always game for a bit of a knees-up so I had no qualms about her blending in.

Mike Stewart's employers, Davies Turner, ship a lot of freight to Austria and he knew several Austrian Reds. We had entertained them in Manchester a few times, now they couldn't wait to return the favour. On the day of the game they took us to a bar only a stone's throw from the ground. The place was rocking, mainly with Rapid fans but we were made very welcome. The beer flowed, the food was like a banquet, folk stood on tables and belted out songs, more beer flowed and all that was washed down with half a dozen rounds of apricot schnapps. The hospitality was so good we nearly forgot the match so it was a quick dash to the turnstiles.

During the Rapid Vienna game United rediscovered their true form. We could have been three up in fifteen minutes though Rene Wagner brought a stunning save from Peter Schmeichel. A brilliant interchange between Cantona and Giggs ended with the Welshman ghosting through to slide the ball home. Cantona

sealed a 2–0 win in the seventy-second minute and the favour-
able news from Turin confirmed our place in the European Cup
quarter finals for the first time since 1969. That was cause for
celebration. We met up with our hosts again in their equivalent of
Manchester's famous Corbieres Wine Cavern. The underground
club played only the finest British rock and roll – not a hint of
Europop and between each record, the Viennese revellers were
treated to a chorus or two of United's legendary symphonies.

On the domestic front, Liverpool were mounting their first
serious title attempt for seven years but Newcastle were the big
surprise. They had failed to build on the previous year's campaign
despite their expensive number nine. The league table a week
before Christmas showed we had some catching up to do.

	P	W	D	L	F	A	Pts	GD
Liverpool	18	11	4	3	35	17	37	18
Arsenal	17	10	5	2	34	16	35	18
Wimbledon	17	10	4	3	30	17	34	13
Newcastle	17	9	3	5	35	17	30	8
Aston Villa	17	9	3	5	22	15	30	7
Man United	17	7	7	3	32	25	28	7

By the end of January 1997 United were top, having won six out
of seven league games. Newcastle, Liverpool and Arsenal struggled
to string together a decent run. Wimbledon ended our FA Cup
interest in the fourth round but the focus was a Champions League
tie with Porto. The Portuguese champions had been on fire in the
qualifying stages and lost only one game all season. We expected a
tough encounter when they visited Old Trafford for the first leg
on 5 March. What we witnessed was one of those genuinely great
European nights at Old Trafford. Keane and Butt were missing
but Giggs and Johnsen were magnificent in their place. May and
Cantona scored in the first half, Giggs and Cole in the second
to give United an unassailable 4–0 lead. The atmosphere was in
keeping with United's finest European traditions.

David May was having his best season yet, having formed
a good partnership with Pallister. Ten days before we played
Porto I went to the league game at Stamford Bridge. The away
fans then were low down in the paddock next to the players'
tunnel right behind the dugout. May was on the bench that

afternoon and late in the second half he started warming up in front of the United fans. A guy a couple of rows in front of me started singing a song I had not heard before, 'David May superstar, got more medals than Shearer.' It brought a wave and a smile from the player before the singer packed it in after a couple of choruses.

On the way home the little ditty kept playing over in my head. I thought no more of it until the Porto game when May popped up to give United the lead on twenty-two minutes. The crowd erupted and for the next quarter of an hour all the great old songs echoed round the ground. When the dust settled I stood up and started singing the David May number I had heard at Chelsea. For a good five minutes I was like a performing seal trying to get this song going. A couple of hardy souls in J and K Stands latched on but my mate Brian said, 'Sit down, Pete, you're flogging a dead horse with that one!' I knew from experience there's a fine line between hanging in there until a song catches fire and standing there like a right prat while everyone around keeps their hands in their pockets. Anyway, I'm nothing if not persistent.

A couple of minutes later I could hear the song picking up in J, slowly spreading along K and a few minutes later it reached the Stretford End and the whole ground was belting it out. It became the anthem of the night and was reprised over the next few years either in recognition of David May or to have a go at Shearer. So, apologies to the nice man at Chelsea for nicking his song but they say imitation is the sincerest form of flattery.

The Porto tie was as good as over but it didn't stop 10,000–12,000 Reds heading over there. We had all booked our trips before the first leg result so the day turned into one big party. Good-humoured Reds took over the city of Oporto, bathing in the warm sunshine and partaking in a few scoops of Superbock, a cheap but powerful local brew that has gone down in terrace folklore. United drew 0–0 in a match that many Reds struggle to recollect.

Borussia Dortmund would be our semi-final opponents. The final was scheduled for Munich and Reds had visions of United lifting the European Cup in the city indelibly linked to our great history. Just before the first leg at the Westfalenstadion Peter Schmeichel failed a fitness test on a back injury he had picked up the day before. Raymond van der Gouw came in for only his fourth outing of the season. United never found their rhythm but managed to create numerous clear-cut chances that were thwarted by bad luck or bad finishing depending on your generosity.

With seventy-five minutes on the clock, fate dealt United a cruel blow when René Tretshok's long-range shot deflected off Butt's boot and looped inches over our stand-in keeper. Many United supporters in the crowd felt Schmeichel would have got a hand to what was the only goal of the night.

Before the second leg Fergie warned his troops against any momentary lack of concentration that could give Dortmund the vital away goal. His prophetic words went unheeded as Ricken nipped in to score after only eight minutes. United had over twenty attempts on goal but couldn't crack the Germans who held on for a 2-0 aggregate win. They would go on to beat Juventus in the final.

In the league United lost just twice in twenty six games following the autumn crash. Solskjær was a revelation with eighteen goals in thirty-three appearances. Liverpool, Arsenal and Newcastle stayed on our tails but we simply out-paced them. On 6 May, United were champions again without kicking a ball as the chasing pack all faltered against lowly opposition. Four titles in five years; Fergie was fast approaching greatness and people started to mention him in the same breath as Herbert Chapman, Bill Shankly, Bob Paisley, Jock Stein and of course our very own Sir Matt. United were dominating the 1990s domestically and our rivals were buckling under the pressure. In early January 1997, Keegan threw in the towel and resigned. Liverpool flattered to deceive under Roy Evans but finished fourth and Arsenal, renowned for the longevity of their managers, had sacked Bruce Rioch after only one season in charge.

Like thousands of other Reds I was delighted with yet another title but it was tainted by the failure in Europe. I wasn't becoming blasé about winning the league. God knows after living through that twenty-six-year dearth I cherish every one. However, I had always put the European Cup ahead of league success and still do. Several of my mates always want the league title before all else, but in my view United should be at the pinnacle of club football and that means winning the European Cup.

That is the journey Matt Busby embarked on in 1956 and it's the benchmark the 1968 team set for United teams to follow. It is where Manchester United belong. Winning the English league title is like headlining at the London Palladium whereas the European Cup is top of the bill in Las Vegas. United's target should always be Las Vegas. Perhaps we shouldn't complain too much though, neighbours City were lucky if they got a one-night stand at the Oldham Coliseum.

Reaching the European Cup semi-final for the first time in twenty-eight years was terrific, United had learned to hold their own against the best in Europe. The 'apprenticeship' that began in 1993 was complete. It was no longer boys against men in cauldrons like the Nou Camp or anything Istanbul could throw at us. Now we had to push on and beat the very best in Europe. To achieve that, we had to resolve our lack of fire power on the highest stage. In the ten Champions League games of 1996/97 we failed to score in six and lost five 1-0. Could Fergie save the day?

20

FLAGS, RAGS, FERRYBOATS, SCIMITARS AND SCARVES, EVERY PRECIOUS DREAM AND VISION, UNDERNEATH THE STARS

On the afternoon of Sunday, 18 May 1997, I was battling with a badly neglected garden that came with the house we had bought the year before. For thirty years I had lived in a terraced house in Salford with a concrete back yard, the only grass down our street was the stuff you smoke. Anyway, the season was over so time to focus on domestic duties. I had the radio on when right out of the blue came an announcement that Eric Cantona was quitting football. The station played a short clip where United's captain said:

> I have played professional football for thirteen years, which is a long time. I now wish to do other things.

With that, the magical adventure was over. Typically, Eric's departure was as unexpected as his arrival four and a half years earlier. United had lost the most influential player in their long history and the supporters had lost an iconic hero. Cantona wasn't the best player I saw in a United shirt, that was George Best, nor was he 'The King', that will always be Denis Law. The Frenchman didn't have the international respect Bobby Charlton attracted, the longevity at the top like Ryan Giggs or the power and drive to lead his team like Roy Keane. Yet as I look back over the last fifty years, the one player I wouldn't want United to have missed out on is Eric Cantona.

Just compare where Manchester United were when he arrived to when he left. The transformation is historic. Furthermore, United would build a lasting dynasty on the foundations he laid. Cantona was an inspiration to his team-mates, the supporters and, I suspect, to Fergie too. I made a cup of tea, sat on me garden wall and quietly thought about what we had witnessed in those phenomenal Cantona years.

Fergie signed 31-year-old Teddy Sheringham from Spurs and raided Blackburn for Henning Berg. Despite losing our leading light, United started the season well and carried it through to the New Year. Challengers to our crown were still very inconsistent whereas United were blowing teams away, 7-0 and 6-1 in consecutive weeks at home to Barnsley and Sheffield Wednesday, 5-2 away to Wimbledon, 4-0 over second-placed Blackburn and 3-1 at Anfield. Andy Cole was back and scoring regularly, Sheringham slotted into Cantona's role and Berg starred in defence. United topped the group stage of the Champions League and won the first five games, including a memorable 3-2 victory at home to the mighty Juventus.

The only stain on the first half of the season was the loss of new captain Roy Keane after just nine games. At Elland Road he tore a cruciate ligament in his knee which ended his season and threatened his career. Initially the loss of Keane didn't faze United. In the FA Cup we annihilated holders and second-in-the-table Chelsea at Stamford Bridge. United led 5-0 after seventy-four minutes, the Londoners' star-studded squad looked completely demoralised until three late goals salvaged some pride. The table dated 11 January 1998 showed us on the way to a third consecutive title:

	P	W	D	L	F	A	Pts	GD
Man United	22	15	4	3	51	16	49	35
Chelsea	22	13	3	6	49	22	42	27
Blackburn	21	11	8	2	38	21	41	17
Liverpool	21	12	4	5	38	19	40	19
Arsenal	21	10	7	4	37	24	37	13

That is as good as it got in 1997/98, United wobbled and Arsenal embarked on an incredible run. We won three of the next eight league games and Barnsley beat us in an FA Cup replay at Oakwell. United's confidence was waning and Giggsy's hamstring injury in late February disrupted the team's rhythm. He missed six crucial weeks including the Champions League quarter-final matches against Monaco and a six-pointer against Arsenal. In the first leg in Monaco, United's marvellous support couldn't inspire the team to more than a goalless draw. On the Saturday before the return leg, we played Arsenal at home. They were on a roll in league and Cup and though still trailing by nine points, had played three games fewer. The game wouldn't decide the title but a win would provide a great impetus for either side.

Arsene Wenger was in his first full season at Highbury and had quickly married the flair of Viera, Petit, Overmars and Bergkamp to the sturdy English defence of Seaman, Dixon, Adams, Keown and Winterburn. Ten minutes from time Marc Overmars, a constant threat that afternoon, sealed a 1-0 win for Arsenal. Four days later United could only muster a 1-1 draw with Monaco and went out on away goals. Once again, a home goal conceded in the opening ten minutes was our undoing.

Arsenal's form was relentless. The Gunners won ten consecutive league games between March and May to claim the title with two games to spare. Just to rub salt in our wounds, the north Londoners won the FA Cup to equal United's double double. Mr Wenger had arrived.

At the time it felt devastating. Second-best was no longer an option for Fergie or the supporters and another failure in Europe left me in despair. Though we had gained a few good scalps in recent years we had been eliminated by Galatasaray, Gothenburg, Dortmund and Monaco – not exactly the cream of Europe. A return to the halcyon days of 1968 seemed a long way off.

Other than the purchase of Andy Cole, Fergie had been picking up shrewd bargains in the transfer market for the previous five years; Solskjaer, Berg, Johnsen, May, Poborsky, Cruyff and Sheringham. He had successfully harvested six top players from United's youth team and still had his reliable generals in Schmeichel, Irwin, Pallister and Keane. The manager could have been forgiven for writing off 1997/98 as an injury-strewn twist of fate, but thank God that adequacy isn't Fergie's driver. His instincts told him to bolster the spine of the team.

Peter Schmeichel was still the best in the business but at centre-back and up front we were making do. Fergie wanted another rock on which to build the defence and opted for Jaap

Stam, the towering Dutch international. United paid a staggering £10.6 million for his signature, a world record for a defender. The search for a top striker led Fergie to Dwight Yorke but it took a bitter battle and £12.6 million to prise him from John Gregory's Aston Villa. Finally, as cover for Ryan Giggs, United bought Jesper Blomqvist for £4.4 million. A total outlay around £28 million and very little financed by offloading other players as only Gary Pallister moved on.

United's faithful were impressed and while no individual signing beat Shearer's £15 million or came near Denílson's world record £23 million that same year, this was a huge expenditure even for a club the size of United. Our annual turnover at the time was around £88 million with net profits around £10 million. Alex Ferguson had taken a step back after the previous season's capitulation and looked at the big picture. Similar to 1995, this wasn't the time to rest on laurels or simply tweak the squad. United stood at the crossroads; one signposted 'PRETTY GOOD' the other 'TRULY GREAT'. Fergie knew there was only one direction for our club.

As 1998/99 got underway it felt great to have Roy Keane back. He had become United's engine, not just his play but his leadership of the team. On the pitch he embodied the manager's devotion, the supporters' passion and the never-say-die spirit of Manchester United. At the back, Stam and Johnsen were the preferred pairing, up front Fergie played Cole and Yorke, using Sheringham and Solskjaer as impact substitutions.

Early season form was steady rather than spectacular; once again it would take ten to fifteen games for the new defensive partnership to knit together. We kept pace with the leading pack, chasing a rejuvenated Aston Villa, and United's Champions League draw threw up a classic 'group of death' containing Barcelona and Bayern Munich with Brondby making up the numbers. United drew all four matches with Barca and Bayern and beat the Danes twice to finish second.

Second place didn't carry automatic qualification to the quarter-finals, the six group winners progressed with the two best runners-up. Fortunately, our ten points edged us through. Barcelona lost back-to-back games against Bayern and went out, ending their dream to win the European Cup in their beloved Nou Camp the following May.

United were scoring for fun. In Europe we racked up twenty in six matches and were top scorers in the domestic league. The defence was leaking goals though; seven times we conceded three in a match by mid-December. At Christmas United were tucked in four points behind the leaders. There was little indication of the extraordinary events the New Year would bring, but something clicked into place as we entered 1999. Middlesbrough were knocked out of the FA Cup, we beat West Ham 4-1 at home and Leicester 6-2 away in the league, then ended Liverpool's Wembley ambitions with a 2-1 win at Old Trafford. Michael Owen scored after three minutes and the Scousers held on until Yorke and Solskjaer scored right at the death. The following week Yorke netted the winner at Charlton in the eighty-ninth minute. United had developed a knack for late goals and it would be a recurring theme through the run-in. The victory at The Valley sent United top for the first time that season.

The Champions League quarter-final pitched us against Inter Milan for the first time in European competition and the prospect was mouth-watering. The home first leg was the night David Beckham came of age; his passing, work rate and creativity were second to none. Add to that a couple of trademark pinpoint, curling crosses for Dwight Yorke to give United a 2-0 advantage.

The big games came thick and fast now, four days later United drew 0-0 at home to Chelsea in the FA Cup sixth round then won the replay 2-0 with another brace from Yorke. Next stop was Milan for the second leg. United took around 5,000 supporters and for many it was our first trip to the famous city. A dozen mates made the journey. One-day excursions now got supporters to the host city well before midday and gone was the Anglo-phobia of the 1980s and early 1990s where fans were unwelcome and shipped in and out as quickly as possible. The eternal debate among the lads was how much time should be given over to sight-seeing as opposed to a drink and a sing-song. We always managed both but some in the group had a very low threshold for the tourist bit.

We passed through the Galleria Vittorio Emanuele II, the oldest shopping mall in Italy housed within a four-storey double arcade in central Milan. On the floor of the main walkway there's a mosaic of the Turin Bull. Legend has it that if you stand on the bull's testicles and spin round it will bring you good luck and possibly increase your fertility. With a place in the semi-finals at stake we gave the bovine scrotum a good pummelling.

After the heady heights of Milan's stunning Duomo Cathedral it was down onto the piazza below to wash the dust from our throats. Hundreds of Reds filled the square that afternoon, enjoying a great atmosphere in the Italian sunshine. We drank, we sang, we made merry and there was no hint of trouble between United's huge following, the police or the locals. Pete Seymour didn't need a bull's balls as he had brought his own lucky mascot with him, a glove puppet of Sooty (Google it if you're too young!) and entertained the troops throughout the afternoon as the famous woollen bear popped up in all sorts of places. During rush hour the traffic was almost at a standstill in the square. Pete's final party piece was to jib a lift on the back of a scooter passing slowly by and present Sooty to the throng of adoring Reds for an ovation befitting royalty.

The sight of the San Siro, or the Stadio Giuseppe Meazza as the Inter fans prefer, took our breath away. Its huge concrete towers, enormous new roof and distinctive protruding red girders, all illuminated by floodlight, gave the appearance of a gigantic space station ready for take-off. Inside, the huge steep sides created a white-hot atmosphere. The received wisdom was not to concede an early goal, keep it tight and hope it quelled the crowd. Inter threw everything at us and the game was played at a frenetic pace. Centre-backs Henning Berg and Jaap Stam stood as tall as the towers surrounding the stadium. Along with Schmeichel they mopped up wave after wave of Inter attacks, often getting a hand, foot or leg to the ball at the last minute.

When Ventola scored after sixty-three minutes the noise was incredible. Our rearguard action dug in even deeper but it was extremely tense with 75,000 Italians baying for a second to level the tie. United stood firm and the clock ran down. With just two minutes remaining the ball fell for Scholes, right in front of the goal and right in front of the United supporters. It seemed to take an eternity for him to swing his leg and hit it sweetly into the net to finish the tie. We danced around like madmen in a shower of lighters, cans, bottles and rotten fruit that rained down on us from the stands above. United were in the semi-finals of the European Cup. The bull had done good!

Fergie said the victory over Inter 'was a massive step forward for this club ... I see Italian big guns as the barometer of our progress.' Wise words but I don't think he wanted to check the barometer again so quickly; United were pitched against Juventus in the semis. The pace of the season was electric with a 'cup final' every weekend and midweek. Arsenal, Chelsea and United were going full-pelt in the title race while April held the promise of semi-finals at home and abroad.

It seems strange now, knowing how the season turned out, that few United supporters were too concerned about the treble at this stage. There was talk of it but the majority of us were simply focused on winning the European Cup. That was now our Holy Grail. The league was important too but the FA Cup was very much an after-thought. We went into the first leg against Juventus top of our domestic league, but after forty-five minutes the gulf between us and the 'Old Lady' seemed wider than ever. Oozing class and packed with star names Juve gave United and the stunned 55,000 a football lesson. But a twenty-fifth-minute goal was all they had to show for their superiority and in the last half-hour United found some form. Just as I was thinking I had wasted my money booking a trip to Turin, Giggsy lashed an equaliser into the top corner in injury time. Out of jail, but our European hopes hung by a thread. To reach the final United would have to do something we had never done before in Italy – win or score twice.

Four days later we faced Arsenal in the FA Cup semi at Villa Park. The Gunners harboured hopes of winning back-to-back doubles, having gone twenty games undefeated since mid-December. United's unbeaten run stretched back one match further. No surprise then that the game ended 0-0, giving both sides the result neither wanted. The replay felt like a massive distraction from the main events but by the end of that night those emotions had been completely swept away.

Quite simply, Arsenal versus Manchester United on 14 April 1999 was the match that had everything. Fergie, fearing fatigue, rotated his strikers and it paid off as United created a string of chances in the first half. David Beckham put us ahead with a beautiful curling shot from just outside the area. The goal brought Arsenal to life and Schmeichel was called into action several times. After the break it was end-to-end stuff and the tackles got more intense as two English giants fought for supremacy. It would be a battle to the death. On the hour, Bergkamp equalised when he created space for himself thirty yards from goal and let fly. Anelka then had a goal ruled out for offside. Keano was everywhere but with seventeen minutes remaining his scything tackle on Overmars saw referee Elleray reaching for the red card.

United re-grouped but in injury time a tired Phil Neville tripped Ray Parlour inside the box. 'Penalty,' said Mr Elleray and the Arsenal terraces erupted in celebration. High on the Holte End terraces our lads decided to move towards the exit tunnel anticipating the outcome. I had edged to the end of the row of seats and I was standing on the aisle steps ready to leave once the ball hit the net. Bergkamp shaped up to deliver the killer blow and there was an 'Oh, Pretty Woman' moment. You know, the Roy Orbison classic where the song reaches a crescendo? The forlorn hero is just about to give up on his dream girl when the Big O stops the music in its tracks, 'I guess I'll go on home, it's late; there'll be tomorrow night, but wait … what do I see? … Is she walking back to me?' … And there was Peter Schmeichel diving to his left to parry the Dutchman's spot-kick. Now it was our turn to erupt, the miss giving United the initiative with the Red Army in superb voice. Meanwhile we sheepishly returned to our seats for extra time.

In a match that just kept giving, a piece of pure gold topped it off. With 109 minutes played, Ryan Giggs scored the best goal ever in the FA Cup to win the match for Manchester United. History has a habit of exaggerating greatness, like the legends that surround Marilyn Monroe, James Dean and JFK. But in fifty years, exaggeration still won't be necessary for this supreme effort. Having intercepted the ball somewhere around Junction Seven on the M6, Giggs' mesmerising slalom dribble through England's best defence before unleashing a rocket into the roof of the net would leave people in complete awe now as it dis then.

The FA abolished semi-final replays after that game as a way of reducing fixture congestion. That was just a smokescreen. They realised nothing could ever come close to matching what we witnessed at Villa Park that night. Out of respect for United's per-formance, and Giggsy's goal in particular, they decided to 'retire' replays at that stage of the competition because it simply couldn't get any better. Well, that's my view anyway.

For the second time in a week, Ryan Giggs had come to
United's rescue at a vital time. Before United's home game
against Sheffield Wednesday the following Saturday Fergie made
an unprecedented pitch-side address to a packed Old Trafford
before the game. Acknowledging the tremendous efforts of the
team so far, he issued a call to arms for the final few weeks of
what was turning out to be a unique season.

Fergie had become very savvy in his handling of the United
faithful. The fixture with Wednesday could easily have been a case
of the Lord Mayor's show with tired players and a subdued crowd
simply awaiting a United romp. His speech whipped up the
passions and United's 3-0 victory was sung home by all corners
of the ground. The win kept us top, four points ahead of both
Arsenal and Chelsea.

Our next port of call was Turin for the second leg of the semi-
final. Around 6,000 Reds travelled but the rain kept most indoors
during the day in the hundreds of bars around the city. I travelled with the usual suspects, Pete Seymour, Mike Stewart and
Simon Rumsey, along with James and Cath Grant from Oldham.
The pre-match banter focused on our chances that night.

Not even the most optimistic were confident. Juventus were
a European superpower and had been for most of the decade.
They were aiming to equal Real Madrid's forty-year record of
reaching four consecutive finals. Perhaps, more tellingly, Juve
hadn't lost a two-legged European Cup tie since 1986. The draw
in Manchester had given us a mountain to climb, but we were
living the dream. We were here and up for it! Fergie's line-up was:
Schmeichel, G. Neville, Irwin, Keane, Johnsen, Stam, Beckham,
Butt, Cole, Yorke, Blomqvist. Sub: Scholes.

The mountain turned into Everest within eleven minutes,
Filippo Inzaghi scoring twice to give Juve a foot in the final.
Ironically, United had settled in their rhythm pretty quickly and
were playing good football. Inside the Stadio delle Alpe it didn't
seem the disaster the scoreline suggested and we knew 2-0 can
be a dangerous early lead. But this was Juventus in Turin, surely
I was scraping the barrel of hope? On twenty-four minutes
captain Keane, leading from the front like never before, powered
home a header from a Beckham corner. The strike gave United
confidence and unnerved the Italians. One more would put us
in front on away goals and it came from Dwight Yorke's head

after thirty-four minutes. Unbelievable! The phosphorous flares, drums and klaxons of the Juve faithful had fallen silent, replaced by shrill whistling as they tried to drown out the celebrations on the Manchester terraces.

A minute before Yorke's equaliser, Roy Keane collected a booking for a clumsy tackle on Zinedine Zidane. The tally of yellow cards in Europe meant he would miss the European Cup Final should we win. Keane never flinched. United's captain was the personification of Fergie's clarion call four days earlier, totally preoccupied with getting his beloved team into the final we so coveted.

The game ebbed and flowed, but once again Fergie had got the tactics right bringing in Ronnie Johnsen to shackle FIFA World Player of the Year, Zidane. As the game progressed the French playmaker had less and less impact. With twenty minutes left it really hit home how close we were to reaching the European Cup Final. Getting through meant everything, defeat now would be unbearable. With every decreasing minute on the giant clock the tension mounted. Six minutes from time the suspense was over as Yorke skipped through an Italian defence in tatters and Andy Cole slid the loose ball home.

There is no point trying to describe how I felt at that moment. Suffice to say there was no place on planet earth I would rather be than right there jumping around hugging fellow Reds who had seen the best and worst of times over the years. Again the Italian whistles tried to mask our songs of praise but that was impossible as the Red Army belted out the 'We shall not be moved' classic. We could hear it, they could hear it and most importantly the rest of Europe could hear it on their TV sets. The message came through loud and clear.

United's performance against Juventus on 21 April 1999 was the best I've ever seen the Reds play. I have little doubt it will stay that way. As United's players left the field the applause from the 55,000 home supporters was warm and generous. This erudite gathering knew they had witnessed an exceptional performance from an extraordinary side. I have never been more proud to be a Manchester United supporter.

The journey home was spent reliving the game and taking in the deep satisfaction of reaching our first European Cup Final for thirty-one years. I bought most of the daily newspapers the next morning, trawling through them to take in every snippet about the match. The press loved us with front and back page coverage.

So now we had two cup finals to think about, Newcastle and Bayern Munich, plus the league title run-in. It was difficult for most Reds to concentrate on anything else. Work, family, etc. were all important but United's finale to the season was becoming all-consuming. Sometimes I had to sit down and calm myself, I was getting that giddy.

There was, however, one pressing appointment I had to focus on. Earlier that year Louise and I had decided to finally start a family. I was 44, she was 33. Procrastination be gone, procreation began. The pregnancy was confirmed in February but like many folk we waited until the twelve-week hospital check before telling anyone. That scan was on Monday, 26 April 1999. I was still on cloud nine from the Juve game but this was important in a different way.

I took a couple of hours off work for the ultrasound tests. Obviously we were just hoping everything was okay, the nurse covered my wife's stomach with jelly and started the sonar machine in motion. There was a furrowed brow on the nurse's face as she told us she wanted another medical opinion and brought in a colleague to listen. They both had furrowed brows but said nothing as they listened through a stethoscope. The second nurse asked if there was any history of twins in the family. I told her no and she kept on listening. 'Any particular reason you asked that last question?' I heard myself say, nervously. 'Yes, I think I can hear two heartbeats.' We moved closer to the monitor and the grainy picture showed two very small babies. 'Congratulations, you're having twins and they're doing fine.'

I had to remain calm because I could see Louise's face draining of any colour. 'Twins?! Twins! Oh my God!' she blurted. It was a massive shock and neither of us had given it a thought. On the surface I was the perfect supportive husband, reassuring her that everything would be fine. Inside I was a mess. Bloody hell, five league games to win the title, we're in FA Cup and European Cup Finals and we're having bloody twins! I must have overdone it with the bull's balls in Milan!

The babies were due on 5 November, so for now I could attend to more urgent matters, although I didn't quite put it like that to Louise. With the two cup finals sorted, it was back to the league title race. Arsenal bounced back from the defeat at Villa Park with four straight wins and cut United's lead, but the Gunners lost

their penultimate game at Elland Road. The title race would go
to the last game of the campaign and United's brave attempt at a
unique treble would be decided by three matches in ten historic
days. The table on the final weekend showed United had to at
least match Arsenal's result:

	P	W	D	L	F	A	Pts	GD
Man United	37	21	13	3	78	36	76	42
Arsenal	37	21	12	4	58	17	75	41

Arsenal entertained Villa while United's final match was home
to Spurs whose supporters turned up with a huge banner carrying a simple message to their own team, 'Let Them Win'! Spurs
players chose to ignore their supporters' wishes and took the lead
through Les Ferdinand after twenty-four minutes. Old Trafford
nerves jangled a little but three minutes either side of half-time
United scored. Beckham equalised then Andy Cole did what he
should have done four years earlier and scored the winning goal
that brought United the title. Arsenal won 1-0, so one point and
one goal separated the top two.

For the first time since 1965, United had won the title on
home ground. It was our fifth title in seven years, our twelfth
overall and the first leg of the treble was in the bag. Time to party
and the Manchester pubs were beckoning. Win two cup finals
and Fergie achieves immortality, but first he had some key selection issues to wrestle. His brave troops had served him well in
an unforgettable campaign. Nineteen players had appearances in
double figures but who would take the field in the biggest week
in the club's 121-year history?

Some decisions were made for him, Scholes and Keane would
play at Wembley as both were suspended for the Bayern game. As
a result, Nicky Butt sat out of the FA Cup Final to avoid injury as
did the suspended Denis Irwin. Fergie felt he couldn't risk losing
Stam or top scorer Yorke for the Champions League Final so
they only made the bench for Wembley. United lined up for the
FA Cup Final on 22 May: Schmeichel, G. Neville, Johnsen, May,
P. Neville, Keane, Beckham, Scholes, Cole, Solskjaer, Giggs. Subs:
Sheringham, Stam, Yorke.

Despite losing Keane to injury after eight minutes United
swept aside a poor Magpies team. Fergie could probably have

rested a few more. Teddy Sheringham came on and netted within ninety seconds and Scholesy sealed a 2-0 victory on fifty-two minutes. It was too easy for United and we used the last thirty minutes to conserve energy. The Newcastle supporters were very subdued as for the second successive year their team had failed to turn up for an FA Cup Final.

The injury to Keane had given United eighty-two minutes to trial a midfield without their inspirational captain. We did well but the test would be a lot harder against Bayern. For now though it was time to raise a glass to our third double of the decade.

All our lads managed to get tickets for Wembley and the Nou Camp. Twelve of us opted for a two-day trip to Spain organised by the infamous 'Scottie'. We arrived on Tuesday afternoon in buoyant mood. The coach dropped off Reds at the other hotels but the driver seemed to be having trouble finding ours, driving round the same block time and time again. Eventually he stopped the coach, put our cases on the pavement and pointed us in the direction of a very big house at the top of a long drive.

Once inside the huge gates we found a corridor with a 'reception' sign. The place didn't look like your conventional hotel but we weren't too bothered. The lads at the front of the queue were having trouble booking in. The little Spanish I remembered from school was enough to understand that the receptionist was mystified about our booking. In a nutshell, Scottie had struggled to find sufficient hotel accommodation and booked us into a religious retreat for teenage catholic girls. Apparently he had told the owners to expect a Norwegian school party planning to use the facilities as a youth hostel over the May holiday.

Now, I've jibbed into some pretty tricky places in my time – bars, matches, concerts etc. – but never a juvenile convent and certainly not accompanied by twelve hairy-arsed Stretford Enders. We smiled politely, backed off and sat outside pondering the best solution. We only had one option, explain the mix-up, promise we would be little angels and throw ourselves on their mercy. We sent in two lads who looked the most respectable to do the talking. Twenty minutes later we were in.

Back home we would discover that Scottie had 'over-stretched' himself, shall we say, with his inventive planning for

Reds in Barcelona. Some supporters didn't receive match tickets that were part of their package and our tour operator had to lay low for quite some time after May 1999. On the Tuesday night our crowd just chilled around Barcelona together. The following day I would watch Manchester United play in the European Cup Final once again. It felt like Christmas Eve when I was a kid. Now, I was privileged to be with the lads who been there for the last three decades following United home and away; through thick and thin.

We all knew how much it meant to each other. My nephew Simon, who was 16, had come on the trip with his dad and Paul Clay, a good mate from Chesterfield, had brought his teenage children Daniel and Natalie. I wondered if the final would provide lifelong memories for them as it had for me in 1968?

On the day of the game we did the tourist bit and chilled some more, but I was itching for the game to begin. Nerves were creeping in. I promised myself I wouldn't get drawn in to a drinking session. I know that sounds like a right wimp but I really wanted to savour the match and the occasion. I knew only too well that they don't come round as often as we would like. So a couple of glasses at lunchtime did the trick. At really big games like this I never feel comfortable until I'm in the ground. That haunting fear that I'll get to the turnstile and be turned away or I'll lose my ticket always returns. There were no such problems and forty-five minutes before kick-off I was in.

The Nou Camp is a cathedral in world football and befitting the top match in European club football. Our view from the third tier was perfect: we were ready for our biggest match in three decades. United lined up on 26 May 1999: Schmeichel, G. Neville, Irwin, Stam, Johnsen, Butt, Beckham, Blomqvist, Cole, Yorke, Giggs. Subs: Sheringham, Solskjaer.

Perhaps we should have expected Bayern to score first given the season we had just had, but Mario Basler's sixth-minute opener rocked United. Unlike the game in Turin, we didn't start with our usual composure and confidence. With Giggsy on the right, Blomqvist down the left and Beckham in centre midfield the shape of the team was distorted. In fact, for over an hour, United looked flat. Perhaps the hectic schedule and the missing players were a bridge too far? Our worst performance of the season came in our biggest match. I knew how the Geordies felt now.

Bayern's early goal enabled them to focus on nullifying United's raids before they reached Cole or Yorke. Our first shot in anger arrived early in the second half. Bayern's coach Ottmar Hitzfeld was employing similar tactics to those that gave his Dortmund side victory over United two years earlier. After sixty-seven minutes Fergie brought on Sheringham for Blomqvist; Giggs and Beckham reverted to their usual positions and our shape improved immediately. Beckham was working like a Trojan to create chances but it was Bayern who came closest, twice hitting the woodwork in the last eleven minutes. Cole was replaced by Solskjaer after eighty-one minutes but time was running out.

I always have faith in United scoring, right up to the last minute. But when I saw the big clock at the other end of the ground showing ninety minutes played I remember looking high into the heavens at the big bright moon and thinking to myself, 'So this is how the dream ends? This is how it's meant to be?' I just felt empty.

Then I saw Beckham collect a German clearance and try another surging run, he passed to Gary Neville whose cross was deflected for a corner. The board had just gone up showing three minutes of added time. There was hope, I was clasping my hands and holding them to my face. I may have said a little prayer, I'm not sure. Schmeichel's dark green shirt appeared in the Bayern area. The corner came in, the ball was all over the place, then suddenly and very clearly right below us was Teddy Sheringham sweeping home the equaliser.

What happened next was sheer pandemonium as 60,000 United supporters erupted with uncontrollable joy. People all around me had wild-eyed, crazed expressions as they jumped and bounced and fell about in absolute disbelief. Never had a United goal been celebrated with such fervour.

We would have been hysterical for the best part of an hour if nothing else had happened that night but suddenly we were off again. United pushed forward and won another corner. Beckham swung it in, Sheringham nodded it on and Solskjaer stabbed the ball high into the German net. Now it was surreal, I was jumping around again, everyone was looking even more crazed than before, some people were still getting to their feet from the first goal and … I had just seen United score the winning goal in the very last minute of the European Cup Final!

No moments up to that point in my life had ever come close to matching those following Teddy's equaliser in Barcelona. The surge and intensity of emotion exceeded all my childhood Christmases, birthdays, summer holidays, my first kiss and the best-ever-sex all rolled into one. It was bliss. If any of that sounds over-dramatic consider this. How often do you wait thirty-one years for your dream to turn into reality? Rarely do any of us have to wait that long for the big events in our life. Be it marriage, children, a new job or promotion. Once we've set our sights on our big goals in life we invariably achieve them within a few years or not at all.

At the tender age of 11, I was mesmerised by the magic and excitement of United's quest to conquer Europe. When I saw that dream achieved in 1968 I knew that winning the European Cup was the benchmark for the team I loved. I didn't know what a benchmark was then, but that doesn't matter. I thought we would win it again many times through my teens and twenties, but it wasn't to be. The spark that was ignited in 1968 had become an eternal flame – and it never dimmed once. Now, in 1999, Manchester United were once again champions of Europe. It was impossible to hold back the tears, young and old were moved by what they had just experienced. Few around us spoke. If they did, it wasn't in joined up sentences, just short cries of disbelief. Words were neither possible, nor necessary.

I reckon many Reds went into clinical shock that night. Everything that followed in the next few hours seemed trance-like. The prolonged and noisy celebrations with each player raising the trophy in front of a wall of noise, meeting Steve Bruce on the way out of the ground, the stifling and slow underground ride back to the city centre – all a blur.

Finally, we reached Las Ramblas which was about to host the best party I've ever known, but the first bar we went in was full of Bayern supporters having the quietest of quiet drinks. As we sat down with our beer, several came over and congratulated us. They were absolutely devastated, and seeing us so delirious could only have added to their pain. Their sporting gesture was a credit to them and we wondered if we would have done the same in those circumstances?

I phoned home to check on Louise. She was fine. She knew how much winning the European Cup meant to me but as I tried to tell her how happy I was I got choked up again. I don't know how much of that call made sense but I think she got the message.

Our crowd stayed together through the night, visiting countless bars. We bumped into dozens of Reds we had not seen for years. It was like an extended episode of *This Is Your Life*. Somewhere along the line we realised United had won the treble! Fergie had given United supporters every precious dream and vision underneath the stars and for the first time in more than a generation we could truly sing, 'We are the champions, champions of Europe! … Europe! Europe! Europe!'

21

IF I TOOK IT FOR A HUNDRED YEARS, I COULDN'T FEEL ANY MORE ILL!

The euphoria from May 1999 stayed with United supporters for months, if not years. No matter where you were or what was going on in your life, you only had to stop for a few seconds and reflect on any aspect of the treble to feel the warmest of glows in your heart. Better still, play a clip of Teddy or Ole's goals and you were 'high' once again.

Not so for supporters of other teams though, especially those who already despised United. They winced at the amount of media coverage the treble brought us. I worked in Warrington at the time. Once a quiet Cheshire town and rugby stronghold in the mid-1990s it became 'Call Centre Valley' thanks to generous Government grants. The west side of Warrington fast became a Liverpool overspill with an exodus of Scousers desperately seeking to better themselves.

That migration brought me into daily contact with far more Liverpool fans than is considered healthy under EU regulations. Nevertheless, it gave me the chance to see up close how they struggled to cope with United's new-found status. Colleague and Kopite, Yvonne Laramee sat opposite me. One morning early in June 1999, after reading the umpteenth taunting e-mail from United supporters, she thumped the desk hard and screamed, 'Bloody hell, the whole planet's turned into a sodding Man United theme park.' I just smiled at her and said, 'I know, it's great isn't it?' She wasn't happy.

To be fair she had a point. United's achievement in winning
the treble brought plaudits of stellar proportions. Not just in
the football fraternity and not just in the UK, everyone became
infatuated with United's fairytale triumph. The TV, papers, magazines and radio phone-ins were full of it for weeks. The English
treble was unprecedented but it was the manner in which we
won it that attracted global admiration.

Firstly, there was the thrilling attacking football. United
scored eighty league goals in thirty-eight games compared with
Arsenal's miserly fifty-nine and Chelsea's fifty-seven. In Europe
we averaged over three goals per game. Secondly, there was the
calibre of the opposition. In the league, Arsenal lost one game
after the turn of the year, Chelsea just three all season. Both
London teams went on twenty-plus match runs undefeated.
The title race had been of the highest order. In the FA Cup,
United played five top-flight clubs including Chelsea and
Arsenal. In the Champions League we faced four of Europe's
giants, Barcelona, Inter, Juventus and Bayern.

Thirdly, there was the indomitable spirit that refused to accept
defeat. The fightbacks against Liverpool, Juventus and Bayern
were breathtaking; no wonder they captured the imagination of
the public. It was derring-do at its finest.

Finally, there was the United invincibility. From 19 December 1998 to the end of the season United were unbeaten in all
thirty-three matches.

Alex Ferguson had achieved immortality and got the acclaim
he thoroughly deserved. A grateful nation looked on as Fergie
had the highest accolade any British citizen can receive bestowed
upon him – the Freedom of the City of Manchester. Naturally,
he was overwhelmed and it complemented his knighthood from
the Queen!

A decade after wanting rid of this Govan man, I now had the
utmost respect for Sir Alex Ferguson. I was so grateful for what
he had done for my team. Now he was ready to make United
even greater.

Before that could happen, a story broke that would grip the
nation and the corridors of Westminster. On 30 June, United
announced they had accepted FIFA's invitation to play in the
inaugural Club World Championship in Brazil in January 2000.
United also accepted the FA's offer to withdraw from the

following season's FA Cup in order to fulfil the FIFA invitation. Initially, United had turned down the invite to Brazil and the German press suggested Bayern Munich, as runners up, should represent Europe. Cue political panic. England and Germany were vying to stage the 2006 World Cup and our bid team felt United's absence from Brazil would cause irreparable damage. United had to go to Brazil but needed to create space in the football calendar.

When the story broke that the preferred option was to pull-out of the FA Cup the nation reeled in horror. The politicians took a step back into the shadows and United were hung out to dry and left to play the pantomime villain. In the end United become the first FA Cup winners not to defend their title. There would be no winners at all amid the shambles. United were eliminated at the first stage in Rio, England lost the World Cup bid and the FA Cup competition was denigrated for several years after. Worst of all, Manchester United were denied the opportunity to defend their treble.

I believe a simple compromise could have been reached. The Brazilian tournament only lasted from 5–14 January. My solution would have been for the Reds to take the first team to Brazil and let our second string compete in the FA Cup fourth round on 8 January. This assumes we would have won the third round tie played on 10 December 1999 (an FA experiment whereby the third round was played before Christmas). The fifth round was scheduled for 29 January by which time United would have been back from Brazil even if we had reached the final.

United had league games against Middlesbrough and Leeds to re-arrange which they did comfortably later in the season anyway. The whole commotion rested on fulfilling that fourth round fixture. A solution was there, I would love to know who blocked it.

The new season opened just seventy-five days after the Nou Camp glory, but even that wasn't soon enough. We couldn't wait to see the Reds play again, meet up with our mates and relive the magic. A colossus was missing though. Peter Schmeichel had retired from English football having played 398 games for United, winning five titles, three FA Cups, and one League Cup. His last act in a United shirt was lifting the European Cup in Barcelona. What a way to go. Peter Schmeichel is the best goalkeeper I've seen play for United and was probably the finest in the world during his career. His impact on United's fortunes was immeasurable; we would struggle to replace him.

The season started well with victories at Highbury and Anfield in the first month. The game against Liverpool had extra special significance. I had longed for United to visit Anfield as champions of Europe and be part of the Red Army singing to a muted Kop. My first trip to Liverpool was 1968, the last time United ruled Europe, but I was just a kid too young to fully appreciate the occasion. Now United's support was in buoyant mood eagerly awaiting the treble-winners.

Prior to the teams coming out and before we were subjected to that dreadful Gerry Marsden dirge, I climbed on to one of the concrete blocks above the entrance to the terraces and bellowed, 'Bring on the champions! Champions of Europe!' Within seconds the chant caught on among United's 3,000 faithful and echoed round the ground. The whistles from the Kop told me they had got the message. Job done. Even two policemen who removed me from my perch seemed impressed. The 3-2 win put further icing on the cake.

My energies would soon be channelled elsewhere however. Louise was becoming … there's no easy way to say this … er … quite big. Twin births invariably arrive early and it was obvious she wouldn't go to the planned Bonfire Night date. Even at Liverpool that day, I half expected a tannoy announcement advising me to get my butt back down the East Lancs Road ASAP.

On Friday, 24 September 1999 the doctors decided to induce the birth and at 10.20 p.m. and 10.24 p.m. my daughters Bethany and Jessica came into this world. Louise, God bless her, did it all on just gas and air. No epidural, no painkillers, just gas and air. The contractions had kicked in around 8.50 p.m. She pushed and toiled for more than an hour and a half. It was tense and it was draining, it seemed like we were getting nowhere, then suddenly out came one baby, minutes later another. The rush of adrenalin was incredible; the jubilation indescribable; tears flowed. In fact, it felt just like a re-run of that night in Barcelona!

Fantastic – the treble and a double in the space of four months. No man should have such luck. The following day, family and friends descended on the maternity ward so I managed to slip away for a couple of hours to watch United's home game with

Southampton, all with my wife's blessing. What a woman – twins on gas and air and I'm off to the footie before they're twenty-four hours old.

United could only manage a draw against the Saints thanks mainly to a dreadful error by new keeper Massimo Taibi. Fergie had brought in Mark Bosnich from Aston Villa but he picked up a hamstring injury two weeks into the season. Taibi was hastily signed and starred on his debut at Anfield two weeks earlier but against Southampton a weak shot from Matt Le Tissier squirmed out of his arms, through his legs and into the net. I couldn't help thinking that if the midwife had shown such an unsafe pair of hands the night before, my babies would have been rolling all round that delivery room floor!

Taibi wobbled the following week in a 5-0 hammering at Chelsea which ended United's long unbeaten run. The match also ended Taibi's short career at Old Trafford, Bosnich returned as first-choice for the remainder of the season.

United stayed in the top two until Christmas and a rejuvenated Leeds led the league. UEFA changed the format of the Champions League, adding a further group stage before the knockout phase. We won both groups comfortably. As well as entering the new Club World Championship, United competed for the good old Intercontinental Cup.

The contest had run for almost forty years between the champions of Europe and South American. Since 1980 it comprised a single match in neutral Tokyo. This was another of my dreams, to see United compete for the title of world champions. However, this is where I got the family planning a bit wrong. My girls were only eight weeks old when United went to Tokyo. Louise and I were still trying to figure out this baby lark, going from none to two kids in four minutes was pretty scary and those first six months were just a blur. So I decided not to go to Japan. I have chalked it up on the board marked 'should have been there'. No excuses, it was my decision – honest!

In the late summer of 1999 my job had taken me to work in Kirkby just on the outskirts of Liverpool. Norweb had morphed into United Utilities and they created an outsourcing arm called Vertex. I had made a bit of a niche for myself managing various projects and was working on a bid to win contracts with the boroughs of Knowsley and Merseyside. As a Manc I was now very much in the lion's den. When I was younger, working every day with Scousers would have been my worst nightmare, but what better year to be among them than 1999? I was the dead fly again, just a different salad. A United supporter with a permanent grin was not what they wanted. In truth, I got on fine with many Liverpool and Everton fans during that time. They realised I was the genuine article and tolerated me. For my part I didn't take the mickey too much.

In that Kirby building Vertex ran a call centre for bookmakers BetDirect. The staff needed live TV screens on the walls as part of their job. For two hours on the morning of 30 November I found an excuse to park myself in that part of the office while I watched the United–Palmeiras match live from Tokyo. Roy Keane's thirty-fifth-minute strike won the game. Anyway, I was on the way back to my desk and I saw four young lads I worked with heading towards me on their way to lunch. They were all rabid Liverpool or Everton supporters. I nodded my head to let on, but just as they passed me I turned and said, 'Oi, lads, I've been meaning to ask you, what's that out there?'

'Out where?' they asked.

'Out there,' I replied, pointing at the window.

'I dunno, the car park?' shrugged Kopite Dave, looking only remotely interested.

'No, beyond the car park,' I told them.

'Er, Kirby?' they all chipped in.

'No lads, I mean after Kirby.'

'Liverpool city centre?' said Mike, from the Gwladys Street End.

'No, even beyond that, lads, come on!' I added.

'Pete, I'm starving, I want me lunch, what the f★★kin' hell is it?' asked Dave.

'Lads, it's the whole of the world! Out there is the whole of the world!' I told them.

They thought I had lost it completely and started to walk away. Then I called after them and smiled. 'And d'you know who are the champions of that world? Manchester United!'

The torrent of abuse and foul language that followed was totally out of keeping with an office environment.

As the second millennium became the third millennium, people across the world became preoccupied with planes falling out of the sky if all the computers failed at midnight on 31 December.

United had their minds on the forthcoming trip to Brazil while my challenge was getting through each day on just four hours' sleep. I was still up to my elbows in nappies, bottles of milk and Farley's Rusks. I had as much chance of going to Rio as I had of landing on Mars. So that went on my list just below Tokyo.

The unsuccessful trip gave United a winter break that recharged their batteries. Title challengers Arsenal, Leeds and Liverpool failed to capitalise on our enforced vacation. We resumed our league campaign against the Gunners on 24 January 2000 and the table that morning showed our rivals' missed opportunity:

	P	W	D	L	F	A	Pts	GD
Leeds	22	15	2	5	37	25	47	12
Man United	20	13	5	2	51	26	44	25
Arsenal	23	13	5	5	42	23	44	19
Liverpool	23	12	5	6	34	20	41	14

We drew 1-1 with Arsenal then put our foot on the gas before slipping into overdrive. United won fifteen of the remaining eighteen games, losing only once. No other team could live with United's blistering pace and scoring rate. The league title was wrapped up five games from the end with a 3-1 win at Southampton.

Where do you start with the superlatives for 1999/00? We won our thirteenth league title by eighteen points; our sixth in eight seasons. Was it getting too easy? The points haul is United's best ever at 79.8 per cent. The twenty-eight wins equalled the club record set in 1906 (thirty-eight games) and 1957 (forty-two games). The ninety-seven goals scored were the highest since 1959/60. The three defeats equalled our least ever (in the previous season) and we remained unbeaten at home in the league for only the fifth time in over 100 years. Aside from the facts, United played great football throughout the campaign to continue their domination. Keane's leadership was second to none again and was rewarded with the Footballer of the Year and Players' Player of the Year awards.

In Europe the knock-out stage paired us with old adversaries Real Madrid. Either side of the first leg United thumped West Ham 7-1 and put four past Sunderland, Middlesbrough and Bradford. Such sharp shooting deserted the Reds in Spain as the two giants fought out a 0-0 draw. At Old Trafford, Madrid ran up a 3–0 lead in fifty-two minutes against a strangely disjointed United team. We pulled back to 3–2 but it was too late; the great European adventure was over.

The exit at the quarter-final stage was a crushing blow. Expectations had been high that this United team could defend our European title and start building a dynasty like the great continental sides of the past.

Despite the avalanche of goals in domestic competitions Fergie was concerned about our strike rate at the highest level. Ruud van Nistelrooy was seen as the answer and a deal was agreed only to be shelved when he damaged his cruciate training with PSV. He was sidelined for twelve months but Fergie promised to wait for the Dutch striker. The manager turned his attention to another area of the team and signed goalkeeper Fabien Barthez. He came with tremendous credentials having won the Champions League with Marseille, along with the European Championship and World Cup with France.

The start of the 2000/01 season saw few other changes to the United squad but the shirt now carried the name Vodafone, the deal with Sharp having finished after eighteen years. United simply cruised through the league fixtures, even defeats to challengers Arsenal and Liverpool failed to peg us back. That New Year's Day table was every United supporter's dream:

	P	W	D	L	F	A	Pts	GD
Man United	22	15	5	2	51	16	50	35
Arsenal	22	11	6	5	38	22	39	16
Sunderland	22	11	6	5	29	22	39	7

The Champions League format still had two group stages. The first proved tricky as United lost at PSV and Anderlecht and drew at Dynamo Kiev. Convincing home wins kept us in contention but we went into the final match, at home to Kiev, needing a win. Sheringham gave us an early lead but we couldn't add to the score. In the second half the crowd became nervous which made the players edgy. With five minutes remaining Kiev missed a golden opportunity to equalise. A draw would have put United out and caused ructions from the boardroom to the terraces. United won 1–0, went through, we thanked our lucky stars and put it behind us.

Well, everybody except Keano. He decided to have a bit of a rant about the atmosphere at Old Trafford; he questioned the football knowledge of some in the stands and whether they were more interested in being served prawn sandwiches than the beautiful game. Our beloved captain had lit the blue touch-paper and stood back.

Those of us who sing at matches couldn't agree more. Despite Old Trafford's capacity having risen to a massive 67,500 earlier that year the atmosphere at some games was lukewarm. There were a few reasons. Firstly, the cost of a season ticket now priced out the more animated supporters. Not the hooligans, just the fans who back United with vocal support throughout the game rather than those who turn up and applaud politely when United score. Secondly, all-seater stadia had quelled the passion on the terraces up and down the country. A church choir stands up to sing its hymns, so too the ardent football follower.

Another spin-off of having seating is that your seat is reserved. You have to sit where the club puts you, not necessarily where you want to be in the ground. Consequently you have the singers and non-singers all mingled in around the stadium. Before the 1990s dawned every ground had its vociferous, singing area for the passionate supporters. Those who wanted to politely applaud would stand or sit elsewhere.

We have to speak in hushed tones about the third reason why the atmosphere at Old Trafford isn't always top notch. As loyal as we are to United, we were becoming spoilt. The years of famine generated a hunger, a sharpness, a defiance among United's faithful borne out of an indignation that we were no longer the top team. By 2000, we had revelled in a decade of perpetual silverware including six league titles, two doubles and a treble. Several home games became predictable United victories, particularly against the less glamorous sides, and many in 60,000-plus crowds seemed uninspired until we scored. My mate Tezzer compared these silent Reds to over-fed huskies in the Arctic that had become too complacent to pull the sledge. He had a point.

Keane's comments stirred up a rumpus in the media because they love one of our own having a go at United. Few genuine Reds felt slighted by his comments, we knew what he was getting at. Twenty rows in front of us in J Stand sat another group of our lads, Mike Stewart, Simon Rumsey, Dave Gabriel, Andy

Henderson and Gary Mullineux, all top Reds who gave it their all at away matches. At home they were surrounded by the more sedate of our brethren and I was forever giving them jip for not getting the singing going in their part of the stand.

The Saturday morning after the Kiev game I was on Walkden market and passed a fish stall advertising two kilo of frozen prawns for a fiver. It was too good an opportunity to miss. I bagged the prawns and took them to the Middlesbrough game that afternoon. I looked like any other day-tripper as I went through the turnstile with my plastic bag although a few in the queue wondered what the funny smell was. Middlesbrough is one of the less glamorous games and though some of the crowd tried to raise the tempo in light of Keano's comments the atmosphere soon melted away. Worse still, Boro took the lead. My little joke would backfire if we lost but finally Nicky Butt equalised.

The crowd were on their feet in celebration. I was on my feet scooping the thawed prawns out of the bag and was hurling them, handful after handful, down the terraces towards my mates. For a couple of minutes J Stand celebrated in a shower of seafood. Our lads knew instinctively who was behind the prank but dozens of Reds looked around bemused as they picked prawns from their hair and coats. I think they saw the funny side!

United's fine league form continued after Christmas. We stretched our lead to fourteen points over second-placed Sunderland when we nicked a 1-0 win at the Stadium of Light at the end of January 2001. Three weeks later Arsenal came to Old Trafford in second place and thirteen points behind. It was do or die for the Gunners. United imposed shock and awe tactics on their closest rivals, rendering them incapable of resistance and running out 6-1 winners. United were making a mockery of the expression 'title race'. With three days of February remaining this great United side were already champions, not mathematically but in reality.

United met Bayern Munich in the quarter-final of the Champions League at Old Trafford on 3 April but once again their performance in Europe was at odds with their breathtaking domestic form. Once again, we failed to win a home leg in the competition's latter stages. In a disappointing showing we lost 1-0 to a late Sergio goal. The week of the second leg was a bitter-sweet affair. On Saturday 14 April we clinched our seventh title in nine seasons. Four days later Bayern completed the job, winning 2-1. A trend was forming. Each year, domestic glory came wrapped in European disappointment.

United joined Huddersfield, Arsenal and Liverpool as the only English teams to win three league titles in a row. Fergie became the first manager to achieve the feat with the same club. Ten years earlier such domination was a pipe dream for United supporters. But a taste of honey is worse than none at all and the 1999 European Cup win provided nectar so sweet that nothing else could satisfy our craving.

Writing in his programme notes Fergie summed up how we all felt:

> The disappointment we suffered this week in Munich was of a totally different order. My hopes had been high and justifiably so, but it was the kind of setback which cuts right through you and leaves you stunned ... It was the kind of experience that leaves you in reflective mood and wondering what should be the next step forward. We want to swing on that star and we are in touching distance ... Everything is under review and I know exactly what needs to be done.

Spot on Fergie. We waited with bated breath. In the meantime we got on with ribbing our rivals throughout the summer.

Shortly after the glorious treble triumph Fergie said he wouldn't continue as manager of Manchester United beyond his current contract which expired at the end of 2001/02. As that season dawned, it was a sobering thought that this would be Fergie's last. When UEFA announced Glasgow as the venue for the Champions League Final the stage seemed set for the great man's curtain call in his home city. In August 2001, the question was, could we do it? My mate Steve Heywood, a deep thinker on football matters, held the view that United's 'failure' to build on the Champions League success of 1999 was because we weren't in the super-league of Europe's transfer market. We bought big domestically but the world's best players still headed to Madrid, Barcelona, Milan or Turin.

Steve believed, as he had told us on many occasions walking back to the car, that if United wanted to emulate these teams they had to put their money where their mouth was. In the summer of 2001 Fergie did just that, buying Ruud van Nistelrooy and Juan Veron for £19 million and £28 million respectively. Steve was happy. We were all happy.

Teddy Sheringham returned to Spurs. Aged 35 he enjoyed a great finale, scoring twenty-one goals in forty-three appearances and became the third United player in six years to win the coveted FWA Footballer of the Year Award. Teddy had made his mark in Manchester not just because of his ninety-second-minute equaliser against Bayern but because of his stylish intelligent play in linking midfield to attack.

Sheringham's exit was expected. The next caused ructions. Jaap Stam was left out of the squad for United's second game of the season at Blackburn. Four days later a bewildered Stam was unveiled by Lazio as their new signing. United supporters were absolutely stunned. The Dutchman was the rock of our defence; a towering figure and a terrace hero. Fergie cited football reasons, however, the waters were muddied by the serialisation that week of Stam's new book in the *Daily Mirror*. The paper focused on the player's disclosure that Fergie had 'tapped him up' while he was at PSV. Within a week, Laurent Blanc was making his United debut. The Frenchman was two months off 36, Stam had just turned 29. More head-scratching in the Old Trafford stands. Fergie asked us to trust his judgement.

Stam's swift transfer unhinged United's defence. Even with a planned transition at the centre of a top defence there is a three-month settling down period as United found when Bruce and Pallister moved on. With United unsteady at the back and van Nistelrooy on fire up front, it was an autumn of high-scoring games. Initially we were up among the leaders but as the days got shorter the fixtures got tougher. By mid-December, after a run of five defeats in seven matches, we were ninth in the table. Eleven points adrift of leaders Liverpool, we were losing our vice-like grip on the title. The signs were ominous for United in more ways than one. Our six league defeats spelt out the reason why. United had lost to Bolton, Liverpool, Arsenal, Newcastle and Chelsea – whose first letters spell B-L-A-N-C. Our latest defeat was to West Ham, or if you pronounce it with a true Cockney accent, 'Where's Stam'. Spooky, eh?

Of course, the blame couldn't be pointed solely at our new centre-back. After all, he hadn't sold Stam. Was Fergie's impending retirement starting to have repercussions? The uncertainty around his own future and the growing speculation about his successor intensified. The pre-Christmas poor form only added to it. The manager, committed as he was, must have been distracted. Discussions had taken place about Fergie being given an ambassadorial role at the club but agreement couldn't be reached on the exact nature of the role or the remuneration. In late autumn 2001, Fergie confirmed he would not stay on in any official capacity, he would go in June 2002.

With Fergie's finishing line in sight, the dynamics among his playing staff will have changed. While the manager's authority might not have been directly challenged, it's inevitable that he would lose more and more authority as the end date approached. It is human nature, some people under your command start to see you as yesterday's man and don't respond with the same urgency, commitment or respect as before. At worst, you gradually become a lame duck. It happened to Tony Blair once he announced he would hand over power at a future date and it has happened to many senior business figures over the years. The best course of action is to say nothing publicly, agree a finishing date with your chairman and just go. Fergie didn't become a lame duck, that was never going to happen, but we were seeing more of Dwight Yorke on the front pages than on the back.

In such situations it takes someone close to you to bring all your thoughts into perspective and advise what's best. Cue Mrs Ferguson. During the Christmas holidays with his family, and while celebrating his sixtieth birthday, maybe the decision to retire was reviewed by the Ferguson clan. A few weeks later, United supporters rejoiced as Alex Ferguson announced he would stay for a further three years. Coincidentally, United's form returned. Between that West Ham setback in December and the start of May 2002 we won eighteen of twenty-one games, scoring fifty-six goals. 'Business as usual' said the sign over Fergie's door.

Unfortunately Arsenal performed a carbon copy of their 1998 double winning run. They too remained unbeaten from December and outpaced United. On 8 May the sides met at Old Trafford and the table showed United had to win:

	P	W	D	L	F	A	Pts	GD
Arsenal	36	24	9	3	74	33	81	41
Man United	36	24	4	8	87	44	76	43

United tried to rough up Arsenal with a first half of crunching tackles but the Gunners rode it, matched it and in the fifty-sixth minute won it with a goal from Sylvain Wiltord. It proved a game too far for United. Arsenal took the title to add to the FA Cup they had won against Chelsea four days earlier.

United's autumn collapse thwarted our title hopes but the European dream remained intact. We thrashed Deportivo La Coruna to meet unfancied German side Bayer Leverkusen in the semis, avoiding Barca and Real. Missing Beckham and Keane we failed to gain an advantage in the first leg at Old Trafford. A 2-2 draw maintained our poor home record but with the Reds just ninety minutes away from another European final the away leg became unmissable. The BayArena Stadium held only 22,500. United could have sold their allocation five times over. None of our lads got tickets, but we had to be there.

Independent Travel ran a day trip and the plane was full of ticketless Reds willing to take a chance that something would turn up in Germany. We flew into Cologne around midday. The ten of us trawled the bars for any sign of tickets. They were like gold dust. Two of our lads decided to pay around £150 each when two tickets became available early that afternoon. They were the only spares we found all day. Six hours before kick-off we took the train down to Leverkusen and decided to eyeball the ground. It was a new stadium with modern security and no obvious chink in its defences. We heard the German police intended to put a 'ring of steel' around the ground to stop ticketless supporters even getting near the turnstiles.

By 3 p.m. we realised the chance of buying a ticket was minimal. We needed a plan B and stayed close to the stadium perimeter to keep inside that ring. Every time I thought about the match I felt sick. The prospect of not getting in was unbearable.

We walked round the stadium half a dozen times, desperately trying to spot an opportunity. There was a McDonald's built on one side of the ground. I spent the best part of an hour discreetly popping in and out, checking for a door or window that might lead into the ground but to no avail. The afternoon wore on, armed police with sniffer dogs patrolled the perimeter fence with their innate German efficiency. At times it felt like a bizarre re-run of *The Great Escape*, only this time the Brits were trying to break into a German stronghold.

We saw one hapless Red who had managed to get into the ground being marched back out of the gates. He had been found hiding in the toilets. As the crowds started arriving, we asked almost everyone we came across if they had a spare ticket. I felt like a beggar but I was desperate. The worst point was when United's hospitality buses arrived at the main entrance. The great and the good queued up within touching distance of ticketless Reds. Angus Dayton and Richard Wilson stood right next to me and I quietly asked him was there any way they could get me in. Both looked concerned and a little sheepish before Dayton politely said, 'Sorry I wish I could but …' and shrugged his shoulders. Oh for that bag of prawns when I needed them most!

With an hour to kick-off we devised a plan. Pete Seymour and Andy Henderson, the two with tickets, would go in and try to pass the stubs back through the fence. We noticed the turnstile operator was giving the tickets a slight tear and maybe we would be able to re-use them. I was kicking myself now for not bringing my stub from the home leg, it looked similar and would have given me a chance. Pete and Andy went in but they couldn't get near the fence to pass the stubs out, security was so tight. We waited about half an hour but nothing was happening.

Time to take stock. It was 7.15 p.m., in thirty minutes my team would be playing a Champions League semi-final. I had been outside the ground for over five hours and still didn't have a ticket. I needed something radical and quick. During our reconnaissance of the ground that afternoon I had noticed a tarmac compound next to the ground which housed the massive vans that carry the TV companies' equipment. The area was screened by a tall, thick hedge. Its road entrance was subject to vigorous security checks. Further along the hedge was a small iron gate. I had pushed the gate and it opened. It was too risky to use that early in the day, with so few people about I would get sussed pretty quickly and I assumed there would be a guarded patrol just inside. I closed the gate but kept a mental note.

Now with kick-off looming I went back to the gate and to my surprise found it still unlocked. It was surreal given the tight security everywhere else, nobody seemed to notice it. I rushed back to our lads and told them I was going to take my chance through the compound. They all decided to wait a bit longer to see if the ticket stubs materialised. My 18-year-old nephew Simon was in our party, his dad Pete had gone in with a ticket. I didn't want to leave Simon so I beckoned him to come with me. On the way I explained he just needed to act cool and follow me.

'What exactly are we going to do uncle Peter?' he asked.

'I'm not sure yet, Simon, we're gonna sneak through that gate and see where it takes us!'

'Are you sure it's okay?' he said, nervously.

'Yeah, of course I'm sure!' I said, lying through my teeth.

Sneaking through the gate, we crept between the parked TV vans. A few technicians were sat around looking at monitors; I just smiled and walked on towards a huge glass-fronted entrance. I realised it was a hotel built on to the ground. We walked into the reception area which was filled with VIPs finishing off their flutes of champagne. I needed a moment to think, I was doing all this on the hoof while whispering discreet instructions to Simon.

We stopped at an empty table, picked up a couple of discarded drinks and sussed what to do next. The TV screens were showing the line-up of the two teams and my heart was pounding, there wasn't much time. The VIPs went through a sliding door which led straight into the ground but it was three-deep with hired suits. We headed for the lifts and had a look round a couple of floors but there was no way into the stadium. My pulse was in overdrive, desperately trying not to panic I considered other options but the hotel staff had eyeballed us so we calmly walked back outside into the compound.

Then it clicked. Along one side of the compound ran dozens of TV cables from the big vans, they must lead into the ground surely? 'Wait here a minute, Simon,' I said and followed the cables down a slope to what looked like the entrance to an underground car park. It was pitch black at first then a right turn led to a long tunnel which opened up into the stadium. Standing at the bottom of that tunnel were the two teams and officials coming out of the dressing rooms, waiting to go out on to the pitch. I scurried back to Simon and told him what I had just seen.

'Well we can't go that way then can we uncle Peter?' he said, in all innocence.

'Simon,' I said calmly trying to reassure my young nephew. 'Manchester United are about to take the field to play in one of their most important matches in thirty years and down that tunnel is our only chance of seeing it. Of course we're gonna go that way!'

We walked down the tunnel unchallenged. The players had entered the stadium and within seconds we were pitch-side. The coaching staff, photographers and stewards were taking their places so I had a couple of minutes to survey the scene before we stood out. The United supporters were massed at the other end. The Champions League theme song was booming out across the German sky. Kick-off was imminent. I remembered how the great United jibbers in the 1960s having found themselves in the wrong part of the ground would feign injury to walk round the pitch then jump into the United end.

'Simon, start limping, I'll support you and we'll head to the other end,' I whispered quickly.

'I can't limp!' he said, laughing as if I was joking.

This was no place for a family argument. I told him to follow me and I limped along the track by the side of the pitch. Still nobody challenged us. We passed within inches of Fergie and the subs but this was no time for adulation either. I had to keep focused. We reached the other end only to find the United terraces enclosed by a huge metal fence. The only entrance gate was locked.

A German steward appeared; he was the size of a barn door and sported a big handle-bar moustache. In broken English I explained I had twisted my ankle on the terraces, been to the first aid room and could he please open the gate to let us back into the United end. At least that's what I thought I had explained. He signalled us to follow him and went down a similar tunnel to the one we'd just come down at that the other end of the ground. I wasn't sure what was happening then realised we were heading towards large doors marked 'EXIT'.

My heart sank. Simon and I looked at each other, we had been sussed. Just before the exit, the steward turned sharp right and took us into a first aid room. He exchanged a few words with the nurse and within seconds I was laying on a table while a doctor examined my ankle. When I was at school I was rubbish at drama, now I had to put on the act of my life. I grimaced as he moved my foot up, down and side to side. The steward had left the room. I noticed Simon trying very hard to keep his face straight as I played out the charade. The nurse then bandaged my left leg from the knee to the toes. The doctor, looking quite concerned, asked me to sign the incident book and explained I needed to wait for an ambulance to take me to hospital.

'Hospital! Shit, I've over-egged this,' I thought. Simon turned away unable to contain himself.

'No, no, I think I will be okay,' I said and with that I got off the table to show I could hobble along. 'I would like to see the match please,' I pleaded.

The doctor shrugged and called for the steward. He asked for our ticket stubs. I explained that our friend had them and he was in the crowd with the United fans. The steward didn't look convinced and told us to follow him again. We left the medical room, me trailing behind like John Mills in *Ryan's Daughter*, but instead of turning left to take us back to the terraces, the steward headed right and took us through the exit doors.

Just when I thought we had got away with it we were outside the ground where we had spent most of that afternoon. I turned to Simon to say at least we had given it our best shot. Suddenly our moustachioed companion shouted an instruction to one of his colleagues working on the United turnstiles nearby. The man waved us forward and ushered us into the ground. I couldn't believe it. We shook the hand of our heroic steward and headed up the stairs to join the Red Army. Simon and I were giddy with delight. We had missed the first fifteen minutes but that didn't matter – we were in!

When Roy Keane scored after twenty-eight minutes we felt like the luckiest people in the world. The hero of Turin was driving us on to another European final. Such an adventure deserves a happy ending but this is no fairytale. Leverkusen equalised and despite wave after wave of United attacks the score remained 1-1 to send the Germans to the Glasgow final. The Munich defeat in 2001 had 'cut right through us and left us stunned'. Against less able German opposition, the 2002 semi-final should have healed that pain. United's best chance of adding to our celebrated triumphs of 1968 and 1999 had gone. Losing to Leverkusen took disappointment to a new level. In the home of the Aspirin, the bitterest pill was ours to take.

22

WATCHING THE PEOPLE GET LAIRY, IT'S NOT VERY PRETTY I TELL THEE

Success invariably changes people. Your personality might not change but your aspirations do. Springsteen sums it up perfectly on his track, 'Badlands':

> Poor man wanna be rich,
> Rich man wanna be king,
> And a king ain't satisfied till he rules everything.

United supporters had yearned for a league title, we got the title. We wanted more league titles. We got them; and doubles, and a treble that put us at the pinnacle of club football. Happy? Yes. Satisfied? Mmmm, kinda. Wanting more? Of course. We wanted to rule Europe! When the dust settled in May 2002, I looked back on the season as a failure of our own making. Despite the injection of around £47 million on two world-class players, United's senior management had jeopardised the season with three poor judgement calls.

Firstly, to go public so far in advance with Fergie's retirement date. The board should have had the foresight to see the pitfalls. The prolonged indecision surrounding Sir Alex's future role was a second own goal and finally, the sudden sale of Jaap Stam. No matter what the real reason for his transfer, Fergie seriously underestimated the impact it would have on the stability of the team. Within a year of Stam's exit, Fergie signed his

long-term replacement in Rio Ferdinand. Why not retain Stam
for that extra year? Laurent Blanc could still have been brought in
as cover on a free transfer. To be fair, Fergie conceded in 2010 he
had been too hasty with the Dutch stopper's exit.

Nevertheless, while United received around £16 million
for the sale, it cost us much more. I am convinced the price we
paid was a history-making fourth consecutive title and probably
another European triumph. There is no guarantee we would have
triumphed in Glasgow but with most of Hampden singing us
home I believe United were capable of beating Real. That would
have given the Reds two European Cups in four years and a platform to emulate Madrid, Ajax, Bayern, Liverpool and AC Milan
as golden teams who towered above their continental peers.

All speculation, of course. In reality the glorious treble-
winning team had missed its chance of European domination. In
the summer of 2002 the curtain was falling. Denis Irwin, Ronnie
Johnsen and Dwight Yorke had moved to pastures new as had
Schmeichel, Blomqvist, Sheringham, Stam and Cole previously.
Heroes one and all.

With the uncertainty around Fergie's future removed, a new
era was dawning. For the second summer running Fergie broke
the British transfer fee, paying Leeds around £30 million for
centre-back Rio Ferdinand. Mikaël Silvestre had established
himself in the defence as had John O'Shea. Ruud van Nistelrooy
was the new star in United's firmament, scoring a remarkable
thirty-six goals, including ten in the Champions League alone.

The 2002/03 season started badly with Roy Keane succumbing
to a niggling hip injury, an operation would keep him out until
Christmas. The man from Cork was still United's driving force and
we missed him. United lost three times in the opening thirteen league
games including the first defeat to City since 1989. After the derby
defeat Fergie called on his players to take a good look at themselves.
The league table on 9 November underlined Fergie's concerns:

	P	W	D	L	F	A	Pts
Liverpool	13	9	3	1	24	10	30
Arsenal	13	9	2	2	28	13	29
Chelsea	13	6	5	2	23	12	23
Everton	13	7	2	4	16	15	23
Man United	13	6	4	3	17	12	22

The crunch came in the first week of December 2002 with consecutive games against the top two. Injury had robbed us of Keane, Beckham, Veron, Butt and Ferdinand. A patched-up United took the field at Anfield on the back of five consecutive defeats there and an animated Kop expecting to see the depleted enemy crushed and their title chances reinforced. We had to dig deep for our defiance on the terraces that day and the players did the same on the pitch.

United stood tall and prevented Liverpool finding any real rhythm. Diego Forlan benefitted from a dreadful error by goal-keeper Dudek, then a Giggs through ball to give the Mancs a 2-1 win. Oh the joy of a silent Kop!

Arsenal proved much tougher. The reigning champions had a formidable team and defeat would leave us eight points adrift. Veron returned but the big surprise was Fergie leaving out Forlan and drafting in Phil Neville to midfield. Once again the great man got it right as United out-played Arsenal in another 2-0 victory. Those results salvaged United's title campaign but the vanquished would gain revenge in the domestic cups.

Our first League Cup Final since 1994 and the delights of Cardiff's Millennium Stadium were marred by a tame two-goal defeat to Liverpool. Arsenal beat us by the same scoreline in an FA Cup tie at Old Trafford. The game was famous for David Beckham copping a cut eyebrow from a spare boot kicked by Fergie in temper. By this time anything Beckham did was seized on by the world media, not just sports journalists. The picture of Becks arriving for training with a plaster on his forehead and his hair held back by an Alice band was splashed across every newspaper. The story ran for weeks.

The Champions League didn't need any extra spice but UEFA added a touch by selecting Old Trafford for the final. United topped both group phases before thumping Juventus 5-1. Real Madrid blocked our path to the semi-finals once again. The Spanish giants had won the competition three times since 1998 to add to the six they won in the 1950s and 1960s. I had missed the away leg in 2000 but now Col Green and I were off to realise our dream of seeing United play in the legendary Bernabeu.

A sun-soaked afternoon in the Puerta del Sol washing down paella with San Miguel was the perfect setting to discuss the mouth-watering prospect ahead. We expected a difficult match as

Madrid had assembled some of the greatest players on the planet. Nevertheless, United were in a rich vein of form and at full strength except for Veron. We were confident. Three years earlier at Old Trafford, it took Real fifty-three minutes to go 3-0 up but this time in Madrid they only needed forty-nine. Raul, again, scored either side of half time to add to Figo's stunning opener after only twelve minutes. In the first half, Madrid played power-ful football brilliantly led by the ubiquitous Zidane. On fifty-two minutes van Nistelrooy pulled one back and would have added a second shortly after but for Casillas' brilliance. The match ended 3-1 to Madrid. The big debate on the flight home was whether we could keep a clean sheet in Manchester because scoring two goals wasn't beyond us.

The Sunday papers following the away leg carried several arti-cles reporting that a deal had been done for David Beckham to join Real at the end of the season. Several journalists had picked up on verbal comments from their Spanish colleagues. I wanted to dismiss it as malicious gossip but Fergie 'rested' Becks for the crucial league matches that followed. When the second leg came round United's number seven was only a substitute despite Scholes being suspended.

The return match was a classic, a showcase for the Champions League and broadcast around the world. Allegedly, it was the match that inspired Roman Abramovich to cut himself a piece of the action and lend a hand to an under-performing West London club. Confidence was high, but concentration was the key. Realistically we needed not to concede.

With almost pathological predictability our big European night faltered in the early stages. Brazilian international Ronaldo squeezed a low shot between Barthez and his near post on twelve minutes. It was a killer blow and took the best part of the first half for United to regain composure. Ruud levelled the scores just before the break but five minutes after the restart Ronaldo struck again leaving the Reds with four goals to find. Level again two minutes later we summoned up that last bit of hope but Ronaldo hit a wicked dipping shot from twenty yards that bemused Barthez. In a gung-ho finale, Beckham rose from the bench to score twice for a 4-3 United win but it was the peerless Ronaldo who grabbed the plaudits with a powerful hat-trick and a standing ovation from all corners of Old Trafford.

No final on home soil then, just more Champions League angst. Comfort was found in a fascinating title race. When we went to Cardiff in early March we had found a little pub near Ninian Park and watched Arsenal beat Charlton. That victory put the Gunners eight points clear with nine games to play and though United had a match in hand the title seemed bound for north London again. After that, United went into overdrive, winning nine and drawing one of the remaining ten matches. Arsenal drew three and lost two of their next seven.

On the penultimate weekend, Leeds' last-minute winner at Highbury handed United a fifteenth title, our eighth in eleven seasons. A pattern was developing whereby Arsenal struggled in the nip and tuck races for the title such as 1999 and 2003. A feature of their successful years of 1998, 2002 and later 2004 was the head of steam they built up after Christmas to power ahead of their rivals.

The chink in their armour was the inability to cope when things went wrong. It might be a defeat, a bad injury or a referee's decision. Their initial reaction was an inflated sense of injustice. 'How can this happen to us when we play such beautiful football?' was the unspoken emotion. It would eat at them to the point where their game was affected and invariably Arsene Wenger strikes the piqued chord or prolongs it. To the contrary, Fergie mastered the art of turning setbacks into positive energy. United didn't need to feel sorry for themselves, they just came out fighting harder than before. I rate Wenger as a manager, his record at Arsenal is to be admired and respected but I believe his innate sense of indignant self-pity has prevented his team dominating the English game the way United have. The trend would continue through the decade.

Anyway, never mind Arsenal. I was off to Goodison Park on 11 May to see United pick up the trophy. It was another mad scramble for tickets but we got sorted. There was concern about safety and whether it was wise to present United with the trophy on Merseyside but common sense prevailed. Everton did their end-of-season lap of honour then our celebrations began. There was no trouble, several Evertonians stayed to watch the ceremony and applaud United.

The partying in the corner of the Park End and Bullens Road went on for an hour. Just like Middlesbrough seven years earlier we were in touching distance of the players and you could see the sheer delight on their faces as they got their medals and danced around. It really meant something to them, let alone the supporters. For Fergie, eight titles now. We were running out of superlatives. The theme of the run-in had been about getting our hands on our property again, and now an almost empty Goodison resonated to the sound of 6,000 Reds roaring, 'We've got our trophy back! We've got our trophy back!'

With the season over, the scribes got busy speculating about David Beckham's future. On 1 July 2003, Beckham was transferred to Real Madrid. The move shocked the public at large who couldn't believe United would release such a 'megastar'. I was surprised but not shocked; disappointed but not distraught. That reflected the views of many United supporters I knew. Beckham was an excellent player for United, I loved watching him and thrilled at his sweeping crosses, free-kicks and 100 per cent pure fighting spirit. However, I wouldn't put him up there with United's all-time greats and I would have been more upset if Scholes, Giggs or van Nistelrooy had left at that time.

People who didn't follow United closely couldn't understand that. They thought Beckham was Manchester United. In my view, Beckham's impact for United stopped progressing after September 2001 when he became the saviour of the national team with a last-gasp goal against Greece to take England to the 2002 World Cup. His focus seemed more on England than United. I am not anti-England but a United player's priority should always be his club rather than his country.

What also stopped our world falling apart was our trust in Fergie's judgement. The manager had made a considered assessment of the player's worth to the team and decided it was best if 'Brand Beckham' moved on. Like Busby, his judgement was invariably proved correct with very few players coming back to haunt United after their Old Trafford days were over. Beckham made 394 appearances, scoring eighty-five goals. He won the lot at Old Trafford and lived the dream of supporting United as a boy then playing at the highest level for the club he loved. For me his finest performance in a United shirt was the 1999 final in Barcelona where he drove a mis-shapen side to football's greatest heights. He will always have a place in our hearts.

Other than the revolution of 1989, when Fergie went mad with the chequebook, we had got used to a couple of comings and goings in the summer transfer market. In 2003, the great man decided the squad needed major surgery. Joining Becks through the 'out' door were Barthez, Veron, Blanc and May. The players coming in raised a few eyebrows – goalkeeper Tim Howard, midfielders Jose Kléberson and Eric Djemba-Djemba, plus wingers David Bellion and Cristiano Ronaldo. Our surprise was the fairly low profile of the newcomers compared to those leaving the club.

Kléberson was well-known having won the World Cup medal with Brazil the previous year but none of the others seemed the finished article. The fee for 18-year-old unknown Ronaldo was £12.24 million, another call on our trust in Fergie. United supporters knew we had to find a replacement for the legendary Roy Keane soon. He was now thirty-two and carrying the scars of battle. Juan Veron had failed to blend into any United formation. Would the new midfielders fit the bill?

One player I would have liked to see at Old Trafford at the time was Claude Makéléle. In the two matches with Madrid in April 2003, Real's Galacticos stole the headlines, but the player who caught my eye was Makéléle. I hadn't heard of him before but his ability to constantly break down our attacks then make a simple pass to a colleague reminded me of Nobby Stiles in his heyday. I wondered if Fergie might put in a bid and use the Frenchman as cover for and successor to Keane. There was no speculation in the papers and I don't know if Fergie was interested, but in the summer of 2003, Chelsea signed him in the very early stages of the Abramovich revolution. Perhaps Roman had noted his presence in that game too. Makéléle would become the backbone of Chelsea's rise to prominence over the next five years. Perhaps, one that got away Sir Alex?

Towards the end of the 1960s there was a chant on the Stretford End at every home match of 'Celtic-Rangers'. Half the crowd shouted for Celtic and the other half for Rangers depending on which Glasgow team you favoured. I don't know when or why it started, it was just a bit of a laugh really. I shouted for the 'Gers because as a kid I was fascinated by the name 'Glasgow Rangers', it had something mystical about it. I was also impressed by the vast numbers both Glasgow clubs took away from home, especially if it meant a raid across the border.

I remember tales of Rangers taking 30,000 supporters to Highbury for a replayed European Cup tie against Red Star in November 1964. I was there when Celtic brought 15,000 supporters to Old Trafford for Bobby Charlton's testimonial on a Monday night in September 1972. Legendary support. I had seen United play at Parkhead and Ibrox but only in friendlies. Passionate friendlies, but friendlies all the same. I yearned for a full-blooded competitive match against either of Glasgow's big two but in forty years it never happened.

In autumn 2003 I got my wish. Rangers survived the Champions League qualifying rounds and were drawn in our group. We played back to back games; the first match in Scotland on 23 October.

Getting tickets for away matches was becoming increasingly difficult. United's fan base mushroomed after 1999, more season tickets were issued as the stadium grew bigger, so more supporters were eligible to apply for away tickets. We had a few good contacts that helped when we really got stuck but there was nothing down for the Rangers game, everyone wanted to go. I put the word out to anyone I knew in Scotland, worked in Scotland or had ever visited Scotland but couldn't get a ticket for love nor money.

Pete Seymour managed to jib a ticket in hospitality through his firm. Mike Stewart couldn't go to the home game so swapped his ticket with a Rangers season ticket holder in return for a seat at the away game. I was determined to see the match so I drove up with Mike on the day. Rangers always bring a big following from Belfast and their ferries dock at Stranraer. Plan A was to stop at each service area after Gretna and ask Rangers supporters for spares. At the first stop two bus-loads of Rangers fans were parked up but the occupants were surrounded by police who were searching the vehicles for drugs and weapons, much to the annoyance of the Light Blue Army. Nevertheless, I was desperate so I went over to the coach but the police stopped me. I told them I was simply trying to buy a ticket for the match but just received one of those 'are you for real, now piss off out of here' looks from the officer in charge.

There were no coaches at the other services. On the outskirts of Glasgow we met Mike's contact to swap tickets. I asked him what my best chance was of finding a ticket. He told us to try the pubs in Paisley Road near the ground. If there were any tickets up for grabs that's where they would be. Good, I had a plan B. We found Paisley Road, parked up and approached the first pub, or to be more precise, bar. Or to be even more precise a single storey, stone shack with steel shutters for windows. It looked as rough as hell. I had no colours on but it was obvious where I was from and why I was there.

Outside it was pitch black, I opened the door slightly and the bright light, smoke and songs came pouring out. The place was rocking with wall-to-wall Rangers die-hards, bedecked in blue and white and belting out their tribal songs many of which didn't sit too well with the Good Friday Agreement. There was no way I was going in; I might as well have slit my own throat. Mike just laughed and said, 'Come on they can't all be that bad, we'll try the next one.' Well they were all that bad and there was very little of the 'we' as Mike kept his distance on the pavement outside. After poking my head into half a dozen similar bars I decided the guy at the services must have been winding us up.

We walked down to the ground but couldn't even find a tout with tickets. It was looking bleak. Then with ten minutes to kick-off Mike spotted a fellow in the middle of the road holding a small piece of paper aloft. I dashed towards him and just caught the words, 'Anybody need a ticket, face value?' I could have kissed him, but this was still Paisley Road. I gave him more cash than he asked for and came clean that I was from Manchester. At that point a look of horror filled his face and for a minute I thought he was going to change his mind.

The ticket was with a group of his pals in the fiercely partisan Upper Broomloan Road and he feared they would be ridiculed if he turned up with a United supporter. I swore to silence and he agreed to sell me the ticket on the condition he would introduce me as cousin Jimmy from Dumfries and I would just nod and say nothing. Deal! He could have introduced me as his 'bitch' for all I cared, as long as it got me in that ground.

By coincidence, Mike's ticket was for the same part of the stadium. There was no sitting down on a night like this, so we headed to Mike's seat and stood together, thus avoiding any Jimmy Krankie impressions. Ibrox was pounding to pre-match entertainment from an accordion band which was whipping up a great atmosphere among the Rangers supporters. Just before the teams came out the band finished with a rousing anthem called 'The Blue Sea of Ibrox'. The club had put a big blue card on each seat for their supporters to hold up during the song. All around us stood burly Scots with cards held high, roaring their devotion to Rangers.

There was no hiding place, Mike and I lifted our cards but hadn't got a clue what we were meant to be singing. The words were on the back of the card but no one, and I mean no one, was reading them. That would have been a dead giveaway, as would staying silent. I tried to imagine what cousin Jimmy would do and started blurting out some words that sounded like what the others were singing. Mike joined in. We looked like John Redwood when, as Secretary of State for Wales and in the full glare of TV cameras, he foolishly tried to mime the Welsh national anthem even though he didn't know a single word.

We got through it with our cover intact and it was all worthwhile. Here we were watching Manchester United play Glasgow Rangers in the European Cup with a white-hot atmosphere – tremendous. Five minutes in and Phil Neville dampened the home passion as he strode through from midfield to put United one up. Mike and I sat on our hands. Rangers huffed and puffed but United's defence was resolute. Keane, booed at every touch, rolled back the years and led United to a valuable 1-0 win. Once Paisley Road had been successfully navigated again we had a good sing-song in the car on the way home.

All Fergie's new recruits had gone straight into United's first team squad as the reigning champions made a strong start. Arsenal, Chelsea and United sprinted off into the distance leaving the chasing pack nine points behind by the end of November. But a hell of a storm was brewing. Rio Ferdinand failed to take a drug test on 23 September 2003. The player said he had forgotten because he was moving house that day. Naturally all hell broke loose. By the time the independent tribunal sat in mid-December we knew the punishment would be harsh with talk of a two-year ban. After eighteen hours of deliberation, Ferdinand was banned for eight months and fined £50,000. The ban would start a month later. Fergie continued to back Ferdinand and play him until it came into effect.

Wes Brown was close to recovering from a cruciate injury and any delay to Rio's absence bought valuable time. Rio's last match was away to Wolves on 17 January 2004 when ironically he went off injured after fifty minutes and was replaced by Brown whose slip cost United the match in a 1-0 defeat. That night United were still ahead of the pack:

	P	W	D	L	F	A	Pts
Man United	22	16	2	4	40	15	50
Arsenal	21	14	7	0	40	14	49
Chelsea	21	14	3	4	40	17	45

Our league form crumbled almost the minute Ferdinand left the Molineux pitch. We won two of seven and shipped fifteen goals, as many as we had conceded in the previous twenty-two. That run ended with 4-1 hammering by City on our first visit to Eastlands. The table of 15 March shows the damage inflicted:

	P	W	D	L	F	A	Pts
Arsenal	28	21	7	0	55	18	70
Chelsea	28	19	4	5	50	21	61
Man United	28	19	4	5	50	21	61

Just like Stam's sudden departure, losing our defensive rock sent us into a tailspin. There was no time for a miraculous recovery this time. Arsenal blazed an unbeaten trail to take the title, United finished third, fifteen points adrift of the Gunners.

In the Champions League, UEFA finally took the hint that fans despised the two phases of group games. After one group stage it was now straight into two-legged knockout with sixteen teams. United drew Porto and lost the first leg 2-1. At Old Trafford we deserved Scholes' thirty-second-minute opener but events in the dying minutes of each half would decide the outcome. Scholes' tally should have doubled on forty-five but he was the cruel victim of a disallowed goal. That would have killed off the workmanlike Portuguese so it stayed 1-0, with United ahead on away goals, until the last minute when Porto won a free kick twenty-five yards out at the Scoreboard End.

Benni McCarthy's curling, dipping shot was covered at the far post by Tim Howard but he seemed undecided whether to catch or punch. He did neither and parried the ball straight into the path of Costinha who shot Porto into the quarter-finals and manager José Mourinho to football stardom. For the first time in eight years United failed to reach the quarter-finals of the Champions League.

The FA Cup was our only hope, United reached the semi-final and waiting for us were Arsenal, undefeated league leaders. A highly-charged meeting at Villa Park on 3 April had United supporters occupying three sides of the ground. The defiance that embodies Manchester United came roaring through, reminiscent of the Forest tie in 1990. Arsenal took on eleven men, 17,000 fanatics and the very spirit of our club.

The singing hardly subsided over ninety minutes in which United edged it 1–0 thanks to that boy Scholesy again. The win thwarted Arsenal's treble aspirations and a record-breaking fourth consecutive final appearance. How the Gunners must hate Villa Park semis against us!

Our first FA Cup Final in Cardiff was against unlikely lads Millwall, who finished tenth in English football's second tier. United's team on 22 May 2004 was: Howard, G. Neville, O'Shea, Keane, Brown, Silvestre, Fletcher, Ronaldo, Scholes, van Nistelrooy, Giggs. Subs: Butt, Carroll, Solskjaer.

Millwall posed little threat and an efficient United ran out easy 3–0 winners. Ruud van Nistelrooy scored twice and won the man of the match award, but the real star of the show was Cristiano Ronaldo with an electrifying display of wing play. The irrepressible 19-year-old scored a thumping header and tormented the Lions' defence all afternoon. The win gave United a record eleventh FA Cup Final victory, Fergie an incredible fifth FA Cup triumph and the supporters a great day out.

Our crew found a smashing little hotel in the foothills of Abergavenny and decamped there for the weekend to celebrate yet another United trophy. Once the party was over we had a summer to reflect on a season where United under-achieved in the top two competitions. The after-glow of 1999 was fading. By 2004, Leeds, Arsenal and Chelsea had progressed further than us in the Champions League. I felt we were pedalling backwards a little.

A tremendous talent had arrived in the boy Ronaldo but Fergie used him sparingly during this transitional period. For me, the problem was the lack of creativity in midfield caused by a combination of poor form and injuries. Keane, Scholes, Fortune, Fletcher, Butt, Kléberson and Djemba-Djemba made over ten league starts each but only Keane and Scholes made over twenty. Too often the other five players looked ordinary and incapable of igniting the spark to make our play catch fire. Fergie's quest to find a suitable replacement for Roy Keane showed no signs of bearing fruit yet.

Arsenal's title meant the home of the champions had been Old Trafford or Highbury for nine consecutive seasons. That unprecedented domination in England was about to be challenged by Roman Abramovich's bankrolling of Chelsea. Claudio Ranieri was replaced in the summer of 2004 with Champions League winner Mourinho. In twelve months those two managers spent a staggering £210 million in bringing nineteen players to Stamford Bridge. The Russian meant business.

At Old Trafford, Louis Saha had arrived in January 2004 followed by Liam Miller, Alan Smith and Gabrielle Heinze in the summer. After 387 appearances for the Reds, Nicky Butt had to move on to play regular football. He was the second of our homegrown 'golden generation' to leave and took with him medals from six league titles, three FA Cups and a European Cup. Butt also took our undying respect for his battles in United's name.

On the final day of the summer transfer window Fergie pulled a real rabbit out of the hat by signing 18-year-old Everton wonder boy Wayne Rooney for around £25 million. The player was recovering from a metatarsal injury and wouldn't play until late September when he burst on to the Old Trafford stage with a hat-trick in a 6-2 rout of Fenerbahce in the Champions League. The Croxteth lad was an instant hero in United hearts – and that takes some doing!

Rio Ferdinand returned from his long exile and his calming influence on the defence was almost tangible. However, United's league games were littered with draws. After nine matches we were trailing leaders Arsenal by an incredible eleven points. Reds were feeling pretty frustrated.

The Gunners didn't lose a single league fixture throughout the 2003/04 title-winning campaign, a feat last achieved by Preston in 1889. When 'The Invincibles' arrived in Manchester on 24 October 2004 their unbeaten run stretched back 49 league games. United were smarting with injured pride.

All the ingredients were there for one hell of a showdown. Not one for the purists, its appeal lay in what was at stake which went way beyond three points. An Arsenal win would herald an underlying shift in power; United's decade of dominance over. A United victory would bring these pompous, preening, arrogant

Cockneys back down to earth. This was football's equivalent to
Ali versus Frazier. United's players matched the passion on the
terraces but neither side could steal a lead. On seventy-three
minutes Rooney won a penalty in front of the Stretford End.
Ruud van Nistelrooy put the ball on the spot. Thirteen months
earlier, in a similar situation, he could have ended Arsenal's long
unbeaten run before it even began but he missed. Prayers were
whispered as the Dutch goal machine stepped up and blasted the
ball past Lehman. Old Trafford erupted. Rooney hit a second.
The Invincibles were vanquished.

At the final whistle, just in front of J and K Stands, Roy Carroll
shook hands with Thierry Henry and offered to exchange shirts.
The Frenchman declined. United's keeper was insistent and
grabbed hold of Henry. Nothing nasty but it looked odd even
from the stands. Henry finally broke away and ran to the tunnel.
Over the next few days it emerged that Arsenal had worn T-shirts
under their tops with the words '50 not out'. Apparently, United
players got wind of this during the match which only redoubled
their efforts.

How pretentious of Arsenal, how conceited of Wenger? Can
you imagine Fergie sanctioning such a public flaunting of success
in mid-season? For the second year running the mutual loathing
boiled over after the game. Outside the dressing rooms Arsene
Wenger exchanged words with van Nistelrooy that didn't please
the Dutchman. Pizza and soup decorated the walls and Fergie's
suit. More mopping-up for the FA, plus a few thousand pounds
in income from the resulting fines.

Chelsea finally emerged as genuine contenders for the league
title. The cocktail of Roman's roubles and Mourinho's management was a powerful elixir and The Blues set a blistering pace.
After losing 1-0 to Man City on 16 October they won twenty-
three and drew six of their remaining twenty-nine fixtures to
take the title with a record ninety-five points. The football was
more efficient than exciting but it made Chelsea champions for
the first time since 1955 when ironically they won it with the
lowest ever points total – fifty-two.

United may have struggled to match Chelsea even in a good
season but 2004/05 was blighted with injury, inconsistency
and our lowest league goals total for fourteen years. Ruud
van Nistelrooy made only seventeen appearances. Rooney

donned the mantle of top scorer with eleven strikes. No other player hit double figures. United failed to score in seventeen of our sixty-one competitive games, that's 28 per cent, and while nowhere near the dreadful 37 per cent in 1989/90 it was on a par with 1972/73 when we were one season from relegation.

United finished third for the third time in four years, lost in the League Cup semi-final to Chelsea, the FA Cup Final to Arsenal and the last sixteen of the Champions League to AC Milan. I appreciate that thousands of supporters across the globe would give their right arm for a season like that. To complain seems churlish at best and spoilt at worst. But, and this is the big BUT, Manchester United supporters set their sights high. We don't expect to win everything every year then stamp our feet if it doesn't happen but we do expect to be seriously challenging for the English title and the European Cup. That's how we measure success at our club.

History and expectation are our drivers. By those standards we had failed. Nobody was calling for the manager's head, but United supporters were becoming concerned by events on and off the pitch over the previous eighteen months. Too many recent signings just weren't up to scratch. Forlan, Djemba Djemba, Kléberson, Miller and Bellion all failed to make an impact at Old Trafford. For the first time in his career at Old Trafford, Alex Ferguson's judgement in the transfer market was called into question. Fergie had always gone to great lengths to ensure we only signed players who were 'Manchester United calibre' – excellent ability, good attitude and the right temperament to play on the biggest stage. Several acquisitions between 2002 and 2004 were far from United calibre and disappeared discreetly via the 'back door' at a reduced fee. Forlan apart, none of those mentioned here made an impression with any club after United – a telling testimony.

The goalkeeping situation had become a running sore. Tim Howard had a great first season until his error against Porto knocked his confidence badly. It was reminiscent of Pat Dunne in 1965. More Howard wobbles early the following season had Fergie turning to understudy Roy Carroll. Now, I'm not being clever when I say this but from the first moment I saw Carroll play I doubted his ability to become a top class keeper. I reckon with goalkeepers you get sixth sense almost immediately. You see how they command their area and whether their physical presence exudes strength, confidence and authority. Harry Gregg, Alex Stepney, Gary Bailey, Peter Schmeichel and Les Sealey all possessed the right qualities and the crowd knew instantly. Others, like Paddy Roche, looked indecisive and edgy. I felt Roy Carroll fell into that category and though he did okay in most league games he always looked likely to get caught out at the highest level.

I was surprised Fergie persevered for so long and in the home leg against AC Milan in 2005 the keeper was found wanting when he spilled the ball to Crespo for the only goal of the game. Fergie was struggling with his transition from the celebrated 1999–2001 team to his next great creation. At the same time our closest rivals, Arsenal and Chelsea, had raised the bar with unparalleled levels of consistency. In 2003/04 and 2004/05 the title-winning teams lost only one league match between them. Despite some mischievous media speculation, the great man hadn't lost the ability to manage overnight and his desire for success at Old Trafford was as strong as ever. I am convinced the reason for our plight on the pitch lay in the distractions off it. I have touched on the mismanagement of Fergie's 'retirement' in 2002 but there was a bigger issue rumbling in the background in the first half of the decade.

By the turn of the millennium Fergie had become increasingly interested in horse racing. It seemed a healthy pursuit to relieve the stress of managing the world's biggest club. He struck up a close friendship and partnership with John Magnier, head of the powerful bloodstock empire Coolmore. Sir Alex's presence at the big race meetings brought great publicity for Magnier's horses and the Irishmen decided to give United's manager a half share in a racehorse called Rock of Gibraltar. The animal became a champion and over two seasons in 2001 and 2002 it set a world record of seven consecutive Grade 1 wins and earned around £1 million in prize money. As such, its stud fees rocketed. Estimates put earnings over ten years in the region of £150 million.

Fergie believed he was entitled to half those stud fees. Coolmore didn't. Compromises were offered, agreement wasn't reached and so began a protracted and bitter quarrel. Sir Alex began legal action and the matter was finally resolved out of court in March 2004 with a one-off net payment to Fergie in the region of £2.5 million.

That part of the story alone would have made a great Dick Francis novel but the plot thickened. In 2001, Magnier and J.P. McManus as investment company Cubic Expressions bought a 6.77 per cent stake in Manchester United shares. By early 2004, the stake had been ratcheted up to 28.9 per cent, making Cubic the biggest shareholder in our club. Just before the 'Rock' dispute was settled the two Irishmen sent United's board a letter with ninety-nine questions querying events under Alex Ferguson's management including certain transfer dealings and wages and bonuses paid to the players.

The Ferguson/Coolmore feud was about betrayal, money and pride between strong-willed powerful people at the very top of their sporting worlds. Alex Ferguson felt he had been cheated out of a £75 million fortune, far more than he could ever earn from football. The conflict may have affected his focus. Then what started as a private matter developed over eighteen months into a situation where United's manager was embroiled in an acrid and very public legal battle with United's biggest shareholder. Imagine the potential implications for the United board and the well-being of the club. Doesn't feel right does it?

Even once the Coolmore dispute was settled another unpalatable distraction loomed. In October 2004, American businessman Malcolm Glazer increased his United shareholding to just under the 30 per cent threshold required to launch a bid. Sharks were circling United and supporters rallied to protest. Over the next six months, individuals and supporters groups took a variety of actions to highlight opposition to United being 'up for sale' to the highest bidder.

I was vehemently against a takeover by anyone who didn't have a genuine affiliation with the club. At the same time I realised that moving to a PLC in 1991 had left the club a hostage to fortune – anybody with the readies could buy 'our' club. Still, it was worth a fight. I joined the animated protests around the ground before the Arsenal and AC Milan games including a rowdy storming of the megastore at the latter. But I couldn't help thinking on each occasion, here we were playing a key game and we were focused on a protest rather than the match. I felt pre-occupied with the potential takeovers. Imagine how it must have affected Fergie.

On Thursday, 12 May 2005, I went to our offices in Huyton to wrap up a project. I took a bit of stick from the Scousers.

Liverpool had wormed their way to the Champions League Final and overnight thousands of Liverpudlians, cured of their agoraphobia, ventured out to talk football again. Having taken as much of that famous Scouse wit as I could stand, I drove back to my Bolton base. Radio 5's headline news announced that Malcolm Glazer had bought the shares owned by Cubic Expressions, securing himself the controlling stake in Manchester United.

Although it wasn't unexpected, I wasn't prepared for the news when it broke. I felt sick, then angry, then scared. What in God's name would this man do to the club I love? I finished work around 7 p.m. that night and considered going down to Old Trafford to protest but had second thoughts. Deep down inside I knew we had lost the fight. Money had won the day; the supporters were just playing at the edges now.

May 2005 turned out to be a black month for Manchester United supporters. On 10 May, Chelsea came to Old Trafford as champions, entered the field to a guard of honour then beat us 3-1 to inflict our first home defeat of the season in our final match. The customary lap of honour felt more like a funeral march as the majority of the crowd quickly disappeared into the night.

Gary Neville's post-match comments summed it up perfectly, 'What happened at the end was the biggest kick up the backside we could possibly have wished for. The whole evening was tough but to walk around at the end, it felt as low as it could get in your own stadium.' Two days later Malcolm Glazer took ownership of the club and on 21 May Arsenal beat us in the FA Cup Final on penalties after we had battered them for 120 minutes.

The last kick to the privates came on Wednesday 25 May. AC Milan versus Liverpool in the European Cup Final and United supporters everywhere were settling down to see the Scousers get their comeuppance. Maldini put the Italians one up in the first minute, Milan then played breathtaking football and raced into a 3-0 half-time lead. For the first time in weeks I was starting to feel good about me football again, but I only had one can of beer in the fridge! At half-time I jumped in the car and headed to Tesco to buy more ale. On the way, Radio 5's Graham Taylor and Alan Green said that Liverpool must focus on damage limitation to avoid a demoralising seven or eight-goal thrashing. 'Stop it lads, I'm trying to drive' I thought!

Back home with beer ready, feet up, kids in bed and mobile phone poised to text anybody west of St Helens, I sat back to savour the humiliation. In six second-half minutes Liverpool pulled it back to 3-3. Both sides shut up shop then the Scousers won on penalties. Somehow they had won the bloody European Cup again. They had played crap most of the season. Best team in Europe? They weren't even the best team on Merseyside having finished fifth to Everton's fourth.

With all our domination of the English game for twelve years we had managed only one European Cup win. Now without having won the league for fifteen years Liverpool had added another one to their haul. The pain of May 2005 went very deep.

23

HOW MANY SPECIAL PEOPLE CHANGE? HOW MANY LIVES ARE LIVING STRANGE?

Distasteful as the Glazer takeover was for United supporters at least it put the ownership issue to bed for the manager. Fergie was finally rid of the non-football distractions that had hung over him for a couple of years. Even so, life would get worse before it got better for the manager, the team and the supporters.

In the autumn of 2005 Fergie would have to dig deep into his management toolbox to keep United's reformation intact. The season started under a cloud as around 5,000 Reds decided the takeover was a step too far and formed their own team, FC United of Manchester. They would play in red and white in the North West Counties League, the tenth tier of English football, at Bury FC's Gigg Lane. We had never known times like it, a public and painful split in the ranks. United supporters no longer united. I never thought I would see that day.

For me, United is a love for life. The only alternative to supporting them would be to walk away completely. I couldn't turn my back on the club and support another team. However, I can appreciate the heartache and mental turmoil those fans went through that did leave to follow FC. The majority were Manchester or Salford born and bred and followed United home and away for years. Their parents and grandparents had followed United – it would have been a heartbreaking decision and I respect it. The only problem I had with the split is that in the short-term it provided ammunition for United-haters across the country who thought we were crumbling. They should have known better.

In the summer of 2005 Fergie finally resolved the goalkeeping problem by signing the classy Dutch international Edwin van der Sar. He also bought Ji-Sung Park after the South Korean starred in PSV Eindhoven's run to the Champions League semi-finals. Aware of Chelsea and Arsenal's phenomenal consistency Fergie stressed the need for a good start to the season. We won the first three league matches then drew the next four. Injuries to Rooney, Giggs, Heinze and Keane within the opening months of the season crippled us.

Meanwhile Chelsea started like a bullet from a gun, winning ten of the first eleven league games. For the second season running they were the team to catch but United just weren't gelling, particularly in midfield, where Smith, Richardson and Fletcher struggled to impress. Following a 4-1 defeat at Middlesbrough on 29 October, a recovering Roy Keane let rip on MUTV about the attitude and performances of his colleagues. I should add 'allegedly' here because very few people watched the footage which was hastily pulled and destroyed before being broadcast. Keano was feeling the same frustrations as most United supporters. In too many matches the standard of football was poor and we were slipping further behind our rivals at home and in Europe. Three days after the Middlesbrough game we lost 1-0 to Lille in the Champions League in another disjointed display.

Fergie didn't react immediately to Keane's outburst. He let the dust settle, did his business behind closed doors and on Friday 18 November the club announced it had parted company with its illustrious captain. His last game had been at Anfield in September where he was carried from the battlefield, injured against the old enemy.

Our captain was 34 and, though still a formidable opponent, couldn't do the fetching and carrying week in week out that was once his trademark. From somewhere around 2001 I'd had recurring cold sweats about what United would do when Roy Keane wasn't there anymore. How would we cope and more importantly who would we get to replace him? I used to put the thoughts to the back of my mind and get on with the day's events, just hoping that Fergie would unearth some gem in time.

Fergie's search for a replacement had been surprisingly unproductive. Now the moment of truth had arrived, Keano was gone. Fergie said Keane was 'the best midfield player in the world of his generation'. Some accolade when you consider his contemporaries included Zidane, Figo, Rivaldo and Sammer but no Red would disagree. Keane played 480 times for United, scoring fifty-one goals, he won seven league titles, four FA Cups, the Champions League and the Intercontinental Cup. The impressive statistics tell only part of the story.

Keano was a massive presence in his thirteen seasons at Old Trafford. Easily United's most successful captain, he was the heartbeat for over a decade. He was you, me and Fergie out there on the pitch, battling proudly in that red shirt until the opposition was defeated and the game won. While Eric Cantona's coming galvanised United, Keane's leadership took us to even greater heights at home and abroad.

Numerous displays of power and skill come to mind but for me there is one performance that stands out in Keane's United career. In his autobiography he dismisses the acclaim heaped on him for that game in Turin in 1999, putting it down to sympathetic praise because he missed the final. Well, sorry Roy, but you're wrong on that one. The occasion, the venue, the opposition and the two-goal deficit left United needing a superhero to turn the tide. That night, our Man of Steel drove the team on against all odds to make sure we reached the European Cup Final, even scoring the goal that got us back in the match. It was his finest hour and United supporters will forever eulogise it. Keane missing the final does not colour my judgment. Turin was the finest performance by a United player in the last fifty years, if not ever. I count my blessings that I was there to witness it.

Exactly a week after Roy Keane's departure, United's faithful were dealt another blow. During the afternoon of 25 November came news that George Best had passed away. He had lost his long battle with liver disease, a consequence of the one opponent in his life he couldn't beat. United's history is littered with heroes and I've adored many of them. Looking back, though, I've only ever had two real idols in my life, Bestie and Rod Stewart. We will park Rod the Mod for now.

The first ten years of our lives are usually filled with memories that our parents create for us. They arrange the fun and we follow.

After that, we start making our own decisions about what gives us a buzz. We might choose music, games, sport, clothes and the opposite sex, and that provides our special moments through teenage years. For me it was football and Manchester United and a genius called Georgie Best. During the winter of 1963/64 my life was lit up by the FA Youth Cup matches that Bestie starred in. I was enchanted by the dazzling dribbling skills, the audacious slalom runs with the ball seemingly tied to his boot and the little tricks that left opponents bamboozled. The charismatic Ulsterman had a captivating presence when he went on a football pitch, supremely confident but never arrogant, he weaved magic before our very eyes.

I was besotted with George Best and that affection just grew and grew as he scaled the heights of his career. I collected anything that had George's name on it from chewing gum wrappers to cigarette cards to posters. Those first five years I watched United, from 1963 to 1968, were far far more exciting than any story in a comic or book or TV programme and while United had a team full of stars Georgie Best was the jewel in the crown.

In the second half of the glorious 1960s our number seven was the finest footballer in the world. I once saw some graffiti which summed it up perfectly – 'Eusebio great, Pele better, George Best'. Even as the United team aged and struggled to win trophies, Best would generate enough magic to make any trip worthwhile. Though the twilight years were painful to watch, nothing – absolutely nothing – could diminish the joy Bestie brought to Manchester United supporters and football fans around the world. George Best is the greatest footballer I've seen. I used to love a song the Stretford End sang in the late 1960s, a little ditty entitled 'Maybe it's because I'm from Manchester'. It was a parody of the 'Londoner' version and contained the line, 'I get a funny feeling inside of me, when I see George Best score.' I always did.

I dearly wish I could find the words to do his greatness justice but that's probably an impossible task. Really, you had to see him play to understand. Some time after George passed away, I was helping my daughter with her homework. She had to prepare a short piece about a supernova and wasn't sure where to start. I suggested we look at the dictionary definition which read:

> A stellar explosion; one of the most energetic explosions in nature.
> Extremely luminous, it causes a burst of radiation that often out-
> shines an entire galaxy, before fading from view. During this time,
> a supernova can radiate as much energy as the Sun could emit over
> its life span.

I read the description a few times, and couldn't help thinking, that was George Best.

United's poor form spilled into the Champions League. We won just one of the first five group games, scoring a paltry two goals, which left United needing to win at Benfica to qualify for the knockout stages. Ever since Bestie's classic 1966 perfor- mance I had wanted to see United play at the Stadium of Light. The original ground was rebuilt in 2003, but it was still on my 'must see before I die' list. Now the tie had added spice and a dozen or so of our lads made the trip. After a great day around Lisbon's regenerated harbour it was down to business. Benfica had never beaten United in a competitive match and when Scholesy gave us a sixth minute lead the omens looked good.

In truth, we were relying heavily on the young and inexperi- enced shoulders of Rooney and Ronaldo. The latter got distracted by a running feud with the home crowd who baited him at every opportunity for his allegiance to Sporting. Eventually Fergie withdrew his young winger to avoid an unnecessary incident. Benfica clawed their way back into the game with a goal from Geovanni and United's luck was out when a speculative drive from Beto got a wicked deflection to give the Eagles the points they needed to progress.

Christmas 2005 saw United supporters wrestling with a few unsavoury truths. A dreadful twelve months on and off the pitch culminated in the failure to qualify from the Champions League group stages for the first time in ten years. In the title race we languished twelve points behind Chelsea. Our problem lay in our inability to break teams down, particularly at home. Between 26 February and 3 December only once did we score more than one goal in a league fixture at Old Trafford, a 2-1 victory over Newcastle in April. Our once legendary and proud midfield lacked bite and incisiveness.

Even staunch evangelists were starting to wonder if Fergie's magic was wearing thin. The transition from the all-conquering treble team had stalled badly. The lads from the 1992 youth team had all turned 30 and we desperately needed to bolster our engine room.

Not for the first time in Fergie's reign, the darkest hour was just before the dawn. The manager set about tweaking the parts of the team that he felt needed most attention. Having kissed a few frogs that didn't turn into princes, his judgement now needed to be spot on. Most United supporters believed we needed a top midfield player and another striker. In the January 2006 transfer window Fergie bought two relatively unknown defenders, Patrice Evra from Monaco and the Serb Nemanja Vidic. The signings raised a few eyebrows as we already had good players in those positions, nevertheless Fergie bloodied both newcomers immediately.

Ryan Giggs had missed most of the first four months but returned to form a surprisingly decent midfield partnership with John O'Shea. Fletcher and Park alternated to partner the two. Fergie started playing Ronaldo more regularly while Rooney, slightly ahead in his development, played almost every game.

The table for 2 February 2006 shows the title race as good as over:

	P	W	D	L	F	A	Pts	GD
Chelsea	24	20	3	1	50	13	63	37
Man United	24	14	6	4	45	24	48	21

United then embarked on a run of nine straight league wins, Chelsea lost two and drew one and the gap closed to seven points with five games remaining. We still had to visit Stamford Bridge and prayed Chelsea might crack. They didn't, we did. United's draw against bottom club Sunderland and 3-0 defeat at the Bridge clinched the London club's second consecutive title.

United had progressed to the League Cup Final for a show-down with Wigan who were revelling in their first season in top flight football. Fergie had been alternating between strikers van Nistelrooy and Saha but played the Dutchman in all the big games. For the League Cup Final at the Millennium Stadium on 26 February Fergie opted for Saha with Ruud on the bench. It shocked supporters and commentators alike. The full line-up was: van der Sar, G. Neville, Silvestre, Ferdinand, Brown, Park, O'Shea, Ronaldo, Rooney, Saha, Giggs. Subs: Evra, Richardson, Vidic.

United cruised to a 4-0 victory. Two goals from Rooney and one each from Ronaldo and Saha gave us only our second League Cup. For over a decade this competition had been fourth on our wish-list every August, but in the absence of any other silverware we relished the occasion. Coincidentally, Wigan were our next opponents in a league match at the JJB Stadium. We all expected van Nistelrooy to return to the starting line-up but Fergie retained Saha. That night I noticed a distinct change in United's play. The speed of movement from defence to attack was much quicker than over the previous twelve months, a throw-back to the Cantona, Kanchelskis, Giggs and Sharp era. There had been signs of it at Cardiff too. United won 2-1, Saha played well and engineered the late winner. The Frenchman's two years at United had been badly hampered by injury but he had forged his way back into the reckoning between December and February and scored ten goals. He played in most of the remaining games.

United beat Charlton in the final match to finish runners-up. Our final haul of eighty-three points equalled our total as champions in 2003, and exceeded our tally when winning titles in 2001, 1999, 1997 and 1996. Before that Charlton match, news broke that Ruud van Nistelrooy had turned up at Old Trafford, had a row about only being on the bench and left the ground in a huff. For some weeks stories had surfaced that the Dutch striker and Cristiano Ronaldo had been involved in training ground bust-ups but these were played down by the club.

The Sunday press reported a rift between Fergie and van Nistelrooy. As with David Beckham three years earlier, United supporters hoped against hope that it was just paper talk but on 28 July the Dutchman joined Real Madrid for around £12 million. The true reason for the sale might remain private. My instincts tell me that Fergie wanted to change United's approach play. For five years we had played balls into van Nistelrooy and he delivered the goals with predatory instincts. His best seasons at Old Trafford were his first two when he benefitted from those wicked Beckham crosses. The problem was, if our goal machine was injured, off-form or well-marked we were less likely to kill teams off. A lot of our eggs were in Ruud's basket.

When Saha was in the team, it complemented the styles of Rooney and Ronaldo. Releasing van Nistelrooy was a big gamble for Fergie though. Firstly, the striker had become a hero to United supporters and rightly so, scoring a phenomenal 150 goals in 219 appearances, including thirty-eight in forty-seven Champions League games and smashing Denis Law's record. Secondly, though United supporters liked what they saw from Saha, we just didn't see enough of him. His susceptibility to injury had earned him the nickname of 'Balsa Boy' on the terraces. Fergie did what he does best, he made the tough decision. We put our faith in him once more.

The summer of 2006 saw the arrival of Michael Carrick from Spurs for around £14 million, our only significant signing. Many Reds believed we needed a second top player to bolster the middle of the park. Fergie, in a moment of disarming honesty, revealed that he had stopped looking for a 'new' Roy Keane on the grounds that it was impossible to find one. I felt the only player in Europe to possess the same qualities as a young Keane was Steve Gerrard. The 'impossible' bit would have been getting him to sign for United. The squad was also boosted by the return of Solskjaer and Heinze from long-term injury.

Fergie reiterated the need for a good start and this time his players responded, beating Fulham 5-1 in the opening fixture and storming to the top with fourteen wins in seventeen games. When Tampa Bay Buccaneers won their only American Superbowl in 2002, their coach Jon Gruden was asked the secret of the team's success, he replied simply, 'Offence wins games. Defence wins championships.' Fergie's seemingly odd purchase of Evra and Vidic now looked inspired and their partnership with Gary Neville and Rio Ferdinand developed into a solid defensive unit backed up by the reliable and experienced van der Sar.

Michael Carrick settled in quietly but effectively. Not overtly vocal like Keane, his timely interceptions, clever reading of the game, accurate passing and superb vision provided steel and sophistication to our midfield play. Scholes returned after nine months out with an eye complaint and, with Giggsy, rolled back the years. Rooney and Ronaldo were fast coming of age and both contributed more than twenty goals over the season.

In the Champions League United drew Celtic, setting up our first competitive clash. Although I had a boyhood soft spot for Rangers, I also admired and respected the legend that is Celtic. A year before United won the European Cup in 1968 I had watched the grainy black and white TV pictures of the Lisbon

Lions beating the great Inter Milan 2-1 to lift the trophy. In May 1976, I was part of a small United following that ventured up to Glasgow for the Jimmy Johnstone and Bobby Lennox testimonial. We received a tremendous welcome stood alongside Celtic supporters in the 'Jungle' which was as fearsome as the Stretford End in those days. The greeting was the same for Danny McGrain's testimonial in August 1980 and the 1992 game to celebrate the twenty-fifth anniversary of Celtic's Lisbon triumph.

As well as these trips, I had enjoyed many games between the two sides at Old Trafford. But all these were friendly matches. Finally, on 13 September 2006 the teams lined up for the real McCoy. Old Trafford was a cauldron and a full house enjoyed a see-saw game that ended with a 3-2 win for United. The ground's capacity had increased during the summer from just under 68,000 to 76,000 with increased seating in the two corners opposite the dugout. The stadium befitted Manchester United.

Both teams were still fighting for qualification by the time of the return leg in November. I managed to get a ticket before I left Manchester this time thus avoiding the trauma of combing Glasgow for spares. The massed, baying legions of green and whites hoops was impressive and the singing of 'You'll Never Walk Alone' was ear-piercing. Once the game started we took control and for most of the first half it was our songs filling the night air.

United's domination failed to produce a goal and Nakamura's devilish free kick put Celtic ahead with nine minutes left. United peppered the Scots' goal and won a penalty in the dying seconds. Saha, on fine form with eight goals in fifteen starts, stepped up looking a bit nervous. Boruc made a flying save. When we had worked out the maths, the win had put Celtic through to the knockout stages while we needed a draw in our final game to join them.

Our city centre hotel was full of celebrating Irish Celts. We had a couple of beers then hit the sack ready for an early start back to Manchester in time for work. When we left at 6 a.m. the Bhoys were still celebrating in the bar! Two weeks later, United held their nerve and beat Benfica 3-1 to qualify.

Chelsea and United went neck and neck in the title race until the Christmas holiday games. In the previous three seasons United had lost ground during this busy period but Yuletide 2006 was different. Chelsea drew three and won one, United won three and drew one. As Alex Ferguson reached pension age, his favourite tipple will have tasted all that sweeter for the six-point lead and the blistering pace his team had set going into New Year 2007:

	P	W	D	L	F	A	Pts	GD
Man United	22	17	3	2	49	15	54	34
Chelsea	22	14	6	2	37	17	48	20
Liverpool	22	12	4	6	32	16	40	16

United's forty-nine goals came from all departments in the team, vindication for the decision to sell van Nistelrooy. Another piece of shrewd business saw Fergie persuade Henrik Larsson to join United on loan during the Swedish close season. The striker would make a valuable contribution with three goals in ten appearances.

Once again, a trip to Stamford Bridge was lurking at the end of the fixture list. We all hoped United could maintain a lead of more than three points for the worst-case scenario. For the first time in four years United were setting the pace while the challengers hoped for a slip-up. Chelsea saw United's fixture at Anfield on 3 March as exactly that. Liverpool hadn't lost a home league match for seventeen months and could disguise another season of underachievement by thwarting United's title chances.

The game was close, tense and goalless for eighty-nine minutes. I was consoling myself that it was a point won rather than two lost when United got a free kick on the edge of Liverpool's penalty area at the Kop end. It wasn't in a central position, more towards the corner of the area. A last-minute winner at Anfield is the stuff of dreams but in forty years of travelling there I had never seen one. Ronaldo whipped in the free kick and the ball appeared to curl low into the arms of Reina stood on the goal-line. As Saha closed in it bounced off the keeper, rolled out to the edge of the six-yard box and there was John O'Shea to side-foot the ball high into the Liverpool net.

That prompted one of those rare occasions in a football supporter's life when even going ballistic to celebrate a goal doesn't seem enough. You feel like you're going to explode. The goal was vital for the three points alone, but to score it in the last seconds at Liverpool directly in front of the Kop was joy unbounded. Eight United players ran to smother O'Shea while Gary Neville and van der Sar joined in with the celebrating United supporters. Meanwhile, Fergie did one of his odd little routines that accompany crucial goals. The great man came rushing out of the dugout ready to cheer as if he were on the terraces, arms aloft, running and jumping. Then he restrained himself remembering he's the manager, stood still and applauded excitedly. He should just let himself go!

Four weeks later, in a league game at home to Blackburn, I saw the signs that convinced me we would be champions once again. The record books show a 4-1 win, Alex Ferguson's 800th league game with United and the highest crowd ever to watch the Reds at Old Trafford – 76,098. However, United had a poor first half, Vidic going off with a shoulder injury and Rovers taking a 1-0 lead. It was one of those games in the run-in that can turn into a banana skin and change the destiny of the title but United came out in the second half and played like true champions. Confident, determined, full of running and skill, United brushed Blackburn aside with four goals in the final twenty-nine minutes to maintain the six-point lead over Chelsea. United had won twenty-one of the previous twenty-five league games, showing incredible consistency which spilled over into the FA Cup and Champions League.

By April this rejuvenated United side were battling on three fronts. In the FA Cup we thumped Watford 4-1 at Villa Park to meet Chelsea in the first final at the rebuilt Wembley. In the Champions League knockout stage we saw off Lille then drew Roma in the quarter-finals. Ever since missing out on that trip to Lazio for the Anglo-Italian Cup in 1973 I had held the dream of seeing United play in Rome. After fifty years of European competition United were finally paired with a side from the Italian capital.

A couple of days before we flew out, the club issued a severe warning on its website for those travelling to the match. I had never read anything like it before, spelling out the strong possibility of trouble from the host fans. The advice specified certain places not to go. The tone of the warning brought criticism from the media who felt United were pre-judging Roma and showing disrespect. I travelled with Tezzer Lomax and Colin Green, veterans of European jaunts, we didn't dismiss the club's advice but there was a mood of 'it can't be that bad' among us.

In Rome we looked around the Vatican, had a few beers, put the world to rights before heading back to our bus for the trip to the Olympic Stadium. The fleet of coaches was flanked by re-inforced police vehicles each carrying a swivelling machine gun on the top. They were basically urban tanks. The guns were manned by officers in full body armour. All traffic on the way was stopped to let us through.

At the ground we were driven into a concrete-walled compound right next to the turnstiles. The compound held four coaches at time, the entrance and exit were huge iron gates which were locked shut while visiting supporters disembarked. Once empty, the coaches left the compound and the next four drove in. Supporters were strongly encouraged to go straight into the ground by the small army of police overseeing the proceedings. There were two hours to go to kick-off so the three of us thought we would try and sneak out of the compound and have a walk around the stadium. We managed to get out okay but the further we walked from the gates we noticed all eyes were on us even though we had no United colours on. This was much less welcoming than Istanbul! We discreetly turned back and went into the ground.

Throughout the next hour a steady stream of Reds came on to the terraces with bloodied faces or bandaged heads. I had not seen this much carnage at a football match since the 1970s. Stories spread of Roma fans attacking United supporters on various approaches to the stadium. It seemed the warnings given out by the club were justified. We were fenced off from the home fans by thick Perspex panels about three metres high. For company we had at least fifty armed members of the Carabinieri, Italy's National Guard. There was continuous banter between the Roma and United supporters but it was low-level stuff, mainly gestures with the odd plastic bottle thrown over.

A minute before half time Roma took the lead through Taddei. In the celebrations their fans rushed towards the fence and so did United's but the barrier was so high and thick the supporters couldn't get at each other. It was all posturing. But that's not the way the Carabinieri saw it. They mounted a brutal full-scale attack on those United supporters near the fence then turned on the rest of our crowd, hitting people indiscriminately with their batons. The behaviour of the police was barbaric. I saw it first-hand.

During the melee I found myself at the front of a stand-off between United supporters and the police. In the middle, lying wounded and bleeding, were several Reds who were victims of the attack. United supporters were so incensed they were ready to launch a counter-attack even though the police had an overwhelming advantage with their protective head-gear, batons and guns. Our blood was boiling and you can only take so much. Then a small, uniformed man with a walkie-talkie appeared in the centre of the stand-off, he directed the Italian police to back off and move to the fence dividing the two sets of supporters. Peace broke out and the injured received medical attention.

The rest of the match passed off without incident on the terraces and we enjoyed a rallying performance from the team. Despite having ten men for an hour after Scholes was red-carded, United put in a spirited display. A superb link-up between Ronaldo, Solskjaer and Rooney brought an equaliser and that valued away goal. Roma went 2-1 up and it was backs-to-the-wall for United's tired defenders. In the end the team held out and our fans got out safely.

Post-match, UEFA launched an enquiry into the treatment of United supporters, as did civil and government representatives from both countries. Nothing of any consequence came of it. In fact, two years later the Italian club were rewarded with host status for the Champions League Final.

The Old Trafford crowd was really up for the return leg against Roma but nobody was prepared for the way United started the match. Firing on all cylinders we were three goals up inside twenty minutes. Roma couldn't live with United's passing and movement not to mention lethal finishing. By half-time it was 4-0 and there was to be no let-up in the second half as United ran out 7-1 winners, 8-3 on aggregate. It ranks as the most devastating performance I've seen from a United side especially when you consider the opposition and occasion. United's line-up for that memorable second leg on 10 April 2007 was: van der Sar, O'Shea, Heinze, Carrick, Ferdinand, Brown, Ronaldo, Smith, Rooney, Fletcher, Giggs.

Only fifteen months earlier, Fergie's side had looked like dispirited strugglers. Now they were on course for another treble. With four games left Chelsea had closed the gap to three points. United had eight games to match the class of 1999 but the season was taking its toll. Vidic and Ferdinand missed crucial games and Fergie battled to keep his team fresh. We managed a 3-2 home victory over AC Milan in the semi-final home leg then travelled to Everton where Fergie rested Ronaldo on the bench. United looked tired and listless. After fifty minutes we trailed 2-0 while Chelsea led Bolton 2-1. Word went round Goodison that Bolton had equalised, but we were struggling to muster a fightback.

On sixty-one minutes John O'Shea pulled one back. He was enjoying his trips to Merseyside. Two minutes later Fergie unleashed Ronaldo. Reds sensed something was on and up went the volume. On sixty-eight we were level through a Phil Neville own goal. Everton were back-pedalling furiously. With eleven minutes left Rooney shot United in front and in the dying seconds young Chris Eagles slotted home our fourth. Bolton held on for a draw. United had a five-point lead with three games to go and our songs of celebration and relief echoed around Goodison Park.

Four days later, AC Milan out-played United, winning the second leg 3-0. There were two factors conspiring against us that evening. One was United's tired legs, the other was an obsessive desire by Milan to join Liverpool in the final and avenge that humiliating 2005 defeat.

A trip to Eastlands brought a 1-0 victory thanks to Ronaldo's penalty. Chelsea played Arsenal the next day and we expected them to win leaving United to avoid defeat at the Bridge the following Wednesday to secure the title in London. But Mourinho's team had gone, Arsenal gained a point and United won their sixteenth title. The anticipated 'decider' at Stamford Bridge on 9 May 2007 would now be a glorious coronation.

This title victory stood for much more than just being champions of England. Abramovich's millions had transformed Chelsea's potential, domestically and abroad. For four years they had been able to buy almost any player in the world as well as top-class cover for those players. Of course, United, Arsenal and Liverpool all had big money but nothing like Chelsea's resources. The other three in the big four had grown organically thanks to success on the park over many years not because of a super-rich benefactor. For United to claw their way back to become English champions so soon was a triumph for Fergie, our supporters and football in general.

So we intended to celebrate accordingly. The most popular song on the United terraces that winter was a defiant reminder to the Chelsea manager that he might not have it all his own way. To the tune of 'Walking in a Winter Wonderland' it went:

Mourinho are you listenin',
you'd better keep our trophy glistenin',
We'll be back in May,
To take it away,
Walking in a Fergie wonderland!

Earlier in the season, many Reds felt the spirit of the song might be a bit too ambitious, but as the season progressed, the chants grew in conviction. Now it was payback time. That Wednesday, I drove down to London with Mike Stewart, Simon Rumsey and his son Stuart. The match meant nothing but the occasion meant everything. United's end was packed; there would be no sitting down this evening. United came out to a guard of honour from the Chelsea players, which was worth the extortionate £50 ticket price alone. Our team was missing most of the players who had won the title but that didn't matter either.

As soon as the game began, the 'trophy glistenin' chant started. Normally it would last around half a dozen choruses then peter out, but United supporters kept it going, and going, and going. Chelsea fans tried desperately to sing their songs but were drowned out by triumphant Reds. In the end the disheartened Cockneys just gave up, they knew they were in for a long night! The song filled Stamford Bridge for twenty to twenty-five minutes by which time my hands, legs, back, throat, all major organs and every muscle ached with the singing and clapping. I remember in 1968, the Stretford End doing a similar party piece with 'We are the champions, champions of Europe!' I think it was a home game against Stoke and the song rang out for almost half an hour. But the display at Chelsea that night was second to none; I've never known a song sung with such gusto and for so long. I believe it came across loud and clear on Sky's live coverage. Message delivered, point made.

The songs of celebration continued throughout the match. It was a throwback to the 1960s and 1970s when United ruled the roost on the terraces with their colourful songs, fanatical support and witty banter. Targets Abramovich, Kenyon and Mourinho all sank visibly in their seats as we reminded them it would take more than just their money and talk to overtake United. The game ended 0-0 but it was one of the best away trips I've been on. When it comes to partying, few do it better than United supporters and here's an important point. It is far better when the supporters themselves conduct the celebrations rather than some suited MC with a microphone and the stadium loudspeakers belting out recorded choruses of 'Glory, glory Man United'. Take note, you bastions of Old Trafford!

The revelry in the final home game was tainted not just by MC Bland but also the 1-0 defeat to West Ham in pouring rain. The truth is, United were battle-weary and it showed a week later in the FA Cup Final against Chelsea where we lost to a late Drogba goal. United had run the title race like a sprint in order to out-pace Chelsea. We equalled our record number of wins in a season with twenty-eight and amassed a magnificent eighty-nine points. That late burst of energy to win the game at Everton left nothing in the tank. We scored just once in the remaining five games – the penalty at City.

By winning the title in 2007, United greatly over-achieved. Fergie's team was still a work-in-progress; most Reds expected it would take another year for the blend to come of age. To win the league, reach the Champions League semi-final and the FA Cup Final was truly incredible. Fergie had got it right again.

24

YOU ONLY GET ONE SHOT, DO NOT MISS YOUR CHANCE TO BLOW, THIS OPPORTUNITY COMES ONCE IN A LIFETIME YO

The week after United regained the league title in 2007 I was summoned to a meeting at work. A big re-organisation was in the offing and about to be unveiled at a hotel in Nottingham. For most of my career I had thrived on such shake-ups, they often provided me with the opportunity to prove myself in a new role. In recent years the object was simply to survive them. As I drove down to the Midlands on a glorious May day I did wonder whether the fat lady might be clearing her throat. We're all just a curly finger away from being called into the office to be told, 'Pete, you've done a fantastic job for us, but we'd like you to bugger off now!'

I was 52, E.On Energy had bought Powergen and the centre of their world in the UK was the Midlands, not the North West where I was based. The writing was on the wall. Sure enough, the company announced several job losses and those posts that remained would be based in the Midlands. The announcement didn't make *News at Ten* but it left me with a choice of relocate or take redundancy.

During the drive home, far from being crushed by the news, I was quite excited at the thought of doing something different. I knew it was time to go. With the redundancy package sorted, I left the energy industry after thirty-six years, on 27 July 2007. Ever since Fergie called off his retirement in 2002, I'd had this notion that I would like to write a book about my travels with United. I could recount the 'Ta Ra Fergie' story plus a number of other anecdotes. For a few years I toyed with the idea but with the demands of work, a young family and a football team to support, there just wasn't the time to write. Never give up on a dream they say, the redundancy was an ideal opportunity to put my keyboard where my mouth was.

While my weekdays were spent writing about the past, my weekends were focused on the present and United's resurgence. Fergie didn't rest on his laurels and signed Owen Hargreaves, Carlos Tevez, Anderson and Nani; awesome additions to a title-winning squad. Credit should be given to the board, the outlay on these four players exceeded £50 million and Fergie spoke of his preference that the club was in private hands rather than a public limited company. The transfers had Reds salivating over the prospects for the coming season.

Football being the wicked temptress she is, we were frustrated for the first month as Rooney sustained a foot injury in the opening game and Ronaldo picked up a three-match ban in the second. Only once in the opening eleven games did we score more than one goal, a run that included six 1-0 victories. A key feature in regaining our title had been goals coming from all parts of the squad. A total of seventeen players netted during the 2006/07 campaign, compared to nine when we last won the title in 2003 and fifteen in our treble season. At the start of 2007/08 that pipeline dried up but the slender wins kept United in touch with early leaders Arsenal and brought victories in the Champions League group stage.

A month into the season came an announcement that rocked the football world. Chelsea parted company with Jose Mourinho. The 'mutual consent' card was played which always adds to the speculation. Chelsea lay fourth in the table with eleven points from six games so results alone were not the issue. Two nights before the departure Chelsea drew 1-1 at home to Rosenborg BK in the Champions League. While disappointing, it wasn't a result to lose your job over. When the dust settled it came down to a power struggle. Mourinho wanted full control of team matters but Abramovich had brought in Avram Grant as director of football in the summer. That was bound to end in tears. Perhaps Abramovich did it intentionally to get rid of Mourinho, who knows? Despite two league titles, the FA Cup and two League Cups in three years, Chelsea were falling short of expectations on two counts.

Firstly in pursuit of the European Cup, the glamour and scale of which seduced Roman four years earlier. Chelsea had failed at the semi-final stage in 2004, 2005 and 2007 and stumbled in the early knockout stage in 2006. Secondly, and perhaps more tellingly, Chelsea's football came more from the School of Science rather than the Theatre of Dreams. Mourinho's teams were experts at wearing teams down but not with width and flair. His tactical nous was unquestionable and it brought results but not friends or admirers.

I had warmed to Mourinho's mix of ability and eccentricity and felt his record at Porto and Chelsea (initially) had put him in the running to replace Fergie when the great man called it a day. However, I think he missed a golden opportunity at Stamford Bridge. With Abramovich's funding and Mourinho's football knowledge it was the perfect blend to build something beautiful in terms of results and performance. Mourinho chose to embrace results and sacrifice flair. If that philosophy was the measure of the man it would be at odds with our whole belief system at Old Trafford. Time would tell. The crowd at that Chelsea-Rosenborg game in September 2007 was just under 25,000; United's three group games attracted an average in excess of 74,000 to Old Trafford. For now, The Special One had failed to produce a special team.

Avram Grant replaced Mourinho and his first game was at Old Trafford which United won 2-0. It had been a very satisfying week for United supporters. After the early goal famine came a flood, United scoring four goals per match in five out of six games. Hargreaves added steel to the midfield, Anderson provided flair and Tevez brought muscle to the attack, a never-say-die spirit and key goals.

But the star of the show was Cristiano Ronaldo. By mid-January he had exceeded his personal best of twenty-three goals the previous season. His performances were absolutely sensational and his free kicks a constant threat. The incredible accuracy and the ability to make the ball move while in flight brought dread to goalkeepers. When dribbling, he skipped past defenders with astonishing close control and his final ball into the area was often a killer for opponents.

Arsenal and United led the title race with Chelsea struggling to recover from their managerial upheaval. The Gunners opened up a five point gap after we lost an emotionally charged derby match against City on 10 February.

That week marked the fiftieth anniversary of the Munich air crash. The media covered the event in depth and with great reverence. The disaster at Munich was never a factor in my becoming a Manchester United supporter, I was four when it happened but knew nothing of it. I don't remember my parents or uncles talking about it at the time. However, once hooked on United from 1963, I was fascinated with the story of the Busby Babes and their tragic finale.

I thought I had read every report and seen every picture in the public domain. During the week of the anniversary I read accounts and descriptions not previously published, stories from young fans describing how they heard the news that day, how small lads had seen their father cry for the first time, the utter disbelief in the city that these fine players would not be coming back to play at Old Trafford and the over-riding feeling of emptiness at the loss of so many young lives.

For everyone connected with United, reliving those events made it a sombre week. In the end I think it got to the players. Before the match, City and United supporters stood in silence to pay their respect to all those who lost their lives. City then inflicted United's only home defeat in the league that season while securing their first victory at Old Trafford in thirty-four years.

A week later United and Arsenal met in the FA Cup fifth round at Old Trafford. Wenger's boys were getting good results and playing exquisite football, but United took them apart in a 4-0 hiding. The defeat rattled Arsenal. In their next league game against Birmingham they were rattled even more, losing Eduardo to a serious leg injury and two points to a late penalty. Captain Gallas imploded at the award of the spot-kick and ended the match in tears sat on the St Andrew's turf. Once more that Gallic, no pun intended, sense of indignation came pouring out from Arsenal over the next few days. Once more, it would cost them dear. They won only one of the next six league games and slipped out of the title race.

For United, the City defeat would be the last serious setback in the league race but Chelsea came up on the rails and pushed us all the way. Grant had stabilised the team and recovered their dogged consistency. From the turn of the year to the end of April, Chelsea won eleven and drew four of their fifteen league games. For the third year running the fixture list took United to Stamford Bridge for a late-season showdown. The table on the morning of the 26 April showed how high the stakes were:

	P	W	D	L	F	A	Pts	GD
Man United	35	25	6	4	73	19	81	54
Chelsea	35	23	9	3	60	24	78	36

A win would secure the title for United, while Chelsea were desperate to regain the supremacy they were accustomed to under Mourinho. United had the second leg of the European Cup semi-final coming up so Fergie gambled by resting Ronaldo, Hargreaves, Scholes and Tevez. Thirteen minutes into the game we lost Vidic to injury and fought a rearguard action for most of the first half. It was nerve-racking stuff and the faces of United supporters at the Shed End looked a lot more stressed than twelve months earlier.

On the stroke of half-time Ballack headed Chelsea into the lead. Rooney was carrying a groin injury sustained earlier in the game and struggled to play through the pain but after fifty-seven minutes Carvalho misplaced a back-pass and the White Pele swooped to equalise. Fergie's gamble was paying off.

Ronaldo replaced Rooney and both sides went for the victory. Four minutes from time Carrick's arm got in the way of a Chelsea cross and Ballack converted the penalty to give the Londoners a 2-1 victory. United now had to keep their nerve at home to West Ham and away to Wigan while Chelsea faced Newcastle and Bolton. United blitzed the Hammers 4-1 and Chelsea won 2-0 at St James' Park. The title race went to the last game for the first time since 1999.

Any nerves about winning the match at Wigan were overtaken by worries about getting in for the game. The demand for tickets was enormous, only Pete Seymour in our crew got one in the United ballot. At the start of that week I contacted Chris Cuerden, a Wigan fan I had worked with at Powergen. I knew his family were season ticket holders and thought they might be tempted to pocket a little profit. Chris got back to me and said his mum wasn't going to the game but wanted £100 for the ticket. Word was getting round Wigan about a possible jackpot! I politely told Chris it was out of the question and bid him farewell.

I was now working on plan C, getting in with a photocopy of a genuine ticket, or a 'snide' as we call them. I made a dozen colour copies of Mr Seymour's original and spent a whole evening meticulously putting tiny perforations in each one to make the tear-off portion look genuine. These tickets were just for our mates, not for sale. The finished product looked good but I was still nervous. It was a must-see game and the police were threatening to surround the ground and check every ticket electronically. I reckoned it was a bluff but it was too big a risk for me. On the day before the game, I swallowed my pride and rang Chris back, 'Is your mum's ticket still up for grabs?' The answer was yes and still £100. It was the most I had ever paid for a ticket but it was starting to look cheap. 'Tell her it's a deal,' I said.

I met our lads in the centre of Wigan and there were hundreds of Reds without tickets. In the pub supporters anxiously phoned one another to check if there was a sniff of anything. Pete and I sorted our lads with the snides and I set off to meet Chris for my ticket. I had to pass the United end and sure enough there was a thick line of coppers accompanied by stewards scrutinising every ticket. I crossed my fingers for the lads. My ticket was in the Wigan end and my 'host' for the day was Shane. Apart from a passionate loathing of Ronaldo, he was a good bloke. For £100 he was prepared to put up with a Red sitting next to him and to see the match I was prepared to keep my colours under wraps.

Tropical sunshine gave way to thunderstorms but it didn't dampen United's spirits as Ronaldo gave us the lead from the penalty spot after thirty-three minutes – a double whammy for my host. Wigan were making a fight of it and one goal might not be enough. Just on the hour, word came through that Chelsea were 1-0 up. Enter Ryan Giggs, at 34 making his 758th appearance for the club to equal Bobby Charlton's all-time record. Within twelve minutes he had scored the goal that wrapped up the game, his tenth title medal and United's seventeenth league championship. You just couldn't write a better story.

Having restrained myself for seventy-eight minutes, I leapt to my feet. So did another couple of hundred Reds spread around the home end. As the Wigan fans poured out, ticketless United supporters rushed in. By now all four sides of the stadium were rocking to 'We shall not be moved'. I saw Tezzer and Col Green come into the stand, all the snide tickets had been detected. None of our lads got in which took the edge off it a bit. They had all been watching in the pub and they didn't seem too bothered, anyway it was time to party!

We had thwarted Chelsea's manufactured might and won a second successive title but the contest between the history-makers and the 'new' money didn't end there. In the Champions League United won the group stage then overcame Lyon, Roma and Barcelona in the tightest of semi-finals. Paul Scholes secured the victory over Barca with a cracking shot in the second leg at Old Trafford.

For the first time in nine years and only the third time in our history United reached the European Cup Final. The stage couldn't be better – the Luzhniki Stadium, Moscow. Ever since I first knew about the European Cup as a kid I had wanted to see United play in Russia. Earlier in the season I had visited Kiev for the group match. Being a former Russian state, that was exciting enough but now this was the real thing. Waiting for United in the final were Chelsea who overcame Liverpool in the other semi. United's first European Cup game against English opposition would be 1,600 miles away, the furthest east a European Cup Final has been played.

The morning after beating Barcelona the focus turned to Moscow. The club had already announced details of which sup-porters would be eligible for tickets and having been to three Euro-aways that season I knew mine was guaranteed. Getting there would be a different matter though. Mike Stewart was on the case right away and found a day trip for £600. He was pretty excited when he phoned to tell me the news.

'But Mike,' I said. '£600, that's ridiculous, I'm not paying that much to go straight there and back!'

'Pete, believe me, that's cheap compared to what the club and others are charging. The number of hotel rooms in Moscow is limited so they're cashing in and the plane companies are looking for a big pay day too!' replied clued-up Mike.

That's when I realised we were all going to be taken for a ride, in more ways than one. The Moscow experience would put a big hole in the pockets of many Reds but it took a few days to get our head round the fact. In the end Dave Gabriel, Andy Henderson and I decided we had to be there and bit the bullet by shelling out over £1,000 each for a two-night stay. We decided we might as well see something of this iconic city while we were there.

At this point I would just like to propose a brief toast to The Understanding Wives Club of Great Britain. May God bless them!

So three of us were sorted but the rest of our lads were in mental turmoil about the cost. Ten days before the match these lads, who had followed United all over Europe for many years, were thinking of giving Moscow a miss. There is a smashing Italian restaurant in Swinton called Isis, run by Brett, a keen Red. He was putting on a special night showing the final live on big screens. Entry cost a tenner and you could eat and drink all you wanted. Our lads felt that would be better than paying the inflated prices to get to Moscow.

It was a difficult situation; I desperately wanted them to come to Moscow with us but knew it wasn't right to tell people how to spend their money. At the same time, I took an historical view of the occasion. This was only United's third European Cup Final in fifty-two years. The previous two had been the best days of supporters' lives – how could they consider missing it? I told these lads about a dream I'd had a couple of nights before. The dream involved a really good friend and was set in the future. I couldn't tell who the friend was but he was on his deathbed and I was there with his family gathered round, comforting him. My mate had had a great life, he was a good man, caring husband and father, *bon-vivre* and loyal Red. But he was now taking his last breaths. In my dream we share a few fond memories; he smiles contentedly, soon he'll be at peace. Suddenly, his face becomes contorted; he seems deeply anxious and upset.

'What's the matter?' I ask sympathetically. He pulls me closer, his breaths are very short now. He grabs my arm firmly and says, 'Pete, oh Pete, no!'

'What is it, my old friend? What troubles you so much after such a wonderful life?' I beg him. 'Pete, Pete … I still can't believe I watched the 2008 European Cup Final in a bloody restaurant in Swinton!' With that my tortured friend fades away.

I don't know if my story helped but within a couple of days all the lads were booked on a flight to Moscow. Sometimes in life we all need a nudge. Just when we thought we could all relax and look forward to the trip of a lifetime came the horror stories of life in the Russian capital. The police were all crooks, they could fine you on the spot for not having your passport, your ticket or just smiling. If they didn't bother you there was a chance the Russian Mafia would target you for a robbery. Drinks would be spiked to make you easy prey or girls used as honey-traps to distract even the most wary. Then there were the pickpockets, gangs of gypsy children who would rush you from all sides and fleece your pockets while you were in a state of shock.

It made us wary but in the end they were just bogey-man stories. Moscow is a huge, thriving, bustling city with a population in excess of 11 million. Everyone we came across was warm and welcoming. The Muscovites don't seem to smile a lot and their world appears very 'grey' compared to the west, but they couldn't have been more friendly or helpful. Several times when using the underground network we were baffled by the station names as they were in Russian and the Cyrillic alphabet is nothing like ours. Within minutes a passing stranger would approach us politely asking if they could help. Some even travelled with us a couple of stops to ensure we made the right connection. Twenty years ago that would have been the KGB; nowadays it is just ordinary folk.

We visited Red Square, Lenin's Tomb, the Kremlin and St Basil's Cathedral to satisfy our thirst for culture although the inflatable rink UEFA commissioned in the city centre did seem at odds with the sense of history around us. Then it was off to satisfy another thirst and have a sing song in the Old Arbat area of the city.

In the last few hours before kick-off my phobia started kicking in about not getting into the ground. I had a ticket, I was in the city the match was being played so the likelihood of being locked out was slim, nevertheless there was still the chance of losing the ticket or it being rejected at the turnstile. It is a phobia, it doesn't get better with age and one day there will be a medical term for it.

Wednesday 21 May was a chilly night in Moscow and the skies were dark grey but as I entered the Luzhniki Stadium I felt a tingle down my spine. I was in Moscow to watch Manchester United in the European Cup Final – the magic never dies! United's line-up was: van der Sar, Brown, Evra, Ferdinand, Vidic, Hargreaves, Carrick, Scholes, Tevez, Rooney, Ronaldo. Subs: Giggs, Anderson, Nani.

United had the best of the opening thirty-five minutes and could have been three goals up, but we only put one chance away. On twenty-six minutes Wes Brown curled a ball in from the right, Ronaldo rose majestically to out jump Essien and head the ball past

Cech from ten yards. It was his forty-second goal in an incredible season and answered the pathetic critics who said he didn't score at the highest level. Ronaldo's goal tally that season has been exceeded just twice in United's history. Law got forty-six in 1963/64 and van Nistelrooy scored forty-four in 2002/03. Ronaldo finished just one goal short of Denis Viollet's record thirty-two league goals in one season, 1959/60. Given he is predominantly a winger, his achievements were nothing short of spectacular and he rightly ran away with several awards for the best player on the planet.

Chelsea were stung into action by United's goal and started to control the game. With seconds of the first half remaining Lampard took advantage of a lucky deflection and rifled home the equaliser. Chelsea opened the second half as they had finished the first and United had to defend deep. With an hour gone I felt Fergie had to change the line-up to prevent us getting over-run. Then United fought back and either team could have won it. An enthralling ninety minutes couldn't separate the teams and neither could extra time although Chelsea hit the woodwork and Giggs had a shot cleared off the line. Crucially though, Chelsea lost Drogba to a red card after the temperamental striker cuffed Vidic in frustration.

The most important game in club football would be decided on penalties. Nerves were already frayed around the stadium. Mike Stewart had smoked at least 100 of his own fags and was now cadging from anyone around him that lit up. It is difficult to describe how supporters cope with a penalty shoot-out at this level. Common sense and logic melt away with every spot-kick. The episode felt surreal, like a mild out-of-body experience. Time seemed to stand still.

United went first. It was all square after two penalties each then Ronaldo failed to bamboozle Cech and the kick was saved. With Chelsea about to take the last of five allocated penalties each it was all square at 4-4. Captain John Terry stepped up with the chance to win the European Cup. By this stage my emotions were completely numb. Desperately trying to make sense of it, I was telling myself that it did not matter that much. How absurd! Of course it mattered! It mattered more than anything in the world at that moment!

Some supporters couldn't watch. I had to watch. My hands were on my head ... and ... he missed it! He missed it! Terry actually bloody missed it!

For a few seconds the relief was tangible but the torture had to continue and for one team it would now be sudden-death. Anderson scored, Kalou scored, Giggs scored, Anelka ... missed! Edwin van der Sar parried the shot to his right and United players raced from halfway to engulf this great Dutch keeper. Manchester United were champions of Europe – the joy was indescribable! It was 1999 all over again.

My emotions were all over the place as it was, then United climbed the steps to receive the trophy to the rousing hymn 'I Vow To Thee My Country'. Among the red and gold back-drop of the Moscow final I saw Rio Ferdinand and Ryan Giggs holding the giant silver trophy aloft. I was the happiest man in the world once again. I had seen United win the European Cup for a third time.

In the hours before the match I had wondered if this final could equal the excitement and drama of Wembley and Barcelona. How could it? They had been magical and sensational occasions that will stay with me until the day I die. Now, at 1.30 a.m. in rain-soaked Moscow, I had my answer. This occasion was right up there with the other two finals. I should have known better.

I had imagined a huge party down in Red Square if we won but it was 3.15 a.m. when the celebrations ended and we finally made it out of the stadium. The Moscow Metro trains were only running until 4 a.m. so most Reds who were staying over dispersed into small groups back to their hotels to avoid getting stranded. Some of our lads were flying out early that morning and went to grab a couple of hours' sleep. Dave, Andy and I headed back with Pete Seymour and Mike Stewart to their hotel in search of a pint.

Just outside the Metro station, down a dark Moscow side street, we came across a small sushi restaurant that was still open. We explained we just wanted some beer and expected a polite 'sorry it's uncooked fish or nothing' ultimatum but the owner waved us in and made us feel at home. We were joined by Garry Mullineux who had travelled by train via Scandinavia and St Petersburg on his own to see the match. There, the six of us sat for the next three hours, we had enjoyed the wild celebrations now it was time for a few quiet beers with good friends, mixed with great chat, and the glow of satisfaction that occurs only during very special moments in your life. We discussed how the match had ebbed and flowed, the unbelievable tension penalties bring, how grateful we were for John Terry's gaffe and all the while it gradually sunk in that United were champions of Europe again.

We talked of little oddities about the match, how it started on 21 May and finished on 22 May. How pleasing that Paul Scholes had played in a European Cup Final after the heartbreak of 1999 and how sad that Keano never did. We drooled over the legend that is Ryan Giggs, coming on in the pouring rain of Wigan and Moscow to deliver the fatal blow to Chelsea's hopes. At the same time equalling, then breaking, United's all-time appearance record. We discussed how remarkable it was that we had won all three European Cup Finals we had played in, but none of them inside ninety minutes.

We marvelled at Ronaldo's forty-two goals in forty-six starts, could he be spoken of in the same breath as Georgie Best? We reflected how, five years on, Roman Abramovich's billions couldn't buy Chelsea what United had – the European Cup.

Finally, we spoke in revered terms of our affection and gratitude towards the man who had made all this possible, the incomparable Sir Alex Ferguson. In leading United to a second European Cup, backed up by ten league titles he had now eclipsed even the great Sir Matt. The man from Govan just kept on re-writing history and was well on the way to Sainthood. Our gratitude knew no bounds. Then, one of the lads asked how I was doing with that book I was writing, 'yer know, the one about wanting to get rid of Fergie!' The dawn was coming up, another Muscovite day had begun, it was time to go!

In June 2008, I got a call from Colin Green, who had spotted a local advert for extras to play football supporters in a forth-coming Ken Loach film. Col had been made redundant a few months after me, we were turning into a right pair of 'wasters' and jumped at the chance of some easy money. We applied to Sixteen Films, the studio making the production, and given our availability we were snapped up. Ken Loach is famed for some excellent gritty films and dramas over the last forty years. For me his iconic *Kes* stands out from the rest. The story centres on young no-hoper Billy Casper, bullied at home and school he finds self-worth by training a wild kestrel. The film perfectly captures school life in the 1960s but is memorable for the classic scene where Brian Glover plays a teacher taking his class of boys for a game of football.

Glover, kitted out in Manchester United colours, plays out the game as if it's being filmed for *Match of the Day*. He imagines himself as the great Bobby Charlton leading his team against the mighty Tottenham Hotspur. He commandeers most of the play, pushes lads out of his way so he can have all the best shots at goal and chastises any kid who gets in his way. Timeless.

Col and I were a bit star-struck as Mr Loach briefed us about our roles on the first morning of filming. He outlined the film's story of a United supporter who has imaginary conversations with his hero Eric Cantona as his life descends into chaos. The film was called *Looking for Eric*, and though the plot sounded a bit weird who were we to question it? It involved Eric, which was good enough for us.

Ken advised the assembled pack of seventy extras that we were needed for a scene where we visited the posh house of a couple of drug dealers on our way to a United away game. The dealers were giving one supporter's son a bit of grief; our role was to smash up their manor using baseball bats, tyre wrenches and wooden staves and put the frighteners on them. These extras were genuine United supporters, all handy lads with fond memories of the 1980s and 1990s terrace culture. This would be method acting at its finest!

The first day's shooting focused on the coach scenes travelling to the 'hit'. All day long we were driven up and down the A6 through Salford re-enacting the riotous coach journeys of yesteryear. We soon realised how meticulous Ken Loach was. The scene would last seconds in the finished film but hours of work went into its making. It set the tone for the week. Col affectionately dubbed our esteemed director 'Once-Again Ken' and it fitted perfectly.

The remaining four days were spent on the raid at the house. The organisers had rented an empty property in one of the most expensive and exclusive roads in Worsley, coincidentally right next door to Ryan Giggs' walled palace. The owners were living away and the studio had recreated the contents out of cheap materials. Plasma screen TVs, beautiful furniture, huge glass coffee tables, artwork on the walls all looked like the real thing before the scenes were shot.

Our role was to get off the coach all tooled-up, approach the gates of the house, confront the gangsters on the front lawn then chase them back into the house before wrecking their ill-gotten gains. This action led to the film's final scene where John Henshaw faces up to the dealers and lays it on the line that we would be back if they didn't leave his friend's son alone. All this was filmed with us wearing Cantona face masks which had become so popular on the Old Trafford terraces in the mid-1990s.

For hours on end we filmed those sequences until Ken was happy. There is a lot of dead time on the set while props are put back in place or the main actors discuss key points with the production team. We whiled away that time swapping football stories with other Reds. Word got round that Eric Cantona himself was in the film and that he might visit the scene at the house. After three days the rumours seemed to be unfounded, then late on the Thursday afternoon the great man casually and quietly joined the set in the grounds of the house.

None of us realised at first, the production team were pushing for one final shoot of the wrecking scene before we wrapped up for the day. One of the lads turned and recognised Eric, guided him to the centre of the lawn and held his arm aloft to hail the returning hero. Cantona smiled. The United supporters gathered round respectfully then a chant broke out of 'Ooh aah, ooh aah, ooh aah Cantona' to the stirring tune of 'La Marseillaise'.

We were all still in costume and the sight of dozens of Reds dressed in Cantona masks, all waving offensive weapons, serenading a laughing Eric Cantona in a posh Worsley garden will stay with me forever. More than eleven years after playing his last match for United, the mutual love and respect between player and supporters was as strong as ever. Ken Loach recognised this was a special moment and for the next half-hour or so filming stopped as Eric took time to meet each one of the United supporters there. He chatted, signed autographs and posed for pictures, he was completely at ease. Eric was among his people. Col and I couldn't believe our luck.

25

BE MY MIRROR,
MY SWORD AND SHIELD,
MY MISSIONARIES
IN A FOREIGN FIELD

After Manchester City stopped being a serious football club, around 1981, they provided United fans and general onlookers with countless comedy moments. For many years City's seasons resembled an extended edition of *The Little and Large Show*. What with their inflatable bananas, their silly little songs about being the only team from Manchester and their pitch being bigger than ours, not to mention having Curly Watts as a celebrity fan. I thought I had seen it all but one afternoon in August 2008 I switched on Sky News and witnessed an amazing sight.

There in front of the cameras were dozens of giddy City supporters running around outside Eastlands with their mam's tea towels on their heads. I laughed so much I thought my pants were never going to dry. The cause of such revelry? City had been bought by the Abu Dhabi United Group led by Sheikh Mansour bin Zayed Al Nahyan, a member of the ruling family of Abu Dhabi in the United Arab Emirates. At a stroke, City became the world's richest club, another futile claim that did nothing to eradicate the fact they had won nothing for thirty-two years.

In a desperate attempt to show they meant business, the new owners tried to intercept Dimitar Berbatov – who was on his way to sign for United – and convince him that blue would suit him better than red. The Bulgarian decided silver was the colour he really coveted and joined United. Earlier that summer we had basked in the glory of winning the league and European Cup. There was only one black cloud in the sky.

Within days of the victory in Moscow the papers were full of speculation that Real Madrid were coming in for Cristiano Ronaldo. The respective clubs made comments about their desire to have him in their team at the start of the new season. The player had signed a new five-year contract in 2007 and could have quashed the rumours but chose to keep his comments ambiguous. An August ankle operation meant he was staying put for now. Meanwhile down at the Bridge, Chelsea's reaction to missing out on any honours was to replace Avram Grant with Big Phil Scolari. Ronaldo missed the first month of the season and United got off to a sluggish start, dropping seven league points in the opening four matches.

This included the annual trip to Anfield. On Saturday, 13 September 2008 I drove to Liverpool with Pete Seymour, Andy Henderson and Craig Cooper. A fairly tame first half saw United take an early lead through Tevez before a Wes Brown own goal levelled it. Since 1968 I had attended every United game at Anfield bar one, in 1983, and know only too well what a powder keg the fixture can be. Oddly, the atmosphere between the two sets of supporters was less volatile than usual. There was a bit of banter but nothing serious.

My seat was on the dividing line between the two sets of fans behind the Anfield Road goal. There was a small no man's land to my left filled with stewards. Towards the end of the first half the home fans started chanting about justice for the ninety-six people who had lost their lives at Hillsborough in 1989. Almost twenty years on from that fateful day, Liverpool supporters were still making calls for a Government inquiry.

Like the vast majority of United supporters, and football followers in general, I regard the disaster as a dreadful event which overrides any rivalry between the fans. But I think I speak for many United fans when I say that by 2008 we felt the matter should now be laid to rest. The disaster had been a terrible combination of events that could have happened to any fans fenced in at the notorious Leppings Lane end. Trying to apportion blame would serve no practical purpose, especially to the bereaved. In fact, I believed that the perpetual call for a further inquiry was prolonging the pain for those who had lost loved ones.

The lessons of that dreadful day had been learnt and the face of English football changed as a result.

So, back to the game, and United supporters responded to the 'justice' calls by having a go at the Scousers to let the matter rest. It provoked a few comments in return but at this stage it was just between individuals. United then responded with a chant of 'justice for Heysel', not a new song but one designed to remind Liverpool supporters how they had been keen to draw a line under the appalling events of the 1985 disaster.

I must stress at this stage, the Heysel chant in no way denigrates what happened at Hillsborough. I joined in with the chant as I thought it was fair comment. The reaction of the home fans around us was well over the top, many flying into a rage and making threats to the United supporters closest to them. If the stewards had been doing their job properly they would have spoken to the home fans. Instead they ignored the intimidation and the one nearest me said I should do the same and just watch the match, which I did.

At half-time I made my way to the toilets and as I went below the stand I felt a tap on my shoulder. One of Liverpool's stewards said he had been watching me and because of my 'continual baiting of the Liverpool fans' he was now going to escort me out of the ground. I couldn't believe it. I asked him what I had done, not original I know but I was genuinely mystified. He just repeated his earlier mantra and asked me to follow him. I told him I wanted to speak to a police officer before I went anywhere. The steward was reluctant, saying it was his decision that counted inside the ground. 'Good God – what have we descended to here,' I thought.

I made my way over to a copper with this jobsworth traipsing behind. I explained the situation; he was sympathetic but confirmed the steward's decision was final. I was on my way out! Clutching at straws I took the steward's full details saying I would write to the club and express my disgust. Five minutes later I was stood in the late summer sunshine on the deserted streets around Anfield. I was 54 years of age and I had been thrown out a football match for the first time in my life!

The great British writer L.P. Hartley opened his classic novel *The Go-Between* with the immortal line, 'The past is a foreign country; they do things differently there.' As I get older I try to avoid the 'Grumpy Old Man' syndrome. I hear many 50- and

60-somethings complain that football, and all that goes with it, was better way back when. My view is that many things have got better, some have got worse but most have simply changed – and that's life.

However, one aspect of football that has sharply deteriorated in the last two decades is the sanitisation of the terraces – or stands to be precise. The advent of all-seater stadia and the ticket prices have almost gentrified football as a spectator sport. In a deliberate attempt to drive out the hooligan element, the authorities have also priced out many vociferous, animated but basically peaceful supporters. That is why many top grounds have less of an atmosphere in the early twenty-first century despite increased capacities.

One instrument of this gentrification has been the rise of the tough-acting steward. Okay, they're not all bad, but too many seem intent on stamping out any sign of passion in a misguided attempt to prevent 'trouble'. These stewards have been given far too much power. Through the week they are probably nothing more than frustrated pickle packers; then on a Saturday afternoon their word carries more weight than the men and women recruited to keep the Queen's peace in this country. Few stewards have experience of handling crime in the real world, whereas a police officer has a balanced view of what behaviour needs a quiet word and what needs strong action. Rant over, you can come out from behind the sofa now kids!

So there I was, walking round Stanley Park, trying to get my thoughts together while I waited for the other lads to come out. At one point I genuinely considered packing in the whole football scene. If it had come to this, did I want to be a part of it? That emotion passed quickly and I sat down on a bench to reflect on the trials and tribulations of coming to watch United at Anfield over the years. Had anything changed since that first trip in October 1968 when our coach windows were smashed by flying bricks and we travelled back along the East Lancs Road with a gale blowing through the bus?

Since then we've had to endure ambushes, bottles, denim jackets robbed off your back, car thefts, darts, flare guns, Stanley knives, CS gas sprays and even an ambulance attack. It got so bad in the early 1980s that Bob Paisley rode 'shotgun' on the United team bus as it arrived at Anfield to discourage assaults. But this was now 2008. Liverpool was revelling in its role as European Capital of Culture. Surely it was a better place? Surely its people had evolved?

Well, I was struggling to witness any signs of improvement on my latest trip to this maritime city. I trudged back to the car, still in philosophical mood. I smiled as I remembered some advice my mate Tezzer gave me about Liverpool's cultural renaissance, 'Yer know, Pete,' he said. 'You can't polish a turd: but you can cover it in glitter!'

United's return to form coincided with Ronaldo's return to fitness. From 23 September we went on an incredible run in all competitions. Twenty-three league games brought a return of nineteen wins and three draws to keep United in the title hunt through the winter. A team littered with players on the fringe of the squad won the League Cup, beating Spurs on penalties, while a similar line-up lost to Everton on penalties in the semi-final of the FA Cup.

The group stage of the Champions League proved a comfortable ride for the holders. Another trip to Tokyo for the FIFA Club World Cup saw United beat Liga de Quito to become world champions for the second time. I didn't make the trip to Japan right before Christmas due to family commitments, missing a third chance to follow United in that competition. Call yourself a supporter, Molyneux? Pathetic. Maybe fourth time lucky?

Liverpool and Chelsea's form was impressive going into the New Year but the first six weeks of 2009 would show all wasn't well with our title rivals. On 9 January, ahead of his team's game at Stoke, Rafa Benitez turned an ordinary press conference into an extraordinary attack on Sir Alex. In an ill-advised attempt to engage Fergie in mind games, the Spaniard spent a full five minutes rambling on about injustices involving abuse of referees, unfair kick-off times and the administration of the fixture list. Benitez claimed United were nervous because his club were top of the table and peppered his rage with assurances that he was dealing here with facts not opinions. It sounded tosh at the time and as the season progressed Benitez's interview looked more ridiculous than Keegan's 1996 tirade.

The tactic backfired immediately. Liverpool drew 0-0 in the Potteries, twenty-four hours later United beat Chelsea 3-0 at Old Trafford. The Scousers won only two of seven league fixtures post-rant. Pressure was building too in West London. Defeats to United and Liverpool saw Chelsea stumble and on 9 February Roman Abramovich replaced former World Cup winner Scolari with Guus Hiddink. As turmoil gripped our rivals, United sailed on supremely, our defence in unbelievable form. From 15 November to 21 February we didn't concede a single goal in fourteen league games. Fergie had stayed quiet, the results and the table at the end of February spoke volumes:

	P	W	D	L	F	A	Pts	GD
Man United	26	19	5	2	46	11	62	35
Chelsea	27	16	7	4	47	16	55	31
Liverpool	27	15	10	2	43	20	55	23

Our procession to the title was dented by consecutive league defeats in mid-March. Liverpool thumped us 4-1 at Old Trafford and a week later at Fulham we lost 2-0. Liverpool closed the gap to one point. The first weekend of April proved pivotal. Liverpool won their Saturday game in the ninetieth minute at Craven Cottage to move two points clear but having played two games more. It is amazing how quickly an apparent crisis can descend over Old Trafford. In our home game to Aston Villa the day after Liverpool went top, United were without Rooney, Berbatov, Scholes, Ferdinand and Vidic. With eighty minutes on the clock Villa led 2-1. A piece of Ronaldo magic got us level but it looked like more lost points until Old Trafford witnessed another Sheffield Wednesday 1993 moment.

Fergie sent on 17-year-old debutant Kiko Macheda in a desperate attempt to spice up a benign attack. Three minutes into five of added time the youngster turned his powerful frame and whacked a twenty-yard shot into the corner of the net in front of the Stretford End. The ground erupted. The goal was critical. It may have saved our season, it certainly reignited it. United won the next six league games, leaving us needing only a point against Arsenal on 16 May to clinch the title. A goalless home draw saw us become the first team in English history to win three titles in a row twice. More importantly, it was United's eighteenth league title. Finally we had equalled Liverpool's record haul. The satisfaction was immense and hundreds of T-shirts, banners and chants reminded Rafa Benitez of the fact.

In the knockout stages of the Champions League United beat Mourinho's Inter and his former charges, Porto. For the third consecutive season three English teams reached the semi-finals.

This time the draw paired United and Arsenal while Chelsea met Barcelona. United shaded a tight home leg 1-0 thanks to John O'Shea's strike. Tickets for the away tie were almost impossible to come by if you missed out in the club ballot. I put the word out to my contacts but twenty-four hours before the game there was nothing. I came across an old number in my phone; a guy called Phil who I had delivered a ticket to in London a couple of years earlier. The errand was on behalf of a friend so I didn't know Phil directly but I sent him a text asking for any Arsenal spares. Nothing came back and by 10 a.m. on the day of the match I had given up hope of going. I was pig sick.

A call came in, it was Phil. He had booked twelve tickets on the club's hospitality rail trip and one of his mates had just pulled out. I could have his ticket but the package cost £300. I went a bit light-headed at the thought of paying that for a domestic game, my first car didn't cost me that much. But what the hell, this was the European Cup, the spirit of 1968, I had to be there. An hour later I was sitting in a first-class carriage as the train pulled out of Piccadilly. The first beer of the day had been served, lunch and wine ordered and most important of all, I had a match ticket in my hand.

I felt a bit of a fraud at first. I don't do the hospitality thing, it's okay for others but I prefer to be with the real supporters. By the time we reached Stockport I knew I was in the company of real supporters. Phil, his mates and the rest of the train were loyal Reds who had followed United home and away for years. Sure, they had dug deep for this trip but there wasn't a part-timer in sight.

United supporters were confident, in great voice and on an unforgettable night the team tore Arsenal to shreds with electrifying moves from defence to attack. The Gunners couldn't live with Ronaldo and Rooney; United raced into a 2-0 lead within eleven minutes and were three up on the hour. The Emirates was silent and shocked except for the away corner where Reds celebrated the prospect of a second consecutive Champions League Final. United ran out 4-1 winners on aggregate, the first time the club had won both legs of a European semi-final. Sadly, Darren Fletcher was dismissed for a trip on Fabregas, bringing him a cruel ban for what would have been the biggest game of his life.

The journey home was a throwback to the late 1960s and early 1970s as hundreds of United supporters poured through Euston singing their Red anthems. In sharp contrast to the normal austere constraints about alcohol on public transport the beer, wine and champagne flowed all the way home – all included in the price and served at your table whenever you wanted it. The train was rocking with non-stop singing of songs old and new. Nobody wanted the night to end but end it must. Around 3 a.m. we pulled into Manchester, I thanked Phil for phoning me back the previous day and set off for the long walk home, belting out United anthems as I made my merry way.

Having already been to Rome in the previous two years, our lads decided on a day trip for the final. Most pundits thought it would be a second all-English affair but Barcelona thwarted Chelsea's chance of revenge for Moscow with a stoppage-time winner at the Bridge. There would be no Roman holiday for Roman.

The night before the final I had a tedious job to do in the garden; Radio 5 did a two-hour show from the Eternal City interviewing several commentators, ex-players and managers. One after another said they were convinced United would win the game and Sir Alex Ferguson would lift his third European Cup to equal the record set by Bob Paisley in 1981. Only Chris Waddle urged caution, and not to underestimate the Spaniards. It made great listening and whetted the appetite.

On a scorching day in Rome, whetting the appetite became an Olympic event as bar after bar stopped selling alcohol in line with a mandate from the City fathers. It wasn't just the beer we wanted but somewhere shaded to sit and conserve energy in the draining heat. By mid-afternoon we had found a suitable place and spent a couple of hours mulling over how great it was being a United supporter. Consecutive European Cup Finals were what we had aspired to since the buccaneering days of the mid-1950s and glorious 1960s. Finally, it was coming to pass. United's team on 27 May 2009 was: van der Sar, O'Shea, Ferdinand, Vidic, Evra, Park, Carrick, Anderson, Giggs, Rooney, Ronaldo. Subs: Berbatov, Scholes, Tevez.

How would Rome 2009 compare with the other three finals? Surely fate couldn't write another script like those? After ten minutes I was convinced this final would be very different as we took the game to Barca with three clear-cut chances. This could be won well within the ninety minutes with a barnstorming United performance, consistent with a great team coming to its peak.

The match was won well within the allotted time but it was Barcelona who stepped up to the mark to win the European Cup for the second time in four years. In the remaining eighty minutes they took control with Xavi and Iniesta running midfield, their silky skills supplying the bullets for Eto'o and Messi to fire in a comfortable 2–0 win. There is no doubt Barca played well that night, but the abiding mystery was the mediocrity throughout the United side. Nobody in a white shirt played anywhere near their normal game, not even the usually irrepressible Rooney and Ronaldo. How rare to see such a lacklustre performance from a United side, a Fergie side, especially on such a night. *The Times* coined the headline, 'Dejected United leave Rome in Ruins'. A clever twist but it was hard to see the funny side.

On Thursday 11 June I was driving into Manchester and my phone buzzed with a text message. I couldn't get it out of my pocket but I would be parking up in a couple of minutes. Before I reached my destination the phone had gone ballistic with messages. I knew something monumental had happened at Old Trafford and for a second I thought Fergie had packed it in.

I pulled over to read that Cristiano Ronaldo was to join Real Madrid for around £80 million. Twelve months earlier I would have been devastated, now I was just sad at what was inevitable. Ronaldo had stayed after the avalanche of rumours the previous summer and had a decent season with twenty-six goals in forty-eight starts but his body language throughout the winter told us his heart wasn't fully in it. Too often he would throw up his arms in frustration if a colleague's pass went astray or a ball didn't reach him. His petulance at times bordered on disrespectful and the chants of 'Viva Ronaldo' hadn't carried the same conviction as in the previous season.

I loved Ronaldo's time at Old Trafford. In five short years he matured from a very promising youngster to become the best player in world. He had everything and was the closest I've seen to George Best in terms of ball control and the ability to fashion something out of nothing. Ronaldo scored 118 goals in 292 appearances. His form in 2007/08 played a huge part in making United champions of England and Europe. Rarely does a great player leave Old Trafford before his peak and of his own volition. However, the lure of playing for Real Madrid and a bit more sunshine proved too much. *Boa sorte e adeus*, maestro!

Rivalling Ronaldo for column inches on the back pages was Carlos Tevez. His 'loan' period at Old Trafford was coming to an end. His agent held the registration and seemed to be offering the player to United for a fee in the region of £30 million, but Fergie wasn't biting. Most United supporters expected to lose either Ronaldo or Tevez in the summer of 2009, but not both.

In mid-July Tevez joined City's growing band of mercenaries at Eastlands. The move contained more vitriol than Ronaldo's and would sour the supporters' relationship with the player. Nevertheless, Tevez made a telling contribution during his two seasons with United, winning the league title twice, the Champions League, World Club Cup and League Cup. His thirty-four goals in ninety-nine appearances was an excellent return. Many of those strikes proved crucial in turning or saving games. Tevez always gave 100 per cent and would make an impact on any game he played in. His contribution would be missed. His poster wouldn't. Fergie bought Antonio Valencia from Wigan, a tricky right-sided winger but United supporters held their breath for the big signing to replace Ronaldo.

One Saturday morning in June 2008, I was in a local garden centre. My wife and the girls wanted to browse so I had a rare chance to grab a coffee and a quiet read of the paper. The football stories were wafer-thin but one article caught my eye. Michael Owen's advisors had issued a glossy thirty-two-page brochure on their client's key virtues and circulated it to several Premier League clubs. The document outlined his 'brand values', summarised his playing career and even provided an expert's medical opinion on his fitness. He was out of contract with Newcastle and available on a free transfer. Much of it was crass PR blurb but I recognised it was a last desperate attempt to resurrect a stalled career that once held so much promise. I chuckled to myself, thinking that some barmy Premier League manager would gamble his reputation in the vain hope that Owen would come good again and keep his team in the top flight. I finished my coffee and thought no more of it. Well, no more of it until a week later when 'barmy' Alex Ferguson signed Owen for United. I can't remember being more surprised.

Other than the purchase of Gabriel Obertan for £3 million, the money received from the Ronaldo deal stayed in the bank, Fergie claiming there was 'no value' in the market. His comments referred to significantly inflated transfer fees in summer 2009 which had been triggered by two factors. Firstly, Barcelona's sweep of domestic and European honours sent Real Madrid into frenzied transfer activity. In one week they broke the world record twice, signing Kaka for £56 million on the Monday and Ronaldo for £80 million on Thursday. The previous record had stood for eight years.

Secondly, City's benefactors were splashing the cash and buying almost a new team for whatever money it took. Fergie wasn't getting involved, preferring to put his faith in last season's squad plus a handful of promising youngsters. Many United supporters were privately concerned about where the firepower was going to come from. The biggest disappointment was the continued absence of Owen Hargreaves following operations for tendonitis. Hargreaves formed a strong partnership with Carrick in 2007/08 when it appeared we had finally got an effective midfield solution to losing Roy Keane.

The 2009/10 season started in a steady, rather than spectacular, fashion but United qualified from the Champions League group stage and reached the semi-final of the League Cup. The league campaign was proving to be a little different though. The 'big four' who had dominated the early years of the twenty-first century were not having it all their own way. In the previous six full seasons only Everton, in 2005, had managed to infiltrate the magic circle. Now Spurs and City were showing the kind of consistency demanded of such an elite placing. At the same time United, Chelsea, Arsenal and Liverpool weren't as strong as in recent seasons.

The loss of Ronaldo and Tevez blunted our ability to relentlessly break down the opposition. An ageing Chelsea were dropping points to teams they usually steamrollered, Arsenal still flattered to deceive and Liverpool had their supporters in torment by failing to build on the previous season's title assault.

Around the turn of the year a few records went tumbling as United lost three home games in different competitions, all 1-0. Besiktas inflicted our first home reverse in the Champions League group stage since 2002; Villa's league victory was their first at Old Trafford since 1983 and Leeds' FA Cup win was their first on our hallowed turf since 1981. The third round exit was our first since 1984 and Fergie's first ever in the FA Cup. There was a genuine concern among loyal Reds that we had lost our firepower. Berbatov and Owen weren't playing or scoring often enough, Nani and Obertan were struggling to hurt opponents down the wings and it was obvious the kids such as Welbeck, Gibson and Macheda weren't ready yet. We were badly missing Ronaldo's class.

Against this background, news of United's financial situation was released. In a nutshell, the £575 million debt used to buy the club in 2005 had reached around £700 million due to crippling interest payments. The Glazers wanted to refinance part of the debt at around 9 per cent interest rather than the existing 14 per cent by selling bonds to financial institutions. To promote the bonds the owners had to go public with a Michael Owen-type glossy brochure. Much more detail of United's finances was in the public domain than in the previous five years. Supporters were appalled at the worsening debt particularly given the club's significant turnover, profits and success in that period.

Many believed the debt had prevented Fergie investing in a suitable replacement for Ronaldo and that Madrid's euros had funded interest payments and consultancy fees instead. Old wounds were re-opened. If anything the anti-Glazer feelings became more animated than in 2005. At the Burnley home game on 16 January 2010, just after United had gone 3-0 up, there was widespread chanting against the Glazers from all parts of the ground. The protests would become a feature of United matches for the rest of the season. The backlash inspired the 'green and gold' campaign where some fans bought and sported the colours of Newton Heath. The Glazers managed to sell all the bonds and successfully refinance the debt but the genie was out of the bottle and it would prove a bugger to get back in.

The League Cup semi-final brought a welcome relief from this internal wrangling when United drew City. The Blues' fans had been revelling in stories of our debt while they wallowed in unprecedented riches. They had replaced Mark Hughes with Roberto Mancini and in their eyes the gap between the two clubs was closing with astonishing speed. For Reds it became a matter of pride: local pride because City supporters were loud-mouthing it all over Manchester, and professional pride because United ruled the roost at home and abroad and we had to show these upstarts we were still number one.

Fergie played full-strength teams in both legs. The matches were a throwback to the last time the two clubs met at this stage of the competition in 1969. Passions were running high, on the pitch and in the stands, and both games provided the very essence of what football is all about. City edged a 2-1 victory at Eastlands. In the return, two second-half goals put United ahead until Tevez levelled the tie fifteen minutes from the end. Almost two minutes into stoppage time Giggs whipped in a cross for Rooney to head the winner and raise the loudest roar I've ever heard at Old Trafford. Reaching the final was almost incidental that night; we had put City firmly in their place.

The City game galvanised United's season, four days later we went to the United Arab Emirates and destroyed title rivals Arsenal 3-1. Early season injuries healed and United started beating teams comfortably, particularly at Old Trafford. After Christmas, Wayne Rooney's performances reached another level as he added the role of deadly striker to his armoury. In the years Ronaldo blossomed, Fergie had used Rooney in a support role often playing him down the left. With 'CR7' gone, Rooney was getting into the six-yard box and it paid dividends with shots and headers flying in almost every week.

It had taken the striker three months to adjust to his new-found responsibility but now there was no stopping him. In the Champions League last sixteen games against AC Milan, United's striker silenced the San Siro with two powerful headers in a 3-2 win. In the home leg he added another brace as United beat the mighty Italians 4-0. Between those two performances he rose from the Wembley bench to head the winning goal as United retained the League Cup against Aston Villa.

United were finding their form just at the right time. The usual suspects jockeyed for position in a three-horse title race. The crunch would be the home fixture with Chelsea on 3 April and this was the table on the morning of the match:

	P	W	D	L	F	A	Pts	GD
Man United	32	23	3	6	76	25	72	51
Chelsea	32	22	5	5	82	29	71	53
Arsenal	32	21	5	6	74	34	68	40

The Chelsea game was sandwiched between the Champions League quarter-final fixtures with Bayern Munich. In Germany, talisman Rooney gave United an early lead but late in the game sprained his ankle trying to stop a Bayern counter-attack. The injury cost United dear. Bayern scored from that attack to win 2-1 and Rooney was out of the Chelsea match. Without him United toiled while Chelsea played well to take three crucial points with a 2-1 win. Carlo Ancelotti's team cruised to the title, scoring eight times against Wigan and seven against both Aston Villa and Stoke during the run-in.

Fergie gambled on Rooney's fitness in the home leg against Bayern and it looked to have paid off handsomely as United raced into a 3-0 lead in forty-one minutes. But the next ten would seal our fate. Bayern pulled a goal back, Rafael was sent off and Rooney limped off. United fought a brave rearguard action but conceded a second to lose on away goals after a 4-4 draw.

The volleyed goal in Munich at the end of March would be Rooney's last of the campaign yet he still finished top scorer with thirty-four strikes in all competitions. Berbatov was next highest with twelve but tellingly no other United player got into double figures. The 2003/04 season was the last time only two players scored more than nine each. I have no doubt that with Rooney fit United would have won a record-breaking fourth consecutive title and progressed to a third successive Champions League Final at the expense of Lyon in the semis.

The eighty-five-point haul was higher than on seven other occasions when United have won the Premier League so it shouldn't be looked on as a failure. Of course, expectation had risen even higher with back-to-back European finals in the two previous years, now with only the League Cup to show for our efforts it certainly felt like a failure.

In early 2010 the atmosphere at Old Trafford became unnecessarily unpleasant, with orange-clad stewards using heavy-handed tactics to quell anti-Glazer protests in the stands. Initially, the dissent from home supporters took the form of chants and the odd banner advising the American owners that they weren't universally welcome in M16. For a few matches this went unchecked, it was a peaceful protest by people who had the right to let their feelings be known. Suddenly, it became obvious the club would no longer tolerate the dissent. Any supporters trying to display a flag quickly had it ripped down and they were ejected. Some stairways were blocked by United's security firm to stop spectators getting to the front of the stand to gain a good vantage point to protest. These goon squads made Neanderthal man look like Stephen Fry.

The club got this action wrong on two counts, firstly it acted only to fuel the protests and they continued far longer into the season than if they had been ignored. Secondly, deployment of these guys to manhandle and intimidate United supporters within the sanctum of Old Trafford was a gross insult to the people who have made Manchester United what it is.

On a lighter note, the anti-Glazer movement did provide one amusing moment. For the League Cup Final against Aston Villa in February we took the service train to London. United fans mixed with ordinary passengers. Behind us sat two old ladies and twenty minutes into the journey their conversation went something like this:

'Who are all these people wearing scarves?'

'They're United fans on their way to Wembley.'

'But I thought United wore red and white, why are the scarves green and yellow?'

'They're protesting against the Glazers, the American owners.'

'But why green and yellow?'

'Because that's the colours they played in when they were Newton & Ridley.'

I didn't have the heart to correct them!

26

TO FIGHT FOR THE RIGHT, WITHOUT QUESTION OR PAUSE, TO BE WILLING TO MARCH INTO HELL, FOR A HEAVENLY CAUSE

The consensus among United's faithful in the 2010 close season was that Fergie needed to bolster the midfield. Scholes and Giggsy had both turned 35 and Owen Hargreaves' eighteen-month battle with injury was ending in heartbreak. Valencia, Fletcher and Carrick were strong but needed support if we were going to re-capture the title and instil fear into Europe. Any newcomer would have to be the finished article. The newcomers turned out to be a trio of promising youngsters. Hernández, Smalling and Bébé were all under 22 and cost approximately £23 million in total.

Commenting on United's transfer policy on the club's website in May 2010 Fergie said:

> We didn't spend £50m on a player last summer, and I think a few people were surprised by that, and there are no plans to spend big this summer either. We're looking at something different. People clamour-ing for big signings are missing the point; £20m is a lot of money to spend on young players, but that's what we like to do, get players who are going to develop in the club, because the long-term view has got to be important here.

It felt like another Christmas with lots of smaller presents to open but no bike or iPad. Yet our faith in Fergie was unshakeable. Not borne out of pure blind faith but based on what he had delivered to United supporters over the previous twenty years – wall-to-wall trophies and football to die for. How those two decades had changed his standing at Old Trafford, from ominous rumblings about the sack to being untouchable. Such job security gave Fergie the luxury of planning two or three years ahead as well as focusing on the here and now. That has enabled him to keep the momentum going through twenty campaigns; never standing still, keeping United on top. Fergie had had to earn that security but now it was self-perpetuating – a bit like owning the recipe for Coca Cola.

The 2010/11 season took a long time to catch alight. United's home form was impeccable and in nineteen league games we would drop only two points, a draw with West Brom in October. Away from Old Trafford we drew seven out of eight up to the turn of the year. Fergie seemed to be using the same formula that brought Busby the title in 1967. A bit of the magic was missing with United making slow, workmanlike starts in several away games and conceding more goals compared to the previous four seasons.

Wayne Rooney was having a wretched time on and off the pitch. Since his March injury in Munich he had struggled to recapture his stunning form. A poor World Cup in South Africa was followed by a stop-start opening to the league campaign. With only a penalty chalked up in the first two months, Reds worried that his damaged ankle might still be causing him problems. Maybe the trouble was slightly more north. His private life was continually in the spotlight with many newspapers carrying stories of his infidelities while his wife Coleen was pregnant. None of us were expecting what happened next.

In a routine press conference on Tuesday 19 October Fergie revealed that Wayne Rooney had told him he wanted to leave United. Within hours the player followed up with a statement saying that during the contract negotiations with David Gill, the chief executive failed to give him any of the assurances he was seeking about the future squad. Those assurances centred on the continued ability of the club to attract the top players in the world. The over-powering inference was that United lacked ambition.

The news went viral and understandably brought a torrent of reaction. Though many United supporters recognised the player's statement as a canny move by agent Paul Stretford to up the ante, they were disgusted by Rooney putting his name to it and grossly disrespecting Manchester United. Talk quickly turned to Chelsea or worse still, City, coming in to sign him. Some Reds expressed their feelings in graffiti. Nike's city centre store in Market Street displayed a giant Rooney poster, sprayed with the stark warning 'Join City and you're dead'. Others took more direct action, choosing to visit our want-away star at his home late one evening for a 'chat'.

Within three days Rooney had signed a new five-year deal at Old Trafford. Those three days had felt like three years for Reds who agonised at the possibility of our best player leaving the club just twelve months after losing Ronaldo and Tevez. It was a critical crossroads for United especially if Rooney had joined City. I felt it showed superb statesmanship from Sir Alex, almost presidential, and had echoes of the great Sir Matt calling Denis Law's bluff in 1966.

I can only imagine that the troublesome time Wayne Rooney was experiencing in his personal and professional life had clouded his judgement and allowed Stretford to talk him into using the 'Glazer' factor to provide a smokescreen for the player's pay rise or transfer. Either way, it left a foul taste and while you might expect such behaviour from some agents, we didn't expect it from our biggest hero. We were glad he had stayed but our loyalty had been betrayed and loyalty at Old Trafford is sacrosanct. It would take a while for Wayne to fully work his way back into our hearts. I guess we knew how Coleen felt!

United remained unbeaten in the league from the start of the campaign until 5 February 2011 when bottom club Wolves won 2-1 at Molineux, a run of twenty-four matches. The unbeaten sequence stretched back to April 2010 equalling the club record achieved between December 1998 and September 1999 of twenty-nine league games. The manager had instilled an 'unbeatable' mentality into his squad and what we lacked in individual flair we made up for in team spirit. In fact the team was the star.

When needed though, a flash of genius would win games for United and none more so than a week after that Wolves defeat when United entertained City at Old Trafford. At 1-1 and twelve minutes remaining the match rested on a knife edge. Around twenty passed two that Saturday afternoon I witnessed the finest goal I've seen at Old Trafford in half a century. A cross from Nani caught a slight deflection of a City defender. Wayne Rooney, with his back to goal, re-adjusted his body and became airborne to hit an unbelievable overhead kick high into Joe Hart's net. The goal had everything – the ultimate execution, incredible athleticism, breathtaking power and radar precision. Add to that the timing, the occasion and the fact it was the winner. The crowd knew they had witnessed something very special. United supporters were back in love with our star player.

The win kept United top of the league with Arsenal, City, Spurs and Chelsea struggling to maintain the pace. From the chasing pack only Chelsea would emerge to mount a serious challenge, closing a twelve-point gap in mid-February to just three by 1 May. A week later the top two met at Old Trafford. A year earlier, Chelsea headed north to nick a vital win from a sluggish United. We were in no mood to surrender another title and blew Chelsea away in sixty seconds, Hernandez beating the offside trap with lightning speed before slotting the ball past Cech. Chelsea were in turmoil as United pummelled their defence. Twenty-three minutes in Vidic's bullet-header ended the contest.

The win left United needing one point from two games, Blackburn away and Blackpool at home. On 14 May 2011, United's Red Army decamped to Ewood Park, packing the top and bottom tiers of the Darwen End. We had come to see United crowned champions of England for a record-breaking nineteenth time. Rovers were in a dog-fight to avoid relegation and took the lead on twenty minutes. Nerves were playing a big part on and off the field but cometh the hour as they say. Actually it was on seventy-three minutes. Paul Robinson came racing out of his goal and scythed Hernandez. Phil Dowd took an eternity to consult with his linesman before awarding United a penalty. Wayne Rooney coolly slotted home and another golden chapter was written in United's history. The goal not only started the party, it launched dozens of banners proclaiming United's dominance of the English game. The Red Devil's trident had nudged the Liver Bird from its perch!

Both teams played out a draw to give Fergie his twelfth league title and put United one ahead of Liverpool in the all-time rankings. When I was a young lad, United and Liverpool dominated the mid-1960s and managed to match Arsenal's record seven triumphs. Over the twenty years that followed, Liverpool won the title almost at will and by 1990 had amassed a record eighteen.

Amid the wild celebrations at Blackburn in April 2011 it was difficult to take stock of the incredible turnaround in United's fortunes under Sir Alex Ferguson. For the first time in the history of English football Manchester United held the record for most league titles. Bizarrely, 14 May was also FA Cup Final day, the first time it had clashed with a set of league fixtures since the 1950s. Manchester City beat Stoke to end their thirty-five-year silverware drought and strangely it didn't seem to matter given our historic triumph early in the day. London and Merseyside looked on as Manchester took the two main trophies for the first time since 1956.

In the Champions League United again sailed through the group stage then knocked Marseilles out with a solid 2-1 aggregate win. The quarter-finals pitched us with old rivals Chelsea, still desperate to live Abramovich's dream and land Europe's greatest club prize. United were equally determined to add to our European Cup honours and beat Chelsea home and away.

The draw for the semi-final was kind and Barcelona and Real Madrid were left to sort out their local differences as United overpowered a surprisingly weak Schalke team 6-1 on aggregate. When I was a kid my dream European Cup Final was Real Madrid versus Manchester United. The Spaniards dominated the competition for five years and were regarded as the best in the world with legends like Puskas, Kopa and the magical Di Stefano. The Munich air crash put paid to the Babes challenging Madrid's reign and Best's cartilage injury prevented us meeting them at Heysel in the 1966 final. The 'perfect match' would have graced Hampden Park Glasgow in 2002 but for a tame semi-final surrender to Leverkusen. So to 2011, my hope was Real would see off the Catalans and United would finally face Madrid on Wembley's lush green turf. Not so. Madrid and Mourinho's indiscipline plus Messi's brilliance meant United and Barcelona met in the European Cup Final for the second time in three years.

Okay, dream match gone but I was still in dreamland. This was United's fifth appearance in the final and our third in four years. In the previous fifty years United supporters ached for this level of performance and consistency and Fergie had found it. After the 2009 defeat in Rome everyone recognised Barca were a special team with a midfield made in heaven and an incredible talent in Lionel Messi. But I also believed they had caught United on a bad day. I was convinced Sir Alex and his management team, having trawled through recordings of that final, would have devised a plan to stop Barca being so dominant again. Publicly, Fergie had said very little about the Rome defeat except that he knew what had gone wrong and it was time to move on.

I had been to four away games in that season's Champions League so a Wembley ticket was guaranteed. Seven of our usual suspects also got tickets so a London hotel was booked and we let the Virgin train take strain. Memories of May 1968 came flooding back in the build-up to the match and during the day. I had splashed out £60 for a personalised big plastic banner with 'The Spirit of 68' on it and a picture of a smiling Matt Busby in the middle. During May I told anyone I met to look out for it as United did a lap of honour with the trophy. I was convinced we would win our fourth European Cup and the team Fergie picked to do it on 28 May 2011 was: van der Sar, Fabio, Vidic, Ferdinand, Evra, Carrick, Valencia, Park, Giggs, Hernandez, Rooney. Subs: Nani, Scholes.

Fabio, Valencia and Hernandez replaced O'Shea, Anderson and Ronaldo from the final line-up two years earlier. Darren Fletcher was unfit and Nani only made the bench but the telling choice was the omission of top scorer Dimitar Berbatov from the squad. A season's haul of twenty-one goals from thirty-two starts wasn't enough to convince Fergie he was the man for the job. Hernandez was having an incredible first season with goals in all competitions.

In many ways the 2011 final mirrored the 2009 meeting. Once again, United looked dangerous for the first ten minutes then Barcelona slipped into gear and simply mesmerised us. Pedro's opening goal after twenty-seven minutes had a certain inevitability about it. The sustained precision and speed of Barca's passing was the finest I've seen by a club or international side. A well-worked equaliser from Rooney gave us all hope and a brief chance of my banner seeing the light of day but nothing could stop the Spaniards. By the seventieth minute Barcelona had won the match in comfort and in style. With a 3-1 lead they took their foot off the pedal otherwise we could have been on the end of an embarrassing scoreline.

In the end Barca had 68 per cent possession, sixteen goal attempts to United's three, twelve on target to our one. We didn't even win a corner. Rome hadn't just been a bad day at the office. Throughout the season, United had beaten the best sides England and Europe could offer. Our supremacy was reflected in long unbeaten runs at home and abroad. Yet in Barcelona we encountered a brilliant team at its peak. Fergie said it was the best team we've ever faced and added, 'No one's given us a hiding like that. They play it the right way and enjoy their football.'

Two European Cup Final defeats in three years was very hard to take. Our first Saturday European Cup Final was going to launch the biggest party London had seen since 1968 but instead it was a damp squib. It is amazing how a defeat at this level just sucks the life out of you. In the pubs around our hotel dozens of glum faces stared into their beer, the banter was scarce and meaningless, nothing could lift us. It was awful. Had we won, sleep would not be an option, in defeat it was our only respite.

Nevertheless, during the close season, United supporters celebrated a truly historic domestic season. Manchester United had now won more league titles and more FA Cups than any other team in the 140-year history of English football. Astonishingly, twelve of the nineteen titles and five of the eleven FA Cups had been won under one manager, the incredible Sir Alex Ferguson.

Having passed the History exam with flying colours, Fergie's next challenge smacked more of Geography. How do you bridge the gulf between Mancunia and Catalonia? More Reds than ever were convinced the great man had to invest in a couple of big-name, finished-article midfielders. Yet Fergie maintained his 'buy young and develop them' strategy.

A wealth of experience left Old Trafford in 2011. Paul Scholes, Gary Neville and Edwin van der Sar retired while Owen Hargreaves, Wes Brown and John O'Shea headed to pastures new. Fergie brought in goalkeeper David de Gea, aged 20, winger/midfielder Ashley Young, aged 26, and defender/one-man-cavalry-charge Phil Jones, aged 19. Danny Welbeck and Tom Cleverley returned from season-long loans at Sunderland and Wigan respectively. So still no top-class signing to bolster United's attempt to reclaim Europe's top prize.

United won the first five league games, the best start since 1985. The nature of the victories whetted the appetite, home wins over Spurs 3-0, Arsenal 8-2, Chelsea 3-1 and 5-0 away at Bolton. United's young bravehearts were running teams ragged. Draws on the road at Stoke and Liverpool plus another home win against Norwich should have put United top. However, having spent £484 million on thirty-six players in three years, Manchester City started to mount a title challenge and led their neighbours by two points. Next up was the Manchester derby at Old Trafford. Time to put City back in their place again.

Exactly a year on from the 'Rooney wants to leave' bombshell, United were hit by a result that shook us to the core. Having won all nineteen home league games in the previous twelve months, United succumbed 6-1 to their neighbours. 'Unbelievable' doesn't even begin to describe it. The result was United's biggest defeat under Fergie, our worst home result since 1930 and but for slack finishing by City in the second half it could have been two or three more.

Let's move on quickly. Fergie blamed it on a cavalier display by defenders rushing forward to pull back a deficit. The players retreated to Carrington and went back to basics. The fans retreated to anywhere that would provide shelter and we licked our wounds. The result – not one goal conceded in the next six matches and four league games won 1-0. The goals started flowing again by Christmas and the Manchester clubs were locked in a two-horse race for the title. City, finally, were serious contenders and the heat was turned up to maximum around Greater Manchester. The spirit of 1968 was back after all.

Incredibly, the FA Cup third round draw paired United and City. Snake or ladder? Revenge or desolation? As we travelled and gathered at the re-named Etihad Stadium the mood was a little heavy, even staunch Reds held doubts. We had just lost back-to-back league games and injuries were mounting. Captain Vidic's season was ended by a ruptured cruciate ligament and Fergie's gamble on a young and inexperienced midfield had been devastated with Cleverley, Fletcher and Anderson missing most of the campaign through injury and illness.

Reds hoped Fergie would bring in that top-notch midfielder in the January window to maintain our title challenge. He didn't let us down. I was chatting with a group of United fans on the Etihad forecourt and suddenly the mobile phones went into text meltdown. The message was as simple as it was unbelievable, 'Scholes has come out of retirement and is on the bench.' The shock was contagious and the response mixed, desperation or inspired? I felt it could galvanise the team. Game on!

United's end was packed and in full throttle, defiant in the face of written and vocal references to '6' on three sides of ground. The pace was frenetic and United were looking assured. On ten minutes City's nemesis Rooney rose to put us ahead with a majestic header. Two minutes later Kompany got a red card and United looked like we could score with each attack. Nani and Valencia were in devastating form down the flanks but the star of the show was Danny Welbeck. His tireless work-rate and impressive link-up play with Rooney had City stretched.

On the half-hour his display was rewarded by a brilliant volley to put us 2-0 up. Ten minutes later Welbeck was tripped in the area and Rooney bagged our third. This was paradise. United were so commanding there was talk on the terraces of hitting them for six but in the second half Fergie shut up shop and almost handed the initiative to City who clawed back to 3-2. Nevertheless it was United who went through with the biggest cheer of the day reserved for Paul Scholes as he rose from the bench in the fifty-ninth minute to resume his remarkable career.

Time for a little rant, I feel. In recent times certain sections of society have displayed appalling judgement and sunk to new depths in our loathing. I am thinking of the greedy bankers who sent us spiralling into recession, and the materialistic MPs who deliberately claimed expenses they were not entitled to. They fully deserve our vilification. Yet their behaviour pales against a dreadful trend that has crept into our wonderful game.

At the City match, I was underneath the stands digesting a pre-match pie and the news about Scholes when a couple came and sat nearby, a lad and a girl in their early twenties. I was surprised to see she was wearing a City scarf. Odd, I thought, and a bit risky. When she turned round I realised it was a half-and-half scarf. I had seen these in the previous twelve months at United games against our lesser rivals like Fulham and Wigan and thought it daft but harmless. But here we were at a full-blooded Manchester derby with passion and tension between supporters running higher than anything in the last forty years and a United supporter is wearing a half City, half United scarf!

'Jesus Christ!' I thought. 'What have we evolved into? What species of life is this? Who are these people?'

Don't get me wrong, having lived through the days of widespread gratuitous violence at football grounds, I know we're in a far better place now than when we used to beat the hell out of rival supporters just because, well, they were rival supporters. But surely the pendulum has swung too far the other way in the post-Hillsborough, post-Heysel, Premier League, all-seater, stewards rule-the roost, gentrified football village we live in today? And surely half-and-half scarves are our wake-up call to stop this creeping sanitisation?

Wearing scarves supporting *both* teams isn't what football is all about. In fact it's not what any sport is about. I don't blame the folk who make or sell the scarves, the buck stops fairly and squarely with the people who wear them. If you must have one, keep it in the bag and take it home as a souvenir, hang it on the bedroom wall if it matters that much but don't wear it to the bloody game.

These people must be discouraged. I don't advocate violence or anything nasty. Humiliation is the key. If you're at a game and you see anyone adorned in a half and half scarf, just go over and tell them they look like a right ****ing muppet!! That should take care of natural selection.

Despite excellent domestic form both Manchester clubs were eliminated from the Champions League at the group stage, United's first such exit since 2005 and only our third in eighteen years. Only one home win and surrendered second-half leads in the other two were our undoing. Fergie bloodied several newcomers and their inexperience was exposed. A decade on from the treble team's unfulfilled European potential we realised the 2008 champions wouldn't dominate the continent either.

We reluctantly settled for our first crack at the Europa League, the old UEFA Cup, but succumbed to a lively Bilbao side. Out of the FA Cup too, the chase for the league title became everything. The Manchester clubs set a punishing pace that winter with rivals Arsenal, Chelsea and Spurs out of it before the traditional run-in. City led most of the way but by early April United had caught their bitter rivals. In the twenty-three league games after City's triumph at Old Trafford, United amassed fifty-nine points with nineteen wins and two draws, a phenomenal recovery. By the end of Easter Sunday, 8 April, the league table looked as tasty as the kids' chocolate eggs:

	P	W	D	L	F	A	Pts	GD
Man United	32	25	4	3	78	27	79	51
Man City	32	22	5	5	75	26	71	49

The football world was united – the title was coming back to the red half of Manchester. City had blown it. It wasn't just the difference in points, Fergie's United very rarely stumble during the run-in. We have come second in neck-and-neck title races where both teams went flat-out but 1992 and 1998 are the only occasions United capitulated. Publicly, Mancini conceded the title and, with the pressure off, City won the next five games, scoring fifteen goals and conceding one. United won two, drew one and lost two, a sequence that included 1-0 defeats at Wigan and City and a 4-4 draw at home to Everton. Going into the final day of the season, City were back in the driving seat:

	P	W	D	L	F	A	Pts	GD
Man City	37	27	5	5	90	27	86	63
Man United	37	27	5	5	88	33	86	55

To become champions of England for the third time, City simply needed to make sure their home result to QPR wasn't worse than United's at Sunderland. Red hearts and heads had known all week that City had it in the bag after a 2-0 victory at Newcastle the previous Sunday. Realistically, that had been the last hope of a Blue slip-up. QPR were fourth from bottom so an avalanche of goals was expected at Eastlands. Every football fan in the world knows what happened next. United won at Sunderland and City scored twice in injury time to beat QPR 3-2 in the most thrilling finale to a title race since 1989, if not 1889.

I travelled to Sunderland on 13 May with brother-in-law and loyal Red, Pete Seymour. He drove and right from the off our conversations centred on why we were putting ourselves through this. United had a chance of winning the league, and not being there wasn't an option, but this was different. The odds were absolutely stacked in City's favour, they were scoring goals for fun again and QPR had the worst away record in the Premier League. City had dropped only two home points all season, Rangers had gained only two from their previous eleven away games. We agreed City would be four up by half-time, the only blessing being we would be out of our misery.

I am sure many such conversations took place among United supporters that day. But then? Mark Hughes was going back to City for the first time since his acrimonious sacking. And he's a

United man through and through. And if anyone can cock it up City can, they've had years of experience. What if eighteenth-placed Bolton took the lead at Stoke, that would make QPR fight harder surely? And if City drew and we won, we were champions? Every few miles we would chew over these possibilities and each time it ended with one Pete telling the other Pete he was talking bollocks and that the title was City's.

Sunderland had too little quality and Rooney's twentieth-minute header meant we were doing our bit. Surprisingly, it took City thirty-nine minutes to lead in Manchester. That was all the Sunderland fans had to cheer during the whole match. Half-time arrived and we still weren't out of our misery.

The next forty-five minutes would be the most tortuous in our long history. Three minutes after the restart, news hit the Stadium of Light that Cisse had equalised for QPR. Suddenly, all those stupid scenarios on the way up didn't sound so stupid. On sixty-six minutes the away end erupted with news of Mackie putting Rangers 2-1 up! This was unbelievable and shouldn't be happening. I found it almost impossible to concentrate on the game in front of us; what mattered now was events at the Etihad.

The timing of the two games synchronised; I watched the big digital clock at the other end slowly move through seventy minutes, eighty minutes, none of us daring to believe. Although no news was good news it was excruciating. I remember the clock moving from eighty-eight to eighty-nine minutes. For the first time that day I let myself believe we were going to do it. The United end was on the brink of celebration but faces were still contorted and twisted with suspense. My heart was pounding so fast I remember thinking, 'Bloody hell I hope I can take this!'

The clock hit ninety minutes and the last clear thoughts that ran through my head were, 'Oh my God! We've done it, even if City equalise now it's not enough … we're champions after all … thank God we made the trip … we're going to see United get the trophy.' I was delirious.

The clarity ended and the surreal took over. During injury time at Sunderland, the radio commentaries confirmed City had equalised. Seconds later our game finished. Fergie, his players and staff tentatively started to make their way to our end. Then from our left came an explosion of noise, the Sunderland supporters going ballistic. 'Why are they cheering a City equal-iser?' I thought. In that second, I realised they weren't, they would only be cheering if it was a City winner.

Ecstasy turned to bewilderment. Radios confirmed City had scored twice in injury time. I knew what had happened but couldn't filter it. I was rooted in that moment, then Pete Seymour shouted, 'Come on Pete, let's get out of here!' That's the last time we spoke until just north of Leeds almost two hours later. There was nothing to say. There was nothing that could be said.

Somewhere along the A1 I did find time to text a couple of good friends a note of congratulations including my old mate Martin Farrar. We go back over forty years. He has been a staunch Blue since the 1960s and I knew how much this day would mean to him. He had taken my ribbing in good spirit for most of those years so how could I begrudge him his moment in the sun?

The facts show United lost the league on goal difference, the first time in our history. Our points haul was eighty-nine. Since 1888 only Leeds in 1970/71, gained more points (ninety-one) as the second-placed team based on three for a win. Leeds played forty-two games, United thirty-eight. Only five times in the previous nineteen Premier League seasons did the champions exceed eighty-nine points. We equalled our record number of wins in a season – twenty-eight. United had scored eighty-nine league goals and only once since 1964 have we scored more in a season.

Given City's transfer outlay of £484 million and the transi-tional nature of United's squad, Fergie did superbly well to get so close to another title. I also believe that only Fergie could have steadied the ship and recovered after the derby defeat in the autumn. That said, having caught City and gone eight points clear in April we should never have surrendered the title. The defeats at Wigan and City were costly but the 4-4 draw at home to Everton on 22 April was the killer. Twice in the second half we held a two-goal lead, twice we let it slip.

City, Blackburn and Everton totalled thirteen goals against United at Old Trafford in 2011/12. In the previous six campaigns United had conceded twelve, twelve, thirteen, seven, twelve and eight home league goals all season. So we ended the season with no trophy and for the first time in ten years United didn't appear in a cup final.

When I got home from that Sunderland game my two young daughters were at the front door ready to console me. They never usually know United's result until I tell them but even they had got caught up in the drama of the afternoon. We had a chat about it then decided the best plan was to take my mind off football completely. The girls had recorded the final of *Britain's Got Talent* from the night before and were keen that we sat down and watched it together. So watch it we did. Or half watch it really, as my mind kept churning over the day's events.

The show was the usual mixture of performers except for a girl and dog act called Ashleigh and Pudsey. The dog pranced around the stage following Ashleigh, performing a number of tricks and dance routines to the theme song from *Mission Impossible*. In the end, the duo won the final. I couldn't quite believe it. In the space of a few hours that Sunday afternoon, Manchester City had become champions of England and I had seen a bloody dog pick up a cheque for half a million pounds! None of it made any sense. Mission Impossible indeed.

Fergie's response to losing the title was emphatic. Shinji Kagawa was signed from German double-winners Borussia Dortmund but the manager pulled a plum from the pie when Robin van Persie was prised from Arsenal on the eve of the new season. Not only had we got a top-class player and weakened our rivals but the Dutchman made it obvious he wanted to join Manchester United for our tradition and his instincts from boyhood. He spurned City and Chelsea's megabucks. The signing lifted everyone connected with the club.

United didn't just get a racing start, they tore through the season. A false Chelsea dawn kept us off top spot until 3 November and by mid-January with twenty-two games played United held a commanding seven-point lead over City in second place. A snapshot at that point gives some indication of the blistering pace the team set. The haul of fifty-five points is a club record. Again, the Babes, the 1960s glitz of Best, Law and Charlton, the Dream Team and the treble-winners couldn't amass points at that rate. The eighteen wins in that sequence had only been equalled or bettered on four occasions in the history of English top flight football.

Yet just as two years earlier, when the team set a club for the longest undefeated start to a season, many people in football failed to appreciate the strength of Fergie's creation. They said we had defensive deficiencies, we still lacked a midfield presence like Keane or Robson, our goalkeeper was suspect, Rooney and Valencia weren't on top form and that Nani was inconsistent. These pundits missed two vital factors, the quality of the squad Fergie had assembled and the determination within the club to regain the title from City.

The manager now had twenty-four first-class players at his disposal, men who had won medals or played at the highest level of club or international football. None could be classed as 'fringe' players. Team changes therefore never weakened the line-up. Our rivals didn't have that strength in depth. As regards the spirit, well you didn't have to be at the Stadium of Light on 13 May 2012 to realise that was the crucible in which Sir Alex forged the club's resolve for the next twelve months. In those few moments, as Fergie and his team looked around for confirmation of our title win only for the dream to be shattered by the cheering Sunderland fans, was born the defiant vow – never again!

Toast plays a small but vital part in the Molyneux household. In that first waking hour it provides the motivation to get out of bed and face the day ahead. My kids reckon I make the best in the world and with my recent CV almost threadbare I'll take any accolade that comes my way.

Wednesday, 12 September 2012 began as just another brilliant toast day. On the 7.30 a.m. news I heard that an independent panel set up to look into the Hillsborough disaster would report its finding later that day. Still juggling margarine and milk cartons, my immediate thought was, 'Bloody hell, that means we're in for an afternoon and evening of Scousers moaning about the latest cover up and conspiracy.'

That day I was working from home and the TV was on in the background. Late morning I heard an anchorman announce that David Cameron was about to address Parliament about Hillsborough. What I heard next was jaw-dropping. The Prime Minister, with the weight of the new evidence to hand, apologised on behalf of the British Government to the families of the bereaved and injured for all they had suffered over the past twenty-three years. He confirmed the evidence shows families suffered a double injustice, firstly the failure of the state to protect their loved ones and secondly the denigration of the deceased in that they were somehow at fault for their own deaths.

Soon after Cameron's speech came a live broadcast from the Independent Panel outlining what they had found. I found myself riveted to the screen as the chair, the Right Reverend James Jones, the Bishop of Liverpool, detailed the monumental cover-up and deceit they had discovered in completing their review. At its core were findings that the police made 'strenuous attempts to deflect blame' for the disaster from the authorities onto the fans for the deaths of ninety-six Liverpool supporters. Most seriously, up to 164 written statements from key witnesses including police officers had been amended to achieve this end. The findings were explained in more detail and corroborated by the members of the panel made up of experts from all walks of human life.

I have got to admit, I was shocked. I have also got to admit I was wrong. While always respecting the tragedy, I had come to the conclusion that the Hillsborough campaigns for justice and all those banners on the Kop referring to it was belly-aching by people who just couldn't let the matter rest. As stated in an earlier chapter about my visit to Anfield in 2008 I found the persistent complaining hypocritical given the tragedy at Heysel. I wasn't alone in that opinion. I guess, also, that having witnessed first-hand many a skirmish in the back streets of Liverpool when United are in town, including fearsome ambushes of innocent Reds in the mid-1980s, I knew elements of Liverpool's support weren't whiter than white. Again, I was not alone in that opinion. Yet, here was something fundamentally different. Right at the core of British society was a conspiracy by those assigned to protect its people, first failing to carry out that duty then falsifying accounts to cover their own backs.

I watched as the families of the bereaved commented on the findings and the announcement in Parliament. You could tell they were genuinely shocked and relieved that finally after twenty-three years the truth was starting to emerge and the wheels of justice would begin to move in the right direction. I have not read the report and more detail isn't for these pages, but I noticed the foreword contains a quote from the fourth-century philosopher Lactantius, 'The whole point of justice consists precisely in our providing for others through humanity what we provide for our own family through affection.' The families of the Hillsborough disaster have had to endure a terrible burden. I wish them well in their pursuit of justice and truth.

By the time March arrived, United were fifteen points ahead of second-placed City. Barring disaster the title was in the bag. All eyes were on a potentially classic tie against Real Madrid – Mourinho, Ronaldo *et al.* – in the knockout stage of the Champions League. The first leg in Spain was an excellent match between two world giants. Welbeck gave United the lead on twenty minutes. Ronaldo, inevitably, headed Real level and both sides missed chances to win it.

The second leg on 5 March was beautifully poised. I couldn't settle all that day, we were born for nights like this. Fergie left Rooney on the bench but the great man got the tactics spot on as United took the game to Real. After forty-eight minutes we got our reward when a Ramos own goal put United ahead. Madrid turned up the heat and we had before us a truly fascinating encounter. The watching millions on TV had the classic we all hoped for.

Unfortunately, 'classic' certainly wouldn't describe the decision Turkish referee Cuneyt Cakir made in the fifty-sixth minute. Nani tried to control a high pass down the left and Arbeloa came racing in behind him. The players collided and fell to the ground. Free kick to Madrid. No one in the ground expected the red card that came Nani's way. Disbelief and despair gripped the supporters, the team and the manager. Sir Alex, rightfully perplexed, berated the officials. Mourinho made two clinical substitutions and twelve minutes later Real led 2-1, the tie over.

Mike Phelan fronted the post-match conferences and talked of a 'distraught manager' in the dressing room. I can't remember being so angry about a refereeing decision since Moran was sent off in the 1985 FA Cup Final, or perhaps Law's disallowed goal against AC Milan in 1969. The Madrid debacle sucked some of the life out of United's season. Chelsea beat us in the FA Cup and careless points were dropped in the league. As always, United recovered and stormed through to clinch the title with four matches to spare.

On 22 April, Robin van Persie scored all the goals in a 3-0 victory at home to Aston Villa including a stunning volley. How fitting our number twenty should clinch our title number twenty. The Dutchman's goals had been crucial especially in the first half of the season with victories over all main rivals. Yet this campaign was a team effort, a club record twenty different players scored in the league. We conceded early leads in too many early matches but the fighting spirit saw us through. Vidic's return after Christmas settled jitters at the back and Carrick was imperious as United's fluid movement and high tempo attacking style blew most opponents away. The presentation of the trophy was scheduled for Sunday 12 May in the final home match against Swansea. By then, our world would have turned upside down.

27

MAY THE ROAD
RISE WITH YOU...

At 10.16 p.m. on Tuesday, 7 May 2013, Colin Green sent me a text saying *The Telegraph* was running a story that Alex Ferguson was giving serious consideration to retiring before the end of the season. Brian Foy confirmed that 'rumours abound' a few minutes later. I checked a few websites but nothing was definite. I poured a beer and wondered if this could be it.

After 2002 we knew Fergie wouldn't announce his retirement in advance but every season I looked for any tell-tale signs. As a keen supporter I've always wanted him to stay, well since 1989 anyway, and with every additional trophy you just hoped he would carry on regardless. Through 2013 almost all the indications were he would stay, he talked in the press of the transfer targets already being lined up for next season and even wrote in his programme notes on 5 May that he had no intention of walking away from this club.

We knew the curtain had to come down on Fergie's reign one day but the announcement still became one of those 'I'll always remember where I was when I heard the news' moments. When I woke on the morning of Wednesday 8 May the 'Fergie's retiring' rumours were still just that, but they were gathering momentum and moving up the news headlines on radio and TV. More importantly, the club made no statement. The silence was deafening.

I managed the toast and the school run but otherwise I was good for nothing. Work could wait, I was glued to the BBC and Sky News. Just after 9.18 a.m. came the announcement that Sir Alex Ferguson had decided to retire as manager of Manchester United. Even when I typed these words a week later I could feel myself getting emotional. Sir Alex would take on the roles of director and ambassador at the club. There was no press conference (Bobby Charlton would have been proud of him!), simply a released statement confirming his decision, explaining what a wonderful time he'd had at Old Trafford and a list of thank yous. Little else occupied my thoughts that day, or in the week that followed. After the numbness came sadness, and after the sadness came gratitude. The gratitude will remain in my heart forever.

Let's summarise Fergie's achievements in his twenty-six and a half-year reign with United, starting with the facts. Our record under Alex Ferguson was:

Played	W	D	L	F	A	W%	D%	L%
1500	895	338	267	2769	1365	60	22	18

No surprise here, Fergie sits in top spot of United's seventeen managers since 1900 based on win percentage, ahead of Ernest Mangnall and Sir Matt Busby. United won a staggering 60 per cent of matches under Fergie. His games-lost percentage is the lowest in our history at a miserly eighteen. Sir Alex Ferguson's trophy haul at Old Trafford is thirty-eight:

European Cup	2
League title	13
FA Cup	5
League Cup	4
Charity Shield	10
World Club Championship	2
European Cup Winners' Cup	1
UEFA Super Cup	1

In 135 years Manchester United have won sixty-one trophies. Fergie has won 62 per cent of that total. He steps down from the Old Trafford throne the most successful manager in our history, in English football and in British football. Sir Alex has made United the most successful team ever in the two main domestic competitions. He has taken charge of more games (1,500) than any other United manager. Matt Busby follows him with 1,141 games. This Govan man will have reigned for twenty-six years, seven months and twenty-four days, compared to Sir Matt's twenty-four years and two months. Mind you, that includes six months when Busby came back to bail us out in 1971. Hopefully Fergie won't have to do the same!

The comparisons between the two knights warrant a mention. Both resolute Scots, they possessed a potent work ethic and an indomitable inner strength. These men took over United at a time when the club had lost its way and each built a dynasty. Or perhaps, Fergie simply built a few more tiers on Sir Matt's? Both kick-started their trophy haul by winning the FA Cup in their third full season and both took seven years to make United champions of England. Fergie won the treble thirteen years into his reign, taking United to the pinnacle of world club football. Matt Busby's thirteenth season was 1957/58. When tragedy struck at Munich, United were third in the league, in the fifth round of the FA Cup and the semi-final of the European Cup. The Babes were in the form of their lives. For most of my life I never thought any United manager could out-shine Sir Matt. It just didn't seem possible. But Alex Ferguson has done just that. Even hallowed luminaries Jock Stein, Bill Shankly, Bob Paisley, Herbie Chapman and Brian Clough all stand in Fergie's shadow.

Okay, the anorak is off, let's move from facts to opinions. Well, my biased opinion anyway. Fergie has upheld the traditions that are the very cornerstone of everything that is Manchester United. For the last twenty-odd years his teams have been a delight to watch. Yes, it took him three years to design the pattern but since then United have played with flair, panache and a never-say-die spirit. Embroidered into this fine tapestry has been the grit, determination and steel to ensure we enjoyed entertaining and winning football. Fergie is a master craftsman at weaving the perfect blend of youth and experience, of taking raw materials and processing them into quality finished products.

Not all these natural resources are homegrown. On 4 January 2011, the side below beat Stoke 2-1: Kuszczak, Rafael, Evra, Fletcher, Smalling, Vidic, Nani, Gibson, Berbatov, Hernandez, Giggs.

Eleven players, eleven different nationalities, a true United Nations. Whether local or imported from around the world, these raw resources had to contain the right qualities. Fergie always talked about bringing in the 'right' players to Manchester United. Any recruit had to be able to perform at the highest level and possess the true desire to play for Manchester United. Just throwing money at transfers or the wage bill often attracts mercenaries and big egos.

United have never had a team full of Manchester lads, even the Babes came from all corners of the British Isles. Yet Busby and Ferguson strived to ensure that any player pulling on that red shirt knew United's history and expectations and quickly embraced the spirit of Manchester United. That player had to go out and play as if he was from Wythenshawe, Collyhurst or Salford.

Fergie has managed to blend Brits with foreigners from across the globe and still retain that 'local' pride. As a consequence he built sides with genuine team spirit, sides that were greater than the sum of their parts. Finished products that proudly bear the trademark 'Made in Manchester'. How fitting that Sir Alex perfected these skills just a goal kick from the Ship Canal and River Irwell and put our city at the top of the football world just as our forefathers did in making Cottonopolis the international centre of the textile trade in the nineteenth century.

Sir Matt built three great United teams, mainly borne out of necessity due to the older players he inherited after the war and then the crash at Munich. Sir Alex became the master of evolution, continuously improving and re-modelling his teams; always striving to stay one step ahead of the game. His judgement on who comes, who goes and when, were honed to perfection.

I remember a TV interview with Sir Clive Woodward where he talked about the battle to get to the top in sport and the challenge of staying there. He spoke passionately about a 'better never stops' mentality. Fergie embodies that spirit – always trying to keep United out in front, always putting the club first, never shirking the hard decisions. There are many important characteristics to admire in this man from Govan; his drive, his desire to succeed, his belief in his own ability, his courage. Those alone don't win games or trophies though. Fergie's tactical ability is shrewd, insightful and intuitive. His knowledge of the opposition's strengths and weaknesses border on encyclopedic.

His man-management and powers of motivation are far more sophisticated than the infamous hairdryer treatment. In recent years many managers have floundered when tinkering with their sides, trying to cope with the demands of the four main competitions. Meanwhile, United's manager has perfected the art of team rotation and still getting results. On 3 May 2008, Alex Ferguson picked the same team to play West Ham that had played Barcelona four days earlier. On 1 March 2011, he played the same side that had played Wigan in the previous game. In the intervening period United went 165 consecutive matches without fielding an unchanged side.

Compare this to the era when Tommy Docherty selected the following United team for eighteen consecutive matches between 6 December 1975 and 9 March 1976: Stepney, Forsyth, Houston, Daly, Greenhoff, Buchan, Coppell, McIlroy, Pearson, Macari, Hill.

In May 2013 I celebrated fifty years supporting Manchester United. As I kicked that ball around with my next-door neighbour in 1963, trying to beat 'his' Leicester City, I could never have imagined the amazing journey ahead. I had boarded the football equivalent of *The Polar Express* and would never disembark. I have always felt blessed to be a Manchester United supporter and the journey from Sir Matt's glorious final years to Fergie's history-makers has been the backdrop to my life. I have seen the world's best footballers play, watched some of the finest club matches of all time, travelled throughout Europe, made countless friends and stored a million great moments on life's memory stick. I have been very fortunate indeed. Some fellow Reds have been mates for thirty or forty years and are godparents to my children as I have been to theirs. Some didn't make the journey this far. I feel privileged to have shared the stage with them all in this story.

For the final home match of each season, twenty or thirty of us meet up in Manchester for a drink before the game, take a barge to Old Trafford, watch the game (and invariably a presentation!) board the return boat, drink to our heart's content in the city's finest public houses and put the football world to rights. It's a perfect day! The May 2013 trip had all those ingredients plus the powerful elixir of saying goodbye to the greatest man in United's history and showing him our gratitude.

I wanted to recreate the 1989 banner but with a more complementary slogan above the 'Ta Ra Fergie'. I'm no John Cooper Clarke but '23 Years of Silver and We're Still Top' fitted the bill. As we all met up in Duke's 92 bar the main theme was the end of an incredible era, a very special day. Everyone was still coming to terms with Wednesday's news. By then we knew David Moyes would be the new manager but for now the focus was on the old one. The over-riding emotion wasn't sadness though, just time to take stock of what Fergie had done for us and that was enough to get any party started.

Inside the ground 73,000 red flags created a superb setting as the two teams applauded Sir Alex out to a guard of honour. In a way, Reds had to witness the proceedings to truly believe it was happening, like biblical disciples. Not since the January 1994 Everton match, in the week of Sir Matt's passing, had a game had less significance.

In the fifty-fifth minute I held up the new 'Ta Ra Fergie' banner. At the same time, from the same seats and with Col, Tezzer and Bri as we had done in December 1989. Full time brought a 2-1 win and a poignant, off-the-cuff address from Sir Alex Ferguson. You could hear a pin drop in the great stadium. Then we sang our anthems and all too soon Fergie's farewell as manager was over. It was time to raise a glass.

Fergie's reign has been almost presidential and if he were to deliver a 'state of the nation' address as he waves farewell, what might be his take on the rivals who most covet United's crown? Well, Liverpool now aspire to a top four finish. I know it provides entry into the Champions League but when they ruled the world, fourth place had us reeling in despair and seeking the Samaritans' phone number. Can you imagine Fergie settling for a top four finish? Never! Shoot for the moon and even if you miss you'll land among the stars is his motto.

Then there's Arsenal, well where exactly? They have spent a decade going from The Invincibles to The Invisibles. Leeds, Newcastle and Blackburn are on an endless 1990s nostalgia trip which brings us to Chelsea and City. Their vulgar new money has brought them trophies but look at the amount they've spent. What respect do they have from fellow football fans? The two clubs make a mockery of the game by sacking managers within months of delivering long-awaited success. In fact it's not the money that's vulgar, it's the people behind it. They care little about our football culture and add no real value. Bad Moon Rising, rather than Blue, in my opinion. I think I've just had my final rant!

Fergie may have left harbouring one regret. I believe he wanted another European Cup, we all did. Well, it wasn't for the want of trying and we know it's a difficult trophy to win. Since the inception of the Champions League in 1992 no team has won the trophy back-to-back and no side has dominated the competition. Maybe the days when Real, Milan, Ajax, Bayern and Liverpool did are gone forever. I think United had an excellent chance in 2013. Kagawa will prove to be a superb signing but injury prevented us seeing him settle into that key midfield role.

If that was unlucky then the turning point in the Real match was a travesty. The sad aspect is we'll never know how that superbly balanced contest would have ended. The football world was cheated thanks to Turkish myopia. When the great man didn't appear for the post-match press conference I did wonder if it was because he knew his last chance had been cruelly snatched away. European domination may have been an impossible dream but those unforgettable nights in Barcelona and Moscow weren't. Nor was knocking Liverpool off their perch and putting my club back at the top of English football. The song playing in Las Vegas, Fergie, is Piaf's 'Je Ne Regrette Rien'.

In 1989 I couldn't picture a United future with Alex Ferguson in charge. In 2013 it's difficult to imagine one without him. Back then I dreamed of seeing United win one league title and possibly another European Cup triumph before I die. Nowadays, it feels like I have died and ascended into a paradise where United's success is perpetual and the football is divine. Anybody with a love of Manchester United enjoys a much better existence thanks to one man. Quite simply, Fergie has made our life wonderful. I want to say thank you, Sir Alex Ferguson, and wish you a long, happy and healthy retirement.

It is difficult to really describe how life was for United supporters in 1986, especially to those who have been reared on the glory years of the last two decades. There was a record around at that time by Brian Walsh called 'Song For Matt Busby'. I came across it on a CD called 'The Red Album: A Mancunian Fantasy' on the Exotica label. It's worth a listen if you get the chance. In Pogues-style, high-speed Irish rock, interlaced with commentary from the 1968 European Cup Final, the singer reminisces about the team of his youth: '...when United are the greatest was the truth'. He celebrates the team's rise to glory in the twenty years after the war, how Busby built three great teams before finally conquering Europe with 'a Scotsman brought from Italy and a balding Georgie lad and an Irishman who danced the field like Nureyev gone mad'. Sadly, he laments our decline under a succession of managers and Merseyside domination, acknowledging that Atkinson and Docherty did their level best 'but they only got the FA Cup whilst the championship went west'. The singer's desolation turns to poignancy as he yearns for a time when he will see his club climb to the top again. The final verse sums it up perfectly:

> Oh the day the Reds if you decide,
> To take their long-suffering fans for a ride,
> To the Championship and Europe that is their rightful place,
> And Sir Matt will go to heaven with a smile upon his face,
> With a smile upon his face,
> With a smile upon his face,
> With a smile upon his face.

A few weeks after this song was penned, Alex Ferguson will have pulled into the car park at Old Trafford, walked through the doors of the famous old stadium and started work. The rest, as they say, is history.

Ta Ra Fergie.

SOURCES

'Anger is an energy', *Rise*, Public Image Limited, (J. Lydon/B. Laswell)

'Thank you for the days, those endless days, those sacred days you gave me', *Days*, Kinks, (R. Davies)

'Yesterday has just departed, and tomorrow hasn't started', *Yesterday has Gone*, Cupid's Inspiration, (T. Randazzo/V. Pike)

'Looks like we're in for nasty weather, one eye is taken for an eye', *Bad Moon Rising*, Creedence Clearwater Revival, (J. Fogerty)

'So I left my home, I'm really on my own at last', *Son of My Father*, Chicory Tip, (G. Moroder/P. Bellotte)

'Everywhere I hear the sound of marching, charging feet boy', *Street Fighting Man*, Rolling Stones, (M. Jagger/K. Richards)

'Don't push your love too far, your wounds won't leave a scar', *In a Broken Dream*, Python Lee Jackson, (D. Bentley)

'Don't you love farce? My fault I fear', *Send in the Clowns*, Judy Collins, (S. Sondheim)

'I need excitement oh I need it bad, and it's the best I've ever had', *Teenage Kicks*, The Undertones, (J. O'Neill)

'Through the coldest winter in almost fourteen years, I couldn't believe you kept a smile', *Mandolin Wind*, Rod Stewart, (R. Stewart)

'Don't need no politicians to tell me things I shouldn't be', *Do Anything You Want To Do,* Eddie and the Hot Rods, (G. Douglas/E. Hollis)

'One man on a lonely platform, one case sitting by his side', *Fade to Grey*, Visage, (M. Ure/B. Currie/C. Payne)

'This indecision is bugging me', *Should I Stay or Should I Go?*, The Clash, (M. Jones/J. Mellor)

'So don't yield to the fortunes you sometimes see as fate', *The Living Years,* Mike & The Mechanics, (M. Rutherford/P. Robertson)

'Is a dream a lie if it don't come true, or is it something worse?', *The River*, Bruce Springsteen, (B. Springsteen)

'Swing from high to deep, extremes of sweet and sour', *Sit Down*, James, (T. Booth)

'He has sounded forth the trumpet that shall never call retreat', *Battle Hymn of the Republic*, Various, (J. Howe)

'Don't these times fill your eyes', *Made of Stone*, Stone Roses, (I. Brown/J. Squire)

'They can lie to my face, but not to my heart', *If the Kids are United*, Sham '69, (Hosen)

'Flags, rags, ferryboats, Scimitars and scarves', *The Whole of the Moon*, Waterboys, (M. Scott)

'If I took it for a hundred years, I couldn't feel anymore ill', *Bitterest Pill (I ever had to swallow)*, The Jam, (P. Weller)

'Watching the people get lairy, it's not very pretty I tell thee', *I Predict a Riot*, Kaiser Chiefs, (N. Hodgson/S. Rix/N. Baines/A. White/ R. Wilson)

'How many special people change? How many lives are living strange?', *Champagne Supernova*, Oasis, (N. Gallagher)

'You only get one shot, do not miss your chance to blow', *Lose Yourself*, Eminem, (Eminem/J. Bass/L. Resto)

'Be my mirror, my sword and shield, My missionaries in a foreign field', *Viva La Vida*, Coldplay, (C. Martin/G. Berryman/J. Buckland/ W. Champion)

'To fight for the right, without question or pause', *The Impossible Dream (The Quest)*, Frank Sinatra, (M. Leigh/J. Darion)

'May the road rise with you', *Rise*, Public Image Limited (J. Lydon/B. Laswell)